Camps, settlements and churches

Eddie J Braggett

Barton Books
Canberra, Australia
2010

This project was assisted through funding made available by the ACT Government under the ACT Heritage Grants Program

Camps, settlements and churches

A history of Anglican centres of worship in the inner south of Canberra 1913–2010

Eddie Braggett

Barton Books
Canberra, Australia
2010

Acknowledgements

All images and photos used in this book have been reproduced with permission of the copyright holder as indicated in the caption.

National Library of Australia Cataloguing-in-Publication entry

Author:	Braggett, E J (Edwin J)
Title:	Camps, settlements and churches : a history of Anglican centres of worship in the inner-south of Canberra. 1913-2010 / Eddie J Braggett.
ISBN:	9781921577048 (pbk)
Notes:	Includes bibliographical references and index.
Subjects:	Anglican church buildings–Australian Capital Territory–Canberra–History.
	Church buildings–Australian Capital Territory–Canberra–History.

Dewey Number: 293.9947

Cover design, typesetting and layout by Graham Lindsay, Barton Books.
Copy editing and checking by Christine Ledger and Tom Frame.
Index compiled by Helen Frame.

Published 2010 by Barton Books, Canberra, Australia
Email: info@bartonbooks.com.au

Printed and bound by KainosPrint.com.au, PO Box 311, Calwell ACT 2905

About the photos on the front cover in descending order:

1. No.1 labourers camp, Westlake, 1924 (© Canberra & District Historical Society; Ann Gugler)
2. Section of the internment camp, 1918 (© The Australian War Memorial)
3. St Paul's near the Powerhouse, 1914 (© St Paul's Archives)
4. Telopea Park, Kingston, Barton, Griffith and Forrest, 1953 (© ACT Heritage Library, DCT Collection.)

Camps, Settlements and Churches

Foreword

The telling of history is an important pursuit. History not only tells us about the past but also informs our knowledge of the present, explaining the place in which we find ourselves, and – if we are thoughtful – providing knowledge of the future and the place we might be.

The Parish of Manuka, the first on the inner south of Canberra, has always tried to proclaim the gospel of Jesus Christ by word and deed. The ministry of word and sacrament has been a permanent feature of the shared life of this Christian community and its witness in the national capital of Australia. Clergy and lay people of each generation have sought new, exciting and appropriate ways to serve God and people and to proclaim the light of the gospel. Sometimes these efforts have succeeded spectacularly and at other times not.

Eddie Braggett's outstanding work shows us in great detail the life and work for the gospel undertaken by many people in the Parish of Manuka. It reveals the struggles of the early days to establish ministry on the southern side of the city and the hopes and plans of many who sought to build the kingdom of God. It seems that effort, tinged with tension and differing hopes, has always marked the Parish of Manuka. Many have laboured and various plans have come to fruition while some have not succeeded.

The Parish of Manuka represents a significant presence in our national capital. The Church of St Paul makes an imposing presence on a major thoroughfare and witnesses to the presence of God, as do its many ministry programs, ensuring the active participation of the parish in the local community and beyond. Part of its mission was to assist in the development of the church at Deakin–Yarralumla and the creation of the new parish in 1959. Change and development continue to be part of the story of the parish and in recent years this can be seen in the establishment and the shared and expanded ministry of the Combined Ministry District of Manuka and Deakin and in proposals for expanded ministry through the shared use of resources. There are still those who wish to plan and act strategically for the future, just as there have been in this past. The future will be a different place from the past and indeed the present. The need for a bold vision and a stepping-out in faith with resolve for the future has become the motivation of the Combined Ministry District Council.

The two inner-south parishes owe a great debt to Eddie Braggett, not only for the detail of the story he tells, but also for the analysis of events in the local area. His insightful interpretation of historical material enhances a sense of thankfulness for the past, reality about the present and resolve to grow and develop into the future, building on the fine tradition of those many fine and godly souls who have gone before us in the service of God.

The Reverend Dr Brian Douglas
Ninth Rector of Manuka

Commendation

The term 'parish pump' isn't used to describe good quality or importance. It is a dismissive phrase, signifying 'of local interest' and 'of little
real importance'. It has a focus upon 'in-house' domestic matters, with
little relevance outside circumscribed boundaries. Some may even see
a history of Anglican parishes in a similar vein. Professor Braggett's
history will change some minds. A parish is strictly a division of a
county with its own church building and representative member of
the clergy ensconced. In England it has both a civil and ecclesiastical
identity. Here in Australia, in Anglican and Roman Catholic circles,
it is entirely a church-determined subdivision of a diocese. Time was
when the rector's 'cure of souls' was balanced by his parishioners' loyalty to their residential parish. In the time scale of this book, the scene
has changed radically. A form of congregationalism now characterises
the church – not only the Anglican Church of Australia but also all
churches. John Wesley famously wrote, 'I look upon all the world as
my parish.' We have turned that on its head! The Episcopal Church
in the United States of America began the trend but we, members of
the Anglican Church of Australia, often choose to worship where we
feel our spiritual needs are mostly met. Our parish is not necessarily
where we live.

The very use of that now official title, 'The Anglican Church of
Australia', is itself an indication of change. If any thought were given to
the nature of the church in the earliest days of the settlement at Port
Jackson, it would have been assumed that the Church of England's
establishment status in England was transferred to the colony. The
interim period from 1788 until 1962, when the Church of England in
Australia came into being with its own constitution, is well covered

in Ross Border's *Church and State in Australia, 1788–1872.* That Archdeacon Border was rector of St Paul's Manuka from 1950 to 1959 only adds to his lustre as a parish priest and historian. The name 'The Anglican Church of Australia' was finally adopted in 1981.

Eddie Braggett's book is a record of radical change. St Paul's, unlike St John's at Reid, is a product of the establishment and expansion of Australia's capital city. It has grown and changed with the city, south of Lake Burley Griffin. At the time of writing, with the addition of the Parish of Deakin–Yarralumla, it is properly known as the 'Combined Ministry District of St Paul's Manuka, St David's Red Hill and St Luke's Deakin'. After World War II the population grew with the arrival of public servants from the state capitals, especially from Melbourne. Although Canberra has often been thought of as a city of public servants, those employed in some form of government service are not in the majority. A critical mass was reached where the city and the territory generally attracted residents whose motivation was that they simply wished to live there.

The name 'Manuka' does not grace a neighbourhood or suburb. St Paul's is properly in Griffith. Manuka Circle surrounds the Manuka Oval. The original bounds included Griffith, Red Hill, Forrest, Barton, Kingston and Narrabundah. They have become attractive places to live, each with its distinctive features. The shopping centre known as Manuka has a good mix of quality shops, a theatre complex and a variety of fine eating-places. Kingston, too has developed a reputation for tasty food and elegant apartments. Forrest boasts perhaps the most prestigious living area in Canberra with embassies, high commissions and diplomatic residences. Schools abound, adding to the attraction of living in the parish.

The siting of the St Paul's church building could hardly have been more favourable, even in the days before the popularity of the motor car. That congregations were growing in the period of Professor Braggett's study is proof of the wisdom of those early planners. Increasing wealth meant, for some Canberrans, the purchase of a holiday home 'down the coast'. There were (are) examples of parishioners with dual parish loyalty, using offertory envelopes for home and 'down the coast'. This raises another marked change in parish life – the introduction in the 1950s of the Every Member Canvass. Many people, especially men, were drawn into the life of the church through planned giving programs. As well, perhaps for the first time, the church had access to funds that gave a fillip to building programs and parish outreach.

Meantime St Paul's has rapidly become an attractive place, not only for worship but also as a community of faith and fellowship. Sunday worship has been the centrepiece of membership but many things contribute to the attraction. Certainly the style of worship, the 'central churchmanship', the thoughtful preaching, the vitality of the congregation – both in and beyond the hours of worship – and the lay leadership and excellent music all contribute to St Paul's being a distinctive city church. It is very much a fellowship with a seven-day-a-week spiritual and social bond. For many, if not for most, it provides the mainspring of their personal and family lives, rooted and grounded in the faith 'that was once for all entrusted to the saints'. The ordination of women to the diaconate, priesthood and the episcopate has been embraced by the ministry and people of St Paul's and the parish as a whole. Notable women have been licensed to the parish as assistants, but only at St Luke's Deakin has there been a woman as rector, the Reverend Elaine Gifford (1996–2003). The role of women in the church has been a very significant change that very few regret.

The 'New Areas' of Canberra in the sixties, seventies and eighties were an almost unique feature of Canberra's growth. Generally, Anglicans were in cooperation with another de-nomination – Presbyterian, Methodist, Churches of Christ and Congregational. After the creation of the Uniting Church of Australia in 1977, cooperation was either with that church or a congregation of the Churches of Christ. The eventual failure of the cooperating scheme was due to a number of factors that deserve their own study. Woden Valley, Belconnen, Tuggeranong and Gungahlin, each with many neighbourhoods, placed a great strain on church leadership and administration, on local congregations and on such social services as were available at the time. In fact, the usually youthful priest-in-charge was often the fount of counselling in areas where young families were settled, far from grandparents and other relatives, as was the situation in the early days of St Paul's. The time, energy and spiritual resources of clergy and lay leaders were stretched to the limit.

Added to this, so far as the nascent church was concerned, was the defection of some would-be valuable parishioners to established churches like St John's at Reid, St Paul's and All Saints' at Ainslie. This was a serious loss indeed. Often they were the very people whose gifts could best be used in establishing parishes. Many promised to return when a *real* church was built! Meantime, worship was conducted in public school assembly halls and community centres. This unsettling but nonetheless exciting period is now almost over yet the balance has only partly been redressed. To its credit, St Paul's materially helped the establishment and building program of the parish of St Mary-in-the-Valley at Chisholm (Tuggeranong), partly in recognition of being at one time 'on the receiving end'. It was an example of the gospel in action.

'Parish pump'? Maybe, but the old pump is still working well, and the water is free yet beyond price!

Bishop Neville Chynoweth
Rector of Manuka, 1971–74

Preamble

Wartime 1943

As his aircraft slowly droned its way over Canberra, Lieutenant-Colonel John Overall surveyed the scattered settlements below before launching himself from the plane and parachuting to the small aerodrome at Pialligo. He was leading a training exercise to capture the airport from the cadets then training at the Royal Military College, Duntroon and had spent many hours studying the layout of the land and the pattern of settlement in order to make the parachute 'attack' a success.

He knew that the population of the capital was a mere 12,000, spread over 'seven suburbs in search of a city', and that the two main residential areas were tenuously linked by 'bicycle and a rickety old bridge across the Molonglo'. He recognised the provisional Parliament House, which 'gleamed white and serene' in the pasture fields designed to be the Parliamentary Triangle, and noted the Royal Military College sheltering among the trees beyond the airport on the other side of the meandering and sluggish river.[1] If he had looked further across the Limestone Plains, he would have noticed a series of small settlements, the remnants of earlier homesteads and their surrounding properties around Ginninderra, Queanbeyan, Jerrabomberra, Tuggeranong and Lanyon. While some stations were still operating, others had closed or been acquired for other uses, one being 'Yarralumla' which had been acquired by the Commonwealth Government in 1912.

John Overall, later to be knighted for his leadership and role in planning and developing the nation's capital while heading the National Capital Development Commission, became a member of the Anglican congregation at Manuka and, when pressed in the late

1990s, quietly discussed the growth of the city while downplaying his own unique contribution. He explained to me that one could not understand the early growth of Canberra or the development of its churches without highlighting the division of the two residential areas of the city by the river (later the lake) – the north and the south – and without underscoring the importance of Kingston and neighbouring Manuka. His assertions are borne out in the narrative that unfolds.

The inner south

It was originally intended to record the history of St Paul's Anglican Church at Manuka as a stand-alone project, one sufficiently formidable in itself considering the scope of the resources available. It quickly became evident that the church's development was so closely entwined with the wider history of the inner south and the extension of surrounding settlements that the project needed to be broadened.

When Walter Burley Griffin designed the Federal Capital of Australia in 1911–1912, he accepted that the Molonglo River was not only the natural division between two segments of the future city but that it also helped to delineate the functions of different sectors of the area. He believed that eventually the Molonglo would be dammed to form a series of lakes, one of which would be named Eastlake and another Westlake. His plan was later modified and a single lake constructed half a century later. Even then, however, the terms 'north' and 'south' continued to be used, despite Canberra's continued development. In time, the 'south' expanded to include the Woden Valley, Weston Creek and Tuggeranong, well beyond the limits originally proposed for the 'south'.

This study concentrates on the original geographical concept, what is now termed 'the inner south', an area encompassing the present-day suburbs or precincts of Yarralumla, Deakin, Capital Hill, Parkes, Barton, Forrest, Kingston, Manuka, Narrabundah, Fyshwick, Griffith and Red Hill. Beginning with church services at two camps in 1914 – the Brickworks (Westridge) and the Power House (Eastlake) – the Anglican Church commenced its witness and gradually extended its influence over nearly a century. It was a faltering, indeed a gruelling, task for the first 30 years but, assisted by the dedication and committed guidance of clergy attached to the Church of St John the

Baptist (on the northside) and the willingness of that parish's leaders to support expansion, the foundations were laid for a vibrant Anglican presence in the south.

Seven themes have emerged and become a focus for this history. They include: Canberra's complex history and the development of camps and settlements within which Anglican services were commenced, together with the later establishment of suburbs and suburban churches; the importance of the parish of St John the Baptist in sponsoring Christian influence on the southside, and the consequent importance of St Paul's Manuka in sponsoring other centres of worship; the crucial role of the rectors and assistant clergy and the considerable involvement of the diocesan bishops within parish and nation; the churchmanship of the clergy, the form of Anglicanism they have promoted and the character of the local liturgy; the changing involvement of the church in the community as the parish sought to become a 'church in society'; the continual requirement for more money, particularly in times of economic depression, armed conflict, population growth and church extension; and, changing societal attitudes to religion and their impact on the church, its mission and ministry. While I have not presented the history that follows under these separate headings, I have been conscious of these themes and their interaction while researching, interpreting and writing this book.

This work honours the sustained efforts of godly clergy and parishioners as they have extended a Christian influence in the community and, above all, sought to serve and glorify God. If this history conveys the determination and grandeur of the vision – the love of God revealed through the devotion of our forebears – I will have achieved a most worthy purpose.

Eddie Braggett

Notes

1   J Overall, *Canberra: Yesterday, today and tomorrow*, Federal Capital Press of Australia, 1995, p. 1.

Acknowledgements

The contribution of the ACT Government to the production of this history is acknowledged and deeply appreciated. Through the generosity of the ACT Heritage Grants Program, I received financial assistance to further my research and to have the completed manuscript edited, designed, indexed and published.

I am most grateful for the patience and assistance of all who have provided original printed material and personal recollections. The archivist at St John's Church in Reid, Diana Body, was a continuing source of inspiration as she located documents, identified photos and found relevant information in the diocesan respositories. I am deeply indebted for her devotion and assistance. At the same time, I was able to gain an overview of the history of St John's, together with specific details of past parishioners and events, in *Firm Still You Stand* (1986), penned by the late Alf Body. My references to his work for the period 1900 to 1950 reflect my indebtedness to his careful research. Jean Salisbury assisted with other aspects of the history of St John's Church and its early parishioners. Photographs from St John's Schoolhouse Archives have been reproduced with permission. While researching the early history of Anglican centres in the Diocese of Goulburn, I was kindly granted the use of a room in the Diocesan Registry, Jamieson House.

Many parish and diocesan records are housed in the Manuscript Section of the National Library of Australia (NLA), including the Burgmann papers, records of St Paul's parish, the papers of the Reverend W Edwards, and the registers of services at St Paul's, St David's, St Barnabas', St Luke's and Christ Church (Queanbeyan) between 1895 and 1987. I am grateful to the NLA staff for their ready assistance and forbearance as they located obscure references and permitted me to photograph documents for research purposes. Likewise, I am indebted to the staff of the National Archives of Australia where I had access to the early records of Canberra, maps of settlements, decisions of committees and commissions and a wide collection of photographs. The staff of St Mark's National Theological Centre kindly assisted my research as well, allowing me access to the photographic collection located in the library's Rare Books Section. The archivists at Canberra Grammar School and Canberra Girls' Grammar School helpfully provided access to all the records and photographs in their collections.

Back copies of *The Queanbeyan Age, The Queanbeyan-Canberra Advocate, The Federal Capital Pioneer, The Federal Capital Pioneer Magazine* and *The Canberra Times* were obtained through the ACT Heritage Library at the Woden Public Library where I had access to its valuable and growing collection. The staff of the ACT Heritage Library encouraged and assisted my research over a three-year period and helped me locate photographs. They are aware of the extent to which I sought their advice. The staff of the Canberra & District Historical Society provided files and newspaper clippings on different suburbs, especially early Kingston, and Val Emerson gave me important insights into the daily lives of those who lived near St Paul's mission hall at Kingston.

While secondary references are listed at the rear of the book, I must acknowledge a substantial debt to Ann Gugler's two books: *The Builders of Canberra 1909–1929* and *Westlake*. Based on her extensive research, these two volumes provided a wealth of minute but crucial detail on the early camps and settlements of Canberra, and gave me a framework upon which some of the early history could be interpreted and presented. Ann kindly permitted me to reproduce photos from her own collection.

The archives of more recent activities held in St Paul's at Manuka proved a most important source, particularly for the period 1950 to 2008. These records had been painstakingly collected, preserved and indexed by Arthur Ingle, saving me many months of investigation. It is probably to Arthur's credit that this history was commenced at all, while his knowledge and quiet encouragement were constant companions. I also enjoyed the complete support and continuing encouragement of the rector of St Paul's Manuka, the Reverend Dr

Brian Douglas, who read rather ponderous drafts of the early chapters before I reduced their length by more than 50 per cent.

Heather Clark had previously collected and filed important documents and reports relating to the history of St Luke's Deakin–Yarralumla in the period after 1957. I appreciated the enthusiastic cooperation of the Reverend Michael Armstrong who introduced me to many of the long-term parishioners and allowed me to work in the church vestry. The history of St Luke's has been enhanced by those who invited me into their homes and shared their recollections and memorabilia.

Duncan Anderson explained the collection of records relating to St David's Red Hill after the 1960s and kindly provided access to them. The Reverend Canon Geoffrey Sibly, who was a curate in the parish during the early 1970s, provided an insight into the planning, construction and opening of St David's Church.

I am indebted to members of St Paul's Church and to numerous people who have had past associations with the church – both at Kingston and Manuka – for providing personal reminiscences, photographs and certificates. The reference list provides the names of almost 90 people who have contributed to the research spanning nearly a century. These people have invited me into their homes, met me over coffee in cafés, telephoned with snippets of recalled information and located drawings and photographs of important events. There were others I had wanted to interview but there was not time. Three people who attended St Paul's at Kingston – Gwen Jackson, Frank Colwell and Morrie Adamson – pointed out the site of the first church and recalled the character of early Kingston, the personalities of rectors and the contributions of leading members of past congregations. Personal contacts added a dimension to my research that is rarely obtainable through written sources.

The opportunity to meet and record the memories of past rectors, assistant priests and clergy with a close knowledge of St Paul's, St Luke's, St Barnabas' and St David's was much appreciated. They include: Canon Peter Bertram, the Reverend Dr John Bunyan, the Reverend Gerald Farleigh, Canon Bill Pryce, Bishop Neville Chynoweth, Canon Scott Cowdell, Archbishop Jeffrey Driver, Canon Robert Withycombe, the Reverend Robyn Lewis-Quinn, the Reverend Robert Willson, the Reverend Hartley Hansford, Archdeacon John Gibson, Canon

Geoffrey Sibly, the Reverend Elaine Gifford, the Reverend David Clark and the Reverend Philip Peters. The daughter of the Reverend James Hardman, Janet Hyslop, provided personal information about her father. Pamela Wright kindly supplemented my knowledge of the Reverend Eric Wright.

I must draw attention to the input of the Right Reverend Neville Chynoweth – former rector of the parishes of both Ainslie and Manuka, Assistant Bishop of the Diocese of Canberra and Goulburn, and Bishop of Gippsland. Although allegedly retired, Bishop Chynoweth is fully engaged in the ministry at St David's, the parish and the wider diocese. He and his wife, Joan, have considerably extended my knowledge of the history of the parish. I am most grateful to them both.

Numerous people have read sections of the manuscript and checked the accuracy of the text. While I have appreciated their suggestions, I am fully responsible for the narrative that follows and for the interpretations it contains.

Finally, I am indebted to my wife, Kay, who has endured a cluttered study for three years without complaint. She proof-read the manuscript and offered much constructive criticism. Kay and I see this history as our contribution to the parish and to the memory of many faithful parishioners whose legacies are a continuing blessing.

August, 2010

1   The Limestone Plains

The Viceroy, Lieutenant-Colonel Lachlan Macquarie, was elated by the glowing reports of fertile grazing lands that had been discovered south of Sydney and was persuaded to explore them for himself. Expedition leaders were summoned, his entourage was organised, provisions were secured, horses were readied and the Governor's own carriage was prepared for the arduous trip. The news of these discoveries had been reported by Charles Throsby, a pastoralist in the Moss Vale district. Throsby was the first European to explore the Limestone Plains while his party was searching for pastures for their ever-expanding flocks of sheep and cattle.[1] Lake George had been discovered in 1820, a stretch of water that 'was brackish and unfit for use extending from N[orth] to S[outh] at least thirty Miles [and] ... widening to about ten miles ... full of Bays and Points on the East side, very beautiful ... '.[2]

By October 1820, Throsby had induced the Governor to visit the region and to gauge the potential of the land for the colony's needs. Macquarie – mindful of his own vice-regal dignity – insisted on being conveyed across 'the virgin country in a carriage' that was alternatively jarred by rutted plains or swamped in 'bogs and sloughs' that 'necessitated the unharnessing of horses'.[3] The trail was 'in appalling condition' but the sight of pastoral lands impressed the Governor who believed that settlement was highly desirable. On the way south, a service of divine worship was held near Lake Bathurst. The congregation numbered between 40 and 50.[4]

Discovery quickly led to settlement in 1824 when Joshua Moore's overseer pushed overland from Goulburn and settled on 2,000 acres at 'Canberry', now known as Acton, near the present Australian National Museum, the Australian National University and Canberra's Civic Centre. The following year, Robert Campbell, the first free merchant in Sydney Town, was granted 4,000 (later 5,000) acres of land that encompassed the present suburbs of Reid, Campbell, Ainslie and Duntroon, and to which he soon added Jerrabomberra, Majura and Narrabundah.[5] Other tracts of land were promptly settled and by 1828 there were an estimated 500 indigenous persons living in the area, together with 91 Europeans, 60 of whom resided on stations at Canberry, Duntroon, Ginninderra (Palmerville), Yarralumla, Weston Creek, Jerrabombera, Tuggeranong and Queanbeyan, with another 31 at Michelago and Jeir. Five of the 91 Europeans were female, two of whom were children.[6]

In one sense, it was a pleasant, peaceful scene of grazing lands, fed by the Molonglo and Murrumbidgee Rivers, and backdropped by nearby hills and far-off mountain ranges – a place where indigenous people and newly arrived settlers lived in relative harmony. Beneath this benign guise, however, there were pressing problems that emerged within a decade and disturbed the placid image. Most of the isolated stations were owned by non-resident landlords who delegated management to overseers charged with clearing the land and enduring the hardships of the rural frontier with the assistance of convict labour. Of the 60 men employed on the stations in 1828, 55 had arrived in the colony 'at His Majesty's pleasure'. It was an unforgiving land for the assigned, an almost totally male environment, where household robbery was not uncommon, bushrangers grew in number and boldness and cattle rustling emerged as a continuing hazard. A harsh climate, lack of facilities, isolation and unrelenting loneliness contributed to an unforgiving and often punitive existence.

Changes occurred by the end of the 1830s, however, and a semblance of law and order was imposed in 1838 with the appointment of a local magistrate and the sitting of the first Court of Petty Sessions 'in a hut on Moore's Canberry Estate'. The number of females in the wider County of Murray rose to 35 in 1833 and 250 in 1836. When transportation to New South Wales was abolished in 1840, the proportion of free immigrants sharply increased and the workforce became more industrious than the previous source of resentful convict labourers.[7]

Religion had a role to play in the transformation of this small society on the periphery of civilisation, partly an outcome of Robert Campbell's increasing participation in the affairs of the Church of England. Campbell, a Scot, increased his holdings near the Molonglo

River after 1825 and named the station Duntroon 'after an ancestral home of his clan'. Yet, despite having acquired 'the choicest selections on the Limestone Plains' by the 1840s, he did not visit the region before 1830 and it was only after the death of his wife, Sophia, in 1833 that he spent more time at his Duntroon property. Campbell was raised a committed Presbyterian, endowing and attending the Scots Church in Sydney but his growing connection with the Church of England led to generous endowments of Anglican church and school initiatives. He supported the establishment of the Kings School at Parramatta; contributed to the building of St Peter's Church at Cook's River; assisted churches at South Bargo, Yass and St Philip's Sydney; and helped to fund the building of an Anglican cathedral in Sydney.[8]

As he spent more time at Duntroon, he came to believe that free settlers were more productive than convict assignees and he encouraged the migration of Scottish highlanders to work on his estates. By 1841 there were up to 85 people living at Duntroon – overseers, shepherds, artisans and cooks – some of them provided with two-room cottages by the owner. While he contributed to their physical wellbeing, Campbell had misgivings about the lack of spiritual guidance available to these people and to others on surrounding stations.[9] Acknowledging that it was impossible for the first resident clergyman of Queanbeyan, the Reverend Edward Smith, to provide adequately for ten different outposts without church buildings in 1838, Campbell turned his mind to finding a solution.

And so this Scot, 'increasingly attracted to the stability of the Church of England', conferred with Edward Smith at Queanbeyan and with his friend, the Right Reverend William Broughton, Bishop of Australia, and offered material assistance.[10] The bishop was requested to visit the Limestone Plains and invited to stay at Duntroon, an invitation he accepted in 1840. Having promised to donate land for a church, Campbell escorted the bishop around the hills and plains of the Molonglo region, before they settled on a site for the future Church of St John the Baptist on the slopes of present-day Reid. It is difficult to visualise the site in the 1840s, surrounded by open fields that gently dipped toward a twisting river, nothing more than a benign brook when the country was in drought but an engulfing expanse in times of deluge.

By an indenture executed in 1844, Campbell conveyed to the bishop two acres of land for the church and a churchyard together with 100 acres for a clergyman's residence and a glebe. It is estimated that he also contributed £1,000 towards the total cost of £2,000 for the erection of the bluestone church that was eventually consecrated by Bishop Broughton on 12 March 1845. Perhaps it was fitting that, late in his life, Campbell received his first communion as a member of the Church of England 'in his own church.' He died at Duntroon in April 1846 but successive generations of the Campbell family continued to donate and bequeath to the church.[11]

The next 60 years formed a period of consolidation and stability for the small Christian community on the Limestone Plains, a time when a link to the English Establishment through the Church of England 'was a sign of gentility and a badge of respectability' without 'a taint of convictism.'[12] While the Church of England was not the Established Church in Australia, the clergy frequently acted as if it were. The rector of Queanbeyan provided itinerant support to the church until May 1850 when Bishop Broughton licensed the Reverend George Gregory, aged just 24 years, to minister to the church and to live in Canberry. Still in deacon's orders, he was well accepted and visited outlying settlements as part of his duties. Tragically, on returning from Cuppacumbalong in torrential rain, he drowned in the Molonglo River as he sought to swim the raging waters below the parsonage at Acton.[13] His friend and former fellow-student, the Reverend Thomas Wilkinson, was then appointed to St John's, a position he held for three years. On his departure, a 28-year-old Scot, was appointed by the new bishop-elect of Sydney, the Right Reverend Frederic Barker. So began the ministry of the Reverend Pierce Galliard-Smith, an incumbency that lasted 50 years and five months from 1855 until he retired late in 1905 at the age of 79 years.[14]

A number of concerns assumed critical importance during these years. They touched on matters that resonated well into the next century, influencing the worship at St John's and spilling over to the other parishes that would eventually be created. In other respects, however, some of the practices adopted and customs taken for granted in the nineteenth century were to be entirely reversed with the creation of the Federal Capital Territory in the early part of the twentieth century.

The congregation at St John's represented, in the main, the upper social order of well-known landowners and their immediate families, including the Campbells at Duntroon and Yarralumla, the Palmers at Ginninderra and later the Craces.[15] While others, such as the Harcourts (who operated the Ginninderra store) and the Shumacks (farmers at Weetangera), were not landed families they were highly respected 'genteel' community members who also nurtured the church. To this extent, St John's was the spiritual home of the upper social class in which the clergyman was also expected to exhibit similar gentlemanly traits. Even in the outlying regions of the parish, landowners predominated. Hence, by the turn of the century, St John's remained the main church in a parish in which 'almost without exception' the congregations were connected with rural pursuits and possessed a degree of influence in the community.

While St John's remained the mother church the clergy ministered to a widely scattered parish, requiring them to roster their time and provide at least two services each Sunday, one at St John's and a second at another centre many kilometres away. Riding their horses (fondly named Goliath, Phoebe, Rodney, Eagle and Snip) in all weathers, often after nightfall, fording flooded creeks and rivers in times of rain, answering calls for assistance and comfort in sweltering heat, rain or snow, and often performing their duties when they themselves were not well, the clergy faithfully ministered to settlements that included Uriarra, Naas, Brindabella, Gudgenby, Tuggeranong, Lanyon, Tharwa, Gundaroo, Ginninderra, Sutton and Bulga Creek (west of Duffy), a sparse itinerant ministry. It was a vast area to tend on horseback and the duties were demanding and constant, so much so that Smith did not have an extended holiday for almost 40 years. Apart from St John's, church buildings did not exist, requiring services to be held in the homes of devoted parishioners by clergy who were equally devoted and self-sacrificing. The challenge of providing for smaller, sometimes transient communities, confronted an overworked clergy for decades.

During Smith's long incumbency, St John's developed and exhibited a particular form of worship and liturgy. It was based largely on the parson's own background and theological predilections. After Bishop Broughton's death in 1853, it was not until 1855 that his successor arrived in Sydney from England. As bishop-elect, Frederic Barker had met Charles Campbell (from Duntroon) at London in December

1854 and had learned that the Reverend Thomas Wilkinson, who had been transferred from St John's Church to Ashfield, needed to be replaced. To fill the vacancy, Barker contacted his cousin, Pierce Galliard-Smith, and offered him the incumbency with 'a salary of £200 a year, three-quarters of which was provided by the state and the balance derived from the glebe lands, together with a rent-free parsonage', a 'very healthy' climate and 'good' society.[16] Smith quickly accepted and he and his family accompanied Bishop Barker in the ship to the colony.[17]

Barker and his cousin were committed Evangelicals. They were convinced that scripture was divinely-inspired, a Holy God could not countenance sin, humanity was depraved and sinful, the death of Jesus had made atonement for sin and redemption was possible through a personal commitment to Jesus Christ. These Evangelical convictions transcended denominational boundaries, emphasising 'conformity to the basic tenets of the faith and a missionary outreach of compassion and urgency'. John Wesley was unable to preserve his 'Methodist' movement within the Church of England and his followers broke with the discipline of the Established Church. Evangelicalism was preserved in the Church of England by a number of leading preachers including Charles Simeon and those who gathered around him at Cambridge, while John Newton, William Wilberforce and others fought social ills and founded Bible and missionary societies.[18]

Others in the church professed a different outlook.[19] Dismayed by the doctrinal and disciplinary laxity and inattention to aspects of the church's rich Catholic heritage, a group of clergymen at Oxford University argued through a succession of published tracts for a higher doctrine of the church approach, the importance of the apostolic succession and the necessity of the sacraments to spiritual maturity.[20]

The 'Tractarians', as they became known, deplored the tendency to reduce an apostolic church to a national institution and formulated a different theological mood with worship styles deemed more faithful to the full deposit of the Church's heritage. In later years, the Anglo-Catholic ritualists sought to restore the full panoply of liturgical ceremony as 'an outward and visible sign' of their high view of Christ's presence in the Eucharist and the church's elevated spiritual charter. Under their influence, such 'innovations' as eucharistic vestments, eastward facing during the recitation of the creed, the use of wafers for Holy Communion, altars dressed with lights and flowers, robed choirs, incense, reservation of the sacrament and auricular confession returned to the English Church.[21] Despite concerted opposition from Evangelicals and some Broad churchmen, many of these practices were steadily incorporated into routine church liturgy and became increasingly widespread over time. As the movement modified during the nineteenth and twentieth centuries, the term 'Anglo-Catholic' was more widely accepted and used.[22]

The differences between the Evangelical and Anglo-Catholic mindsets became evident at St John's in Canberry. The first cler-gyman, the young George Gregory, admitted to his 'unfortunate leaning to Romanism in times past' and believed that it prevented his advancement in the church. When Pierce Galliard-Smith arrived,

Reverend Pierce Galliard-Smith, 1897
© St John's Schoolhouse Museum

he asserted the strong Evangelical attitude of his cousin, Bishop Barker. Indeed, Smith de-cided to study at Durham University to avoid the Tractarian influences of Oxford.[23] While the Sydney church was more High Church than avowedly Tractarian, it was about to change under Barker's influence.[24]

Smith moved the liturgy at St John's in a distinctly Evangelical direction. He referred to his home as the 'parsonage' and not the 'rectory', he called himself 'Parson Smith' or 'Minister' and not 'Rector', and his carefully crafted ser-mons emphasised sin, repentance and salvation. Communion was not celebrated each week but held once a month (sometimes every two months) towards the end of Smith's incumbency.[25] While he followed the usual practice of wearing a clerical collar, this rather shy and austere man frowned on formal vestments within the church. He was more likely to wear his aca-demic hood over his white surplice. In characteristic Evangelical style he disliked frivolity and disapproved strongly of 'lotteries and raffles ... and especially of dances, fancy dress

St John's Rectory (Parsonage) 1890s
© St John's Schoolhouse Museum

balls, concerts, theatricals, Punch and Judy shows and other like modes of providing the stipends of those who share in the sacred Ministry of God's Church'. As Alf Body remarked 90 years later: 'It was an austere religion that was preached at St John's at the time' although very much in keeping with Evangelical piety and practice popular at the time.[26]

Like many in southern New South Wales, Smith would have pondered the future and his own prospects when it was decided in 1861 to create the Bishopric of Goulburn. The subdivision of Sydney diocese would separate him from his cousin and end the close relationship he had enjoyed with his diocesan bishop. Any apprehension was unwarranted. The first Bishop of Goulburn, Mesac Thomas, was a graduate of Cambridge and a man with 'a sense of mission flowing from his evangelical faith'.[27] He had been Secretary of the Colonial and Continental Church Society, a body that stressed personal conversion and exhibited an enthusiasm 'similar to that of the Wesleys and Whitfield'. Moreover, Thomas himself had conducted evangelical missions 'to the [horse] cab drivers and the bus drivers of London'.[28]

On his arrival in the colony, the new bishop maintained his commitment to Evangelicalism, holding traditional morning and evening prayer services, celebrating Communion only infrequently so as 'to impress the meaning of our Lord's atonement', and disapproving of 'long disused rites and ceremonies' and any reinterpretation of the Bible along rationalist lines. These were 'novelties' associated with Tractarianism to which he could not subscribe.[29] According to the diocesan historian, Tom Frame, Thomas was at times intolerant. He 'looked upon Roman Catholic priests as usurpers and Non-conformist ministers as interlopers', and set out to convert as many as possible to the Anglican faith.[30] It was only after the appointment of William Chambers as the second Bishop of Goulburn in 1892 that the theological mood of Goulburn diocese became broader and inclusive.[31] While Frame maintains that the 1890s marked the end of a particular form of Evangelicalism in the diocese, its influence was extended another decade at St John's.[32] Whatever the form of churchmanship, however, the church was clearly the transplanted Church of England, one that lacked a distinct Australian character.

In one sense, St John's was fortunate that Smith remained the incumbent for half a century as it resulted in a secure source of funding for the church. The *Church Act* of 1836 (NSW) had provided government subsidies for clerical stipends and, although this was discontinued for clergy appointed after 1862, it continued in Smith's case until his retirement in 1905.[33] This meant that the church had at least three sources of income: an annual government grant of up to £150; rents and other income from the glebe lands located between the church and the river; and fees from parishioners for reserved pews in the church. Most of these funds were forfeited after 1905, resulting in considerable insecurity during some difficult years. Mesac Thomas foresaw some of these potent challenges when the Goulburn Church Society was established in 1864 to support the church's work in the furthest reaches of the large diocese.

The resignation of Pierce Galliard-Smith in October 1905 ended a significant era in St John's history on the Limestone Plains, one of consolidation and consistency. It might be argued that, like Bishop Thomas whom he outlived, Smith retained the attitude of an English clergyman 'who never seemed quite to accept that his Church no longer enjoyed the privileges and status of being established by law in the Colony'.[34] After all, state support for his stipend was assured until his resignation. Additionally, the congregation at St John's was drawn mainly from the landed gentry and he was afforded a commensurate level of respect throughout the district. Even at the turn of the century, Smith fitted Patricia Curthoys' description of mid-nineteenth century Anglican clerics: 'They were clergy of the majority religion, were usually gentlemen, and saw themselves as part of the colonial gentry'.[35]

Smith's legacy was enduring. It is said that he changed the name of Canberry to Canberra in the early 1860s and, when the first post office was opened in January 1863, it assumed the name that he had chosen, 'Canberra'.[36] The wife of the Governor General, Lord Denman, confirmed the tradition in 1913. But neither the clergy nor the congregation realised the far-reaching events that were about to transform this rural community.

Notes

1. L Gillespie, *Canberra 1820–1913*, Australian Government Publishing Service, Canberra, 1991.
2. J Wild to C Throsby, 1820. Cited in E Lea-Scarlett, *Queanbeyan – District and People*, Queanbeyan Municipal Council, 1986, p. 2.
3. Gillespie, *Canberra 1820–1913*, p. 3.
4. A Body, 'The cross beside the lake – some background notes', *Diocesan Historical Society Journal*, April, no.1, 1986, pp. 3–8.
5. A Fitzgerald, *Canberra in Two Centuries. A Pictorial History*, Clareville Press and the Limestone Plains Partnership, Canberra, 1987, pp. 12–14, 16–17; and Lea-Scarlett, *Queanbeyan*, pp. 10–11.
6. '1307.8 – Australian Capital Territory in Focus', 2007, *Australian Bureau of Statistics, http://www.abs.gov.au*
7. Fitzgerald, *Canberra in Two Centuries*, pp. 8–9; Lea-Scarlett, *Canberra 1820–1913*, p. 17.
8. M Steven, 'Campbell, Robert (1769–1846)', *Australian Dictionary of Biography*, vol. 1 (pp. 202–206), Melbourne University Press, 1966.
9. There were '557 persons in the area including Gungahlin, Lanyon and Queanbeyan, 120 of whom were female'. Yarralumla had ... 108 persons ... Queanbeyan seventy-two, Palmerville 68 and Lanyon fifty-nine. 'Australian Capital Territory in Focus'.
10. Steven, 'Campbell, Robert (1769–1846)'.
11. A discussion of the site selection, the laying of the foundation stone and the opening and consecration of St John the Baptist Church is provided in, A Body, *Firm Still You Stand*, St John's Parish Council, Canberra, 1986, pp. 7–17.
12. B Fletcher, 'The Anglican ascendancy' (pp. 7–30) in B Kaye (ed.), *Anglicanism in Australia. A History*, Melbourne University Press, 2002, p. 20.
13. PN, May 1957.
14. The aim is to sketch the background history of St John's Church in order to analyse developments and practices that were later to influence the parish, especially the inner south of Canberra. I have relied heavily on: Body, *Firm Still You Stand*; and L Fitzhardinge, *St John's Church and Canberra* (2nd edition), St John's Parish Council, Canberra, 1959.
15. Jean Salisbury has researched the history of St John's Church and disputes this generalisation by referring to the number of manual workers and artisans who were buried in St John's Churchyard. Burial in the church grounds, however, did not necessarily denote church membership. Additionally, the workers when attending sat upstairs away from the general congregation. Personal communication, 2009.
16. Body, *Firm Still You Stand*, pp. 36; 45; 97.
17. R Willson, 'Jane Barker's Letters from Canberra', *MARGIN: Life & Letters in Early Australia*, April 2008, *http://findarticles.com*
18. R Pierard, *Evangelicalism, http://www.mb-soft.com/believe/text/evangeli.htm*

19. L Radford, 'The Oxford Movement. I. Its antecedents' in J Moses (ed.), *From Oxford to the Bush. Essays on Catholic Anglicanism in Australia,* Broughton Press and SPCK, 1997, p. 4.

20. *Anglo-Catholic, http://www.answers.com/topic/anglo-catholicism*

21. 'The Oxford Movement', *The Columbia Encyclopedia* (6th edition), 2008, *http://www.encyclopedia.com/doc/1E1-Oxfordmo.html*

22. P Curthoys, 'State support for churches 1836–1860' (pp. 31–51) in Kaye, *Anglicanism in Australia*, p. 42.

23. See Body, *Firm Still You Stand*, pp. 24–26, 35.

24. Willson, 'Jane Barker's Letters'; and Fletcher, *The Anglican Ascendancy*, p. 24.

25. StJ Register of Services, 1899 to 1905.

26. Fitzhardinge, *St John's Church*; and Body, *Firm Still You Stand*, p. 89.

27. B Wright, *Shepherds in New Country. Bishops in the Diocese of Canberra and Goulburn 1937–1993*, WE Wright, Moruya, NSW, 1993, p. 37.

28. JR Border, *The Founding of the See of Goulburn*, St Mark's Library Publications, no. 1, Canberra, 1956.

29. T Frame, *Anglicans in Australia*, UNSW Press, Sydney, 2007, pp. 74–75.

30. T Frame, *A Church for a Nation: The History of the Anglican Diocese of Canberra and Goulburn*, Hale & Iremonger, Sydney, 2000, p. 59.

31. Wright, *Shepherds in a New Country*, p. 37.

32. Frame, *A Church for a Nation*, p. 79.

33. The Church Act, 1836, *http://www.sl.nsw.gov.au/discover_collections/ history_nation/religion/places/act.html*

34. Frame, *A Church for a Nation*, p. 59.

35. Curthoys, 'State Support for Churches', p. 40.

36. Body, *Firm Still You Stand*, pp. 42–43.

2   The Southside: beginnings

The Reverend Frederick Ward (and dog) with Bishop Barlow, Barmedman 1911. © *St Mark's Library Archives*

It was a long and tiring journey for Frederick Ward as he travelled from Barmedman in the central west of New South Wales to the newly proclaimed Federal Capital Territory in 1913. While it was possible to travel by train for part of the way – even to engage a 'motor service from Yass to the Capital' – there were sections by coach or buggy and he was glad to arrive.[1]

After migrating from Middlesex at the suggestion of Bishop Christopher Barlow at the turn of the century, he had become a lay reader in the Diocese of North Queensland where Barlow was bishop. When Barlow was elected and enthroned as the third Bishop of Goulburn in April 1902, Frederick Ward and his brother John, a priest, were two of the team who followed the bishop to Goulburn. Fred was licensed as a lay reader in the parish of Young on 22 August 1904. He later entered Bishop's College at Goulburn to study theology, was made a deacon in February 1905 and ordained a priest in November 1907.[2] After serving as assistant minister at St Saviour's Cathedral, curacies at Temora and Wagga Wagga, and an incumbency at Barmedman, Ward succeeded the Reverend Arthur Champion as rector of St John's in April 1913 at the age of 37.[3] (Arthur Hopcroft and Arthur Champion succeeded Pierce Galliard-Smith at St John's in the period 1906–13.)

A few weeks earlier, special trains had brought almost 500 guests from Sydney and Melbourne to Queanbeyan and Yass from where they had been transported over rough and irregular tracks to the Territory. Together with local residents who arrived in wagons and buggies, the assembled dignitaries had seen cadets from the Royal Military College form a guard of honour, heard a salute of nineteen guns echo across the plains and listened expectantly to Lady Denman as she announced that the new city would be named 'Canberra'. After another salute of twenty-one guns and the singing of both 'Advance Australia Fair' and the national anthem, 'God Save the King', the crowd dispersed and quietness returned to the Molonglo Plains.[4]

Bishop Barlow, who had been asked by the Primate to represent the Church of England, may have stopped at the rectory overnight and visited St John's where the new rector was expected within the month.[5] Barlow had arranged for Ward to preach at the Easter Sunday Service at St John's on 20 April but the new rector arrived unexpectedly before that date.[6] As Arthur Champion had vacated the rectory and his furniture and effects had been auctioned for sale on 5 April, the rectory was available for Ward's use from early April.[7]

The crowds left Canberra after the naming ceremony and Frederick Ward arrived quietly in his new parish soon after. He was invited to serve as Chaplain to the Royal Military College at Duntroon, an appointment confirmed the day before his first service at St John's.[8] He must have experienced mixed emotions as he walked the short distance from the rectory to the church on that Easter Sunday, the bell tolling its welcome and a happy but curious crowd arriving in sulkies, on horseback or on foot. While he was keen to lead the parish and provide spiritual guidance with compassion and humility, he was well aware of disturbing challenges confronting him and the congregation.

Finance was a major concern. Indeed, it extended to the ultimate ownership of church property. Land ownership had overnight become a problem when the government decreed that no-one was to own land in the Territory, thereby allowing the Commonwealth to resume all property over time. Compensation would be paid on 1908 valuations. St John's was not immune from this provision and lost ownership of all its lands – 119 acres of glebe, the rectory and even the churchyard.[9] The pre-emptory decision was to result in years of wrangling between the bishop and the Commonwealth as both parties sought to determine acceptable compensation. When added to the cessation of government assistance towards the rector's stipend in 1905, the gradual phasing out of rented pews in the church and the loss of glebe rents, the delay in settling compensation was one of many major concerns for the rector and the parish council.

Moreover, rapid changes were occurring in the congregation at St John's, largely a result of laws prohibiting freehold ownership of land. The church had drawn its membership from landowners and their employees in the past. When the Federal Capital Territory was proclaimed, a number of landowners could see the uncertainties that might eventuate, sold up and moved from the region. The government had resumed Yarralumla and the Duntroon estates, and St John's was to lose the support of the Campbell and Hudson families 'together with many close supporters of the Parish', all of whom 'were severe losses to the Church'.[10] Other landowners were scrambling to negotiate compensation claims before leaving the district.

While these challenges loomed large, the new rector was even more concerned about the potential expansion in population with the arrival of tradesmen and labourers, together with the widespread nature of settlements across the territory. With the resumption of Duntroon and the establishment of the Royal Military College, there was now a permanent settlement of workers on the Duntroon site with a consequent demand for weekly church services and chaplaincy support. Ward would need to ride to Duntroon each Sunday as well as travel to outlying centres on a rotational basis. Additionally, there were increasing numbers of children at Duntroon, creating the need for a Sunday school and for weekly religious instruction.

The decision to declare Canberra the nation's capital led to major geographical surveys, the laying out of sites and the construction of numerous buildings over a short period of time. Ward knew that work had commenced on cutting a pipe track from the Cotter River to Canberra and on the construction of a storage dam to provide the city's water supply, works that required over 120 persons.[11] He was aware that the Brickworks at Westridge were employing over 60 workers, that the railway line under construction from Queanbeyan to Eastlake involved an additional workforce and that the Acton work camp and administration centre had become a permanent site.[12] Then, as a final reminder of actual growth, he could look out from the rectory across the river to the rising steel skeleton of the

Powerhouse, a facility that employed substantial numbers of workmen in its construction.[13]

During May and June 1913, he had time to assess the overall situation and ponder how he might provide for the spiritual needs of the diverse settlements: 80 persons at Ainslie, 127 at Canberra, 252 at Duntroon, 195 at Ginninderra and 57 at Tuggeranong, just to mention five of approximately 30 scattered settlements in his parish. As an initial measure, Ward wrote to the Administrator in July and sought permission to conduct church services in the galvanised-iron Canberra Recreation Hall at Acton on the second and fourth Sundays of each month, a request that was granted with 'much pleasure'.[14] Then he turned his mind to the Brickworks and the Powerhouse.

The Brickworks was situated on 38 acres of land that formed part of the Yarralumla property owned by Fred Campbell who had allowed the government to erect the buildings and to mine the shale nearby. Ward watched as the workmen's camps were laid out in June 1913, one of tents (mainly for single workers) and the other of hastily erected humpies (for married men and their families) in an area near to present day Banks Street in Yarralumla.[15] Near the future intersection of Banks and Schlich Streets a nursery had been established by Charles Weston to determine the most appropriate trees and shrubs for Canberra's climate and to grow seedlings that could be transplanted to cover the empty plains.

Less than a year later, the rector decided it was time to act in a concerted way. When he rode to the camp in 1914, he looked for a building in which to hold services and most likely settled on the Single Men's Mess as there was virtually nothing else available that was suitable. Hard-pressed to meet his existing commitments, Ward approached Assistant Professor Frederick Robinson at the Royal Military College and informed his parishioners that Professor Robinson 'has willingly come to my assistance and will hold a fortnightly service at the Brickworks'.[16] The first service was held at 3.30pm on Sunday 17 May 1914 but it proved impossible to maintain a fortnightly schedule. Monthly services were conducted instead in May, June, July and August 1914 and actually ceased for eight months before resuming in March 1915. Nevertheless, Ward had taken the first step in broadening the Anglican presence in Canberra from its nineteenth-century rural emphasis to a more inclusive gathered community. The rector then turned his attention to the Powerhouse camps which posed a different problem.

The founders of Canberra were far-sighted and planned for an all-electric city of 25,000 people at a time 'when electricity had only recently been made available in Sydney and Melbourne on a restricted basis'. A powerhouse was planned south of the river despite Walter Burley Griffin's objection to siting it on the flat area above the Molonglo River at Eastlake because it was grazing and farm land with hardly a tree in sight. The Powerhouse would stand out as a tall, unbecoming structure on a bare landscape. The site was strategically located, however, as the condensers of the steam generating sets could be cooled from a small dam on the river 150 metres away. Griffin's objections were overridden and construction of the Powerhouse commenced in October 1912 on the bare stretch of land.[17]

By the time that Ward arrived in 1913, a small weir dammed the river, construction of the Powerhouse had been underway seven months and the railway line from Queanbeyan to the Powerhouse was being prepared.[18] In a bustle of activity, the 'enormous' steel structure gradually rose and the concrete walls were poured, while one and half million bricks were fired at the Brickworks and delivered to the site for the internal, non-supportive walls.[19] Unfortunately, the bricks were defective and were never used. A host of other temporary or semi-permanent buildings gradually surrounded the tall structure, all designed for the engineers, painters, fitters and electrical engineers and for the workers in the stores office. Other iron sheds housed timber, pipes, crushing material, general works offices, stables for horses and petrol for trucks.[20] The railway from Queanbeyan to the Powerhouse was completed in February 1914 and trains then transported heavy materials to the site and to other parts of Canberra.[21]

Swagger Camp: the married men's quarters near the Powerhouse before 1921 © *Ann Gugler*

When Ward rode his horse 'Bayfield' across Scott's Crossing to the Powerhouse area in 1914, he knew that the tradesmen sought to keep separate from the navvies, while the married families usually lived separately from the single men.[22] He came to Swagger Camp, the first established settlement next to the Powerhouse on a site that included what is now Wentworth Avenue up to Gosse Street.[23] Designed for married couples, the men and their families lived in 'humpies made out of galvanised iron, hessian and wood'. Separated from them were the single workers who apparently lived closer to the present railway station in tents rented on a shared basis for 1s 6d a week while others built temporary huts from whatever materials they could purchase or pilfer from government works.[24] For two streets of huts and tents, there was one common water tap, a central ablution block and 'six water closets for each 20 dwellings'. It was a cold and spartan exist-ence. Another site, established two years later across the road from the Powerhouse, was the Engineers' Mess, containing living quarters and a mess hall.[25]

Frederick Ward was troubled by the absence of a Christian pres-ence at Swagger Camp and other nearby settlements and discussed the need to intervene with members of the parish council. He was shrewd, however, realising the importance of having the Powerhouse workers on side and contacted the Secretary of the Railway Workers and General Labourers Association, J O'Neill, and outlined a plan to him. O'Neill was impressed, calling a meeting of the workers and inviting Ward to address the men. The result was described as a big event when 'the workers rolled up to a man, including those belonging to the small craft unions'.

The church decided to erect a hall 'by voluntary labour as a place of worship and recreation' and Ward announced the decision from St John's pulpit, seeking volunteers to assist.[26] It was twelve months since he had come to the parish but the workers at the Cotter Junction, Powerhouse and Brickworks had 'received no ministrations of the Church during that time'. With the assistance of a curate, he hoped 'to do something' for the workers, announcing that 'a church hall is being erected at the Powerhouse (April–May 1914) in which we intend to hold regular services'.[27] In response, Fred Campbell, continuing his family's support of St John's over a period of 70 years, guaranteed a loan of £60 from the newly-founded Commonwealth Bank for 'build-ing a Church of England Hall at the Power Station Centre'. This gesture was made at the time of his retirement from Synod and immediately before he left the district. It is unknown whether all of the loan was required as some of the costs were covered by local efforts.[28] The parish council was particularly cautious in 1914 as church funds were low and negotiations with the Commonwealth for compensation over lost assets were continuing.

The Sydney-based firm, Saxton and Binns, provided a quote for the provision of building supplies while JB Young's store in Queanbeyan provided minor items.[29] Tenders were not called. Voluntary labour was employed to construct the building 'with enthusiasm' and even the local doctor 'turned up to lend a hand' dressed in 'frockcoat and gaiters somewhat after the style of a nineteenth century bishop'.[30] Two church members, Frank Dowthwaite and a Mr Green, acted as building overseers and provided the necessary skills to erect the small building that was slightly modified at the last moment because of the costs involved. When all the bills were later received, the total cost of the building was £89 8s 9d of which £30 was paid for the labour and almost £43 for building materials.[31]

As eight members of parish council met on a winter's evening at the rectory on 10 June 1914, they realised that the hall would be finished in a few weeks' time and that plans for the opening needed to be made. As it was far too complex an item for eight people to consider together, a small sub-committee was formed under Mr Maytum's

St Paul's Church Hall, 1914   © St John's Schoolhouse Museum

direction to 'be responsible for the arrangements' while the rector and Mr Ireland formally agreed 'to make the necessary plans for a concert and evening'.[32] One wonders whether Ward invited the Canberra Glee Club to participate as he himself was a well-known member of the local singing group.

On a 'very cold and stormy' day on Sunday 12 July 1914, the rector conducted an early service at Duntroon, returned through the rain for the morning service at St John's and then prepared for two more duties. Before conducting the evening service at Duntroon at 7pm he was delighted to ford the river to the Powerhouse Centre and conduct the first Sunday school in the hall at 3pm – an unofficial but important opening.[33] Located in the middle of an open field on short piers, amid the soil churned up by the builders and now turned to mud, was a small and unpretentious building of galvanised iron with a wooden door and adorned by two small wooden crosses on the gables. (When the area was eventually surveyed, the hall stood near the corner of Wentworth Avenue and Gosse Street.) The building, which probably still required a few finishing touches, was not lined nor was it lit or heated. It had only a few stools with no backs.[34] The clatter of children's feet echoed on the wooden floor, while its tin roof and walls accentuated the reverberating noise of the afternoon's rain. One wonders how many attended the first Church of England venture in the future suburb of Kingston. No records survive.

Twenty days later, the hall designed for 30 people, was officially opened at 5pm on Saturday 1 August 1914 when a group of enthusiastic people crowded into the building lit by kerosene lamps. The

St Paul's opened 1 August 1914. ©St John's Register of Services, 1914 rector blessed the mission hall which he named St Paul's – the new spiritual home of the Eastlake workers – and outlined his vision for the future.[35] A collection of £2 14s amounted to nearly one-thirtieth of the total cost of the building. Then everyone settled down to an enjoyable evening of entertainment arranged by Mr Ireland and the rector – a few violins, an accordion, a piper, solos and duets, humorous, sentimental or patriotic recitations and a supper were usual concert fare.[36] While the building was undoubtedly blessed by the rector, it was never consecrated nor was the land on which it stood ever acquired by the church. The consecration of a mission hall still encumbered by debt on uncommitted ground was neither seemly nor canonical. It also reflected the policy introduced by Bishop Thomas that permitted only substantial permanent (stone) buildings to be consecrated.

As he rode back across the fields to the rectory in the dark with a lantern in hand, Frederick Ward must have felt a further sense of accomplishment. Apart from outlying districts, he and his helpers now conducted weekly services at St John's and Duntroon, two services each month at Acton and a monthly service at the Brickworks, as well as a Sunday school at Duntroon and the proposed services at St Paul's mission hall. God's work was being extended and it encouraged the rector to do more to meet the needs of the growing population.

The next day (Sunday 2 August) the rector conducted the evening service at Duntroon where he learned of ominous developments overseas. A month earlier, Archduke Ferdinand had been assassinated in Serbia and this had led to escalating tensions in the Balkans, culminating in Austria–Hungary's declaration of war on Serbia. *The Queanbeyan Age* noted a Russian comment that the situation 'was the biggest upheaval since Napoleon'.[37] Ward then heard the frightening news that Germany had declared war on Russia a few hours before and, the following day, learned that Germany was at war with France. A terrible international conflagration had commenced. When German troops marched into Belgium, Britain declared war on Germany 24 hours later.[38] The rector could not help but be involved: he was chaplain to officers and cadets who could and would be sent into battle.

The reaction in Canberra, Queanbeyan and surrounding districts was immediate. The clergy extolled 'loyalty to the great (British) Empire', their congregations heard 'appropriate' sermons, all stood and sang the national anthem with fervour and church groups discussed ways of helping the war effort.[39] The 3pm service on 9 August was significant in its own right: it was the first service of divine worship held in the Powerhouse mission hall. The sermon centred on the outbreak of war the preceding week. In a sombre mood, Ward outlined the problems, agreed that war was justified against blatant aggression and spoke of Australia's obligations to Britain. All knew of his affiliation with the military college a few miles away and recognised his absolute commitment to the military forces as he explored ways in which the little congregation could combine with others to assist England, Belgium and the allies. His sentiments accorded with those of the bishop (Christopher Barlow) and the majority of the Church of England clergy who were 'thoroughly imbued with Imperial loyalty, based on an established tradition of supporting British military campaigns'.[40] As Brian Fletcher has pointed out, Christian values needed to be safeguarded at a time when there was a 'struggle between rival ideologies – the ideals which the church sought to defend were embodied above all in the British Empire which had at all costs to be preserved'.[41]

The Powerhouse congregation was not to know, however, that their rector would write to the Vicar-General within two weeks, applying to join the AIF as a military chaplain for overseas duty.[42] It was not acceptable for the clergy to engage in combatant duties which conflicted with their ordination vows but ministry to those who fought and those who supported them was deemed a worthy calling. Consequently, together with 174 other Anglican clergy across Australia, Ward volunteered as a chaplain and was accepted.[43] Fortunately for St John's, he was able to remain in Canberra for another year as rector with oversight of the fledgling centres before departing for overseas service.

At first, it was not possible to conduct services in the mission hall each week owing to the burden of other demands on his time but this changed with the appointment of a young curate, the Reverend Frederick Berry. Ward and Berry were able to alternate and hold Evensong at 3pm or 7.30pm until Christmas 1914. Following Berry's sudden departure, Ward obtained the assistance of a young stipendiary lay reader, Cyril Ashley Wilson, who assumed an important role at a time when conditions worsened and it became increasingly difficult to maintain a Christian presence at the Powerhouse.[44]

St Paul's mission hall could not have been opened at a worse time. It was meant to serve the workers in the region, the majority of whom were employed at the Powerhouse and workshops but, even as the hall was being constructed, the number of workmen was declining. As the Powerhouse neared completion in June, men were discharged and even more were put off when the machinery was installed in April 1915. Moreover, the Queanbeyan–Canberra Railway was completed early in 1914 and 'the men paid off' together with carpenters and other back-up staff. A correspondent for *The Queanbeyan Age* reported that 'unless further works are approved … it will be necessary to further reduce hands', a most unfortunate outcome 'considering the depression existing owing to the war and the outlook for the pastoralists'.

The government was also forced to implement cost-saving measures because of the war effort. Pipeline gangs were cut back and later closed down. Road gangs were reduced from four men to two and 'every suggestion to spend money at the Capital was objected to' in the federal parliament then situated temporarily in Melbourne.[45] Men left Canberra as soon as work ran out or as their contracts expired – the labour force of 754 in the territory in September 1913 fell to 690 in November, to 568 in January 1914 and to 359 in March 1914.[46] The exodus was not confined to labourers and semi-skilled workmen but extended to public servants who had recently arrived from Melbourne and Sydney. Will Rolland, then a child, later recalled how his father moved back to the Melbourne Department of Works because of 'the cessation of all building operations' in Canberra. His mother and three small children were driven to Yass over 42 miles of unsealed road on a 'bitterly cold night' with the wind whistling through the car that had no side curtains (windows). Even the journey south was coldly interrupted at Albury when they had to change trains because of different gauge railway tracks.[47] Canberra was in the doldrums.

With a diminishing population and restricted sources of funding, St John's sought ways of clearing the outstanding debt on the Powerhouse hall. Six parishioners contributed £9 among themselves, a mission service at Duntroon raised extra money and a vocal and instrumental concert netted over £33, raising the total contributions to over £46.[48] This left the daunting sum of £43 still owing and the members of St John's parish council searched for a novel way of generating funds. Then a creatively minded person suggested that they 'pelt the Kaiser'. A widely advertised sports day was arranged for May 1915 at the Canberra Recreation Reserve and an innovative program was designed. On the day, a 'goodly crowd' turned up despite the 'cold and bleak' weather and a piercing wind that funnelled down from the snow-capped mountains around the emerging city. Apart from a wide range of athletic events, people guessed the weight of fat sheep and the height of tall poles, taking time to warm up at the refreshment bar with hot drinks and food. One of the main attractions, however, was a shooting gallery and a chance to 'pelt the Kaiser' by throwing balls and rubbish at a figure dressed as the German monarch. Given national sentiment it was 'well patronised'. 'The Reverend FG Ward mingled with his parishioners and had an encouraging word for all.' At the end of the day, the receipts totalled just over £43 and the debt on St Paul's was paid off.[49]

Repaying the debt so quickly was even more remarkable at a time when the population was solidly focussed on financing the war effort. Patriotic funds, such as the FCT War Fund, were immediately opened to which residents could contribute on a fortnightly basis. Collection boxes were placed in public places including the Powerhouse, grand military displays were organised across the region and a wide range of community events was organised throughout the war years. The Canberra Patriotic Sports were arranged, musical and dramatic concerts were held, addresses were given on Germany, the Red Cross collected donations and bazaars were a frequent occurrence. They were all designed to raise funds to assist soldiers overseas. By May 1915 the Federal Capital Territory War Food Fund amounted to £1,240, 'a magnificent result when it is considered that the whole population – men, women and children – (was) under 2000 and comparatively all in humble circumstances.'[50]

Public giving was bolstered as local men enlisted and their names were publicised in *The Queanbeyan Age*. Patriotic sentiment was further stimulated as heavy losses of life were reported at Gallipoli during April 1915 and news was received in May of the death of General William Bridges, late of Duntroon. The general's body was returned to Canberra where the rector participated at the funeral held in St John's. The return of others from active service, many incapacitated, reinforced the feeling of loyalty and encouraged men to enlist although the heavy casualties among the graduates of Duntroon

shocked the local population.⁵¹ Chaplain Ward assumed the difficult
task of communicating with the families of former cadets who were
killed or wounded.

As Ward prepared his Easter sermons in 1915, he expressed some
very personal feelings. 'The joy of Easter is darkened this year by the
fearful war now raging in Europe' and there was never 'a time when
your prayers were more earnestly needed than now'.

> The call to service is to all, not merely by taking up arms or by
> monetary assistance but in a much more powerful way, namely
> by interceding to God for those who fight, that strength may
> be given them to uphold our honour. The Empire, as a whole,
> needs your prayers and not it alone but also the State as well
> as the Diocese … surely we need to turn our faces more to
> Him who is the giver of all good things.⁵²

Five months later Ward sailed for Egypt as a chaplain with the expe-
ditionary forces, a day or two after having learned of the death of his
old friend, Bishop Barlow, who had died in the rectory at Cooma, the
home of Fred Ward's brother and mother.

Barlow's successor, Bishop Lewis Radford, had the challenging
task of finding clergy and lay people who could lead the church during
the war years. The Reverend Albert MS Wilson took over from Ward
as *locum tenens* at St John's and maintained services in the major
centres with the assistance of lay readers, including the young Ashley
Wilson, the stipendiary lay reader who, according to Ward, came 'with
all the freshness and enthusiasm of youth'. With this commendation
and Ward's trust that 'the richest of God's blessing will be on his
work', Ashley Wilson and the locum conducted morning prayers and
Evensong at two or three week intervals at St Paul's Hall during 1915
and 1916, while maintaining some services for the children.

Unfortunately, 'owing to parents failing to send their children' to
the Sunday school and the relocation of families from the district, the
Sunday school was discontinued early in 1916. A demanding time was
made even more difficult by Ashley Wilson's decision to enter St John's
College, Armidale, to train for the priesthood.⁵³ Matters became increasingly desperate for the church toward the end of that year with
the local newspaper reporting that there were very few men employed

and, but 'for the desire to avoid creating further unemployment, the whole of the works would have been closed down.'[54]

Numbers became so depleted near the Powerhouse that services were held only once a month at St Paul's early in 1917 while in both March and April 1917 'no congregation' turned up at all. As a result, St Paul's closed its doors, a casualty of war, depression, population exodus and a parish stressed beyond its human resources. On the night of Sunday 15 April 1917 or soon after, another lay reader, Wilberforce Brooke, collected the small heater that had been donated by St John's, removed the altar cloth, put the church key in his pocket and returned despondently to the rectory.[55] He left two lamps in the hall just in case they were required on a future occasion. And so the church stood closed, swept by the red dust that blew across the paddocks, overlooked by the small settlement still living near the Powerhouse and waited for the end of war and a gradual upturn in the economy. In the meantime, St John's treasurer duly paid 10s 6d each year to insure the building for the sum of £90.[56]

Four weeks later the acting rector, the Reverend Arthur Champion, read the annual report of his predecessor – another acting rector who had filled in during Ward's absence. Its contents worried him exceedingly as he considered the best way to respond. Champion had been the rector of St John's in 1913 and had now been asked by the bishop to return and act *in locum tenens* until permanent arrangements could be made. He read that there had been 'many losses by removal; in fact the majority of the old church people, interested in the Parish Church' (those who had previously been his parishioners), had now 'left owing to the Federal Government resumptions,' and that seven church officers at St John's had resigned in one year 'either to go on active service, or on account of removal.'[57] Clearly, there was a crisis and Champion decided to raise the issue at his first parish council meeting.

It was a rather sombre council that met in the rectory that Saturday in May 1917. The acting rector asked to be 'made acquainted with the condition of the Parish' and turned first to the Brickworks settlement. When he consulted the Register of Services, he found that services had begun in May 1914 and that, apart from an eight months' break when there was no-one to lead the worship, they had continued without any interruption. From March 1915 until March 1916, there had been a monthly service conducted by the lay reader, Ashley Wilson, except when 'the river was up' and there was no access to the camp from the northside. Moreover, Ashley Wilson had introduced fortnightly services from April 1916, a schedule maintained by Wilberforce Brooke when he took over in December 1916. Consequently, the council members were aware that the fortnightly services were still provided in May 1917, although there were ominous signs that the camp numbers were falling. Nevertheless, the council was cautiously optimistic about the continuation of worship at the centre.

Brooke had a different story to relate about the Powerhouse settlement. There was no congregation at St Paul's, no services had been held there for three months and the Sunday school had been discontinued over a year ago.[58] After discussion, the council agreed that services could not be sustained at the Powerhouse and, when the acting rector asked for possible suggestions, Mr Lea suggested that St Paul's should be permanently closed and the building moved to the Brickworks. Others contended that such a decision might be premature because the council was still awaiting the government's decision on church property and the amount of compensation to be received. Unable or unwilling to make a binding decision, Champion and the seven council members 'decided to leave the matter ... till the next meeting' in six weeks' time.[59] Another debate ensued at the July meeting and it was 'decided to postpone the suggested removal of the Hall at the Powerhouse'. Champion was probably reluctant to make a long-term decision in Ward's absence and the issue was not formally discussed again. It could wait until Chaplain Ward returned.

In the meantime, much had occurred in Chaplain Ward's life. After saying farewell to his mother and his brother at the Cooma rectory in September 1915, Ward – 39 years of age and unmarried – left Canberra and was inducted into the Australian Imperial Force as Captain FG Ward (Chaplain 4th Class) on 1 September. He embarked for Egypt on the *Beltana* on 9 November. As part of the 8th Australian Infantry Brigade, he was paid 19s a day and asked to represent the Empire.[60] His calling was not to fight or to kill but rather to assist the soldiers, to offer help and compassion and to cater for the spiritual needs of uniformed personnel.

The 8th Brigade joined the newly raised 5th Australian Division in Egypt and Sinai and proceeded to France where they were involved in numerous bloody battles, resulting in 458 of their number being killed and 1,207 wounded.[61] It proved to be a long, arduous campaign for the chaplain especially during November and December 1916 when losses were high. He was mentioned in despatches when Major General Hobbs, the Commanding Officer, wrote:

> *Chaplain Frederick Greenfield Ward*: The work of Chaplain Ward deserves special mention. During the period November 21st to December 12th 1916, this officer had charge of the soup kitchen at Waterlot Farm and worked day and night, not only in providing hot soup and drinks to men of all units returning from the trenches, but also in helping to keep up the morale of all ranks by his cheerful disposition and unremitting attention. In addition to this, his services were being continually requisitioned by Brigade Headquarters to read Burial Services, in different localities and in all sorts of weather.

This was not an isolated incident. Ward won the Military Cross in 1917 for 'acts of exemplary gallantry during active operations against the enemy on land.' The official citation, held in the Australian War Memorial, reveals his dedication and compassion.[62]

As he worked long hours in his food kitchens and comforted wounded and dying men, the chaplain had the chance to remember his parishioners at home while reading from the small service books that his Canberra congregations (including the people at the Brickworks and the Powerhouse hall) had provided for him and administering the sacraments from the small communion set they had presented to him in a leather case as a departing gift.[63]

The Battle of the Somme was to remain imprinted on his memory for the horror, fear and gallantry involved, prompting him later to comment that 'any man who went over the top into the front line and said he had no fear is not only a liar, but a damned liar.'[64] One day the bullets and the searing shells came too close, severely wounding the chaplain and forcing his evacuation to England. Sometime later, *The Queanbeyan Age* recorded the event abruptly and without due ceremony: 'The Reverend FG Ward of Canberra, who went to the front and very nearly stopped there, cables that he hopes to be discharged from hospital shortly and able to return to Canberra.'[65] One wonders whether he met his brother (Chaplain John Ward and Archdeacon of Monaro) who was also in France 'delivering lectures to soldiers' and expecting to return to Cooma by Christmas. Fred Ward, still affected by his injuries, received a transport chaplaincy back to Australia, arriving in Canberra at the end of November 1917.[66] While still recuperating, he attended Christmas and New Year services and was in Canberra until mid-January when he seemingly disappeared.[67]

While Ward was missing from Canberra in January 1918, visitors noticed that the rectory was tended by a small group of enthusiasts who worked each Saturday to put the building and the grounds in order but the rector's whereabouts were unknown. It was left to *The Queanbeyan Age* to solve the riddle. According to the newspaper correspondent, the rector had come 'back from somewhere in France a few weeks ago only to hurry off to New Zealand to become betrothed to the lady who in future is to preside at the Rectory.'[68]

After Fred Ward returned with his bride, Margery, whom he had married at Auckland on 30 January, almost 300 people came to the rectory on 23 February for a party to welcome the rector home from active service and to congratulate the married couple. The Duntroon band played 'See the Conquering Hero Comes', the Reverend R Elliott gave a 'rattling' good speech, the rector's reply-speech was 'capital', the bride and bridegroom busily shook hands all afternoon and the afternoon tea was enjoyed 'in the prettiest part of the ground'. There was even a rumour that the parish council had 'decided to obtain a parish motor car' for the rector.[69] And so, Ward with Margery's assistance, resumed leadership of the Canberra parish in March 1918 while he was still suffering from his war wounds.[70]

Throughout the rest of 1918, Ward was still deeply concerned about events overseas. He was grateful as the allies gradually overcame enemy attacks and German morale collapsed leading to the armistice in November 1918. It was in a state of happiness and relief that bells were rung, processions held, ex-diggers lauded and thanksgiving services were organised across the country. Chaplain Ward MC led a Sunday evening service for 500 people at the Royal Military College where he offered 'thanks to the Almighty for the recent great blessing of peace' and the consequent armistice.[71] He was also to participate in both sad remembrance services and joyous reunions over the next twelve months, including those organised for members of his own Canberra congregation.[72] Moreover, as returned servicemen met and formed groups throughout the country, it was not surprising that Ward was elected as Vice-President of the Returned Sailors and Soldiers Imperial League (Duntroon Sub-Branch) in October 1919.[73]

The end of war did not bring immediate prosperity to Canberra. Practically all public works had been suspended and there was indecision as to how the internment camp built at Molonglo (now Fyshwick) early in 1918 would be used.[74] There was a vague understanding of the threat of Bolshevism in other countries and there was widespread industrial disruption in Australian cities. Additionally, the country was devastated by a virulent 'flu epidemic in 1919 that led to thousands of deaths. Bishop Radford directed that 'no more than two persons were to sit in the one pew in service or at Holy Communion' and that the chalice was 'not to be passed from person to person but the bread (was) to be dipped in the wine and given to the communicant.'[75]

The Powerhouse near the Molonglo River 1918–19. Red Hill is in the background. St Paul's Hall is indicated by the white arrow. ©*St John's Schoolhouse Museum*

Despite all this, the rector looked to the future and prayed 'for the power of the Holy Ghost to guide those who are thus called to work for the extension of Christ's Kingdom amongst us.'[76]

He certainly needed guidance and a great deal of faith in view of the parlous situation in the settlements on the southside where St Paul's mission hall was still closed with no hope of reopening under the stringent conditions of mid-1918. Moreover, the demand for production of bricks had slowed considerably in 1917 as building in Canberra had virtually ceased. The men at the Brickworks had been put off and the Single Men's Camp had been effectively deserted only two weeks after the members of St John's Council had considered moving St Paul's mission hall to the Brickworks. During July, August and September there had been 'no-one present' when Wilberforce Brooke had attended to conduct worship. Services were discontinued.[77]

Despite these setbacks, the rector still had continuing commitments, often in outlying areas of the parish, where horseriding was tiring and time consuming. The parish council then offered him a tantalising choice: would he prefer the appointment of a curate to assist him in the parish or the purchase of a parish motor vehicle for his own use? The funds were not sufficient to cover both and perhaps a car was more economical than a curate. A car it was to be. The purchase of a Morris in August 1918 allowed the rector to cover over 80 km each Sunday and conduct services at seven different centres on a rotational basis. The Powerhouse and the Brickworks were not, however, included.[78] While another building, the Mess Hall, had been established less than 100 metres from St Paul's and a few additional houses had been built for the engineers in the middle of what is now Wentworth Avenue, the mission hall still stood on the verge of open paddocks stretching across to Red Hill where rabbits in increasing plague numbers were trapped and sent by train to the Sydney food markets.[79] Unfortunately, there was no increase in the church population.

The parish revived steadily during 1919 and 1920. Finances improved, the Sunday school at the Royal Military College increased to 47 pupils and church services were stabilised in seven centres.[80] A dilemma, however, revolved around the two centres, the Brickworks and the Powerhouse, as nothing could really be achieved until the population returned and numbers substantially increased. The matter was partially resolved in late 1920. While the Federal Capital Territory had been created a decade before and Canberra had been named the future home of the national government, there had been a renewal of lobbying during 1919 and 1920 for the original decision to be overturned and the capital to be located elsewhere. The Queanbeyan Age recounted bitter attempts by Melbourne to become the capital, particularly in the lead up to the Estimates Debate in 1920. Eventually, however, the Minister for Home and Territories, Austin Chapman – who was also the Federal Member for Queanbeyan – proposed that £150,000 be allocated in 1921 for the development of Canberra, resulting in strong moves in both the Lower House and the Senate to defeat the proposal and to divert the money to another site. The New South Wales and Victorian members were intensively lobbied. After a close vote, the Estimates Bill was passed against 'determined opposition by the Melbourne Press and their political supporters'. As the newspaper editor pointed out, the Melbourne people realised 'how much it meant to them in prestige and coin' to have the parliament and the ministries located in their city and 'they spared no effort to block (Canberra's) path in every conceivable way ... at times they almost succeeded'.

By November, the Minister indicated that the Commonwealth would spend £30,000 on Canberra's roads, railway, water sewerage and electric light 'to cope with the first influx' of public servants, which was estimated to be between 10,000 and 15,000 people. He also planned to order construction of the first of 30–50 homes at a cost of £600 each, some of which would be located near St Paul's mission hall. A few weeks later Chapman brought the Prime Minister, William Hughes, and other Cabinet Ministers to Canberra. They toured various sites including the Powerhouse and the internment camp and inspected 'the proposed site for the cottages'.[81] The Prime Minister was 'impressed'. The site of the future Eastlake (Kingston) was sealed and the revitalisation of God's work in the tin church was thereby revived. In the words of Edward, the Prince of Wales, who visited Canberra in June 1920: 'At the present moment, Canberra consists chiefly of foundation stones ... the fault of war ... (but) we are going to build a very fine city here.'[82] Part of that 'very fine city' grew out of the internment camp inspected by the Prime Minister in December 1920.

Notes

1. QA, 6 March 1914.
2. J Vockler and B Thorn, 'Barlow, Christopher George (1858–1915)', *Australian Dictionary of Biography*, vol. 7 (pp. 176–177), Melbourne University Press, 1979; R Wyatt, *The History of the Diocese of Goulburn*, Edgar Bragg and Sons, Sydney, 1937, pp. 36–37; Fitzhardinge, *St John's Church*, p. 47. Frederick's brother, the Reverend John Ward, was appointed by Bishop Barlow as Domestic Chaplain to the Bishop on

1 May 1902. Frederick was unmarried and probably arrived with his brother.

3. RA&P, 22 August 1904; 24 February 1905; 1 March 1905; 3 November 1907; 8 November 1907; 17 June 1909; 9 September 1911; 19 May 1913. The bishop had previously accepted of Barmedman from 13 April 1913, RA&P, 12 April 1913. He was issued a licence as 'Acting Incumbent of Canberra' on 19 May 1913.

4. W Rolland, *Growing up in Canberra – Birthpangs of a Capital City*, Kangaroo Press, Sydney, 1988, pp. 29–30; QA, 14 March 1913.

5. QA, 18 March 1913.

6. Body, *Firm Still You Stand*, p. 110.

7. QA, 4 April 1914.

8. *Civilians employed at the Royal Military College of Australia, Duntroon, from 1911 to 1931*, Mimeo (November 2000), R Howarth, Archivist. (ACT Heritage Library).

9. QA, 29 November 1912.

10. Warden's report, StJPC, May 1914.

11. QA, 26 November 1912.

12. J Gibbney, *Canberra 1913–1953*, Australian Government Publishing Service, Canberra, 1988, pp. 11–12.

13. W Shellshear, 'Railways', in A Fitzgerald (ed.), *Canberra's engineering heritage* (pp. 47–71), Canberra Division, The Institution of Engineers, Australia, 1983, pp. 48–49.

14. A Gugler, *The builders of Canberra 1909–1929. Part one – Temporary Camps and Settlements*, CPN Publications, Fyshwick, ACT, 1994, p. 42. Also: Correspondence between F Ward, the Administrator and Secretary of the Recreation Hall, *NAA*, A 206–1, vol. 9, Admin 13–1806, 11–18 July 1913.

15. Gugler, *The Builders of Canberra*, pp. 77–81.

16. Rector's report, StPPC, May 1914.

17. H Jones, 'Electricity' (pp. 127–140) in Fitzgerald, *Canberra's Engineering Heritage*, pp. 127–129; also Gugler, *The Builders of Canberra*, p. 139.

18. It was begun in October 1912. Gibbney, *Canberra 1913–1953*, p. 9.

19. QA, 21 November 1913.

20. Gugler, *The Builders of Canberra*, p. 143.

21. QA, 17 February 1914.

22. StJPC, 26 February 1915.

23. QA, 17 February 1914.

24. Gugler, *The Builders of Canberra*, pp. 147, 149.

25. Gibbney, *Canberra 1913–1953*, pp. 9–11.

26. *Cross-Way*, vol. 1, no. 4, July 1967.

27. StJPC, May, 1914.

28. The council acknowledged the assistance of Fred Campbell, retiring synodsman, for acting as guarantor, StJPC, 1 May 1914.

29. QA, 10 June 1913; StJPC, April 1915.

30. *Cross-Way*, July 1967.
31. StJPC, 10 June 1914. The actual amount for labour was £29 8s 5d.
32. StJPC, 10 June 1914.
33. StJ Register of Services, 12 July 1914.
34. A secondary source suggests that the hall was lined with pine boards but the parish council called for a quotation to line the building in 1922 (StJPC, 17 October 1922).
35. The name 'St Paul' was entered in the StJ Register of Services, 1 August 1914.
36. StJ Register of Services, 1 August 1914; StJPC, 10 June 1914.
37. QA, 28 July 1914.
38. Spartacus Educational, *http://www.spartacus.schoolnet.co.uk/FWWtimetable.htm*
39. QA, 11 August 1914.
40. Frame, *A Church for a Nation*, p. 119.
41. B Fletcher, *The place of Anglicanism in Australia: Church, Society and Nation*, Broughton Publishing, Melbourne, 2008, pp. 64, 69.
42. RA&P, 1914–1939, 28 August 1914, p. 5.
43. Fletcher, *The Place of Anglicanism*, p. 71.
44. StJ Register of Services, February 1915 to December 1916.
45. QA, 17 February 1914; 16 June 1914; 28 August 1914; 30 April 1915; 23 June 1916.
46. Gibbney, *Canberra 1913–1953*, pp. 11–12.
47. Rolland, *Growing Up in Canberra*, pp. 35–38.
48. QA, 7 August 1914.
49. StJPC, 9 June 1915.
50. QA, 11 May 1915. These events were advertised in the QA from August 1914 to 1918.
51. QA, 21 May 1915 and 11 January 1916. Reports of Duntroon casualties were wired from Gallipoli and cited in the QA during February 1916.
52. Rector's letter, StJPC, April 1915.
53. Acting rector's letter, StJPC, April 1916.
54. QA, 30 May and 23 June 1916.
55. StJPC, 15 June 1915 and 14 April 1916.
56. StJPC, 9 September 1916; 17 December 1918; 19 November 1920.
57. Acting rector's letter, StJPC, April 1916.
58. StJ Register of Services, 1915 to 1918.
59. StJPC, 25 May 1917.
60. Australian Imperial Force – Nominal Roll. 8th Infantry, 30th Infantry Battalion, AWM, p. 15.
61. Churchwarden's report, StJPC, 2 May 1920; and 30th Battalion, AWM, *http://www.awm.gov.au/units/unit_11217.asp*
62. *Recommended for Mention*, 8th Infantry Brigade, 5th Australian Division, 9 March 1917, AWM, *http://www.awm.gov.au/cmsimages/awm.pdf*

63. Acting rector's letter, StJPC, April 1916; Body, *Firm Still You Stand*, p. 117.
64. Body, *Firm Still You Stand*, p. 117.
65. QA, 27 July 1917.
66. Warden's report, StJPC, 2 May 1920; QA, 30 November 1917.
67. StJ Register of Services, 1917–1918.
68. QA, 8 February 1918.
69. QA, 8 and 26 February 1918; Body, *Firm Still You Stand*, p. 119.
70. Warden's report, StJPC, 2 May 1920.
71. QA, 19 November 1918.
72. For example: QA, 27 June 1919. He welcomed home Private EG Crace.
73. QA, 4 November 1919.
74. QA, 5 July 1918; A Foskett, *The Molonglo Mystery*, Canberra, 2006.
75. QA, 25 February 1919.
76. Rector's letter, StJPC, 2 May 1920.
77. StJ Register of Services, 1917.
78. Warden's report 31 March 1920; StJPC, 2 May 1920.
79. The sale of rabbits and their fur provided a lucrative market well into the 1920s as reported in QA.
80. StJPC, 2 May 1920. The seven centres were St John's Canberra, Royal Military College, St Peter's Sutton, Ginninderra, St Luke's Upper Gundaroo, Duntroon and Sunday School at Duntroon.
81. QA, 8 October and 7 December 1920.
82. QA, 22 June 1920.

3   Camps and settlements, 1920–1924

The next stage of Canberra's development began in 1918 when a British Government cable in February resulted in a flurry of building activity previously unseen in the territory. In the ten weeks between February and April 1918, 40 long wooden huts with malthoid roofs were constructed on 80 acres of land overlooking the Molonglo River between Queanbeyan and the Powerhouse in the area now known as Fyshwick. Amid the secrecy, it gradually emerged that the British Government wished to house 3,290 German and Austrian interns, including 1,724 women and children from different parts of the world. Each tenement block was to accommodate fourteen family units while stores, guard houses, barracks, stables, a lookout tower and a commandant's residence completed the enclosed complex which stood starkly on a treeless stretch of land sloping down to the river. The camp was connected to the water, sewer and electric light. It even had its own railway siding.[1]

When the German Government learned about the camp and its intended use, it threatened not to release prisoners-of-war if the British persisted. As a result the project was hastily dropped and the Australian Government sought other uses for the expensive, unused camp. It was then decided to transfer about 150 German and Austrian nationals from the Bourke and Berrima internment camps in New South Wales and others from the Pacific area to Molonglo. Most arrived by train in May 1918. The internees were 'mostly of a superior type' and, under a relatively caring and fair administration, the guards and their prisoners played in local sporting competitions, 'prisoner' families shopped in Queanbeyan and local youths played tennis on the camp courts.[2] Frederick Ward, the former military chaplain whose comrades had opposed German militarism, contacted the camp officials and obtained permission to conduct a service for the internees in March 1919. The extent of his involvement with the internees is unknown but he noted that he held a service of worship for them on Friday 14 March at 7.30pm.[3]

Between May 1919 and early 1920, the Germans were forcibly repatriated to their homelands (not to their places of capture), even though some had earlier made their home in Australia. Hence, a sprawling camp designed for 5,000 internees, guards and support staff was standing idle when visited by Prime Minister Hughes in December 1920. Even before the Prime Minister's visit, there had been discussion of alternative uses for the complex. The Queanbeyan entrepreneur, JB Young, realised its potential and claimed that 'the buildings recently erected for internees would make splendid accommodation for the employees engaged on Capital construction work.'[4]

Section of the Internment Camp 1918 (later the Molonglo Settlement). © *Australian War Memorial*

The new Federal Capital Advisory Committee, appointed in January 1921, decided to remove some of the internment camp buildings to other parts of Canberra including Eastlake, near the 'sandwash' on the Molonglo River at the end of Telopea Park, a few hundred metres from St Paul's mission hall. The 60 people who lived in the 15 Eastlake tenements – spartan housing with communal washing facilities, toilets, showers and baths – probably contributed to the revitalisation of St Paul's from 1922. (The site of the Eastlake Tenements was later flooded when the lake was created 40 years later.) With the availability of wooden tenements, the roughly constructed Swagger Camp humpies around the Powerhouse disappeared. A new era had arrived.

The twelve buildings that remained at the internment camp were divided into single and married quarters and rented out at 1s 6d a room with fuel supplied. The married units comprised three to six rooms, effectively forming a house.[5] Conditions were not satisfactory as these structures were cold and draughty, the wind whipping under and through the raised buildings. The rain came in through warped timbers. Facilities were manifestly inadequate and a lack of privacy a constant issue.[6] Complaints were numerous and frequent, the local press repeatedly commenting on the acute need for improvement.

During the early months of 1922, *The Queanbeyan Age* reported on improving catering services in the tradesmen's mess, the gradual reintroduction of electric light and water, the development of an amusement hall and a range of social activities, the introduction of a gymnasium and the opening of a post office. Fortnightly newspaper reports from the Molonglo Progress Association indicated a quickly growing and well-functioning community of over 200 people in 1922 with workmen 'preparing additional blocks of tenements for families waiting to move in'. By January 1923 there were 90 families – about 400 people – housed at the centre and the workmen 'were hurriedly engaged in roofing extra blocks of tenements for occupation' but were unable to keep pace with the demand. A year later, the population of the camp had reached 530 and a 'single men's mess to accommodate 90' was required as well as new quarters for the caretakers.[7] Despite its inadequacies, the Molonglo settlement provided a much needed home for a growing number of workers and their families on the southside of the river.

The rector of St John's was quick to respond to the spiritual needs of the settlement and organised a service of 'Evensong and Sermon' at the end of July 1921, probably in the tradesmen's mess.[8] Hence, an Anglican presence was extended to the camp which, despite its inadequacies, developed a community spirit. The children played and swam in the river, the women formed interest groups and performed a constant round of 'home duties' (according to the 1928 census) and the tradesmen bonded together in their daily work and social activities. Ward's initiative was successful and developed into a monthly service of Evensong that he himself conducted. Throughout 1921, 1922 and 1923, a sizeable congregation (judging by the collections received) met every fourth Sunday at 3pm until the meeting time was changed to 7pm during 1924. After the Molonglo Camp Public School opened in a former camp hospital building for fifteen children in January 1922, church services were held in a schoolroom while a weekly Sunday school with 'large' attendances was commenced in a separate room by Mr Naveau and Mr Paynting.[9] Annual prize-giving ceremonies rewarded regular attendance and even larger numbers enjoyed the popular annual picnics for children and their parents.[10] By 1924 the Molonglo settlement had a well-established Anglican outreach to both adults and children.

Down the dusty road near the Powerhouse, St Paul's had languished since May 1917 when the doors had been closed. Ward had inspected the building on his return to the parish in 1918 and had found that, by the use of a duplicate key, 'the Hall and all that it contained was at the disposal of the men at the Powerhouse'. The parish council asked Frank Dowthwaite to replace the lock and sought to discover who had removed the two lamps that had been left in the hall.[11] Thus secured, the hall had stood its lonely vigil waiting the reappearance of a congregation and a renewal of its Christian witness.

By early March 1921, the Federal Capital Advisory Committee finally prepared plans for ten brick cottages facing Waratah Parkway (Telopea Park), Gosse Street and Jardine Street at a total cost of £8,800. In June, their construction was 'well advanced'. Supplied with water, sewerage and electricity, the cottages were fenced, supplied with iron gates and surrounded by shrubs to enhance their appearance. The construction of ten additional homes was recommended in February 1922 but the growing demand for accommodation was barely relieved. While 'further homes were required for staff already in the territory,' the need was even greater for married officers 'who would otherwise be transferred to Canberra' but were unwilling to leave Melbourne or Sydney 'on account of the shortage of cottages'.[12]

Unfortunately, St Paul's hall now stood in the way of this critical housing development. When Ward had approached the administration for permission to build the hall in 1914 the Powerhouse area had not been surveyed and the building had been erected in the middle of a field, 'subject to the condition that it be removed at any time should the Commonwealth require its removal'. Now, eight years later, it stood on land newly zoned for homes and needed to be relocated. With the noise of builders' hammers echoing from home construction in Gosse Street in April 1921, the church hall was slowly jacked up, telegraph poles slid underneath and a traction engine, belching smoke and steam, inched the building 90 metres south where it was aligned behind sites 28 (Giles Street) and 31 (Jardine Street) and occupied a new site, rent-free, for the next 23 years. When the Secretary of the Federal Capital Advisory Committee recommended a further ten cottages in March 1923, adding that this would result in 'a complete architectural group' of 30 homes on the 'block set apart near the Powerhouse', he did not mention that St Paul's mission hall would be located on a reserve or park that was immediately adjoining the back

The Powerhouse and railway line circa 1926. © ACT Heritage Library : Val Emerton Images

fences of homes on two sides and accessible only by walkways from Giles, Gosse and Jardine Streets.[13]

By February 1922, Ward believed that the time had come to resume services in the relocated hall. Mr Naveau replaced broken glass windows, covered them with netting, installed a different door lock and cleaned out the birds that had found a divine home for four years. The floor was swept and scrubbed, the cobwebs removed, the temporary altar and wooden seats dusted, the blinds repaired and the altar cloth returned and spread once again for services. A letter was forwarded to the government asking for the return of the two lights that had been removed as the hall was not connected to electricity. St John's Parish Council even considered lining and painting the building but decided that the time was not right for such an investment.[14]

As Ward set out for St Paul's in April 1922, the circumstances were quite different from those when he had first arrived a decade earlier. Instead of fording the Molonglo on his horse, he now drove the parish car across the small wooden Commonwealth Avenue Bridge (built in 1916) and continued along the south bank until he came to Interlake

Avenue (later renamed Wentworth Avenue) which was lined by the small trees cultivated and planted by Charles Weston, the curator of the nursery. Gravelled streets had been formed near Telopea Park, including Gosse, Jardine and (presently named) Giles Street, while a number of homes had been finished, partly hiding the church hall in a small enclave in which children played. According to the local newspaper correspondent, 'the locality is already taking on a new aspect.'[15]

The first service in the reopened church started at 7.30pm on Sunday 9 April 1922 when the rector conducted Evensong and preached to a congregation that came close to filling the lamp-lit hall designed for 30 people.[16] It must have been a satisfying occasion for Ward but he was careful not to move too quickly or to stretch the limited resources too far, informing the gathering that there would be monthly services at 7.30pm. He did not foresee, however, that his health would interfere with his plans on some occasions or that increasing numbers at the mission hall would require fortnightly services four months later.[17]

History was made on 28 January 1923, just after the Feast of the Conversion of St Paul, when the rector held the first service of Holy Communion in the hall at 8am.[18] Services since 1914 had been confined to 'Evensong and Sermon' but for the seven communicants that day, it seemed that the mission hall had attained a deeper level of reverence and was nearing the status of a church. During 1923 and 1924, two services were held each month, one being Holy Communion at 7.30am or 8am and the other Evensong at 7.30pm.[19] The Sunday services on 23 December 1923 were notable for other reasons. The rector may have been running late for early morning Communion at St Paul's , prompting hime to take a short cut. Ward drove his car through the river at Scott's Crossing where a bridge was yet to be constructed. The rather plaintive entry in the Register of Services records the result:

> Dec. 23 [1923]. Power House Holy Communion. 7.30am. No service. Stuck in the Molonglo River. F. Ward.[20]

In one sense, Ward's timing was fortunate. It was one of the last occasions on which he would need to use the small Morris. The church council had already placed an order for a new five-seater Ford at a cost of £250. Nevertheless, the rector needed assistance to save the old

Morris which realised £40 as a trade-in a few days later. Undeterred, he returned to St Paul's more circumspectly during the afternoon and held a children's service at 3pm where he could tell the youngsters of his river experience.[21] The inclusion of a children's service was, however, premature. After two such services Ward found the pressure of work too great and he reverted to two regular gatherings at St Paul's each month.

It was a difficult period for the rector as he worked without the assistance of a curate. His congregations were increasing and the number of small settlements across Canberra was burgeoning. Homes were being constructed at Blandfordia (Forrest), for example, and Ward held a mission service and another of Evensong there in June and August 1923.[22] The city's population, which was a mere 1,150 in 1921, rose to 2,600 in 1924 and to 3,500 in 1925, compelling him to commence further new ventures although it placed unsafe pressure on his health.[23] He had already spent time in Sydney Hospital in 1920 and in June 1922. He suffered a relapse in 1924. But Ward never relented: God's work was an obligation to him – both a duty and a love.[24]

It was no surprise, therefore, that the rector sought to relaunch services on the other side of Capital Hill as well. Church services had ceased at the Brickworks in June 1917 when brick production had been halted and the single men's camp had been closed. When Ward returned to duties at St John's in March 1918, he visited the remaining workers who resided at the camp and organised a small service on March 24. There were so few who attended that it was impossible to schedule regular Sunday gatherings. Undaunted, he gathered small groups for worship in August and September on Wednesday evenings and then introduced a morning service in November 1918. Believing there was a greater need, he advertised a service of Holy Communion for the workers at 'Camp Yarralumla' in December and was encouraged when twelve communicants knelt on the bare boards of the mess and received the Lord's Supper.[25]

Despite Ward's continuing efforts, the church's witness at the camp was limited to four services during 1919 (including an afternoon children's service in April) and it became evident by July that services were no longer viable for the few workers and their families. Services were reluctantly discontinued in July and awaited their resumption more than two years later with the assistance of the Federal Capital

Territory Advisory Committee. Dressed in dignified suits and hats, the members of the advisory committee arrived by train at the end of January 1921 to inspect the sites for 'the hostel at Canberra, the workmen's cottages and [the] proposed temporary hall for the meeting of parliament' (soon to be named the provisional Parliament House).[26] A few days later, the secretary, Charles Daley, recorded the committee's decision: it agreed 'to facilitate the speedy commencement and completion of various buildings' in the slowly emerging city and recommended 'that the Brickworks be restarted'.[27]

In order to provide accommodation for additional workers, brick homes were planned and some of the tenement buildings from the internment camp were relocated along Banks Street between the dirt tracks that later became Hooker and Schlich Streets.[28] By May, the construction of seven new cottages at a cost of £6,185 was 'well in hand'. They were situated on the rise above what was to become the Yarralumla shopping centre.[29] While the numbers in the settlement varied from month to month depending on the need for bricks and tiles, the combined population of the married and single men's camps together with families in the new cottages rose from 31 men in 1922 to 170 in 1923, prompting the Advisory Committee to arrange for the development of a recreation ground, the construction of a recreation hall and the building of tennis courts and a cricket pitch.[30]

Early picture of the Brickworks (Yarralumla).   ©National Library of Australia

Just as the first families were moving into their cottages in October 1921, Ward with the approval of the church council resumed services at the Brickworks. Having finished his Sunday morning services at the Royal Military College and at St John's on 30 October, he had a hasty lunch and set off to conduct a 2.30pm 'Evensong and Sermon' for the long-term inhabitants and the new arrivals. Wondering whether numbers would be sustained, he advertised another gathering for a Wednesday evening a few weeks later.[31] Encouraged by the numbers who attended but still not fully convinced about the viability of regular services, he decided to hold a monthly Evensong from January to April 1922, probably in the single men's mess, but again the venture was premature. It was not until March 1923 when a new recreation hall was completed on a site in present-day Schomburgk Street that a schedule of monthly services was begun and continued without interruption, each consisting of 'Evensong and Sermon'.[32] Fortunately the growing number of permanent residents, including newly arrived office workers, compensated for reduced numbers of labourers in slack times at the Brickworks. The services throughout 1923 and 1924 were well attended.[33] Planning then became more complicated.

When the advisory committee had inspected sites in 1921, they were planning for the construction of the future Parliament House and a 'hostel' nearby to house politicians and other dignitaries who would visit the city. The hostel, known as Hostel No.1, proved to be a grandiose structure. It later became known as the Hotel Canberra and today is the Hyatt Hotel Canberra on Commonwealth Avenue. In May 1922 approximately 200 unemployed men arrived in Canberra, some to work on the foundations of the hostel and others preparing the site of the future Parliament House. John Howie & Son won the contract to construct Hostel No.1 and, in order to house the workers, built a settlement of 25 timber cottages, 18 huts and a recreation hall, together with ablution blocks and mess rooms. According to Ann Gugler, the contractor's camp for single men was known as 'Hostel Camp' and the married quarters as 'Howie's Cottages'. From 1922 to 1924 the Commonwealth erected tent camps nearby for single trades-men and for men working on the installation of Canberra's sewer system. Work was completed on 51 portable cottages at 'The Gap'. This entire area became known as Westlake and today covers part of

Stirling Park and the embassy precinct of Darwin Avenue, Empire Circuit, Perth Avenue and Alexandrina Drive.[34]

The growth of Westlake created a dilemma for Ward. Ideally, he would have preferred the residents to walk through the scrub to the Brickworks service or, alternatively, for the Brickworks service to be transferred to the new hall at Westlake. Unsure of the better move, he continued services at the Brickworks and commenced a mission service at the Hostel Camp in July 1923, most likely in John Howie's recreation hall. It proved relatively successful and the rector continued the mission-type gathering once a month on either Wednesday or Thursday evenings. The informal gathering seemed to appeal to the workers more than formal Evensong and Ward himself was apparently comfortable with the approach. Nevertheless, realising that the numbers at Westlake would fluctuate considerably, he did not introduce regular Evensong but continued with midweek mission services once a month until the end of the year, only conducting Evensong on two occasions in March and August.[35]

By the end of 1924, there were four scattered settlements on the south side of the Molonglo, a conglomeration of ex-internment camp huts, new brick homes, 'temporary' wooden houses, hastily constructed shanties and rows of tents. Ward faced a challenging task in providing for the spiritual needs of these diverse centres in contrast to the long-established traditions at St John's, the routine and order of his work at Duntroon and the relative predictability of rostered services in outlying settlements. He was required to be flexible, to adapt, to experiment and could not be discouraged if a particular approach did not succeed. With little time to probe complex theological questions or the finer points of churchmanship in the embryonic centres, the rector's approach was simple, direct and evangelistic.

Ward relied on the mentoring he received from Bishop Christopher Barlow and the Archdeacon Wentworth F Wentworth-Shields (who later became Bishop of Armidale). Ward had closely observed Bishop Barlow in North Queensland as he widened the church's influence, encouraged mission work among indigenous people and extended the church's activities among both Pacific Island cane workers at Mackay and Chinese workers in a number of smaller centres. The bishop was interested in all classes of people, taking the church's message to workers in smaller settlements and to those on the edge of society. It seems that Ward never forgot the content or conduct of those outreach programs.

Originally of Evangelical sentiment, Barlow gradually changed 'towards a more moderate liberalism with its emphasis on spirituality in worship and the personal faith of the clergy'.[36] Those who knew him described him as a warm, humane person – a peacemaker with a simple faith and a man of tolerance who could accept different points of view. Frederick Ward, Barlow's personal friend, seemed to exude similar qualities, perhaps as a result of Barlow's influence. Ward trained for the ministry in Goulburn where Barlow had established a theological college in 1906 under the wardenship of Wentworth-Shields, the bishop's cousin. The Warden was a 'superb preacher' who attracted crowds 'by the sheer force of his pulpit oratory and the spiritual intensity of his message'. At the same time, Wentworth-Shields downplayed high churchmanship, promoted a form of moderate ritual, smoothed old parish resentments, conciliated diocesan authorities and argued for a liturgy in the language of the people, one that could even reach children without 'verbosity and pomposity'.[37]

Influenced by his mentors, Ward displayed a flexible, easy approach in the pioneering centres. While he always wore a clerical collar, there were no vestments, no candles and no ritual in the camps and early settlements but rather a simple style that proved effective and engaging. He commenced with mission services that evolved into 'Evensong and an Address' when the congregation was more stable. Under his drive, the church had a missionary zeal, propelled by a vigorous approach that transcended tradition and dogma. Ritual and formal liturgy, as important as they were, could come later. While he was quick to introduce children's services in the camps, Communion was not offered until the gathering was relatively permanent (one that resembled a 'congregation') or when a special occasion demanded it. This three-step formula – mission service, leading to Evensong and finally to Communion – was his successful paradigm in the developing centres.

When the Adelaide church historian, Brian Dickey, surveyed Anglican trends at the end of the nineteenth century, he concluded that 'the parochial model of the settled ministry was becoming a potential burden' to the church, a 'static model unable to respond to the changing patterns of community life'. Moreover, 'Anglicans found difficulty in sympathising with working-class activists' because the 'style and content of popular Anglicanism' were 'increasingly distant from working-class issues and made the church appear less than sympathetic'.[38] This was not true of the new Canberra centres, however, as Ward's form of Christianity and the nature of his parish did not permit him to settle into the comfort of a formal liturgy designed for middle-class people possessing socially conservative views. He conferred with the union bosses and took his Saviour's message into rough tent camps among hard-drinking workers whose sympathies were not necessarily church-oriented at all. Reports confirm that his friendly manner was well received and that he had a close affinity with those who were still suffering the traumatic consequences of war during the 1920s. It was well known that 'Chaplain Ward, M.C.' could provide understanding and spiritual comfort.

Even when addressing his regular parishioners at St John's and St Paul's, his message was clear and simple. He exhorted them to pray 'for the power of the Holy Ghost to guide those who are called to work for the extension of Christ's Kingdom amongst us' and he asked people to be 'living witnesses who are prepared to make some sacrifice for Christ'. From the men's group, he called for 'a band of men whose hearts are touched by the Love of God … men who are out to fight … not for the dogmas of the Church but for the principles for which the Church stands'.[39] Emphasising unity and compassion, his orientation was one of inclusion, of compassion and Christian devotion as he steered the church along a middle course, avoiding extremes of either Evangelicalism or Tractarianism.

Ward increased the frequency of Holy Communion at St John's and Duntroon from monthly to bi-monthly celebrations and introduced the Lord's Supper at Christmas and on some saints' days. Moreover, when their first son was born in October 1919, the Wards presented a pair of candlesticks to St John's for use in the sanctuary.[40] During the period of his incumbency, the liturgy moved from the deeply held Evangelicalism of Pierce Galliard-Smith to an equally caring expression of Broad Anglicanism in which the church was active in society, a Christian witness that was dynamic and outgoing.

Ward's ability to experiment and adapt was clearly evident at St Paul's. The mission hall at the Powerhouse was erected to be 'a place of *worship* and *recreation*', not a building reserved for church services alone. It was used by the Co-operative Store for regular meetings, by the Powerhouse employees, by sporting associations and by community groups for a range of purposes. The local newspaper reported, for example, on 'a meeting in the Church Hall Eastlake to consider steps to assist … in opening the new school' at Telopea Park in 1923. When the school was opened in September, Bishop Radford, Frederick Ward and other dignitaries were present to meet 600 children collected from all over Canberra.[41] From its commencement in 1914, St Paul's was a church and a social centre, God's church in society and for society. It was only in 1923 that the rector believed it appropriate to introduce services of Communion to a relatively permanent congregation judged ready to receive the sacrament. Communicants were previously asked to attend St John's.

Clearly, Ward's approach was sufficiently flexible to meet the needs of different groups in the now disparate community. What did not change was the depth of his own spirituality, his abiding concern for his parishioners and a deep and overwhelming desire to take the message of God to all. Often feeling the burden of his divine calling, he wrote to his parishioners: 'I would ask you to pray for me that God may indeed use me for his glory and his service. (Signed) Your sincere friend and Rector. F. G. Ward.'

By the end of 1924, Frederick Ward and St John's parish council could regard the extension of God's work on the southside of the Molonglo with a feeling of satisfaction although they had wished to accomplish more. They had maintained services each Sunday at St John's and the Royal Military College, while providing ministry at outlying centres such as Sutton, Gundaroo and Uriarra on a roster basis. In addition, the rector had continued his heavy program of hospital and home visits, provided instruction at Telopea Park School and been engaged in Sunday schools, confirmation classes and community involvement. Despite the workload he did not neglect visiting the rapidly emerging new camps, meeting the men and their families and commencing church services and missions at a number of the larger settlements. This had been achieved by the rector and a small band of faithful lay people without assistant priests, curates or stipendiary lay readers. It was a worthy accomplishment given the limited resources.

Despite these advances, there was an expectation by 1924 that even more would be required by the parish. It had been decided that land on the southside could be leased for business purposes – allowing private enterprise 'to build up the city' at the same time as the government 'erected its buildings.'[42] Auctions were then planned. There was mention of a printery, a new development at the Causeway, expansion at Blandfordia (Forrest) and the sale of land at Manuka. Above all, it was anticipated that the construction of the provisional Parliament House would open a new era in the region's history. The church's mission and ministry would need to expand as well.

Notes

1. The story of the internment camp has been research by Foskett, *The Molonglo Mystery*; A Fitzgerald, *Historic Canberra 1825–1945*, AGPS, Canberra, 1977; and Gugler, *The Builders of Canberra*.
2. Foskett, *The Molonglo Mystery*, pp. 40–41.
3. StJ Register of Services, 1919.
4. QA, 23 May 1919.
5. Gugler, *The Builders of Canberra*, pp. 152, 161.
6. See the reports of those who lived at Molonglo in Foskett, *The Molonglo Mystery*.
7. QA, 19 May 1922; 12 January 1923; 1 February 1924.
8. StJ Register of Services July 29, 1921. There was no other suitable building available in July 1921. An amusement hall was available from early 1922.
9. StJ Register of Services, 1922; QA, 23 May 1922.
10. See Foskett, *The Molonglo Mystery*, pp. 109, 125, 127–128.
11. StJPC, 18 April 1918; 30 May 1918.
12. 'Plan of the Layout of cottages in the Power House neighbourhood', FCAC, *Cottages for Power House Staff*, NAA, A414 A414–1. no. 23 and Sulman's Memorandum of 4 March 1921; also 24 June 1921; 16 July 1921; 17 February 1922; 17 March 1923.
13. Surveyor-General to Archdeacon Robertson, 23 June 1942, NAA, 'St Paul's Church Hall, Kingston', Series A659 (A659–1) Control # 1941–1/3451.
14. StJPC, 17 October 1922.
15. QA, 2 June 1922.
16. As the collection amounted to 11s 6d – a substantial amount for a regular service in 1922 – it appears that the service was well attended.
17. StJ Register of Services, 1922–1923.
18. StJ Register of Services, 28 January 1923.
19. StJ Register of Services, 1923–1924.

20. StJ Register of Services, 23 December 1923.
21. Body, *Firm Still You Stand*, p. 137.
22. StJ Register of Services, 1923.
23. *Estimated Population: Australian Capital Territory and Canberra, 1911 to 1963*. ACT Statistical Table.
24. QA, 16 June 1922; and Body, *Firm Still You Stand*, p.140.
25. StJ Register of Services, 1918.
26. QA, 28 January 1921.
27. 'Brickworks', NAA, Series A414 (A414/1), Control # 21/1, 2 February 1921.
28. Gugler, *The Builders of Canberra*, p. 81.
29. 'Cottages for Power House Staff', Memorandum to Hon. LE Groom, 22 July 1921; QA, 13 May 1921; Gugler, *The Builders of Canberra*, p. 23.
30. Gugler, *The Builders of Canberra*, p. 78.
31. StJ Register of Services, 1921.
32. Gugler, *The Builders of Canberra*, p. 81.
33. This assessment is based on the monthly offerings received. See StJ Register of Services 1923 and 1924.
34. This account of early Westlake settlements relies on: A Gugler, *Westlake. One of the Vanished Suburbs of Canberra*, CPN Publications, Fyshwick, 1997, pp. 55, 57.
35. StJ Register of Services indicates mission services from July to December, 1923; see also StJ Register of Services, 1924.
36. Vockler and Thorn, 'Barlow, Christopher', pp. 176–177.
37. K Cable, 'Wentworth-Shields, Wentworth Francis (1867–1944)', *Australian Dictionary of Biography*, vol. 12 (pp. 443–444), Melbourne University Press, 1990; also Frame, *A Church for a Nation*, pp. 110–111.
38. B Dickey, 'Secular Advance and Diocesan Response 1861–1900' (pp. 52–75) in Kaye et al (eds), *Anglicanism in Australia*, Melbourne University Press, Melbourne, 2002, pp. 64, 73.
39. Rector's letter to parishioners, StJPC, 2 May 1920.
40. Body, *Firm Still You Stand*, p. 119.
41. QA, 14 September and 16 November 1923.
42. This new development was mentioned as early as 1922. See QA, 4 July 1922.

4   Patterns of development, 1925–1929

There was a sense of expectation when the first auctions were held in Canberra on Friday 12 December 1924. A dais was set up on Capital Hill, maps of the various subdivisions were posted on boards and two Sydney auctioneers joined the local men, Bill Woodger and Harry Calthorpe, to offer the first lots. Almost 300 potential buyers and curious onlookers, dressed in suits, ties and hats and with a sprinkling of ladies standing under parasols in the warm sun, listened to speeches by politicians and civic leaders before the auction began. *The Queanbeyan Age* outlined the order of the sale: (1) Eastlake business and residential sites; (2) Blandfordia residential sites; (3) Red Hill residential sites; (4) Manuka shopping centre; (5) Civic shopping centre; and (6) Ainslie business and shopping sites. It was an important day for Canberra.

Some idea of Canberra's expectations may be gauged from the preliminary report:

> The Eastlake site [Kingston] is about six miles from Queanbeyan and already there are between 30 and 40 cottages of the bungalow type with attractive garden frontages. The subdivision is on gently undulating ground of rich red soil ... Twelve business sites are included ... About a mile further is Manuka, a retail business site subdivision of about 30 blocks, designed to supply the better class residential area provided for in the existing cottages at Blandfordia [Forrest] and Red Hill subdivisions. [Blandfordia and Red Hill] appear to be the cream of the residential part of the city ... They have a general easterly aspect commanding fine and extensive views over the whole city.[1]

View of Kingston 1924. © *National Library of Australia*

Blocks on the southside attracted the most interest at the auction described as 'highly successful indeed'. The first commercial lot at Eastlake, diagonally opposite St Paul's hall (now the site of the Kingston Plaza) had a reserve of £650 while residential lots between Jardine Street and Wentworth Avenue ranged from £150 to £200. To the excitement of the crowd but not necessarily that of the buyer, Lot 1 with a reserve of £650 attracted spirited bidding until it was knocked down to JB Young of Queanbeyan for £2,050.[2] All the commercial sites at Eastlake were snapped up, together with 58 residential allotments, while 9 were purchased at Blandfordia, 25 at Red Hill and 23 at Manuka.[3] Church folk did not then realise that the auction would commence a period of development, resulting in the consolidation and eventual expansion of St Paul's at Eastlake and leading ultimately to two new church buildings in the nearby suburbs of Manuka and Red Hill.

During 1925 and 1926 the shopping centre at Eastlake took shape as stores were erected, roads and footpaths formed and trees and hedges planted. The Canberra Co-operative Society's store at the Canberra Railway Station, the only shop of any substance before 1925, was soon to close. No longer would shoppers have to travel to Queanbeyan to shop or to buy from a catalogue and have their goods railed from Sydney. As George Colman, an old time member of St Paul's recalled: 'We had canvassers taking orders and the customers were used to it.' All that was about to change.[4] One lad was glad that he would be able to buy shoes at a store without having to trace his feet on a piece of paper for someone at the Marcus Clark store in Sydney to match his size.

The opening of JB Young's Store in 1925 changed Eastlake completely. Food was now available locally as well as produce, hardware, men's and women's wear, drapery and fancy goods. With streets now being formed, Young's opened on Fridays for late night shopping, an exciting event that drew people from all over Canberra. According to Morrie Adamson, a lad who attended St Paul's Church, Friday night was a 'real social occasion'. Families would come from the northside 'because of the better shopping facilities' at Eastlake or walk across from Manuka 'which was a disjointed arrangement' of houses and shops mixed together.[5]

JB Young's, Kingston, decorated for the visit of the Duke and Duchess of York, May 1927.
© ACT Heritage Library

The shops expanded from Young's on the corner, to Dunnes Federal Newsagency next door, to Taylors (men's and women's outfitters and shoe store), Gunn's Southern Cross Tearooms and to Woodger and Calthorpe's motor shop and petrol bowser. A personal relationship developed between the motor shop and St Paul's when Harry Trevillian (a strong supporter of St Paul's) worked after school and on Saturdays as a bowser boy, pumping the stiff handle to raise the petrol from the tanks below ground; and when Jim Hardman worked in the motor shop as an accountant. Both would become significant figures in parish life. It was not long before shops at Kingston stretched around the corner into Kennedy Street.

There was further expansion when a contract was let in August 1925 for the erection of a building 'which would temporarily house the Government Printing Office' in Wentworth Avenue and 24 semi-detached homes were constructed and occupied in August 1926 by the workers near the shopping complex in Kennedy Street.[6] Known as the Printers' Quarters, it catered for 140 persons in 1927 and its communal dining room was used for local gatherings.[7] Growth continued throughout 1927, 1928 and 1929 as semi-skilled, skilled, commercial and professional men and their families moved to the area, now named 'Kingston', expanding the suburb in the direction of the future suburbs of Barton, Forrest and Manuka. Kingston had assumed a specific character – neither lower nor upper social class – and St Paul's mission hall was acquiring the same characteristics.

Across the open fields from Eastlake was the developing centre of Manuka where 23 leases had been snapped up at the auction in 1924. Conceived as a retail trading centre from the outset, it was planned as a two-storey commercial arcade with other shops interspersed between residential lots radiating out in an arc with a large institute, a bank and a post office facing the arcade. By December 1926, the first three shops had opened and by August 1927 another 27 were in course of construction.[8] When the Federal Capital Commission developed Manuka, it was envisaged as serving the 'better class suburbs' of Blandfordia [Forrest] and Red Hill, an overt expression of social distinction and the affluence that went with it. With the transfer of the national parliament from Melbourne to Canberra that year, it was expected that a number of politicians and senior public servants would reside in these areas and that the homes would reflect private enterprise rather than government provision. *The Canberra Times* lauded Red Hill as a 'superior residential suburb ... where would be seated higher class residentials of Canberra ... [a] class of residence somewhat different from the general class of residential raised in other parts of the city'.[9]

When the transfer of public servants was delayed until 1927 and beyond, there were complaints that the Manuka retail area was being neglected at the expense of Ainslie and Eastlake but this trend was partly reversed when plans for an institute were changed, permitting the construction of the Capitol Theatre on land sold for £7,000.[10] On a gala night in December 1927, the theatre was opened with lights illuminating its portico entrance, 'and the whole of the building became visible from afar'. It soon became a hub of social activity in the developing city, not only as the main cinema but also as a venue for large functions including those of the Anglican Church on the southside of the river. After the construction of St Christopher's Roman Catholic School and Convent in 1927–1928, Manuka was set to develop as a retail district, a residential area and a new centre of activity for the two major Christian denominations in Canberra.

The building boom at Eastlake, the development of a commercial centre, the influx of workers at the Printers' Quarters and the growth of surrounding 'suburbs' all had an immediate effect on both the small congregation at St Paul's and the ability of St John's Church to cope with the enlarged demands on its human and material resources. By February 1925, electric light was installed in the church hall, allowing a more comfortable use of the building at night and two dozen small service books were purchased for use by the congregation. The rector was able to maintain two services each month, Communion early in the morning and Evensong at 7.30pm.[11] Moreover, it was noticeable that the number of communicants was increasing on special occasions (20 communicants were recorded at the August 1925 service). The building was frequently crowded, something that gladdened the members of parish council but taxed their ability to respond. 'St Paul's in–the-tin-shed' was developing as a spiritual home for those who lived around the hall and it had become an accepted part of the community, next to the children's swings and see-saws.[12]

At the same time, there were increasing requests for the use of the hall by other bodies. The parish council agreed that the Eastlake Progress Association could

St Paul's hall in the reserve at Kingston, 1927-28.
© Canberra & District Historical Society; Ann Gugler.

hold its meetings in the hall each month and that the Girl Guides could 'use the hall free for meetings but pay for electric light' and cleaning. The Eastlake Amusement Association continued to meet in the hall, organising sporting events such as tennis and cricket and a growing number of social activities. The building was hired to the Chief Electoral Officer during elections for 15s a day and the Federal Capital Commission increasingly requested its use.[13] Unfortunately,

the community's need for the building was greatest at the time when
St Paul's own activities were increasing. Consequently, the Canberra
Community Library was informed reluctantly in April 1928

> that the [Parish] Council had given sympathetic consideration
> to their request for the use of St Paul's Hall, but that as the
> Hall is used so many nights for Church purposes the Council
> regret that they cannot make it available.[14]

Financially, the church benefited from outside use of the hall as it
charged a fee for its use and paid a cleaner 2s each week. By mid-
1927 voluntary workers fitted backs to the seats, offering a little more
comfort to parishioners. The council decided to line the interior of
the building with timber.[15] Some of this renovation was carried out
with the help of the Methodists who did not have a church of their
own. Their clergyman, the Reverend Edward Vercoe, held services
from 1926 to 1929 in – what he later reported was – 'an unlined
galvanised iron shell' owned by the Church of England 'and hidden
behind the cottages somewhere opposite JB Young's store.'[16] Probably
as compensation for their use of the hall, the Methodists provided
some of the voluntary labour to renovate the building while the
church council paid for the timber. Moreover, it was the Methodists
who provided the first permanent organ at St Paul's until June 1929.
The Methodist Church Ladies Aid made donations towards the cost
of electric light.[17] It is not known whether the Presbyterians also contributed to the improvements but they held services 'at the Anglican
Hall at Eastlake' whenever a retired Presbyterian minister was sent
from Sydney to 'supply' Canberra's growing Presbyterian numbers.[18]

Despite the improvements made to the building between 1925
and 1929, St Paul's was too small and lacked basic facilities. There
were no toilets and the hall was not connected to the water supply.
This meant the cleaner and church members had to beg water from
the surrounding homes when it was needed. Fortunately, some of
the nearby residents were church members who assisted. As early as
1925, St John's parish council members discussed these problems and
the overcrowding at the church and sought a solution. The council
did not own the land and could be requested to relocate the building
which was landlocked, tucked away behind new homes and not visible to the general public. Some considered extending the building,

a suggestion that might have come from the bishop himself but the council opposed the idea. The members met with Bishop Radford, explaining that they were:

> of the opinion after consideration that the St Paul's Church Hall building and site at Eastlake are unsuitable for additions to cope with the needs of the south side of the River.[19]

After discussing the matter informally during the remainder of 1925, the council members met in January 1926 and the rector moved that a sub-committee be established to 'determine the new location of the Hall'. A few believed, however, that too much attention was being given to the southside leading to neglect of the north. When the council met again a month later, it was moved that 'the new locality of St Paul's Hall be Ainslie'. The argument was persuasive and it was agreed that St Paul's hall be moved to the northern suburb.[20]

In the meantime, the rector and the sub-committee approached the Lands Department of the new Federal Capital Commission and applied for a site for a church on the southside, leading to a resolution that 'the removal of the hall to Ainslie be suspended' and the matter 'urgently referred to the Site Sub-Committee'. Realising that 24 new homes were about to be occupied at the Printers' Quarters thereby placing additional pressure on the hall, Clyde Finlay, the doctor with a surgery near St Paul's and a few streets from the Printers' Quarters, persuaded Everard Crace to change his opinion. They moved 'that the hall, if moved, should be in Manuka locality and that, with a view to selecting the site, the Rector and Percy Sheaffe interview the Commission'.[21] Other council members were persuaded to change their opinion. It was agreed in May 1926 that Manuka was to be the new locality if an appropriate site could be obtained.

By 1929 one of the patterns of Anglican development on the southside had clearly emerged. Over fourteen years, the Powerhouse settlement had become a permanent suburb with established commercial and residential centres. A small but growing middle-class population and two major industries provided employment possibilities to support tangible church growth. Regular services were now a permanent feature at St Paul's. The congregation's future seemed assured, albeit on a different site when resources permitted.

It was during this period that church planning became more complicated. Eastlake was burgeoning, Manuka had been chosen as a desired locality for St Paul's, and more homes were expected at Red Hill and at Blandfordia when the provisional Parliament House was opened in May 1927. At the same time Bishop Radford was vigorously pursuing the idea of a Church of England cathedral on the southside not far from St Paul's. Then, as the Molonglo settlement was continuing to grow and to demand attention, a new centre, named the Causeway, entered calculations.

The Causeway provided a second and different pattern of church development on the south side of the river. With the growth of Canberra's population – 3,500 in 1925; 4,900 in 1926; and 6,150 in 1927 – there was an urgent need for even more housing despite the building efforts of the Federal Capital Commission and its predecessor, the Advisory Committee.[22] It was believed that additional 'temporary accommodation' was required for workers involved in the construction of Parliament House and other public buildings. However, as demand would eventually decline, a temporary settlement at the Causeway was proposed as partial solution. When Walter Burley Griffin had originally designed Canberra, he had planned a series of lakes that were to be formed by dams across the Molonglo. One of these dams would stretch from Eastlake to a point on Constitution Avenue near the present Department of Defence Offices at Russell Hill, an embankment that would not only raise the water level but also provide a causeway across which a railway line could be built into Civic Centre. The proposed causeway was never constructed and the idea of a railway was later abandoned, although the name 'Causeway' was retained. It covers an area near the present Canberra Railway Station.

In February 1925 the Federal Capital Commission called tenders for 'the construction of 60 timber cottages near the Causeway, Canberra', believing that the settlement would be temporary and last no more than five years. The first homes were occupied in the winter of 1925 (with those on lower ground being promptly submerged by the disastrous floodwaters that engulfed the Molonglo Valley in June) and by October 'the final group of 120 portable cottages' was practically completed.[23] Within twelve months, the Causeway Progress Association was formed, 'bus services were introduced, tennis courts were being constructed for the local tennis club and a ground for the Causeway Cricket Club had been reserved 'behind the old Co-Op Store'.[24]

When the rector visited the Causeway, he noted the rapid construction and quickly became involved in Causeway activities. He participated in a Christmas treat for 175 children at the end of 1925 when the 'Social Services Officer (Mr Joe Honeysett), Dr Finlay and the Reverend FG Ward' organised an evening program at which each child received two toys, sweets and ice cream. A contemporary account noted that pleasant entertainment was provided for children and adults. On this occasion, the rector, Clyde Finlay and Bert Jackson were able to mingle with the adults and inform them of an important date – 21 February 1926 – when the first Anglican service would be conducted at the settlement.

The Causeway Progress Association had been encouraged 'to provide recreation and to promote the welfare of residents' and, with the assistance of the Commission, had embarked on an ambitious scheme of building its own hall. Over eight weekends, volunteers constructed the 'Causeway Hall' with the help of 'tradesmen, quill-drivers [clerks], refreshment staff and Boy Scouts'. Bert Jackson of St John's and St Paul's took a leading role in its development. The opening on 6 February 1926 was a gala occasion for the Causeway community. With the Canberra Brass Band playing, the crowds arrived 'in a continuous stream by car, horse and the ever-reliable *Shank's pony*', so that by the time the curtain went up, all available seating was filled to overflowing in 'the largest hall in New South Wales' and the Federal Territory, 'south of Goulburn'.[25] The hall quickly became a centre for cultural, social and religious activities as it pre-dated the completion of the very grand Albert Hall by almost two years.

The rector had long-term plans for the Causeway Hall. He wanted to commence church activities as quickly as possible not only to provide for the rapidly rising population but also to counterbalance the strong Roman Catholic influence at the Causeway. (He might have heard some of the residents claim that, while there would be domestic fights in the settlement, there would be few divorces because 75 per cent of the people were Irish Catholic.[26]) In the short-term, however, he believed that a Causeway church might help to alleviate the overcrowding that was looming as a problem at nearby St Paul's. He

booked the new Causeway Hall for church activities on 21 February
1926 and drove Bishop Radford to the Causeway to conduct the
7.30am service of Communion, a solemn and joyous occasion with
23 communicants.[27] It was the beginning of an enthusiastic Anglican
presence at the settlement.

Those who lived at the Causeway later recalled the sense of
community that developed among the inhabitants.[28] The men
were involved in the construction of Parliament House, the laying
of sewers, the making of roads, the fashioning of joinery work at
Gorman House and the treatment of timber at the two local saw-
mills. While they shone their shoes and used excessive amounts of
Brylcreem when seeking employment, as manual labourers they
came home covered with dust and grime. They also feared alienat-
ing the employers who had a policy of 'last on – first off' in times
of hardship. They were the construction men, the working class of
Canberra. Their wives looked after the homes, reared the children
and developed daily routines such as boiling water in coppers for the
Monday washday, scrubbing lino floors on hands and knees, tending
the vegetable patches and 'chook runs' in the back yard, and taking
their babies to the Mothercraft Centre next to St Paul's at Eastlake.
If they had time for employment, they worked at the printery, took
in laundry and ironing for the Roman Catholic Church, acted as
waitresses in the Kingston shops or milked cows at the dairy situated
near the Dairy Flat Bridge.

The children enjoyed games, swam in the river and frequently
had rides on steamrollers (safety regulations were frequently ig-
nored). When the 5pm Powerhouse whistle blew, it signalled a hasty
return home. If the family owned a cow, children did the milking
before school, made butter and cream from the milk, trapped rabbits for dinner, helped make soap from caustic soda in kerosene tins,
polished brass taps and cleaned tin mugs. Sometimes they were sent
to Kingston to buy 'a bag of broken biscuits' and they were known
to collect empty bottles from the crates behind the stores and take
them into the same shops to claim the deposit money. JB Young's
even gave them 'a bag of lollies' when they paid the weekly bill. To
end the week each Saturday night, the fire under the copper was lit,
the water was boiled for the bath and the children were systematically cleaned ('if you weren't quick, dad would get in first'). It was in

this labouring-class environment that the Causeway Hall became the centre of community life. A cinema was established (characteristically known as 'the flicks') and became a weekly attraction. Dances became a regular feature, boxing matches were organised and attended by enthusiastic onlookers, gymnastics and first aid classes were organised. The gramophone and 'the wireless' were introduced to many at social functions. The use of the hall was so intense that the churches had to make bookings well in advance to ensure they were not overlooked.[29]

The rector saw the Causeway as an important part of the parish and sought ways to integrate the new venture with existing ministry at St Paul's. With the opening of the Causeway Hall, however, the demands on Ward's time were again excessive and he was forced to discontinue services at St Paul's for more than four months, requesting the Eastlake congregation to attend at the Causeway or St John's.[30] Devoting one Causeway service each month to Evensong and the other to Communion, he sought ways of providing for both centres. It was then that the bishop came to his assistance. Radford had been searching for a suitable curate who could assist the rector, being conscious of the difficulties Ward was facing. His prayers were answered when Walter Fletcher contacted him and volunteered his services for Canberra. Fletcher had left the legal profession to enter the ordained ministry and, after gaining his ThL qualification, was ordained in 1907. He was initially appointed to St Stephen's, Willoughby, became rector of Darwin in 1912, and later served at the cathedral in Rockhampton. With relief, Bishop Radford licensed him as assistant priest at Canberra in May 1926, knowing that Fletcher had served in Holy Orders for nineteen years and was devoted to God's work.[31]

As soon as Fletcher arrived in Canberra the rector asked him to take over duties at St Paul's and the Causeway. Together they formulated a plan that allowed weekly services at both centres between 1926 and 1929. Services of Communion, Matins and Evensong were rotated so that both congregations enjoyed consistent and regular gatherings led by two clergy who worked well together and built up the congregation in a complementary way. Fletcher declined parish council's offer of a motor cycle describing motorcycles as devices 'of uncertain temper and antics'. But, after the sustained misery of bicycle-riding from his home at Brassey House, he purchased a Morris Cowley car with the council reimbursing him 8d a mile in travel expenses. Fletcher had a similar approach to ministry as Ward. He visited the homes of new residents, introducing himself and inviting all to participate in the church's activities.[32] As new hostels were constructed for the workers he met the men and displayed sincere concern for their welfare. He became well known and much respected in Canberra, his life being described as 'an example of Christian piety to all who … came in contact with him.'[33]

The rector too received recognition for his dedicated services when he was made a Canon of St Saviour's Cathedral in September 1926. It was a fitting tribute to Ward's untiring efforts. The report in *The Canberra Times* seemed to reflect the sentiments of his parishioners:

> Few honours which have been conferred on residents of Canberra have been more fitting than that which was received by Canon Ward … a recognition of his 13 years of labour in the parish.[34]

Work with children was a priority for both the clergy and the Sunday schools assumed an important aspect of their outreach program. In November 1926 *The Canberra Times* reported on a Children's Festival Service at the Causeway Hall. A 'large congregation' listened to 'the Causeway Sunday school' children, together with youngsters from St Paul's, 'in the singing of well known children's hymns' under the direction of George Harper, the Superintendent at both centres.[35] He led a team of six teachers at the large Causeway Sunday school and under his guidance the number of children at St Paul's reached over 50 in 1928. This integration between St Paul's and the Causeway benefited both churches and constituted an effective use of resources.

The next step was to create a combined Eastlake Choir with choristers drawn from both centres. The 'newly formed choir' made its first appearance at the Children's Festival Service in November 1926 and sang 'at the Services at St Paul's Hall, Eastlake and the Causeway Hall' on a rotational basis, choir practice being held each Thursday evening at St Paul's where there was both a piano and a small organ.[36] (It is possible that the rector took his own portable harmonium to the Causeway for services.) Considerable enthusiasm accompanied the efforts of the choir. Less than twelve months later, the members presented a cantata, *Under the Palms,* in the Causeway Hall as part of Evensong. It was deemed an occasion 'which reflected great credit on their devoted work'. Over time, the choir under Harper's direction built up a library of anthems which 'assisted in carrying on the musical part of the Church services' and which, it seems, contributed to the eventual formation of a parish choir at St John's. [37] The period 1926 to 1929 was marked by sustained growth for the two congregations under the able leadership of Ward and Fletcher. The two men worked as an effective team with Fletcher's quiet spirituality and caring approach complementing Ward's own spirituality and evangelism. Both extended God's work in the permanent suburb of Kingston and the 'temporary' settlement of the Causeway.

Further down the road beyond St Paul's and the Causeway was the Molonglo settlement, sited below a ridge that was to become Newcastle Street, Fyshwick. Its population, which had risen to 530 in 1924, continued to climb. By 1925 it numbered 750, almost 600 of whom lived in the family tenements and 150 in the tradesmen's mess. Despite the growth of the settlement, the quality of the buildings deteriorated further and the living standards of the people were the cause of continuing bitter complaints. Warped timbers, gaping holes between boards, no internal lining and the absence of fires or heating in the living quarters led one trade union representative to write in frustration that at Molonglo 'people are herded … into frowsy vermin-infested dens that are a standing disgrace to our so-called civilisation,' a place where a 'decent night's rest is out of the question'.

The newly appointed Federal Capital Commission, to its credit, responded to these harsh criticisms and upgraded the facilities so that by 1927 the tenements were remodelled into cottages with electric light, sewerage and fencing, and provided with shrubs and plants to beautify the surroundings. While there was no children's playground, by 1928 the settlement had become 'a good type of Australian working class' area with a relatively 'high standard of personal hygiene' seen in the 'cleanliness and tidiness of the children' and the gardens and yards of the inhabitants. It was still accepted, however, that residents could graduate to a higher standard of habitation by moving to the Causeway.[38]

While Ward had conducted monthly services at the settlement from July 1921 to the end of 1924, these had always occurred during the afternoon or early evening and had taken the form of 'Evensong and an Address'. At the start of 1925 he implemented a number of changes in an attempt to provide for the needs of different groups. First, he reintroduced the mission service, one designed to reach those who did not attend regularly and to attract residents to the church through friendly and inspirational gatherings in the school building. For others, he continued with the usual Evensong, one that was well attended and apparently much appreciated. Then as a third form of worship, he introduced a quarterly celebration of Holy Communion at 7.30am for the ten to 20 communicants who attended. He even managed two or three services in some months.[39]

It was a heavy schedule that could not be maintained because of his ever-widening duties and the fragile state of his health, forcing him to revert to monthly services during 1926 and 1927, continued only with the assistance of the Reverend Walter Fletcher. Fortunately the services were held in the 'spare' classroom which was lit by electricity (allowing the clergy to introduce Lantern Services) and had a brick fireplace that warmed the room in winter. This was particularly important for the Sunday school children who met in the afternoon.

The Molonglo School where Anglican services were conducted.
© A Foskett

The size of the Molonglo settlement was dependent largely on the construction of public buildings in Canberra. While construction activities were expanding, the population of the settlement increased. But with the opening of the provisional Parliament House in 1927, the completion of the Hotel Canberra, Brassey House and other hostels and the conclusion of a number of sewerage projects across the suburbs, the need for workers began to decline. The numbers at Molonglo fell to 650 in 1927 with the school population contracting as well.[40] Throughout 1927 and 1928, Ward and Fletcher saw their congregation diminish leading to the cessation of early morning Communions, a reversion to Evensong and cancellation of occasional services. Only six services were held in 1929.[41] The settlement was not, however, destined to close as there was a continuing need for some construction work in Canberra, the growing effects of the

Depression curbing the provision of alternative accommodation. For some reason not immediately apparent, there was little or no attempt to combine activities at the Molonglo settlement with those of other centres a few kilometres away.

One may therefore discern a second pattern of Anglican development south of the Molonglo in the period to 1929. Unlike in Kingston, with a settled and growing population, the number of Molonglo and Causeway residents rose rapidly, peaked and then declined over years, requiring first an expansion and then a reduction in services but still demanding a church presence and a commitment of resources. While these 'temporary settlements' were destined for eventual closure, they lingered for decades, providing living quarters for workers desperately in need of accommodation in the remnants of the internment camp or in 'Hudson prefabs' meant for a five-year occupancy. In these circumstances there was little possibility of constructing church buildings as the clergy were reluctant to expend resources on centres whose futures were uncertain. Moreover, both 'temporary' settlements were on a 'bus route' to St Paul's mission hall after 1926.

A third pattern of Anglican development became apparent at the small settlement of Westridge (the future Yarralumla) which continued its intermittent growth, dependent on the varying need for bricks and tiles. Production dropped during 1924 and 1925. It was not until 1926 that demand rose sharply again necessitating the installation of two grinding mills and an additional eighteen-chamber kiln.[42] At that time much of the portable housing had been removed and Westridge consisted of 'about ten cottages of brick and timber', most of them erected before 1925.[43] The profile of Westridge altered, however, when it was decided to move the National School of Forestry from the University of Adelaide to Canberra to take advantage of Weston's pioneering research on tree species, especially conifers. The facility was built a few hundred metres from the Brickworks at the intersection of Banks and Schlich Streets and was completed and occupied in November 1927.[44] An elaborate building with a magnificent domed octagonal hall, it was opened by the Governor-General in the presence of the Prime Minister, Stanley Melbourne Bruce, and a host of dignitaries, auguring well for the future of the area.[45]

Church attendances in the Westridge Recreation Hall had been encouraging during 1923 and 1924 and continued so during 1925 until the rector was physically unable to maintain his demanding schedule. Reluctantly he was forced to discontinue services in October and the congregation did not meet again for seven months. Again it was the arrival of Walter Fletcher that allowed the revitalisation of Anglican services in May 1926. This impetus coincided with the expansion of the Brickworks and the opening of the National School of Forestry.[46] A cottage construction program of 20 homes was begun in 1927, Westridge House (known as Tudor House) was built as a residence for the Principal of the School of Forestry, and 27 lined cubicles were hastily erected for the forestry students who used three empty houses in Solander Place for dining, recreation and ablutions.

With a growing number of children at Westridge, Ward and Fletcher introduced two services each month. The first was a children's service at 3pm and the second Evensong. These continued regularly during 1926 and into the following year but were thrown into chaos when Ward's health declined at the end of 1927. At the beginning of 1928 'the spiritual work' of the parish 'was at a high pitch' and the rector was heavily involved in the preparation of candidates for confirmation, a duty to which he attached great personal importance. Eventually, however, he could carry on no longer and was taken to St Luke's Hospital in Darlinghurst for 'a rather serious operation' that required three months' rest and recuperation.[47] During Ward's absence Walter Fletcher carried on alone, curtailing activities and reducing the number of services at Westridge although maintaining the children's work as a priority.[48] In the midst of this upheaval, it was announced that the Brickworks would close at the end of March 1928 because of the diminished demand for bricks. The growing stockpiles in the yards resulted in the loss of 60 jobs. Fletcher had no alternative but to discontinue Evensong as the Depression contributed to the rapidly downward–spiralling economy.

The first of the Westlake cottages, 1926. © *National Library of Australia*

The fourth form of development was evident at The Gap (Westlake) where the transitory population involved in construction work made it impossible for the rector to contemplate a regular ministry. He simply provided occasional services during 1925 and 1926. By 1927 the camps were reduced in size or removed to other sites as the population was reduced. The Federal Capital Commission made the Westlake Hall available for church services but it was not until mid-1927 that services were resumed following 'several requests' from the Westlake Progress Association to hold 'Anglican Church Services ... in Westlake Hall'.[49] The clergy then conducted Evensong once a month until October 1927 but services ceased altogether as more than 400 workers left or were transferred to other sites.[50] This coincided with Ward's illness and hospitalisation.

Four patterns of Anglican development had therefore emerged by 1929. First, the Powerhouse settlement had become a permanent suburb and the future of St Paul's seemed assured at either Kingston or Manuka. Second, the 'temporary' settlements of Molonglo and Causeway had expanded, peaked and begun to decline. Yet they still provided living quarters for workers desperately in need of accommodation. Under these circumstances, there was little possibility of constructing church buildings as the clergy were reluctant to expend resources on centres whose future was unknown. Third, Westridge (the future suburb of Yarralumla) was still embryonic, preventing regular church services or the construction of a dedicated building. It was waiting for future growth. And fourth, the Westlake settlement was virtually a construction camp for workers involved in specific building projects that would certainly close when the projects were finished. The clergy provided what assistance they could – virtually

Number 4 Sewer Camp in 1926–27. © Ann Gugler

on an *ad hoc* basis – but realised the limited contribution they could make.

Well before 1929 both Ward and Fletcher realised that no single formula for development existed and that long-term plans for con-solidating an Anglican ministry were difficult to devise. Indeed in some centres it was next to impossible. It was only the positive situation at St Paul's Kingston that gave a guarantee of permanence and stability.

Notes

1. QA, 9 December 1924.
2. 'Canberra – Maps', NAA, Series A414 (A414) Control # 26 Attachment 1.
3. QA, 16 December 1924.
4. G Colman, 'The live firm with the live staff – JB Young's' (pp. 51–57), in V Emerton, *Past Images, Present Voices*, Canberra Stories Group, 1996, p. 52.
5. M Adamson, 'The Adamson family' (pp. 1–6), in Emerton, *Past Images*, p. 4.
6. *Queanbeyan-Canberra Advocate*, 6 August 1925.
7. Gugler, *The Builders of Canberra*, p. 312.
8. 'Plans for Retail Trading, Manuka Centre', 8 November 1924, NAA, *Canberra – Maps*, Series A414 (A414) Control # 26 Attachment 1; and *Federal Capital Pioneer Magazine*, 20 August 1927.
9. CT, 28 October 1926.
10. CT, December 1926.
11. StJPC, 18 February 1925; and StJ Register of Services, 1925–1926.
12. Val Emerton who lived next to the hall recalled that this was the day-to-day name for St Paul's in the 1920s and 1930s. Personal communication, September 2008.
13. StJPC, 26 March 1926; 28 August 1928.
14. StJPC, 19 April 1928.
15. StJPC, 22 May 1925; 9 June 1927.
16. R Winch, *The Red Bricks of Reid*, Reid Uniting Church, Canberra, 1977, p. 10; and J Udy, *Living Stones: the Story of the Methodist Church in Canberra*, Sacha Books, Sydney, 1974, p. 61.
17. StJPC, 9 June 1927 and 10 July 1928; PN, June 1929.
18. Rolland, *Growing Up in Canberra*, p. 100.
19. StJPC, 9 October 1925.

20. StJPC, 23 January and 23 February 1926.
21. StJPC, 26 March and 20 May 1926.
22. *Estimated Population ... 1911 to 1963*.
23. QA, 13 February 1925; *Federal Capital Pioneer*, 20 June and 20 October 1925.
24. *Canberra Community News*, 14 October 1925 and 11 September 1926.
25. *Canberra Community News*, 14 October 1925 and 11 February 1926.
26. J Waterhouse, *Canberra: Early Days at the Causeway*. ACT Museums Unit: Environment, Culture & Heritage, Dept. of the Environment, Land and Planning, 1992, p. 51.
27. StJ Register of Services, 1926.
28. The description of Causeway life is from Waterhouse, *Canberra: Early Days*.
29. *Canberra Community News*, 11 September 1926.
30. There were no adult services at St Paul's from 3 January to 9 May 1926.
31. CT, 12 January 1929.
32. Body, *Firm Still You Stand*, p.141.
33. CT, 15 December 1928.
34. CT, 1 October 1926.
35. CT, 11 November 1926.
36. StJPC, 7 August 1928. 'all the girls who were learning to play the piano would take turns in playing the hymns', Gwen Jackson, Personal communication, 2008.
37. StJ Register of Services, 1926–1927. See also the rector's letter, PN, October 1928.
38. Foskett, *The Molonglo Mystery*, pp. 81; 87; 103.
39. StJ Register of Services, 1925.
40. The exact number was 655 (Foskett, *The Molonglo Mystery*, Appendix 9.)
41. StJ Register of Services, 1929.
42. *Supplement to the Federal Capital Pioneer*, 22 April 1926; and *Federal Capital Pioneer Magazine*, 15 October 1926.
43. CT, 8 July 1927.
44. *http://www.library.act.gov.au/find/history/frequentlyaskedquestions/Place/Stories/forestryschool* and *http://dspace.anu.edu.au/manakin/handle/1885/314*
45. CT, 25 November 1927.
46. The National School of Forestry was later reconstituted as the Department of Forestry, ANU in 1965 and moved to the ANU campus in 1968.
47. CT, 28 April 1928.
48. StJ Register of Services, 1926 to 1928.
49. *Canberra Community News*, 14 October 1925.
50. Westlake's population in 1925 was approximately 700 of whom over 450 lived in the camps, which were progressively closed or transferred by the end of 1931. Gugler, *Westlake*, pp. 71, 171.

5   Nation, diocese, city, 1923–1929

The developments on the south side of the Molonglo in the period to 1929 were challenging and resource-intensive for both St John's parish council and the clergy. There were also wider challenges that emerged at the diocesan and national levels. The opening of the provisional Parliament House and the consequent transfer of parliamentary sittings to Canberra led the General Synod of the Church of England to consider a national cathedral. This coincided with Australia's slump into economic depression and Bishop Radford's plans to establish two church schools in the fledgling capital. There were further complications at the parish level where the illness of the rector preceded the resignation of both clergymen at St John's.

After the traditional 'turning of the first sod' for the construction of Parliament House in 1923, tradesmen and labourers from the Westlake, Molonglo, Capital Hill, Causeway and other settlements made the daily trek to Camp Hill where a building for 'the seat of government' gradually took shape over a four-year period. Hills were removed and the soil carted away by teams of horse-drawn vehicles. Galvanised tin sheds were erected around the working area. Railway lines were constructed to the site from the brickworks, steam shovels dug foundation pits and Thornycroft trucks with solid rubber tyres transported materials from Kingston to the site. Traction engines hauled heavy consignments or compacted soil in their noisy, ponderous fashion. Extra bricks were produced at Westridge. The painters arrived, the carpentry and joinery workshops at Kingston increased production and construction became more intense and frenetic. Interested and curious onlookers contemplated the size of the building from the boulevard named Commonwealth Avenue while, almost incongruously, crops of wheat and sheep farms were undisturbed a short distance away.

On 9 May 1927 the Duke (later to become King George VI) and the Duchess of York opened the building with due pomp and ceremony. Dame Nellie Melba sang the National Anthem, royal salutes were fired, a flypast of biplanes winged slowly overhead and a religious service was conducted jointly by the Anglican Primate of Australia, the Presbyterian Moderator and the Methodist President-General. (The Roman Catholic Church held its own separate function at Manuka as it believed the Anglicans should not have been given precedence at the ceremony although the Church of England had more adherents than any other in the Commonwealth.)[2] While dignitaries who arrived by special train from Sydney were granted a particular vantage point to view proceedings, ropes held back the local folk who had walked, driven, bicycled, ridden horses or caught one of Canberra's 'rectangular' buses.

The transfer of parliament to Canberra had a number of consequences for the Church of England and for the people of St Paul's at Kingston. While a sudden and substantial increase in the number of public servants in the capital did not eventuate as expected, there was a gradual move of government departments and public figures to Canberra over the next few years. A number of these men and their families were Anglican adherents and gave devoted service to St John's and St Paul's during the 1920s and the 1930s.

Sir Robert Garran and Lady Garran (left); Sir Littleton Groom and Lady Groom (right). © *National Archives of Australia*

One of the most notable contributors was Sir Littleton Groom, barrister and politician, who, after serving as Minister for Works and Railways and being responsible for construction programs at Canberra, became the Speaker of the House of Representatives. Despite his busy schedule, he devoted considerable time to the church as a lay reader in Canberra (conducting a service at St Paul's in 1928) and serving as a member of the General Synod.[3] Working closely with Canon Ward, he assumed a leading role in the Church of England Men's Society and became a well-known and popular speaker at church functions. Another was Sir Robert Garran, lawyer and public servant, who was the permanent head of the Attorney-General's Department for 31 years. He served as Chancellor of the Goulburn diocese from 1939 to 1956.[4] The spouses of these two men became closely involved in church work on the southside and contributed much to St Paul's. Sir Geoffrey Whiskard, the British High Commissioner to Australia and Lady Whiskard were also close friends of the church during their time in Canberra and contributed significantly to its development.

Other devout Anglicans included James Colwell of the Patents and Trade Marks Office (a church treasurer for a number of years); William Weale from Intelligence who was secretary of the parish council and worked tirelessly for the transfer of St Paul's to Manuka; John Starling, Secretary to the Prime Minister's Department and also the Department of External Affairs (a church warden, lay reader and financial supporter of St Paul's); and Bill Parkes, Clerk to the House of Representatives. These men (and usually their families as well) were active in the church and gave their time to the parish council. They personally supported St Paul's and were involved in fund-raising activities for the southside.

The Church of England took some time to be convinced of the strategic importance of a strong and visible presence in the national capital. After the creation of the territory was announced, the Primate of Australia, Archbishop John Charles Wright, called on the Minister for Home Affairs at Melbourne in 1912 'to learn what action would be taken to provide a site for an Anglican Cathedral at the Federal Capital'. The Minister, King O'Malley, assured the Primate that sites for the churches would be surveyed 'as soon as the design for a new city had been adopted' and that 'all churches would be met on just and equitable conditions'.[5] There was a clear expectation from the outset that an Anglican cathedral, representing the entire church, should be built in Canberra although Walter Burley Griffin's design did not originally include such a provision. The matter was delegated to local representatives – Sir Littleton Groom and Bishop Radford – to progress.

By 1923 it was apparent that the development on the south-side would eventually result in the need for an expanded Anglican presence, one that coincided with the bishop's plans for a subdivision of the diocese. Championing Canberra's position as the nation's capital, Radford wrote to Groom in October 1923 about 'the erection of church buildings' that adequately corresponded 'to the national dignity of the seat of government of the Commonwealth'. He submitted an application 'for a site for a church which might serve as the cathedral of an Anglican diocese'.[6] Radford's ideas were well in advance of most of his contemporaries. He was also one of few diocesan bishops able to transcend regional and local self-interest in the hope of embracing a national vision.[8] Radford proposed the creation of a new diocese based on the Federal Territory and envisaged its bishop serving as the Primate. The idea, in embryonic form, was expressed in a personal letter to Groom:

> At this stage [1923] it may be sufficient to intimate that on the site for which I am now making application would be erected in due course a building which would serve in the first instance as a church for the growing population of the city and which would be of such a character and design as to form ultimately part of the building of a cathedral in the event of the city becoming the see of an Anglican bishop. Those buildings would include a cathedral, a synod hall or chapter house, a residence for a bishop, etc.[7]

Two years later, the government accepted the bishop's preferred site for a cathedral on Rottenberry Hill overlooking the present King's Avenue Bridge in Barton. Feeling elated and seemingly acting on behalf of the Diocese of Goulburn and the General Synod, the bishop arranged provisional sketch plans for a large complex, believing that the church had limited time in which to commence the project.

While it is unnecessary to trace the history of the ill-fated venture in detail, it is important to realise the implications of the bishop's letter and of subsequent developments. The cathedral site was only a few kilometres from St Paul's mission hall. As noted earlier, the parish council did not believe that either the mission hall site or its building was suitable 'for the future needs of the south side of the River'. St John's was fearful, therefore, that it would be asked to contribute heavily to the construction of the cathedral which would be in its parish – thereby replacing St Paul's. Alternatively, it might have been asked to finance a temporary structure (a hall) on the cathedral site, pending the completion of the main building.

With an element of haste and a degree of alarm, the parish council informed the bishop that it did 'not feel justified in financing a temporary building on the Cathedral site', although it was prepared 'to pay rental' for a new hall (church) which it understood the Federal Capital Commission was proposing 'to erect at Manuka Circle and to supply the requisite ministration, if the hall may be rented from the Commission'. In short, the council's preference was to close St Paul's mission hall, open a new church at Manuka and administer this facility as part of the parish. Knowing, however, that the bishop was strongly committed to the construction of a cathedral, the parish council formulated a fall-back position. It informed the bishop that, 'if a hall [not the cathedral itself] be erected on the cathedral site *by the Diocese* as a half-way measure, 'the Council is prepared to pay rental

Manuka 1928 and the Capitol Theatre © *National Library of Australia*

thereafter so long as it is used by the Parish', and also 'meet the cost of the ministration'.[10] Frederick Ward was able to keep a watchful eye on developments as he was appointed to the committee convened to consider the cathedral proposal in 1926.[11]

By this time the General Synod had authorised the erection of a building 'which in its simplest form would serve as a church and hall and ultimately become the Synod Hall and Chapter House when the cathedral ... has been erected' on the site.[12]

In the meantime, with the date for the opening of the new Parliament House set for May 1927, it was decided to hold an appropriate ceremony on the cathedral site the day before parliament opened. Beneath a large white cross donated by the Canberra Branch of the Church of England Men's Society, 'huge crowds attended the open air service' when Archbishop Charles Riley, Acting Primate of the Church of England in Australia, formally dedicated the site and launched 'an all-Australian appeal for funds for the building of the proposed Cathedral.'[13]

While it was relatively easy to organise an architectural competition for a cathedral design, to name the planned structure St Mark's and to launch an appeal for funds, it was more difficult to circumvent tension, indeed open hostility, when the nature of the proposed see, its bishop and his relation to the Primacy were debated. As proceedings dragged on, Bishop Radford was asked to act as Commissioner to the Cathedral Project but little progress was made in attracting funds or resolving difficulties. Eventually a full-time Commissioner, Canon Charles Shearer Robertson, was appointed in July 1929, his appointment coinciding with the onset of the Great Depression. Without intending to be involved, St John's Parish Council faced a very awkward situation. While it sought to avoid a costly commitment to a parish hall that would principally serve the national interest, it was still obliged to deal with additional numbers at St Paul's mission hall and to provide services at other southside settlements. Moreover, two other recent developments demanded attention and funding.

Bishop Radford was keen to see Anglican schools established in Canberra and was personally associated with two foundations on the south side of the city. Neither school was a diocesan venture after the Synod determined that church schools were not within its responsibility. Yet, both were to have substantial resource implications for the parish and the diocese.[14] Schools in the Federal Territory were administered by the New South Wales Department of Education and operated under the provisions of the *Public Instruction Act* of 1880 which had abolished state aid to denominational schools from December 1882. The Commonwealth Government was equally firm in its decision not to fund church schools, favouring strong public schools such as that at Telopea Park. This policy did not satisfy Bishop Radford.

Inspired by the ministry of the Sisters of the Church at Waverley in Sydney where St Gabriel's (Girls) School was well-known, Radford sought their assistance in Canberra. Jill Waterhouse has described how the Sisters were approached by the bishop to commence a school in Canberra and how, with 'vigour overriding caution', they shopped for furniture in Sydney and 'set off for the twelve-hour drive to the national capital in two taxis laden with luggage' to begin their new venture.[15] St Gabriel's opened on 10 June 1926 in the old rectory (built during the time of Pierce Galliard-Smith) and accepted boys as well as girls in the lower junior forms. Although a new rectory was being built for the Wards at the time, it was not occupied until October 1926. For almost four months the rector's family, teaching staff and ten pupils shared the old rectory.[16] This would have suited Teddy Ward, the rector's eldest son, who needed only to walk downstairs to his Form 1 classroom.

In December the school's 'auspicious beginning' was celebrated at the inaugural Speech Day in Reid when it was revealed that the first wing of the new building on the southside was expected to open in June 1927. This was a somewhat optimistic forecast. (The foundation stone was blessed by the bishop on 8 May 1927, the same day on which the church dignitaries dedicated the cathedral site on Rottenberry Hill.) While the bishop lauded the efforts of the staff and students at the Speech Day ceremony, Canon and Mrs Ward felt a sense of personal pride when Teddy came first in General Progress and won the prize for Form 1 Divinity.[17] They were not to know that Teddy would one day be ordained and serve as chaplain in the Royal Chapel at Windsor.

As 'rapid progress' was being made on the new building at Melbourne Avenue on Red Hill, Mrs Margery Ward and the women's committee organised the annual fete at Reid and planned future Speech Days. They achieved highly effective publicity for the school when the 1927 Annual Prize-giving Day was hosted by Sir John Butters. The prizes were presented by Lady Garran, the assembly was addressed by Sir Robert Garran and 'His Excellency the Governor-General and Lady Stonehaven were present in their capacity as parents'.[18] Canon Ward informed the gathering that although the first wing of the Red Hill School had been opened just three months earlier, extensions would probably be required in two or three years.

The rector took a close interest in the school and immediately commenced a weekly service of Holy Communion for the staff and visitors. Ward and the Reverend Walter Fletcher then alternated month by month. Weekly services continued at both centres until both the junior and senior departments were moved to Red Hill early in 1928. The Register of Services shows that, in addition to weekly Communion services held in St Gabriel's School Chapel, children's services were also held on special occasions.[19] These commitments added to the already heavy load carried by the clergy, one made even more onerous when Ward accepted 'the kind offer' of the Sisters of St Gabriel's School 'to start a monthly Evensong' in the entrance hall of the school.[20]

In a parallel venture, the bishop was involved in the foundation of Canberra Grammar School. A co-educational school, which had been established in Cooma in 1906, was purchased by the Rector of Cooma in 1908 and became the Manaro (later Monaro) Grammar School for boys. It was inevitable that its operation would be relocated after the Reverend William Edwards 'accepted the Headmastership [of Canberra Grammar School] on the understanding that he would work to move the School to the new National Capital'.[21] The directors secured 20 acres of land at Red Hill and 'admirable plans' for a complete school were obtained from Burcham Clamp and Finch of Sydney. This development led *The Canberra Times* to report in November 1927 that construction was soon to commence on the Canberra Church of England Grammar School at Red Hill.[22] The Cooma directors subsequently withdrew from the project prompting Radford 'to constitute an association of limited liability for the foundation of a new school, the foundation stone eventually being laid by the Prime Minister, Stanley Bruce, in December 1928'.[23] As the school was opened and dedicated by the bishop before the building was completed on 5 February 1929, the headmaster, staff and 63 boys occupied the old rectory at Reid for eight months before moving to the new building in September 1929. A short time afterwards Edwards presented his first annual report noting that 'the work of the school' covered 'the whole of the Secondary School Curriculum from First Year [Year 7] to Leaving Certificate Honours, together with one from below First Year [Primary School]'.[24] Edwards had formerly occupied a number of influential educational and pastoral positions: staff member of Trinity Grammar School, Acting Director of Education for the Diocese of

Sydney and Rector of St Augustine's at Bulli, as well as serving in the AIF and studying at Queen's College, Cambridge.[25]

With an Anglican priest as headmaster, the school did not require the clergy of St John's to conduct chapel services for the boys. Nonetheless, Edwards very quickly established a close working relationship with Canon Ward and with the Anglican centres on the southside. The headmaster was proud to accept 'a presentation of unique value and historical interest' from Canon Ward – 'the Holy Communion vessels presented to him by the parish and used by him while on service with the AIF' at the Somme.[26] Edwards was to provide much-needed assistance in the parish at a difficult stage when the national economy declined and resource shortages became more acute.

At the end of 1927 Canberra's population had reached 7,591. The rate of growth was, however, soon to slow. After the completion of the provisional Parliament House and other public buildings in 1927, the need for construction workers fell, a decline reflected in the numbers of people employed by the Federal Capital Commission.[27] Peaking at 3,086 in January 1927, the number dropped to 2,115 five months later and to 1,920 in December.[28] In the midst of this reduction, the national economy began to falter causing parliament to reduce expenditure on Canberra and to retrench even more men.

Hotel Canberra 1951, originally Hostel 1   © ACT Heritage Library

As a consequence, the commission's 'retrenchment axe fell [again] …
when 400 constructional employees' opened their pay envelopes and
discovered the 'unseasonable intimation that their services would not
be required after the Christmas vacation.'[29] By the end of March 1928,
the Brickworks closed down as the demand for bricks, tiles and pipes
dried up, the number employed by the Commission fell further to
1,463 in March 1928 and to 1,348 in June, and the transfer of further
public servants from Melbourne was delayed and, in some instances,
deferred. The calendar year 1928 proved to be 'an eventful, troubled'
one, *The Canberra Times* voicing the feeling of the people: 'the boom
period has gone.'[30]

It was during this 'eventful' period that the Sisters of St Gabriel's
were transferring their school to Red Hill, planning an expansion of
the buildings and seeking funds to reimburse their original outlay of
£20,000 while requiring additional money for future expansion.[31] Not
far away at Canberra Grammar School, the council was paying £750
a year to lease the site, repaying a debt of £5,000 for the first wing of
the school and entering into a second mortgage of £10,000 for the
second wing to be built in 1929. At the diocesan level, the bishop
was pushing ahead with plans for a national cathedral and seeking
£25,000 to £50,000 as a deposit for a scheme valued at £150,000.[32]
There was predictable angst when the economy began to deteriorate,
creditors became more insistent and appeals for funds met with less
than enthusiastic responses.

While these ominous issues were played out at the diocesan and
national levels, they impinged on the Parish of St John the Baptist and
involved Canon Ward and Walter Fletcher. These events conspired to
occur at a time when Ward was very unwell. He had suffered periods
of illness since his return from the Somme and was occasionally hos-
pitalised as his strength ebbed away. In early 1928 Ward was a weary
man. Without Walter Fletcher he would not have been able to carry on.

It was then that Fletcher broke the devastating news: he wished
to resign and return to England. Soon after, Ward fell ill again and
was taken to Sydney for surgery. Fletcher delayed his departure and
carried the burden of the entire parish with limited support. Finally,
after a challenging three-year period 'in the work of establishing the
churches in a fast growing community', Fletcher departed in January
1929. He was farewelled by 200 people in the old rectory grounds.[33]

Ward not only lost 'a very true friend and colleague' but was left with a difficult decision to make. After three months recuperating from his illness, he received a remarkable display of affection and support from the church centres in the parish. It took the form of a monetary gift and a signed address that read in part:

> Those who had been in close touch with Canon Ward fully realised the constant personal sacrifice he had made during the past few years. The growing city had made its demands upon him but he responded unselfishly and with a whole heart. His personal touch had made the newcomers feel at home [and] ... the older residents had written affectionately, paying their tribute to his devotion to them and personal attention to their needs.[34]

Ward felt an obligation to his congregations but now, only six months after their fulsome and generous expression of kindness, he had lost his assistant and the full weight of the parish descended on him again. Could he continue? Even the appointment of the Reverend GAM (Monty) Nell a few weeks later did not completely settle his anxieties. He had serious discussions with Margery about their future.[35]

Aware of his failing health and diminishing strength, Ward worked at a frenetic pace to prepare the parish for his eventual departure. With 'the scattered nature of the city' in mind, he encouraged a monthly publication in September 1928, *Parish Notes,* to provide regular information on church activities to parishioners in all centres including St Paul's, the Causeway, Molonglo, Westridge and St Gabriels at Red Hill.[36] He placed increasing emphasis on the work of the parish branch of the Church of England Men's Society (CEMS), one he helped to revive in 1926. Men from St John's, St Paul's, the Causeway and other centres held lively discussions, conducted monthly church services at the various centres, arranged excursions, took a major role in welcoming new members to the church centres and became involved in community activities. The rector encouraged CEMS, arranged Communion services for the group each month (followed by breakfast and a speaker), supported their library and quickly accepted the men's offer to publish *Parish Notes.*[37]

CEMS members printed a card that was personally handed to male newcomers to Canberra informing them of the men's group and

St John's	8.00am	2nd, 3rd 4th Sundays Holy Communion
	11.00am	Every Sunday (1st and 3rd Holy Communion)
	7.30pm	2nd, 3rd and 5th Evensong
Causeway	8.00am	3rd Sunday Holy Communion
	11.00am	2nd Sunday Matins
	7.30pm	1st and 3rd Sundays Evensong
St Paul's	8.00am	1st Sunday Holy Communion
Eastlake	11.00am	4th Sunday Matins
	7.30pm	2nd Sunday Evensong

inviting them to join its membership. On the back of the card was a list of church services held in 1927.

The rector also realised the potential force of the women in the parish. With the assistance of his wife, Ward widened the scope of the Sanctuary Guild and renamed it the 'St John's Churchwomen's Guild'. It boasted 53 members in September 1928. Some of the women on the southside joined St John's Guild but found difficulty attending meetings because of the irregular bus service to Civic and the walk to the rectory.[38] Consequently, Ward called a meeting of the churchwomen on the south leading to the formation of the St Paul's Women's Guild in 1929. Mrs Mollison, who had recently arrived in Canberra, was elected president, Mrs Nell the vice-president and Mrs Rowley the treasurer. The women immediately agreed 'to raise the money to buy a small organ for the hall' to replace the one on loan from the Methodist congregation and arranged 'American teas, snowball teas, bridge parties and musical events' to raise funds.[39] Mollie Mollison later recalled that the Guild was 'the first to introduce jumble sales to the southside of Canberra' and they proved such a success that they were

The Reverend (later Canon) FG Ward, Rector of St John's from 1913 to 1929
© St John's Archives

extended to 'the Causeway Hall, Molonglo and Westlake'.[40] Canon Ward, Monty Nell and their wives did not realise the vibrant force that was created on Wednesday 29 May 1929. The Guild was a vital body that would successfully lead the drive for a new church building at Manuka over the next decade.

While he was particularly appreciative of the help of others and sought to involve them in the work of the church, Ward was especially energetic in welcoming Edwards as Headmaster of Canberra Grammar School late in 1928, believing that he had a significant part to play in Anglican ministry on the southside. Additionally, Ward supported and nurtured the talents of a young man, James Hardman, asking him to be superintendent of the St Paul's Sunday school from January 1929, supporting his election to synod and accepting his appointment as secretary of the parish council in March. Ward was consciously preparing people for a time when he would no longer be with them.

Even when considering his resignation, the rector's mind was preoccupied with the southside and its future. While the Causeway Hall allowed joint services between the Causeway and Kingston congregations, the mission hall was totally inadequate to meet the needs of the local people. It was in urgent need of extension. Ward again raised the issue in May 1929. After a long council discussion, 'definite steps were taken to organise the work of the Church in the southern portion of the parish,' with local residents asked to take a leading role.[41] Organising committees and guilds were established, new goals were devised and 'additional services' were planned for church people 'in and around Kingston'.[42] Despite all his efforts, the rector acknowledged that there was 'so much which I feel has been neglected by me' even though 'I have honestly tried' to do more.[43]

The pace was demanding – indeed too intense – and he realised that he could not continue for much longer. After discussions with Margery, the bishop and the assistant priest, he requested 'leave of absence from the Diocese for a year', explaining to the parishioners, 'I feel that I cannot go [on] without a thorough rest and I hope to leave at the end of June with my wife and children and do light work in an English village'.[44] Less than two months later, he accepted the futility of continuing in any form and submitted his resignation to the bishop, with effect from 30 June 1929. He entreated the parishioners to 'stand fast in that one Spirit' and not retreat from the advances that had been made 'by the grace of God' so that 'my successor may be able to do what I have been unable to do'.[45]

Farewell gatherings were held in all the church centres, the Hotel Wellington and the Albert Hall. Each occasion concentrated on the contributions Ward had made to a specific centre. One address 'on behalf of the residents of the parish' summed up the totality of his effort:

It is given to few clergymen to serve a community during three
... phases of development ... For the first few years the parish
was a typical rural district and there is ample testimony from
the settlers of your influence among them. Then followed a
period of constructional activity which introduced an urban
industrial element, to whom your ministrations were equally
grateful and lastly, since the establishment of the national capital
with the attendant influx of population and the development
of civic and rural problems of every kind, your personality,
sympathy and kindly interest have been the most valuable
help to all classes of the community.[46]

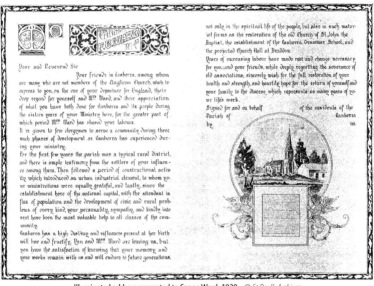

Illuminated address presented to Canon Ward, 1929 © *St Paul's Archives*

On 23 June the rector conducted an 8am service at Canberra, a 10am
Church Parade Service at Duntroon, an 11am Choral Communion for
112 communicants at St John's, a 3pm Children's Service and a 7.30pm
Evensong at St Paul's. Perhaps it was symbolic that his last service was
held on the southside. He then walked into the vestry, took his pen
and noted in the Register of Services, 'Thus ends a happy ministry in
this Parish. FG Ward'.

After a farewell evening program the next day at the crowded
Albert Hall (24 June 1929), Frederick and Margery Ward, together
with their two young sons, Teddy and David, boarded a late night train

for Sydney. They sailed for England two weeks later where they settled in the Diocese of Southwark and served God at a more sustainable pace. In 1936 they moved to the Diocese of Norwich where Ward ministered for another 20 years. Ever remembering his association with the national capital, he kept in touch with the parish and followed closely the development of Anglican mission and ministry on the southside, recalling again in 1953 that 'the sixteen years spent at Canberra as Rector were some of the happiest of my ministry'. He met up again with Walter Fletcher and their friendship continued over many years. It was significant that Ward attached a plaque to the front of his home on which was inscribed the name 'Canberra'. He died in 1963, having seen his two sons enter the Anglican Church as priests.

An assessment of Frederick Ward's sixteen-year incumbency reveals a continuing but successful struggle to extend a Christian influence in the parish, particularly on the south side of the Molonglo River. The rector, with recurring periods of illness, worked alone for much of the time, escalating his efforts to extend God's work and the Anglican witness. It was never an easy task – one that was gruelling at times – but one that was performed and guided by devotion to God and by unwavering compassion and concern for his parishioners. He provided an increasing number of services at St John's each Sunday, served the outlying centres of Sutton, Ginninderra and Gundaroo and maintained Sunday services and a chaplaincy at the Royal Military College. He eventually ministered to six southside centres, in addition to his community involvements, without the assistance of another priest until 1926. As the gloom of the Great Depression was about to descend, an important era in Anglican outreach to Canberra came

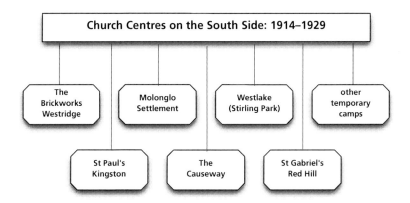

Church Centres on the South Side: 1914–1929

The Brickworks Westridge — Molonglo Settlement — Westlake (Stirling Park) — other temporary camps

St Paul's Kingston — The Causeway — St Gabriel's Red Hill

to an end. The 'lengthened shadow' of Canon Frederick Ward would endure for decades. Ward left his young assistant, the Reverend 'Monty' Nell as priest-in-charge.

Notes

1. A description of the events was recorded in CT on 11 May 1927.
2. Gibbney, *Canberra 1913–1953*, p. 129.
3. D Carment, 'Groom, Sir Littleton Ernest (1867–1936)', *Australian Dictionary of Biography*, vol. 9 (pp. 130–133), Melbourne University Press, 1983.
4. Robert Garran, *http://en.wikipedia.org/wiki/Robert_Garran*
5. QA, 21 June 1912.
6. Radford to Groom, 17 October 1923, NAA, 'Ecclesiastical Building Sites', Series A414 (A414), Control # 75.
7. B Fletcher, 'Anglicanism and the shaping of Australian Society' (pp. 293–315), in Kaye, *Anglicanism in Australia*, p. 307.
8. Radford to Groom, 1923.
9. See for example: Frame, *A Church for a Nation*, Chapter 7.
10. StJPC, 9 October 1925.
11. R Wench, 'The cathedrals that didn't happen and the early urban churches of Canberra', *Canberra Historical Journal*, March 1977, p. 15.
12. Report of the 1926 Diocesan Synod in CT, 28 October 1926.
13. CT, 9 May 1927. Tom Frame in *A Church for a Nation* stated that the cathedral site was dedicated by the Archbishop of Perth, Henry Le Fanu, but this was not possible as he was not installed as Archbishop of Perth until 1929.
14. Report of the 1926 Diocesan Synod in CT, 28 October 1926.
15. The following account is heavily dependent on Jill Waterhouse's, *A Light in the Bush*, Old Grammarians Association, Canberra, 1978.
16. CT, 24 September 1926; Body, *Firm Still You Stand*, pp. 125–126.
17. CT, 16 December 1926.
18. CT, 2 August 1927; 9 December 1927.
19. StJ Register of Services, 1926–1929.
20. PN, October 1928.
21. A Keenan (ed.), *Catching the Vision: The Foundation of the Canberra Grammar School*, Canberra Grammar School Foundation, 1997, p. 11.
22. CT, 25 November 1927.
23. CGS Report of the Council, Annual Meeting 11 March 1930, CGS Archives, Headmaster's report 1930 File.

24. CGS Headmaster's first annual report, December 1929, CGS Archives 1929 Report File.

25. CT, 2 February 1929.

26. Headmaster's first annual report.

27. CT, 24 January 1928.

28. CT, 4 July 1928.

29. CT, 30 December 1927.

30. CT, Editorial, 1 January 1929.

31. Waterhouse, *A Light in the Bush*, p. 35.

32. P McKeown (ed.), *Deo, Ecclesiae, Patriae. Fifty Years of Canberra Grammar School*, ANU Press, Canberra, 1979, pp. 4–6.

33. CT, 12 January 1929.

34. CT, 9 July 1928.

35. CT, 23 February 1929.

36. PN, September 1928.

37. PN, September and October 1928; March 1929.

38. *The Pauline*, June 1954. p. 2.

39. PN, June 1929.

40. *The Pauline*, June 1954, p. 4.

41. StJPC, 23 May 1929.

42. CT, 25 May 1929.

43. PN, June 1929.

44. PN, March and April 1929; CT, 9 March 1929.

45. PN, May 1929; CT, 8 May 1929.

46. Copy of address presented to Dr [sic] Canon FG Ward on his retirement from St John's Anglican Church, NAA, Series A3560 (A3560), Control # 5660.

6   Depression years and setbacks

The decade after Ward's departure in June 1929 was a difficult period for the Canberra parish, particularly for centres on the southside. The church was restricted by limited staff, continuing financial stringency as a consequence of the Great Depression and its aftermath and decreasing congregations at Molonglo, Westridge and Westlake as workers left these districts. At the same time, the council was called upon to provide additional resources to meet the demands of a rapidly expanding community at Kingston.

It was an overwhelming task for the assistant cum-temporary-priest-in-charge, Monty Nell, to take over the entire parish in July 1929. With less than five months experience in Canberra, he had responsibility for all services at St John's, Duntroon, St Paul's Kingston, the Causeway, St Gabriel's Red Hill, Molonglo and Westridge as well as centres at Ginninderra, Sutton and Gundaroo.[1] Additionally he provided religious instruction in schools, chaired the parish council, attended the Men's Society meetings, edited *Parish Notes,* visited the sick and sought to maintain normal home visits. The small Morris Cowley car, which the council purchased for his use, was essential as he moved among the centres and tried to cope with an almost impossible situation.[2] Fortunately, his wife, Marjorie, assisted in the Churchwomen's Guilds at St John's and St Paul's.

Within weeks, Nell advised parishioners of the regrettable cancellation of services at Molonglo and St Gabriel's Red Hill, the reduction of services at St Paul's and the curtailment of home visits.[3] He did maintain all services, however, at St John's and the Royal Military College and became well known for his Sunday sermons that were reported in *The Canberra Times.*[4] Moreover, his understanding of oriental religions resulted in requests to address local associations.

When working with young people, Cubmaster Nell took the initiative and established scouts' troops at St John's and St Paul's, ventures that proved so successful that a full quota of 24 boys was quickly reached at Kingston and a waiting list for membership had to be established.[5]

In the meantime, Bishop Radford searched for a suitable replacement for Ward while beset with a range of problems relating to the proposed cathedral and its funding, the two denominational schools and the Depression. Moreover, the bishop's wife, Maud, died after a long illness leading the bishop to withdraw from his duties for a time.[6] During these challenging months some of the St John's parishioners wrote to the bishop and alleged that the 'church is falling to pieces'. The bishop curtly replied that it was 'the parishioners who were falling to pieces [and] not the Church'.[7] Not surprisingly, there were difficulties following Canon Ward's sixteen-year incumbency but Monty Nell was not without loyal support. He publicly acknowledged 'the most valuable assistance' of Bill Edwards who conducted services at St John's and permitted the use of Canberra Grammar School's new premises for meetings and parish activities.[8] James Hardman, a layman, also provided valuable and continuing assistance, unaware at the time of the personal influence he was later to exert on St Paul's, on other southside centres and on the impetus for a new church at Manuka.

What kind of priest was needed to lead such a disparate ministry? The Diocese of Goulburn 'had clergy representing every shade and expression of Anglicanism' – 'Low', 'Broad' and 'High'. Radford, a convinced High Churchman, searched for one who reflected his own predilections and theological leanings and found the potential appointee already working with him, Canon Charles Shearer Robertson.[9] Born at Sydney in 1889, Robertson was educated at Wahroonga Grammar, leaving school at the age of sixteen to work at Central Railway Station to support his mother. As a young man he listened to an Open Air Mission in the city and heard a dynamic speaker, Bishop George Merrick Long of Bathurst, whose influence led him to enrol at Moore Theological College. One of his classmates was Bill Edwards. The two men were to continue their friendship in Canberra. Made deacon in 1912 and ordained priest in 1913 (by the Bishop of Bathurst), Robertson spent over twelve years as curate of Dubbo and rector of Trundle, Wyalong and West Wyalong in the central west of New South Wales as well as one year working as secretary of the

Brotherhood of the Good Shepherd.[10] He had gained wide experience
in two dioceses by the time he was 40 years of age.

As early as 1918, he had written to Bishop Radford, by-passing
his own bishop, indicating that the 'ultra-Protestants are fighting
me … in Wyalong [but] so far the battle has gone against them'. The
following year he had again contacted Radford about altar lights,
seeking the bishop's opinion on whether churchwardens could refuse
to approve their installation. Apparently attracted to Radford's Anglo-
Catholicism, he had written, 'I would like some day, sir, if you have
any suitable vacancies to come into your diocese.'[11] Eight years later
the bishop was searching for an organising secretary for the diocese,
one who could 'muster enthusiasm for the task of collecting money'.
Radford offered the position to Robertson who accepted the challenge
in 1926.

From 1926 to 1929, 'Robbie' as he was commonly known to his
friends, travelled 'up and down the length and breadth of the Diocese
of Goulburn', seeking to 'sway people to give their wherewithal' as he
met town leaders, preached in churches, sought contributions and
bequests and motivated his fellow clergy to do the same. Achieving
'excellent results',[12] he became well known in the diocese where his
name was recorded in numerous registers of services over a four-year
period, including St Paul's Kingston in November and December 1929
when he assisted Monty Nell.[13] Most of his work aimed to raise diocesan funds, including those for a cathedral, but it became increasingly
evident to him and to the bishop that the descending financial gloom
of 1928–1929 militated against the cathedral project. It was put on
hold and eventually abandoned.

In mid-1929 the bishop suggested that Canon Robertson might
accept a half-time appointment to St John's while continuing his
money-raising travels in the diocese. The parish council did not accept
the proposal. By the end of the year, however, the council members
unanimously approached the bishop and requested that Robertson
be appointed as full-time rector. In characteristic fashion, Charles
Robertson set down his terms. He would accept the appointment
provided the council permitted his continued involvement in the
cathedral project and the two denominational schools, paid him
a stipend of £450 plus fees and allowed him to retain his own car.
Significantly he added 'that, if he occupied the parish, it was his

intention to wear the eucharistic vestments, a policy agreed to by the council as 'this was entirely a matter for the Rector'.[14] He accepted the position. Squeezing himself and his prized books into his small Austin car, Robertson set off for Canberra. He preached his first sermon on 5 January 1930.

Speaking on the theme, 'go forward', Robertson's message was clear, his voice authoritative and his presence reassuring.[15] A week

Canon (later Archdeacon) CS Robertson, early 1930s.
© Mrs A Price and Mrs J Salisbury

later the church was crowded as the new rector was installed and the bishop addressed the congregation, outlining the ways in which the parish could 'go forward'. After referring particularly to St John's, Radford addressed the needs of the newer centres, stressing that 'the Canberra Church of England parish must have a place of worship other than St Paul's Hall, Kingston, on the southern side of the city'. While the construction of the cathedral was not possible for the time being, he queried whether 'the Church of England people of Canberra [were] going to let visitors think that all they were capable of was the St Paul's Hall? Of course they were not.'[16]

Robertson highlighted three aspects of his new ministry. First, he set down the main tenets of his Christian message with an emphasis on worship and the sacraments. Second, his commitment was to 'go forward' and expand the influence of the church. Third, the church's position on the southside had to be addressed as a matter of urgency. Canon Robertson – popular, dynamic and infectiously enthusiastic – quickly restored the numbers at St John's and St Paul's through 'his engaging personality and ability to project his thoughts' to others.[17] Communicant numbers rose across the parish centres from 3487 in 1929, an average of 67 each Sunday, to 5,325 in 1930, an average of 102. Moreover, collections increased from £763 to £1,098 in the same period, the rector displaying his typical flair for raising funds. 'In a year of depression, we have gone forward and not back,' he informed the parishioners.[18]

He then turned his attention to St John's aged church building. The parish council agreed to refurbish the chancel, restore the original stonework walls, recondition the entrance to the vault underneath the chancel, improve the drainage around the church, rearrange the seating in the church and install a new organ (at a cost of £850). The western entrance to the churchyard was remodelled and a memorial lych-gate was constructed. The churchyard was restored and enhanced by the planting of hedges, shrubs and roses. To his credit, Canon Robertson was able to enthuse the council and to spearhead attempts to raise more than £4,000 to restore the church building and its environment.[19] Parishioners from the southside were impressed with the changes when they attended St John's for confirmations, church anniversaries and other special occasions. They could not help but compare their 'tin shed' to the attractive, historic and consecrated church. The comparison helped to raise a feeling of discontent among St Paul's parishioners who 'felt ashamed of their own building' and became increasingly determined to erect a substantial structure to glorify God.[20] Unfortunately, the Great Depression prevented any attempt to relocate the mission hall or to construct a new church despite the embarrassment. No-one knew at the time the devastating effect that the Depression was to have on the church and the entire society.

Surviving the Depression and providing help to the destitute actually constituted one of two major challenges facing the parish during the 1930s. This was a formidable task even for Canon Robertson who was an acknowledged fund-raiser in the diocese. The beginnings of the Depression were felt early in Canberra with the completion of public buildings in 1927 including the provisional Parliament House. The effects were varied among different groups in the emerging society. At the top of the social order were the permanent public servants concentrated mainly in the Prime Minister's Department, the Treasury, the Attorney-General's Department and the Department of Home and Territories, most of whom were housed in the East and West Blocks near Parliament House. While all sectors of society felt the effects of the Depression, the 'public servants were safe from the spectre of unemployment' although they endured a salary reduction of over 20 per cent in 1931.[21] As a group, they 'contributed generously' to the

Unemployment Relief Committee which was set up in June 1930 to provide relief for unemployed workers. This scheme was subsidised pound for pound from Commonwealth funds.[22]

For a second group – the semi-skilled and manual workers – the story was quite different. This was highlighted by an AWU representative who remarked, 'There is practically no other employment outside that offered by the Government' and workers 'are totally dependent on the Government for their existence'.[23] When the Federal Capital Commission closed the Brickworks in 1928 and retrenched 60 men, followed by 40 from the Labouring and Trades section in July 1929, another 47 from the Engineers and Lands Department in September and an additional 68 a week later, the situation became bleak. The workforce of the Federal Capital Commission dropped from 3,086 in 1927 to 977 in November 1929.[24]

The Federal Government postponed the transfer of departments from Melbourne and devised policies for stabilising employment with preference being given to 'married returned soldiers domiciled in Canberra'. It was accused of making 'severe and inhumane' cuts to Canberra's services on 'Black Thursday' when 200 employees were dismissed and lost their accrued sick leave as well. In a city that boasted of its parks, hedges and flowers, it was virtually 'impossible to carry on services provided by the Parks and Gardens section'. Even worse followed in October 1930 when it was announced that the Royal Military College at Duntroon would be moved to Sydney 'to save money'.[25]

While political factions squabbled over appropriate courses of fiscal action in 1929–1930, a crowd of 350 to 400 men frequently gathered outside the administrative offices at Acton 'in the hope of securing work'. On a typical day in June 1930, only 30 of the 400 were hired to construct a road to Duntroon. They received employment for one week in every four. Others were engaged in seasonal burr-cutting and tree-planting along the Queanbeyan Road.[26] Many lived at the Molonglo settlement and the Causeway and, for those who retained their work, the cash in the 'little brown envelopes each week' was very welcome.[27] For others there were ration tickets or coupons to the value of three shillings that could be exchanged for food (not tobacco) after their cases were vetted by Mr Goodwin, the welfare officer. By July 1930, almost 1,700 ration orders had been issued to local single men, many of whom were also given relief work for 'one week on and five weeks off'. They usually sought to supplement their money by putting up fences, chipping thistles and begging work wherever it was available.[28]

Feeding a family was a continuing challenge. A garden in the Causeway backyard provided vegetables while fowls were kept in enclosures some distance from the homes (allowing boys to pilfer eggs and birds for their own supply). 'Many times we would have gone hungry except for the little rabbit,' wrote one resident. 'There were lots of them up around Mt Mugga.' Others later recalled that they were virtually 'brought up on a diet of rice, rabbits, cornbeef and pickles' and that potatoes were a real treat as they cost sixpence for 5 lbs (2.3 kg). Lindsay Perry from the Government Stores 'did a lot of good for us when times were hard,' recalled one man. 'We'd get him to drop a bag of potatoes off the government truck and then we'd share them around.' Despite adversity, men were reluctant to take individual action to better their cause for fear of recrimination and loss of employment. Yet they were quick to join in large unemployment rallies in the 1930s and marched to Parliament House, led on occasions by Father Patrick Haydon, Canon Robertson and Dr Lewis Nott (a local doctor and politician) who sympathised with their plight and espoused their cause.[29]

A third group in Canberra was even more severely affected by the Depression. Interstate workers moved through Canberra between 1929 and 1935 in search of employment, believing that the Federal Government would provide work for them. They were not entitled to employment – not even casual relief work – and had to seek aid at No. 4 (Single Men's) Camp, a complex comprising 43 cubicles, a mess, kitchen, drying room, stores and ablution blocks. Assistance was provided for a 'short stay' of two weeks but it was known that some were actually 'domiciled' for months. Another camp at Ainslie provided for a small number of family groups. By June 1930 about 700 ration orders for three shillings each had been distributed to single men, while a small number of itinerant families received between 12s 6d and 30s, depending on their circumstances.[30] Relief orders and coupons rose from 79 orders in one week in May 1930 to 200 a week, occasionally peaking at 300 by Christmas. By the winter of 1932 the average had dropped to 25 and in August 1933 the system of working for the dole was introduced for 40 people.[31]

Robertson had to pass No. 4 Camp when he drove over Scott's Crossing and went up the slope towards Parliament House on his way to Kingston, Molonglo and the Causeway. The site is now under the lake in front of old Parliament House. He was well aware of the conditions so many faced. The clergy of the various denominations discussed the plight of the men and decided on joint action 'to ameliorate the lot of the itinerant unemployed'. A soup kitchen was set up in March 1930 with the men in the camp providing the labour and the churches supplying 'the necessary ingredients' on a weekly basis.[32]

A concerted Anglican response gained momentum when Canon Robertson approached the Men's Groups[33] and the Women's Guilds at both St John's and St Paul's to organise a sit-down meal for the men. He later wrote in the Register of Services: 'Afternoon tea was given to the unemployed in the No. 4 Camp at 4.45 at which over 100 men were present.'[34] Over the following months, a routine was established when 120 of the ladies from the various Anglican church centres each prepared about four gallons (eighteen litres) of soup. The soup was bucketed into milk cans and transported to the camps by the rector in his car which was aptly known as 'the Soup Cart'. Robertson was typically amused when he heard that some of the men sold the soup to the steward and made a profit.[35]

Over several months Anglican assistance broadened as church people from all denominations were invited to donate 'gifts of cakes, scones, bread, butter, sugar, cigarettes and tobacco' for a tea at No. 4 Camp. By Christmas a parish relief fund was distributing food parcels and clothing while work was offered to some of the unemployed to renovate the churchyard at St John's.[36] Robertson was acutely aware of the oppressive effects of the Depression on the parishioners and the distress that resulted as economic hardships lingered. 'Many of you have lost your positions altogether and are on relief work,' he sadly acknowledged to his various congregations. Some were 'greatly reduced in salary' and others were 'on the road'. Adopting a characteristic Anglican response, he condemned 'a system of world finance under which such things are possible'. He could not 'subscribe to repudiation' of Australia's overseas debts but he believed 'that an adjustment should be made in the rate of interest and that, if necessary, payments for interest should cease for a period of years.'[37]

Matters did not improve quickly. As 1932 dawned, he noted in the Register of Services that 'the full force of the Depression hit Australia at this time'. Most government departments 'were cut down', civil servants had their salaries reduced and their living allowances were taken away.[38] Robertson and the assistant priest accepted their own share of the burden and took reduced stipends in an effort to assist the parish.[39] Many appreciative stories were told during the Depression years (and for decades thereafter) of Robertson's care and personal contribution to those in distress as his family provided food, shelter and support for the unemployed and destitute. Even in 2008, there were older parishioners who still lauded his contribution and indi-

---

The Canberra Times

THURSDAY, DECEMBER 31, 1931.

THE PASSING YEAR

FROM the sore trials of 1930, a worried world looked with hope twelve months ago to 1931 as the year which would see its troubles mended. From the disappointments of 1931, hope springs eternal and flows to the beginning of 1932, for the passing year has not proved to be a time in which the world has rid itself of its troubles. It has been a time for the world in general of ups and downs, of hopes and disappointments, but withal it ends with the prospect of human affairs being decidedly better in the New Year. For the world in general, 1931 has proved a term of purgatory for its failures and misdeeds of the past, and in this term of expiation there has been a sufficient spirit of repentence to inspire serious effort to avert their repitition and to repair their consequent ills.

Extract from *The Canberra Times*, 31 December, 1931

cated that the Robertson family members went without themselves in order to assist others.

It was not until November 1933 that Prime Minister Joseph Lyons asserted that 'conditions generally were better than at any time since the beginning of the depression' as the states accelerated their works programs, loan appropriations increased, trade gradually revived and private employers began to employ more workers.[40] In Canberra the number of food relief orders dropped to 36 in June 1934, while by 1935 the weekly average of work orders was only four. With a thankful sigh, the authorities ordered the demolition of No. 4 Camp. Canberra became 'less attractive to the forced *tourist*,' and the policy of issuing 'food relief and work dockets' was virtually finished.[41]

Although the Depression was not over by 1933, its worst effects had passed and Robertson surveyed the position of the church and his own standing as rector. On his arrival, he had the assistance of Monty Nell until June 1930 when the bishop had appointed the young priest to the Parish of Moruya. Nell had been succeeded by the Reverend George Wheeler who had also been moved within months. At this point the rector had decided to 'go alone' until a suitable curate could be found and the financial situation had improved.[42] It was a desperate time without assistance. Finally on 15 May 1932, Bishop Radford ordained the Reverend Alban Elliott who joined the staff at St John's and assumed some responsibility for the southside centres. The Archdeacon knew, however, that St Paul's required a leader to supervise the work personally. When the Reverend James Hardman was ordained at the end of 1932, he was given major responsibility for the southside centres.[43] It was on Hardman that much of the burden of leadership was concentrated.

This initiative permitted Canon Robertson to devote more time to what he saw as a continuing concern – the doctrinal integrity of the church and the inertia of nominal Anglicans. Being a high church-man who referred to Holy Communion as 'the most important part of our worship and chief means of grace', he was adamant that it was an absolute obligation on every Anglican to attend church regularly.[44] Almost as a creed, he insisted that Anglicans pray daily, read the scriptures every morning, 'be present *every Sunday* at the Service of Holy Communion and on the Saints' days and weekdays when possible', observe Friday as a day of fasting and abstinence and set apart some of their income each week for God.[45] For much of the time, however, he was powerless to engender enthusiasm and watched with dismay the stagnation and falling attendances at four southside centres. Not only was there a declining interest in the church itself but the effects of financial restraints and changing demographic patterns were obvious as well.

Consequently Robertson turned his attention to the second major challenge facing the parish between 1930 and 1937, the four southside centres of Molonglo, Causeway, Westridge and Westlake. In the first instance the population of the Molonglo settlement, after peaking about 750, declined as unemployment become widespread and as workers left to seek work elsewhere. Whereas the 1928 electoral roll included 224 adults at the settlement (plus children), the number dropped to 186 in 1935.[46] It was widely agreed that the 97 'patched up' tenements needed to be demolished and the population moved. The Depression prevented demolition, however, and the buildings lingered as low-cost housing at five shillings a week for three to five rooms.[47] As the settlement decayed the public hall fell into disuse and was destroyed by fire. The 'untenanted' post office went up in flames and 'vandals set fire to the old internment camp's observation tower in 1934'.[48]

The official intention was to 'abolish the Molonglo settlement' and to 'transfer the present residents to the Causeway'. When this was delayed, the Molonglo 'Slum' became political ammunition in the Senate. The buildings were alleged to be 'worse than hovels, dank, dark and vermin-ridden' and it was a crime 'that men who had fought to save the country should be compelled to live in huts built to accommodate our wartime enemies'.[49] By 1934 the conditions had not improved and there were further demands for change and for transfer of the dwindling population.[50]

It was in this environment that the clergy and members of the Church of England Men's Society sought to maintain a presence at the settlement. After Canon Robertson organised lay readers to rotate services during 1930, declining numbers and a falling interest in Anglicanism within a heavily working-class neighbourhood forced him to reduce services and then to terminate them.[51] Alban Elliott started services during 1931 and 1932 but they were again discontinued as the population steadily declined and the fortnightly collections gradually dropped to nothing.[52] When regular adult services ceased, the clergy placed even greater importance on children's work despite the difficulty of attracting dedicated Sunday school teachers.[53] Transfers in and out of Canberra during the Depression years caused continuing problems with staffing while some teachers lived on the other side of the river and lacked transport each Sunday. To overcome these problems a bus service was provided for children from Molonglo to St John's but the venture proved too costly and soon had to cease.[54] As the difficulty of recruiting Sunday school teachers became more acute, Robertson lamented that his frequent appeals for assistance during the 1930s were 'fruitless'.[55]

Eventually, James Hardman provided a degree of stability during 1935 when he visited the Molonglo settlement regularly. He advertised the resumption of services, prepared the school classroom, improvised a temporary altar and conducted a midweek service two, three or four times a month, for a relatively constant and viable group. Perhaps it was the traditional Sunday form of service that was the earlier problem or, more likely, that Hardman had a particular approach that attracted people. Whatever the reason, his success prompted Canon Robertson to inform Ernest Henry Burgmann, who had succeeded Radford as Bishop of Goulburn in 1934, that James Hardman was 'a keen and faithful priest and knows the mind of the people'.[56]

After Hardman's departure from the parish, fortnightly Evensongs continued on Wednesday evenings until the arrival of the Reverend Tom Whiting in mid-1937. Because few Molonglo families owned a car, those who desired to take Holy Communion were required to walk or bicycle to St Paul's or St John's or to catch a local bus that operated at irregular times and via a rather circuitous route. It was obvious that the 'temporary' Molonglo settlement would eventually be demolished and that church services would cease. It was, in fact, only a matter of time. Before this happened, it was to the credit of the rector, his assistants and the lay readers that services continued and were organised for the dwindling number of residents.

The Causeway had also been designed as a 'temporary' settlement with a life expectancy of five years but again the Depression changed the government's plans. The 120 modularised houses, fourteen other tenements and locally constructed hall were considered an improvement on Molonglo and, while they may have 'looked like rows of butter boxes' known as 'the cubicles', Causeway homes came to assume some character when the residents cultivated gardens and sought to improve the settlement's appearance.[57] Years later when reminiscing about life at the Causeway, the former residents recalled the pride of having a two-bedroom house with electricity, an internal laundry with a bath in it and 'a landlord (the government) who would come round and attend to maintenance and even clean the chimney'. Modern comforts provided a sense of luxury with an open fire in the house, a chip-heater in the bathroom and a wood stove in the kitchen. One lad was impressed to discover 'an inside toilet with a real chain'. Social status certainly increased when one moved from the Molonglo to the Causeway.[58]

Despite these differences, all was not well at the Causeway in the 1930s as the cheaply constructed homes began to deteriorate and as buildings became increasingly difficult to maintain. An official verdict in 1930 indicated that the Causeway homes were 'in fair condition and will serve the purpose for a few years yet' but such predictions were often optimistic.[59] When the Leader of the Opposition, John Curtin, visited the Causeway and Molonglo in 1935, he declared that Molonglo should be demolished, the rents at the Causeway should be reduced and that new houses should be erected, giving householders of the Causeway 'the opportunity of moving into them to make room for residents of Molonglo'.[60] Social distinctions arose based on the housing provided and the rents charged.

Unlike the Molonglo settlement, the Causeway maintained a relatively constant population from 1930 to 1937 because of the better housing, the attractions provided at the Causeway Hall, the sense of community that developed and its location closer to Kingston shops. This allowed the various denominations to provide services on a regular basis and to develop semi-permanent congregations. While the Catholic Church continued to have a strong following, the Salvation Army was also well known for its open-air meetings in the streets and for its brass band playing 'Onward Christian Soldiers' and 'Bringing in the Sheaves'. At other times, the 'Salvos', as they were known, 'went around every street, playing the organ that was strapped to the running board of the car'. The car was hit by a train at the Causeway but fortunately the organ escaped to play again.[61]

Anglican services had been predictably cancelled after Canon Ward left the parish and after Nell rationalised his time.[62] When Robertson arrived in 1930 it was decided to discontinue Causeway services altogether, none being held again until November 1937, a gap of almost eight years. A number of reasons accounted for this change of policy. First, it was difficult for Robertson with limited assistance to meet commitments in all the parish centres and it was felt that other provisions might be made for the Causeway residents – St Paul's at Kingston was close by, allowing the Causeway congregation to attend the mission hall where additional services were scheduled. Second, there was a cost involved in renting the Causeway Hall for each service, an unwanted financial strain during the years of economic Depression. Third, Canon Robertson had ideas for expansion on the southside by using the new Manuka Theatre for combined missions. As a result, church services at the Causeway were terminated in 1929 although children's activities were continued.

The Causeway Sunday school was one of five Anglican Sunday schools in Canberra during this period, others being at Ainslie, Kingston, Molonglo and Duntroon. With the cessation of regular services, the Causeway Sunday school was organised from St Paul's where teachers were trained and prepared, rosters were organised and training schools were occasionally held to improve teaching methods and presentation.[63] A combined Sunday school picnic for a number of centres was held each year, usually at Russell Hill, with buses transporting the children to the picnic grounds and the Canberra City Band providing music.[64] By 1935 the Kingston and Causeway schools held their own picnic when 160 children crammed into overcrowded buses (disregarding issues of safety) and had a day of 'fun and romping' at Duntroon before joining 'lustily in singing on the homeward journey.'[65] Despite the emphasis on the children, regular services were not possible.

On the other side of Capital Hill, Westridge was such an isolated settlement in the early 1930s that the local bus terminated at the Prime Minister's Lodge, requiring the residents to walk the rest of the distance home.[66] The settlement comprised seven homes constructed for the staff of the Brickworks, more than twenty others built between 1923 and 1927, the National Forestry School, the principal's residence and basic student accommodation. Two street lights did little to illuminate the isolated area, particularly for those residents who trudged to and from the milk bails in winter, 400 metres away. The Westbourne Woods arboretum, planted by Thomas Weston and the nursery staff, stretched away towards the Molonglo River, while adjacent to the settlement were 131 acres set aside for the Governor-General's residence not far from the large woolsheds of the Yarralumla property. By 1928 there were 123 adults on the electoral roll for the Westridge area.[67]

Anglican services ceased here also as Nell rationalised his time but revived when the new rector organised a roster of laymen from the Men's Society to conduct regular Evensongs in the Westridge Recreation Hall, sometimes three or four times a month. There were gaps between church services during 1931 and only two services were conducted in 1932 until James Hardman and lay readers provided continuity during 1933. It proved to be a losing battle, however, as the numbers dwindled and services were discontinued from November 1933.[68] The rector persisted in advertising Westridge services in *Parish Notes* during 1934 but it was a forlorn hope and from January 1935, he informed parishioners that services would be held 'by arrangement'. Only two were recorded, one in October 1935 and another for two people in August 1936. Services at Westridge were no longer viable under the prevailing conditions and had to wait fourteen years before they were revitalised.

A short distance away, the settlement of Westlake gradually changed character as it declined in numbers from a peak of 700 in 1925. Twelve of Howie's 25 cottages were removed by 1926. By July 1927 the Old Trade's Camp was demolished and the men transferred to the Parkes Barracks (No. 4 Camp) in front of Parliament House. The camp, which had housed 110 workers, disappeared while those who lived in No. 1 Labourers' camp – about 100 tents of hessian and canvas – were also moved in 1927 to wooden cubicles at Red Hill. Finally, by 1931–1932 all temporary camps as well as Howie's cottages were demolished or removed, leaving only the portable cottages for 250 to 300 residents.[69]

These cottages (below the site of the present American Embassy) stretched along the hillside that gradually sloped towards the Molonglo River and had an appearance of permanency, each painted green to fit into the surroundings, with vegetable gardens at the rear and flowerbeds in the front. The area officially comprised '61 four-roomed wooden buildings', the majority of which had been 'erected in 1924 for the temporary accommodation of workmen'. The houses gradually deteriorated during the Depression and there were proposals in 1933 to provide fireplaces and chimneys, the latter detached entirely from the woodwork'. Even this modest improvement was a concession because the 'majority of tenants' were 'considerably in arrears' with their rent because of the Depression.[70]

Over a nine-year period Robertson and the assistant priests found it difficult to minister to the Westlake residents because of the rapidly declining population up to 1932, the proximity of Westridge where some church services were held and the seeming indifference of the adults to Anglicanism. The rector asked the assistant priest, Harold Marshall, to assume responsibility for Westridge and Westlake early in 1933 but, after two ineffectual attempts to hold services in the old Recreation Hall in August and October 1933, there were no further services at Westlake between 1933 and 1938.[71] The Westlake residents were informed that a service could be held 'by arrangement' but apparently no-one accepted the invitation.[72]

And so, the adverse effects of the Depression, falling numbers and a decline of interest in the Anglican Church were experienced in these four centres between 1930 and 1937. They were working-class areas which might be expected to suffer the worst effects of economic stringency but their plight was also affected by the temporary – yet lingering – nature of the settlements and the changing demography that resulted from government policy. Nevertheless, it was not only the lower socio-economic groups that were affected during the 1930s.

The economic downturn also affected the two denominational schools on the southside. St Gabriel's School, which had moved all classes to its Melbourne Avenue site early in 1928, had an enrolment of 90 in 1928 (22 boarders and 68 day pupils). This number had fallen to 80 in 1930 and to 61 in 1932 as many parents could not afford the fees. Unable to meet the demands of the creditors, the sisters announced the closure of the school at the end of 1932, the news galvanising the local parents into action. Robertson was not only the school chaplain but also had four of his own children in attendance and eventually proposed that the school be leased from the sisters in Sydney. There were difficult negotiations and an anxious search for funds during 1933–1934 but eventually the Church of England Girls' Grammar School was created with the sale of the school to the Parents and Friends Association at a cost of £12,500 in 1935.[73] While financial woes persisted as the school struggled to attain financial viability, the rector continued a close relationship with the students and the parents. He introduced an early morning Communion Service each

Thursday and then, to assuage hunger pains, the students, staff and rector had 'puftaloons and golden syrup in the school dining-room' where Robertson chatted with the headmistress and the girls. He must have consumed many puftaloons as he attended most weekly services during the 1930s. After breakfast, the rector conducted religious instruction classes, underlining his concern for the youth of the parish.

The Canberra Grammar School, which had moved from the its temporary premises in the old rectory to Red Hill in 1929, also passed through a period of financial turmoil as the school directors sought to extricate themselves from the debts and misunderstandings resulting from Bishop Radford's involvement.[74] An association named 'Canberra Grammar School' was incorporated in 1929 as a non-profit company and the school was managed by a council of at least fifteen, comprising clerical and lay representation. Numbers dropped during the Depression and the staff were paid a mere pittance but with the assistance of Sir Robert Garran, Sir Littleton Groom, Percy Sheaffe and others, and with the added proceeds from numerous fetes, balls and appeals for funds, the worst days were over.[75] By 1935 there were 74 boarders and 35 day boys at the school and numbers began to increase.

While the headmaster was frequently invited to participate in services at St John's and St Paul's, all prayers, chapel services and religious instruction classes at the school were led by Edwards himself, avoiding the need for parish involvement except on formal occasions. Gradually the school acquired an academic reputation but it was Radford's retirement message that is often best remembered: 'I cannot expect to live long enough to hear of a young Bishop or a Prime Minister' having been a former student of the school, he wrote, but he was certain that it would eventuate. One of the students at the time was Edward Gough Whitlam who became Prime Minister in December 1972.[76]

Another step was taken to develop Canberra's embryonic educational facilities when the Commonwealth Government 'decided to pass an Ordinance to create a university college at Canberra', one that removed the need for public servants and their children to leave the district in order to further their education. The college gave further meaning to the two denominational schools that provided studies to Leaving Certificate (university entrance) level. From 1930, degree courses were established in cooperation with the University of Melbourne when University Extension lectures were commenced and a scheme of bursaries was instituted.[77]

When Robertson looked back over the first seven years of his incumbency in 1937, he was acutely aware of the financial difficulties that had been endured and the changes that had resulted on the southside. The Molonglo Communion services had been discontinued, Evensong services rescheduled to weekdays and the regularity of gatherings continually interrupted. The Causeway ministry had been combined with St Paul's at Kingston resulting in the termination of regular services at the Causeway Hall from 1930 and an increased emphasis on the education of youth. Falling numbers at Westridge and Westlake had led to the virtual cessation of services at these centres after 1933 indicating a need for the church to concentrate on more populous districts but also pointing to a weakening of Anglican allegiance and a degree of parishioner disengagement. The situation challenged him to attempt even more to defend and extend the faith of his church. And yet, despite these problems, there had been evident success at Kingston where 'St Paul's-in-the-tin-shed' had prospered and God's work had been enhanced.

Notes

1. 'Church Services', PN, 1928–1929.
2. CT, 9 March 1929.
3. Changes were advised in PN November and December, 1929.
4. Nell's sermons were reported in the 'Churches Column' of the CT.
5. PN, April 1929; November 1929; April 1930.
6. PN, December 1929.
7. See Body, *Firm Still You Stand*, pp. 150–151.
8. PN, July 1929.
9. Frame, *A Church for a Nation*, pp. 79, 134.
10. *ABM* [Australian Board of Missions] *Review*, December 1956. pp.189 ff.
11. Robertson to Bishop Radford, 14 November 1918; 21 May 1919; 14 November 1919, NLA Manuscripts, MS1998, 'Diocese Correspondence with Archdeacon CS Robertson', Papers of Ernest Burgmann, Box 34.
12. *ABM Review*, December 1956.

13. Christ Church Queanbeyan, Register of Services, 21 February 1926, NLA, Manuscripts 3085/13/12; CT, 19 August 1929; StJ Register of Services, St John's and St Paul's, 1929.
14. StJ PC, 9 December 1929.
15. Canon Robertson's sermon, CT, 6 January 1930.
16. PN, February 1930.
17. J Woolven, *A Stitch in Time: Charles Shearer Robertson – Recollections and Reminiscences of some who knew him.* Mimeo, 1992, pp. 22 ff. Robertson was a Canon of St Saviour's Cathedral in 1929, relinquished the canonry when he was appointed to St John's and was again appointed Canon in March 1930.
18. PN, Feb/Mar. 1931.
19. See details in PN between March 1930 and April 1934; and in Body, *Firm Still You Stand*, pp. 159–166.
20. Gwen Jackson, Personal communication, 2008.
21. Gibbney, *Canberra 1913–1953*, pp. 159–164.
22. Gugler, *Westlake*, pp. 327–328.
23. AE Gardiner, President of the Canberra branch of the AWU, CT, 1 October 1930.
24. CT, 20 March 1928; 11 July, 10 September, 17 September and 18 November 1929.
25. CT, 24 July and 23 August 1929; 24 April and 18 October 1930.
26. CT, 23 August 1929; 5 June 1930.
27. The accounts of former residents of Molonglo and Causeway are found in Waterhouse, *Canberra: Early Days*, Chapters 3 and 4; and Foskett, *The Molonglo Mystery*, pp. 124–128.
28. CT, 31 July 1930.
29. Waterhouse, *Canberra: Early Days*, Chapter 2 and p. 21.
30. CT, 31 July 1930 and 20 February 1932; Gugler, *The Builders of Canberra*, pp. 268–269.
31. CT, 7 June 1935.
32. CT, 21 February 1930.
33. PN, July 1930.
34. StJ Register of Services, 27 July 1930.
35. PN, September 1930.
36. CT, 21 February and 18 November 1930; PN, January 1931.
37. T Frame, 'Local differences, social and national identity 1930–1966' in Kaye (ed.), *Anglicanism in Australia*, p. 103. Also PN, September 1930.
38. StJ Register of Services. The entry was made between 27 December 1931 and 1 January 1932.
39. StJ AGM, CT, 20 February 1932.
40. CT, 8 September 1933.
41. CT, 7 June 1935.
42. PN, July and September 1930.
43. RA&P, 1914–1939, 15 May 1932 and 7 December 1935.

44. PN, October 1936.

45. PN, May–August 1932.

46. Figures are calculated from the 1928 and 1935 electoral rolls for the Molonglo Settlement. Roll lists are found in Foskett, *The Molonglo Mystery*, Appendix 7.

47. Foskett, *The Molonglo Mystery*, p. 108.

48. CT, 24 March 1931; 10 September 1932. Joyce Daly's reminiscences cited in Foskett, *The Molonglo Mystery*, p. 108.

49. Senator Collings, Senate speech on 'Canberra Slums', CT, 2 December 1932.

50. CT, 11 September 1934.

51. PN, June 1930.

52. StJ Register of Services 1929 to 1937 provides information on all services.

53. PN, November 1928.

54. PN, June 1929.

55. PN, September 1930.

56. Robertson to Burgmann 25 November 1935, NLA, Manuscripts, MS1998, Diocese Correspondence with Archdeacon Robertson, Papers of Ernest Burgmann, Box 34.

57. A review in March 1930 revealed 134 'temporary or tenement houses' at the Causeway, CT, 19 March 1930

58. Reminiscences of former Causeway residents in Waterhouse, *Canberra: Early Days*, Chapter 3.

59. CT, 19 March 1930.

60. CT, 22 October 1935.

61. Waterhouse, *Canberra: Early Days*, p. 87.

62. Causeway Church Services in PN were omitted from August 1929.

63. See PN October 1929, June 1933, May–June 1934, October and November 1935. Sunday school meeting times were advertised in PN from 1930 to 1936.

64. CT, 3 October 1931.

65. PN, November 1935.

66. Eunice Burton, Personal communication, 2009.

67. Gugler, *The Builders of Canberra*, p. 96. Gugler reproduces the 1928 electoral rolls for Westridge and the Nursery. The number of adults totalled 123.

68. StJ Register of Services 1930–1938. Two services were recorded, one on 13 October 1935 and another on 18 August 1936. Only two or three attended.

69. Gugler, *Westlake*, pp. 71, 171, 377.

70. Department of Interior report, March 3, 1933, in Gugler, *Westlake*, p. 273.

71. PN, November 1932.

72. StJ Register of Services 1930–1938; also PN, December 1934.

73. PN, November and December 1934; September 1935. This resumé of the Girls' Grammar School and of Canon Robertson's involvement is based largely on Waterhouse, *A Light in the Bush*, Chapter 5.

74. Frame, *A Church for a Nation*, pp. 140–141; Wyatt, *The History of the Diocese.* pp. 126–127.

75. J Pulford, 'Deo, Ecclesiae, Patriae' (pp. 18–48), in McKeown, *Deo, Ecclesiae, Patriae*, pp. 26–29.

76. B Porter, 'A backward glance' in McKeown, *Deo, Ecclesiae, Patriae*, pp. 8–9.

77. CT, 11 December 1929.

7   St Paul's-in-the-tin-shed, 1930–1937

In contrast to the decline that occurred in other southside centres between 1930 and 1937, the congregation at St Paul's increased, the small hall was extended and the church assumed responsibility for children's work at the Causeway. These developments resulted largely from the growth of Kingston and the surrounding suburbs and from the leadership provided by Canon Robertson and an assistant clergyman who lived in the area. Eventually the congregation planned a new building on another site, opened a 'Building Fund' in anticipation and began to work with gusto on fund-raising activities, causing a degree of consternation at St John's in the process. The one responsible for much of the church's development was James Hardman.

Born in Lancashire England, Hardman spent a few years in Africa before arriving in Sydney with his father and brother in 1907 at the age of nine. After his father was killed on military service in France in 1917, Hardman eventually found his way to Queanbeyan where he lived during the 1920s.[1] First mentioned in the Register of Services of Christ Church, Queanbeyan, conducting Evensong in January 1923 (followed by others when the rector was ill or absent from town), 24-year-old Hardman was a clerk and became involved in a range of youth activities: the Warrigal Football Club, the Dramatic Club, the local hospital and a range of Sunday school projects for which he became well known.[2] It was his involvement in youth work at Christ Church, however, for which he had an abiding passion. After an illness he indicated that he would leave Queanbeyan because of lack of work whereupon local meetings were convened to recognise his contribution to the town and to make presentations of money and a silver watch 'suitably inscribed by the pupils of the Sunday school'.

The rector said 'good bye to a faithful worker who had been untiring in his labours' and was 'deserving of the highest appreciation'
especially among the children 'for whom he had worked unstintingly'.
The Mayor of Queanbeyan wished there were more 'young fellows of
the stamp of Mr Hardman', regretted his departure from the district
and 'hoped that something might be found for him to do which would
prevent his leaving'.[3] Apparently Hardman did remain in Queanbeyan
for his name was listed on the electoral roll in 1925 and the following year he was a member of the Queanbeyan Hospital Committee.[4]
Moreover, he conducted church services at Queanbeyan and Tharwa
during 1924, 1925 and 1926, standing in for the local rector when
assistance was required.[5]

He then moved to Queensland where he attended St Francis'
Theological College at Nundah for two years and married Lillian at
All Saints, Brisbane, in December 1927. He returned south without
having completed his studies to Diploma or Licentiate level. Moving
to Canberra at the end of 1927, he lived in Dawes Street Kingston and
worked as a 'Company Secretary' at the motor garage a few doors from
JB Young's Store.[6] Despite his move to Kingston, Hardman continued
his contacts with Christ Church and was licensed as an honorary
lay reader in Queanbeyan by Archdeacon Joseph Pike in December
1928, whereupon Ward promptly announced that Hardman would
superintend 'the St Paul's [Sunday] school', effective three days later.[7]
By April 1929 he was a diocesan synod representative and twelve
months later Robertson nominated him as a lay reader on the revised
list for the Canberra parish.[8]

Lillian Hardman became deeply involved in the activities of St
Paul's mission hall – only a short distance away from the Hardman
home – collecting for *Parish Notes* each month, supporting fund-
raising schemes for St John's and St Paul's, working for the Kingston
Women's Guild and encouraging her husband through the demanding
times of the Great Depression.[9] Hardman worked up to 48 hours a
week at the garage, became increasingly involved in the work of the
church, accepted the position of parish secretary during 1929–1930,
conducted services as a lay reader and was drawn ever closer into the
work of the Christian ministry.[10]

As he had previously made out the monthly accounts for customers at the motor garage, Hardman knew the people of Kingston

1930 view of Telopea Park School (centre); Powerhouse and Kingston (top right). © *National Library of Australia*

well – his friends and acquaintances at the Government Printing Office, the retailers in the Kingston shopping centre, the engineers and mechanics at the Powerhouse and his fellow residents. Kingston's 319 adult residents in 1928 included artists, musicians, photographers and chauffeurs, as well as a sprinkling of gardeners, labourers, railway workers and dairy farmers. Some of the 124 women were typists, clerks, or shop assistants while others held managerial positions in shops or restaurants but the majority were married and were listed under the rubric of 'Home Duties'.[11] Overall, Kingston was developing its own character and was 'Canberra's most vital suburb ... the retail and social centre of the small [Canberra] community'.[12] In close proximity and contributing to Kingston's development, were Manuka with 34 adults on the 1928 Roll, Griffith 111, Mugga Mugga 45, Forrest 178, Barton 88 and Telopea Park 49.[13]

A range of stores and emporiums filled the Kingston block by the 1930s. There were grocers, delicatessens, jewellers, hairdressers, butchers, fish and chip shops, chemists and dental surgeons. Milk bars were popular, the tea rooms were a respectable retreat for ladies and Pat Norgrove obliged customers with the best breads and cakes at Ogilvie's bakery. The smoke-filled billiard room catered for the men and the Canberra Café (the first licensed premises in Kingston after the liquor laws were changed) was a lively spot after work. With the end of Canberra's prohibition in 1928, the residents jokingly affirmed, 'No longer did the emu on the coat of arms at Parliament House look longingly over its shoulder towards Queanbeyan when it felt thirsty.' Radio Station 2CA, located in Jack Ryan's radio shop in Giles Street, was operated by George Barlin who advertised for the Kingston shopkeepers and for national advertisers 'like Colgate Palmolive, Arnotts biscuits and people selling pills'. George could always rely on an enthusiastic listening audience as he relayed a summary of the day's test cricket, especially when it involved Don Bradman's exploits in the 'bodyline series'.[14]

Late shopping on Friday nights promoted a festive atmosphere as people arrived by car, bus and on foot from the surrounding streets and from Barton, Manuka, Forrest, the Causeway and the Molonglo settlement. Woodger and Calthorpe's motor shop and bowser provided car service for those who travelled from the northside and from Queanbeyan. The female bowser attendant bewildered and disgusted the Kingston ladies by wearing pantaloons when working in grease and pumping the petrol.

Children walked to the nearby Telopea Park School, raised the Union Jack and sang 'God save the King' each day. After school the boys played cricket behind the Powerhouse, the girls enjoyed hockey, others played in the reserve beside St Paul's hall and those who owned bicycles explored Red Hill. Morrie Adamson and his friends sank tins into the open stretch of rough ground between Kingston and Manuka and constructed their own golf course while others climbed over the 'Big Gun' captured from the Germans at the Somme in 1918. The gun is now located outside the Australian War Memorial. Fortunately the signal to return home, the Powerhouse whistle at 5pm, could be heard as far as the Manuka Swimming Pool. The pool was opened in 1931 and immediately became popular during Canberra's hot summers.[15] The residents claimed that Kingston developed a cooperative community spirit in the late 1920s and 1930s and was a safe and happy place in which to live.

Living near the Kingston shops, Hardman knew the environment well and was aware of the role that the church could adopt. He observed Radford's attempts to stall the development of St Paul's as the bishop planned a cathedral, frustrating the actions of St John's parish council as it searched for a 'suitable allotment on the south side of the Molonglo River for Church extension purposes'.[16] Hardman was one who desired a more appropriate building and was only partly assuaged by Canon Robertson's moving comment in *Parish Notes*:

> The only building we have at Kingston, in which we can join together to worship God, is the little tin shed that we call 'St Paul's Hall'. Nevertheless, though we long for a structure more worthy of our God and more inspiring to ourselves, we remember that Christ was born in a dirty old stable and also that we worship the same God in Kingston hall as we would in the finest Cathedral.[17]

Hardman was gratified when Robertson called for £5,000 for a church hall in Manuka in 1930 and St John's council agreed as an interim measure to improve the existing mission hall in April so that it took on the appearance of a church.[18] An unpainted ceiling was fitted, making the building 'much warmer on cold nights', a small porch added over the door to provide a sense of privacy and a bell erected in the grounds to be tolled before each service.[19] As attendances continued to increase during 1930, the rector informed parishioners that a new church hall on 'the south side of the river was still the most important work waiting' to be accomplished and needed to be 'attempted as soon as possible.[20] In the meantime, however, further changes were required to the existing hall if progress were to be made.

As the number of communicants at the 9am Communion service increased to 25 and sometimes 30, the members of the congregation at St Paul's became more vocal as they realised that no new church would be constructed in the foreseeable future.[21] Finally Robertson contacted the bishop, outlined a plan to extend St Paul's hall and received his consent as there was 'money in hand'. Mr Doddrell, the secretary of St John's council, wrote to the Civic Administrator seeking to enlarge the hall by 12 feet (3.5 metres) 'in a workmanlike manner … finished to match the existing portion of the building. Upon completion the entire structure would be painted'.[22] Permission was granted in June 1931, *The Canberra Times* informing its readers that tenders had been let for the extension at the end of July, just three weeks after 80 people unsafely crammed into the hall to farewell Monty Nell.[23]

The extensions took three weeks and were completed in time for special services on Sunday 30 August 1931. As the 9am congregation arrived they found the interior of the hall lined and painted, a small vestry curtained off for privacy and curtains erected so that the altar and sanctuary could be 'completely closed off apart from times of service'. The servers wore 'the Sarum or Old English robes as distinct from the Western' type, giving an added sense of ritual to the occasion.[24] The hall was filled as the rector reminisced about the changes – less than two years before there had been no altar, altar linen, or altar step and not even a Bible or missal, while the hangings had been faded and they had used a borrowed organ. Since then the Kingston Women's Guild had bought a new Estey organ for £32 10s and the cost of the extensions and renovations had been partly covered by the hard work of the women.[25] After the sermon, 52 people received communion.

Fortunately the weather was fine that Sunday night because the congregation was 'too much for the building' when Robertson, Edwards and Hardman conducted choral Evensong. With additional space in the building, Mr Scriven (ACM, TDLCM, MusDipMelb, MusDip London) led 25 St Paul's choristers in the anthem *Sun of my Soul* and the *Te Deum*, after which the overflowing crowd listened to well-known solos: *Open the Gates of the Temple; Consecration; There is no Death;* and *Just for Today*.[26] As a result of the extensions it was possible to open the new door on the side of the building and for the preachers and soloists to stand in the doorway so that those inside and outside could follow proceedings.

The Reverend James Hardman, 15 May 1932, the day he was made a deacon.
© St John's Schoolhouse Museum

By this time Hardman believed that he was being called to the full-time ministry and approached Robertson and the bishop for guidance. Bishop Radford accepted him as a postulant for Holy Orders and he entered Moore College at Sydney in March 1932 where his training was shortened considerably because of his previous theological studies. As he left for Sydney his 'services to the parish in many capacities' were recognised and the Women's Guild acknowledged Lillian's 'faithful work' for the church and the Kingston guild in particular.[27] As a special concession, Hardman received £26 to work during vacation time in the parish commencing in May 1932, again receiving the parish council's appreciation for the 'splendid work' he performed for the church.[28]

Priested at St Saviour's Cathedral on 18 December 1932, Hardman left the cathedral and drove back to Kingston in time to conduct the evening service at St Paul's where the congregation reacted with favour (and perhaps a degree of pride) as he was the first to enter Holy Orders from 'St Paul's-in-the-tin-shed'. Robertson was equally pleased that he had an assistant priest and promptly asked him to concentrate on the southside centres where he became the unofficial priest-in-charge of St Paul's.[29] As Hardman contemplated the changes required to meet Canberra's rising population (from 6,880 in 1929 to 7,325 in 1933) he realised that the mission hall, so close to the centre of population in 1925, now served a much wider district with an increasingly diverse population. There were increasing numbers of public servants, politicians and business people who resided in Forrest, Barton and Manuka, while others were beginning to move up the slope towards Red Hill. Consequently, St Paul's was no longer the centre of the populated region but found itself on the periphery, requiring people to walk longer distances to church or to find some other means of transport. There was clearly a need for change and a new vision.

A morning and evening service each Sunday at St Paul's was insufficient, Hardman believed, and with Robertson's approval he commenced early morning Communion services each Tuesday and Friday to supplement the Sunday service that now provided for 40 communicants.[30] By December 1934 he added a third service on Wednesday mornings increasing the total number of communicants during 1934 to 2,359, an average of 45 each week. Perhaps the transfer of the Patents and Trade Marks Office to Canberra in 1933 helped to swell numbers.[31] By 1935 the total number of communicants climbed to 2,476, almost 48 a week, a figure that was maintained during 1936.[32] It led Robertson to pay tribute to the work of the assistant priest who was 'not only holding the congregation of St Paul's together in love and harmony' but was also 'building up on right lines in his work with the young.'[33]

With the same enthusiasm that he had shown at Queanbeyan, Hardman introduced a 10am children's service by mid-1933, one that proved particularly popular not only for youngsters but also for adults

who were encouraged to attend with their children.[34] Depending on
the season of the year, numbers at the children's service rose to 50
or 60, while the 'regularity in attendance shown by the majority' was
most encouraging.[35] By the end of 1935 the 10am service was attracting large numbers and Robertson hoped that it would 'not be long
before we have a full church', requiring the churchwardens to provide
'more accommodation'.[36] Specially designed stamps were distributed
to the children each week and prizes were awarded at the end of the
year for faithful attendance. Moreover, the 7.30pm Evensong attracted
gratifying numbers and, depending on weather conditions, occasionally reached 60.

During 1933 Robertson and Hardman discussed a joint venture
with the Community of the Ascension, the first Anglican religious
order for men in the Australian Church. Robertson had been the
secretary of the Brotherhood of the Good Shepherd in 1915 – a 'bush
brother' at the age of 26 – and was well aware of the work of such
communities.[37] Founded by Anglican chaplains who had served in
the 1914–1918 War, the Community of the Ascension with its Anglo-
Catholic orientation helped the clergy of the diocese through 'parish
missions and retreats, school religious instruction, clergy training and
the testing of vocations'.[38] It was no surprise, therefore, that Robertson
looked to them for assistance, involved them in five services at St
Paul's between 1930 and 1933 and planned an extended mission in
December 1933.

The proposed program was refined, the mission advertised and
Father Campbell, Brother Peter and James Hardman launched into an
eleven-day venture of evangelism comprising 32 meetings that were
integrated with regular church services. Communion was celebrated
early each morning for a total of 309 communicants and mission
services were held each evening, the rector urging the congregation to
'attend each night' and indicating that, should the hall prove too small,
'the door will be used as a pulpit and the seats will be put outside'.[39]
While the mission may have sought to reach non-Christians, it was
primarily aimed at those who wanted 'to build up their Christian life'
and others who wished 'to get the help that only the Christian religion
can give'.[40]

As Robertson devolved considerable responsibility on Hardman in
the south, he kept a tight rein on financial issues and ensured that his

authority was never successfully questioned. Even before Hardman's ordination, a Kingston church committee of six members had been created in 1930 but the rector had retained chairmanship.[41] This advisory committee had discussed the needs of St Paul's and made recommendations to St John's council, its role broadening when St Paul's had assumed overall responsibility for the Causeway congregation. After the Kingston church had been enlarged, a committee of management with nine persons had been created in 1932 and invited to *share* 'with the Rector in the management and organisation of St Paul's'. Messrs Weale, Hewitt, Randall, Rowley, Hopkinson, Jackson, Scriven, Terrill and Worrall served on this committee.[42] After his ordination, Hardman, who 'knew the mind of the people', worked closely with the committee for three years as church activities expanded and as new ventures were undertaken but there was no doubt as to the rector's ultimate authority.[43]

The committee dealt with day-to-day matters, sometimes challenging, but one has to appreciate the wit of the treasurer who reported two broken windows at St Paul's and their replacement.

> It is hoped that would-be William Tells try their markmanship elsewhere and leave Church property immune … We have all passed through the stage as boys when window panes succumbed to volleys of pellets, but after the satisfaction of hearing the crash, came the realisation of having to bend to the dictates of parental authority as well as the ruthless stoppage of pocket money … Should this [report in *Parish Notes*] come to the eyes of the delinquents, the hon. Treasurer will be pleased to accept 'war reparations' which will be acknowledged …

As Canberra gradually climbed out of the gloom of the Depression and St Paul's increasingly progressed and prospered, it was natural that the church at Kingston should accept increasing responsibility for its own financial position, an advance that came at a price. The southside congregation was required to meet its 'Kingston quota' (an annual recommended sum paid by the parish for diocesan purposes), a sum of £300 a year in 1935, 'a fair and equitable' figure, according to Robertson, despite the hardship it caused the congregation.[44] Fortunately, the stipends of the clergy, motor vehicle expenses and general items of parish expenditure continued to be met by the mother church.

As part of the plan to separate the finances of the two churches, the parish council commenced a 'Kingston Hall Alterations and Repairs Account' in April 1931, a move that permitted the small church to assume a greater responsibility for its own welfare.[45] Hardman had a wider vision, however and spoke of the day when a new church would be built at Manuka. In response, Ken Knight, a very loyal parishioner at St Paul's, approached Hardman on 5 March 1933 and gave him a £1 note, indicating his wish to be the first to contribute to a new church.[46] When others added smaller amounts of 5 shillings or more, Bill Parkes wrote to the council about the need for a dedicated fund to build a future church, prompting the parish council in March 1933 'to establish a St Paul's Building Fund' and noting that 'contributions to such a Fund have already been made.'[47] Hardman strongly supported this decision and continued to press for a new building, making financial contributions himself when he was the unofficial priest-in-charge.[48]

The task of raising the requisite money for a new church appeared virtually impossible. After nine months there was an amount of £17 in the fund and, by November 1934, less than £40.[49] As the parishioners contemplated the thousands of pounds they would require for a church (not a hall), they realised the titanic enterprise that lay ahead. It was then that the Churchwomen's Guild accepted the challenge. The guild had already become a driving force, providing social and spiritual support for its members and developing into the chief fund-raising organisation within the church. It had raised money for a church organ, improvements to the interior of the church, the erection of a porch, the extension of the church building itself and the enhancement of the ventilation system. Smaller items were also financed by the guild including kneelers for the congregation, a piano to accompany the organ, a set of candlesticks, a purple fall for the lectern and new hangings.

From 1929, Mollie Mollison and her sub-committee devised means of raising money: selling clothing, crockery, books, magazines and other household goods at Kingston, Molonglo and the Causeway; holding jumble sales; organising children's fancy dress parties; and staging musical afternoons. In this constant round of activities they donated 10 per cent of all proceeds to the parish general account as required before liquidating any debts on purchased items and making contributions to worthy projects.[50] One of the chief sources of income was the annual bazaar or fete, a major event that became well known. The first in 1929 raised £33.

Most of the money-raising events were designed to improve the church and its surroundings but the guild also catered specifically for the spiritual needs of the women. They met once a month for a special Communion service, organised inter-denominational gatherings, arranged speakers who explained the work of the church, were actively involved in mission work, held musical afternoons and enjoyed devotional meetings that were 'largely attended and helpful to those who came.'[51] Nevertheless, from 1934 the women became increasingly focussed on raising money for the building appeal – a new church on the southside – and with Lillian Hardman's assistance began a continuous and sustained round of competitions, sale of works, flag bridge afternoons, balls, fetes, 'dollar drives' (they apologised for 'using an American expression referring to five shillings'), cake stalls, raffles, fancy dress parties and small bazaars – anything that could raise funds for the cause. Small contributions of 5 shillings or 10 shillings were usual while garden parties could raise £10 or £15. It was an arduous process but by the end of 1936 the fund stood at almost £270, of which a 10 shilling note was earmarked for a baptismal font for the future church.[52]

The eventual success of the venture was even more remarkable when one considers the continuing costs that had also to be met: annual assessment fees paid off in monthly instalments, maintenance on the existing Kingston church, appeals to assist St John's Church, advertising costs in newspapers and donations to missions and others in need. Moreover, ten per cent of all monies raised went to the St John's general fund for parish costs. The women were so successful in their efforts that St John's parish council intervened in August 1934, asking 'that all efforts for raising funds for St Paul's by the Church people' of that centre temporarily cease 'so that all helpers will be free to devote their time and labour to the main parochial efforts held towards the end of the year.'[53] As the guild had became a major driving force in the life of St Paul's, such requests from St John's were not always accepted with grace by the Kingston folk who sought to focus on their own project.[54]

Another strong group in the 1930s was the Church of England Men's Society, a focal point for the social, intellectual and spiritual needs of the men of the parish. Spurred on by its National Vice-President, Sir Littleton Groom, it organised regular Communion services, introduced 'quiet days' for reflection, planned debates, addresses and formal lectures, arranged visits to neighbouring branches and held family picnics and luncheons. Family church attendance was encouraged through 'Father and Son' Sundays and the men did much to support the Boys' Society. When a social gathering was advertised for the men 'in the Tennis Pavilion on the south side of the city', 170 enjoyed 'a happy and jolly time' of fellowship together.[55] Its activities were appreciated so much that, on the ninth anniversary of its founding in Canberra, it had become 'an integral part of the Parish', prompting the rector to write in 1935 that 'one cannot think of Canberra Church life without the CEMS.'[56]

Two months after his arrival at St John's in 1930, Robertson had asked the Society to be responsible for church services in the parish, encouraging the parishioners at Kingston, Molonglo and Westridge to be part of the venture and inviting several members 'to become lay-readers'. Over years, members of the Society conducted Evensong at St Paul's, Causeway, Molonglo and Westridge and the names of Bill Parkes, David Israel, John Starling, Sir Littleton Groom and Charles Wickens (Commonwealth Statistician) figured prominently in the Register of Services at St Paul's. Although organised on a parish basis, the Society was a dynamic influence on the Kingston church and other southside centres, one that enhanced fellowship and promoted spiritual growth.

Other groups revolved around the children and young people of Kingston, Molonglo and the Causeway. Expecting Anglican children to attend church, Robertson referred to the 'old family pew' 'with father at one end and mother at the other and a stairway of more or less restless children between.'[57] Years before, as a deacon, he had set up a gymnasium for local boys in his church and he showed the same concern for young people in Canberra.[58] When young people from St Paul's attended Evensong at St John's on special occasions, they were asked to join the 'Younger Set' who crowded into the rectory for scones and cakes on Sunday nights. Having been a District Scoutmaster, he introduced a Scout troop, encouraged the Cubs commenced by Monty Nell and found appropriate leaders for the Girl Guides.[59] Heralds of the King (a missionary organisation for children) was commenced at St Paul's in 1932, the Sunday schools at Kingston, Molonglo and the Causeway were encouraged, children's festivals were organised, teaching methods were updated and annual picnics were held to maintain the interest of the youngsters.

The youth group, known as the 'Pastime Club' or the 'Younger Set', organised a full schedule of events involving social gatherings, talks and debates, dances, visits and picnics and was encouraged to join the sanctuary team as servers. The St Paul's cricket team formed in 1933 won the Cup for the Junior Association of Church Teams the following year while the St Paul's Football Club made a name for themselves as 'good sports ... always fielding a team punctually and taking their losses in the right spirit.'[60] The same competitive spirit existed among the Canberra Grammar School, Telopea Park School and St Christopher's in tennis and football.[61]

One of the challenges facing the rector and assistant priests was to continue Canon Ward's work in schools, a more difficult task as Telopea Park Public School expanded and as St Gabriel's consumed more time. As Robertson said in 1930, the clergy 'are teachers as well as preachers and the religious instruction of the young means a big demand on their time.' He spent time on two mornings each week at St Gabriel's and on Thursday and Friday mornings in the public schools.[62] As the task increased, Robertson gave 678 lessons in the schools in 1933, in addition to those provided by other loyal parishioners.[63]

Church historian, Ruth Frappell, has referred to 'the plethora of guilds and groups' that developed across the Australian Anglican Church before 1929, a trend that was replicated in the Canberra parish during the 1930s.[64] The church was a focal point for the social and spiritual life of parishioners, a place where young children found instruction, where young people enjoyed entertainment and spiritual guidance, where women socialised, took part in devotional activities and raised money for the church and where men found like-minded fellowship and inspiration. Such group activities were integral

The Reverend James Hardman.
© Mrs J Hyslop

to church life at St Paul's and Hardman was instrumental in their development and support.

By the end of 1935 James and Lillian Hardman knew that it was time to leave the Canberra parish. He had been offered a parish of his own in the Goulburn Diocese on three occasions between 1933 and the end of 1935 but had refused each offer, opting instead to develop the church at Kingston.[65] Robertson informed Bishop Burgmann in November 1934 that Hardman 'does not want to leave Canberra for twelve months yet ... he is doing useful work and we are good pals. I couldn't find any priest who would work more effectively and more loyally'.[66] Nevertheless, Hardman was keen to serve in Queensland and eventually informed the rector and the bishop of his intention to move to the Parish of Toowoomba in January 1936. The 'church hall was packed' as he was farewelled amid a genuine show of affection from the Kingston parishioners and others.[67] He knew, however, that his devoted service for God had built up St Paul's Church and that there was a faithful band of workers who would one day move to the Manuka precinct. He wondered whether he would ever witness that day.

For the next fourteen months, St Paul's was the partial responsibility of the curate, Cecil Faulkner, but his services were widely spread as there were only two parish priests instead of the normal three for much of the time. The Tuesday Communion Service was cancelled and the usual 'St Paul's Column' in *Parish Notes* was discontinued as the services at St Paul's were taken by (the now) Archdeacon Robertson, the Reverend James Benson (Community of the Ascension), Canon Edwards, the Reverend H Morton (organising secretary of the Australian Board of Missions), lay readers such as Bill Parkes and James Colwell as well as visitors to the parish. All these performed their work well but they lacked the concentrated zeal of James Hardman who had lived in the suburb and had taken total responsibility for the church's growth and development. Cecil Faulkner resigned from his position in April 1937 and, when farewelled by the Kingston congregation, expressed the hope that, on his return from England in two years' time, 'he would see at least a part of his dream of a church at Kingston fulfilled'.[68] He never returned but was to make another contribution two years later.

In the meantime the Kingston church was held together by its community spirit, the drive of the Women's Guild that continued to raise funds for a new church, the assistance of the Church of England Men's Society, the devotion of loyal Sunday school teachers and the input of the clergy who were restricted further by the intermittent absences of the archdeacon as he sought to stabilise the situation at the Girls' Grammar School. In a sense, St Paul's marked time waiting for its next priest-in-charge but, to the credit of the Kingston folk, the small church did not falter and remained a vibrant congregation.

In retrospect, therefore, there was a marked contrast between the success and prosperity of the Kingston church between 1930 and 1937 and the difficulties experienced in the other Anglican centres on the southside. St Paul's flourished as the population expanded, profiting from the guidance of Robertson, Hardman and St John's council and the dedication of the Kingston laity. The congregation was not aware, however, that a young priest had applied for the position of assistant priest and that his skill and dedication would lead them to even greater success.

Notes

1. Janet Hyslop, Personal communication, 2009.
2. Christ Church Queanbeyan Register of Services 1923–1928, NLA, Manuscripts 3085/13/12. According to Janet Hyslop, Hardman's daughter, he was born in Lancashire, UK, on 22 September 1898. See also QA, 8 February 1924; CT, 14 October 1926.
3. QA, 8 February 1924.
4. Electoral rolls 1925, Eden–Monaro, Subdivision of Queanbeyan. Entry No. 748 listed: Hardman, James c/- CA Leslie, McQuoid St Queanbeyan, Clerk (m). Also: CT, 14 October 1926.
5. Christ Church Queanbeyan Register of Services 1923–1928, NLA Manuscripts 3085/31/12.
6. CT, 12 March 1932. Janet Hyslop indicated that her parents were married on 17 December 1927. Lillian was born in Normanton, Queensland, on 23 April 1904. Hardman's name was listed in the 1928 electoral roll (Eden-Monaro, Subdivision of Queanbeyan): No. 1089. Hardman, James, Monaro Street, Queanbeyan, Clerk (m). On the electoral roll for the Territory of the Seat of Government in 1928, there were two entries: No. 1766, Hardman, James, Dawes Street, Kingston, Coy Secretary, (m);

and No. 1767, Hardman, Lillian Eleanor, Dawes Street, Kingston, Home Duties (f).

7. RA&P, 1914–1939, 28 December 1928, p. 319.

8. PN, December 1928; April 1929. Also RA&P, 1914–1939, 21 March 1930, p. 350.

9. *Parish Notes* indicate her involvement in the Women's Guild and collections. Morrie Adamson (Personal communication, 2008) indicated the loyal support she gave to her husband and his work.

10. CT, 9 March 1929.

11. 1928 electoral roll in Gugler, *The Builders of Canberra*, pp. 384–388.

12. Emerton, *Past Images*, p. ix.

13. All figures are calculated from the 1928 electoral rolls reproduced in Gugler, *The Builders of Canberra*, ch 9.

14. 'George Barlin on air with Radio 2CA' in Emerton, *Past Images*, p. 118.

15. This overview of Kingston in the 1930s is based on interviews with Val Emerton, Marie Lehmann, Frank Colwell, Gwen Jackson and Morrie Adamson; and on recorded interviews in Emerton, *Past Images*.

16. PN, March 1930.

17. PN, April 1930.

18. PN, May 1930.

19. PN, September 1930.

20. PN, February–March 1931.

21. StJ Register of Services, 1930–1932.

22. Letter from Honorary Secretary of St John's to Civic Administrator, 28 February 1931, Federal Capital Commission, NAA, A414 (A414) 'Ecclesiastical Building Sites'.

23. Civic Administrator to P Scheaffe, 5 June 1931, NAA, A414 (A414). Also CT, 1 August 1931.

24. CT, 29 August 1931.

25. This was the price paid by the Church at Hall, ACT, in 1930. PN, January 1930.

26. PN, August–September 1931; CT, 29 August 1931.

27. CT, 19 March 1932.

28. StJPC, 10 March 1932, 14 April and 23 June 1932.

29. PN, November 1932.

30. StJ Register of Services, May 1933.

31. PN, June 1933.

32. Hardman recorded these figures in StJ Register of Services at the end of December 1934 and 1935. See also StJ Register of Services, December 1936.

33. PN, March–May 1933. The rector continued such comments during 1934–1935.

34. PN, June 1933.

35. PN, April 1935.

36. PN, November 1935.

37. *ABM Review*, December 1956, 'Former Rector of St John's, a much beloved priest'. Also Wyatt, *The History of the Diocese*, p. 155.
38. Frame, *A Church for a Nation*, p. 149.
39. StJ Register of Services, 1933.
40. PN, October–November 1933.
41. PN, July 1930.
42. PN, May–August 1932.
43. PN, April 1934; May–June 1934; November 1935.
44. StJPC, 23 February 1933. PN, April 1935.
45. StJPC, 16 April 1931.
46. PN, November 1934, reported that Kenneth Knight donated £1 to the Building Fund; PN, February 1936, mentions he was the first subscriber. A letter from William Weale dated 30 December 1937 states, 'This fund was started on the 5th March 1933 by Kenneth Knight, since deceased with a donation of £1.' (StP Archives)
47. StJPC, 16 March 1933.
48. James and Lillian Hardman contributed to St Paul's financially from their arrival in 1928 and collected for the church over eight years (1928 to 1935).
49. PN, November 1934; PN, Financial Statement: St Paul's Building Fund at 31 December 1939; StPPC, 1940.
50. PN, July and November 1934.
51. PN, July 1935.
52. PN, February 1937.
53. StJPC, 21 June 1934.
54. Gwen Jackson, Personal communication, 2008.
55. PN, March–May 1933.
56. PN, March 1935. CEMS activities were reported in the PN between 1928 and 1937.
57. PN, May 1930.
58. Woolven, *A Stitch in Time*, p. 49.
59. PN, January, February and March 1939
60. PN, October–November 1933; May 1935.
61. PN, June–July 1931.
62. PN, July 1930.
63. PN, May–June 1934.
64. R Frappell, 'Imperial fervour and Anglican loyalty 1901–1929' (pp. 78–99, in Kaye et al (eds), *Anglicanism in Australia*, p. 80.
65. PN, December 1934.
66. Robertson to Burgmann, 14 November 1934. Diocese Correspondence with Archdeacon CS Robertson, Papers of Ernest Burgmann, NLA, MS1998, Box 34.
67. PN, February 1936.
68. CT, 15 April 1937.

8 Church and war, 1937–1944

The next stage of St Paul's history, 1937 to 1944, embraced the important incumbency of the Reverend Tom Whiting at Kingston and Manuka, the construction of a new church, the outbreak and escalation of World War II, the restrictions experienced during the war effort and the constant struggles to pay off loan debts and to maintain financial solvency.

With James Hardman's departure, Thomas Whiting, a 28-year-old curate from Cowra, applied for the position at St John's and sent his details to Robertson. The rector contacted the two nominated referees who did not question Whiting's 'moral character or his work as a priest' but had some doubts as to his suitability for 'the type of work wanted'. Robertson, in characteristic haste, sent a telegram to Whiting indicating 'References Unsuitable', an action he later confessed to the bishop as being 'stupid' and a result of being in a 'tremendous hurry'. Whiting persisted and Robertson relented, informing the recently installed Bishop Ernest Burgmann that 'we will give him all the help and friendship he needs' and reminding the bishop that the previous curate, Cecil Faulkner, had come 'under a cloud' but had 'done excellently'. 'We'll hope for the same from Tom Whiting who has more guns than Faulkner.'[1] The archdeacon did not realise the force of Tom Whiting's 'guns'. Given one week to transfer, Thomas packed, prepared final sermons, attended farewells and caught a train to Canberra.

Born in Bournemouth in 1908 and educated at Salisbury, he had migrated to Australia in 1926, studied for matriculation and entered Moore College in 1928 with the double purpose of reading for a degree at the University of Sydney while studying theology. He had used his time well by graduating with a Bachelor of Arts degree in 1933 and a masters degree in anthropology in 1935, winning the Francis Andrew

Memorial Prize in Psychology, gaining his Licentiate of Theology and tutoring in Greek at Moore College.[2] He then served as assistant chaplain of All Saints' College at Bathurst for three years and spent one year at Cowra.

On his arrival in Canberra, he was met at the station by Dr Clyde Finlay who drove him to his own home in Wentworth Avenue near the Powerhouse where Whiting was to board. The next day he conducted the 9am service at St Paul's Kingston; three days later he was involved in the visit of the Bishop of Tanganyika to the parish; the following day he was commissioned and conducted two more services for Anzac Day; and he was then drawn into preparations for the official services for the coronation of King George VI.[3]

As the assistant priest, Whiting ministered to all parish centres but was also designated as the first official priest-in-charge of St Paul's. Twelve months later he acknowledged 'the utmost pleasure and happiness I have found in my work under such a spiritual leader and instructor' as the rector and publicly thanked him for 'his ministrations and help during the year'.[4] For his part, the Archdeacon recommended 'the raising of Whiting's salary to £300 per year' and informed the bishop that he was 'going to hold him in Canberra ... I am more than pleased with the work he is doing and for the ... increased results at Kingston'. Robertson added, 'He has defects, so have we all, but he is worth holding.'[5] In the meantime Whiting had qualified for the award of Scholar of Theology (ThSchol), a master's level qualification.[6]

St Paul's-in-the-tin-shed experienced the 'fullest activity [in] all aspects of church life' during 1937. Much of its vibrancy centred on the women's group whose efforts were 'directed almost entirely towards the Building Fund'.[7] A men's committee was formed under the leadership of Whiting and Bill Weale, one that played an integral part in the planning and organisation of a new church. The young priest urged the St Paul's 'Younger Set' to organise dances, table tennis tournaments and excursions and to set itself a goal of raising £50 for the Building Fund over a few months. The group enjoyed fellowship, prompting Whiting to report that it was 'a very happy experience' to be 'associated with so many keen young people in the life of the church'.[8]

While he was fully involved in these church organisations, his overriding concern was the spiritual welfare of the congregation and the extension of 'the work of Christ in this southern portion of our city'. He observed the increasing congregation – about 42 taking communion each week during 1938 – and 75 to 100 regular attenders at the popular children's service on Sunday, 'a big feature of our church life'. Whiting was not complacent and urged people to be 'more regular and more infective' in their spirituality and counselled them to 'see that we finance every aspect of our church life'. 'Let us work for our new church by all means ... but remember the other calls on our finance as well'.[9]

Despite the caution, Whiting was solidly behind the escalating desire to erect a new church somewhere in Manuka. He accepted that £325 in the Building Fund in May 1937 was a promising beginning but still far short of what was required and he pondered how the fund might be advanced more quickly.[10] When he spoke to the rector about the issue, Robertson was cautious for he had been involved in a long and unsuccessful drive for a cathedral, had been caught up in the austerity of the economic depression and had more recently spent months campaigning for funds for the Girls' Grammar School.[11] What was more, the newspapers were filled with pessimistic reports about the future.

The world was in a parlous position as Britain appealed to Germany to 'cease arming and enter European Concert', as Churchill warned of the 'danger of war', and as Mussolini waged a propaganda campaign against the English. There was friction in the Middle East, Japan had moved against China and Hitler had retaliated against the Spanish who had attacked the German warship, *Deutschland*.[12] The editor of *The Canberra Times* referred to the prodigious 'expenditure in preparation for the next war ... more terrible in its ravages than the last and ... more serious unless civilisation can save itself'. Alarm was justified and the last thing that Robertson desired was a 'crippling debt' at St Paul's 'from which St John's would derive no appreciable benefit'. While he agreed that a new church was essential, he and the bishop required firm financial guarantees.[13]

As a first step, Whiting invited the rector to the first meeting of the men's committee on 11 August 1937 to discuss the issue. As they sat in the small church at Kingston that Wednesday evening, Whiting was able to inspire the men to form the St Paul's Church Committee with Bill Weale as treasurer and outlined schemes for 'a big collection drive', recommending a date on which to lay the foundation stone in March 1938 if sufficient funds were raised in time.[14] A consequent meeting of the church congregation endorsed the decision and elected Whiting and Weale as a sub-committee on their behalf. The Archdeacon, however, was 'suspicious' of the enthusiasm and insisted on a second meeting at which he could speak. His message was stark:

> All decisions concerning the new church were the concern of the whole parish and must have the full approval of the Parish Council, which represented both St John's and St Paul's ... a further £1,000 must be collected before any thought of plans, sites, etc. could be entertained; ... the costs of the new church must be borne [exclusively] by the parishioners of the south-side; and no solicitations for funds must be made among the Anglicans of Mugga Way.[15]

There was indignation that St John's regarded 'the select area' of Mugga Way as 'its own special preserve' and some accused the Archdeacon of putting deliberate obstacles in their path.[16] In retrospect, one may understand the rector's caution (even the Mugga Way claim – the area was affluent and contributed to St John's funds) but the effect was to create a greater resolve to succeed 'in spite of the opposition'.

The new thrust of St Paul's was bold, leading to an official Building Fund Appeal, the distribution of leaflets seeking donations, the canvassing of local people and an even greater zeal to succeed. Fetes were held at the Causeway Hall, cake stalls, jumble sales and Christmas gift stalls were conducted, the annual bazaar was arranged and the 'Younger Set' organised dances and planned a moonlight excursion to raise funds. Canvassers collected from the local inhabitants at a time when the 1934 basic wage was £3 5s (or 65s) a week, when a donation of 1 shilling or 2 shillings was the best that some could afford and when a gift of 5 shillings or 10 shillings was often a considerable sacrifice.[17] And so, 'the consuming interest at St Paul's' rose to £525 by the end of January 1938.[18] St John's parish council sought the help of a Melbourne architect to 'make a rough sketch' for a suitable building while Whiting approached Ken Oliphant, a local architect, to assist. Despite these overtures, it was left to Bill Weale and happy serendipity to intervene.[19]

As Captain William Weale was having a 'wee dram' at the Kingston Hotel, he spoke to an unknown fellow-imbiber, Bernard Clamp, who proved to be the architect in charge of extensions to Canberra Grammar School and the son of Burchamp Clamp who had designed the parish church of Moree. 'Just by chance', queried Weale, 'do you have any spare designs of churches in your pocket? I really need one.' It is likely that Weale even paid for the next two rounds of drinks. The ploy succeeded and within weeks a number of plans arrived and were guardedly distributed among the members of the congregation. Fearing the Archdeacon's censure, Whiting reminded the people that any decisions had to be submitted to the rector, the parish council and Bishop Burgmann.

Meanwhile the balance in the Building Fund crept up to £650 in February 1938 and to £730 in March, leading the Building Committee to renew its appeal 'for the first one thousand pounds' and set a closing date of 4

Mrs AE Jackson, Reverend T Whiting, Mrs Mollinson, Captain Weale, Mrs Rowley. © St Paul's Archives

September 1938.[20] To boost funds, the foundation ball in the Albert Hall in July netted over £54, *The Canberra Times* claiming that the 'interest and enthusiasm' of 350 people provided 'a good indicator of the public support for the new church.' Another £60 came from the annual fete, encouraging the congregation to renewed efforts.[21] And so the fund rose: almost £800 in July, £850 in September and £1,000 (indeed, 7 shillings above the initial target) in October. Not only was the aim achieved but the Archdeacon announced in September that 'sufficient funds would be on hand to commence building operations during 1938'.[22]

There followed a bewildering flurry of events: the congregation compared drawings and determined its preference; Weale steered the proposal through parish council and negotiated 'with the Department of the Interior a site for the new church' on the 'corner of Captain

Cook Crescent and Canberra Avenue ... a main intersection of traffic but not seriously affected by it'. It was a 'most convenient meeting place' for the people of Kingston, Barton and Griffith and Captain Weale was assured by the town planners that 'no housing development was contemplated further than one mile from the site'.[23] The parish council was prompted by Weale to accept a plan for a total complex including a church with a tower, a hall, a rectory and a tennis court. At the last moment the members were reminded to include a toilet block, a slight oversight. Bishop Burgmann accepted the proposal without difficulty, warning Whiting and Weale that 'the supervision of the overall concept would be a lasting test of their ability and zeal'.

Despite the success, Whiting was worried that the project might not commence before the world was plunged into devastating armed conflict again. A new date to lay the foundation stone was set for 11 December 1938 but there were further obstacles when Robertson insisted that only three bays of the church be constructed to provide for a congregation of less than 200, a basic structure without a sanctuary or vestry and with a blank fibro-cement front wall to remind the congregation of the need for future extensions. No arguments were encouraged or even desired, because of political developments in Europe and the ominous threat of war. Haste was essential. As a last concession, Roberson permitted tenders to be advertised for both a three-bay and four-bay church in red brick, with the sanctuary and tower being deferred until a later extension. The six tenders ranged from £3,075 to £3,733 for three bays and from £3,485 to £5,237 for four bays and, after investigation into the financial viability and expertise of each firm, the tender of WJ Perry was chosen to construct three bays, an early start being projected. Jim Perry, a local builder, realised that financial economies could be effected if the entire project (a large church, sanctuary, tower, vestry and rector's residence) was completed at the one time and offered to construct the overall complex for £10,000 but Robertson flatly refused.[24]

It was calculated that there would be at least £1,200 in the Building Fund, requiring a bank loan of £2,500 to construct three bays. One bank refused the church's application and the project appeared doomed until Weale approached a second bank which agreed, provided twelve guarantors were found and the church transferred all its business to the bank, conditions that were accepted.[25] Perhaps

Bishop Burgmann gave a chuckle when he heard how the names of the guarantors were found. After Whiting had been assured of eleven signatures but was feeling despondent as one more elusive name was required, he called into a Kingston café and met the new proprietor who enquired how the building project was progressing. The priest confessed that another name was required and was staggered when the lady replied, 'Why not ask me?' Tommy Whiting promptly asked her, she agreed on the spot, signed as a guarantor 'and the curate left with a cheque for the appeal'. He cycled home as fast as possible, hastened to the telephone and informed Bill Weale.[26]

There was further frustration when Charles Daley from the Department of the Interior objected to the truncated building, exclaiming that a structure 9.75 metres high, 10.97 metres long and 9.15 metres wide would be 'an eyesore and a silly cube' to 'disfigure the Manuka environment'. 'Surely there are enough Anglicans in Canberra to build the complete church,' he tersely commented. Whiting – knowing that Daley was an Anglican who attended St Andrew's Presbyterian Church and was the church organist – quickly replied, 'Yes sir and that would be possible, if all Anglicans in Canberra

Franklin Street, Manuka 1934 © *National Library of Australia*

would give us their full support and attend their own church as they ought'. Daley agreed without further discussion.[27] Finally the contract was signed and the date for the laying of the foundation stone was confirmed. Then, just in time, the parish council remembered that it had not considered the proposed wording on the foundation stone.[28]

The 'shopping precinct' of Manuka was now fourteen years old with shops and houses in a strange mixture that characterised the area until the early 1940s. By 1938–1939, shops stretched along Franklin Street to St Christopher's School, through the arcade and around the lawns between the lane and Bougainville Street with Kelly's café, Miss Yelland's newsagency, Cusack's furniture store, the Capitol fish and chip shop and Adam's butchery being well-known establishments. Eight semi-detached, two-storey homes had been constructed in Bougainville Street in 1933 and others in Forrest, while residences began to appear in Flinders Way and Mugga Way. La Perouse Street was yet to be constructed.[29] The Catholic church had extended its ministry at Manuka by erecting a church opposite St Christopher's School and Convent, a venture that cost in excess of £15,000.[30] This church (later named a cathedral) was completed in June 1939 and, when Robertson had his weekly game of cards with Father Haydon, he assured the Catholic priest that 'Anglicans will not be backward with their congratulations and with their prayers.'[31] Nevertheless, the completion of the Catholic church helped spur the Anglicans to achieve a similar success.

Sunday 11 December 1938 dawned fine and pleasant and a large crowd gathered in the afternoon to watch the official cars arrive for the ceremony, headed by His Excellency the Governor-General, Lord Gowrie (whose name had *very* recently been inscribed on the foundation stone) and Her Excellency, Lady Gowrie. Other cars conveyed Sir Geoffrey Whiskard, the British High Commissioner, and Lady Whiskard, Mrs Olive Robertson, representatives from other churches, the wardens of St John's Church and the architect, Mr Clamp, and Mrs Clamp. In the unavoidable absence of the bishop, Robertson officiated at a ceremony where the choir of St John's led the singing, speeches were presented and prayers were offered. The ladies held their hats as the wind rose during the dedication service but it was less disruptive when they retired to the marquee for afternoon tea. Captain Weale and his committee gleamed with pride as they later inspected the stone and found £220 in donations lying on the top.[32] Tom Whiting sought to disguise his pride, a weakness considered unbecoming in a clergyman, and elected instead to mingle with the visitors and accept their congratulations. By evening the crowd had dispersed, the foundation stone stood its lonely vigil held firm by wood supports and the Building Fund had climbed over £1,200. It was a portentous day for St Paul's.

Jim Perry and his team launched into the construction without delay, digging the foundation trenches, pouring the concrete and constructing the walls to a metre high, but the builder was most unhappy despite the quality of his work. The building with only three bays looked cropped or pared, a fourth bay would be more aesthetically pleasing and the cost of an extra bay would be relatively small compared to the benefit derived. In early March 1939 he made an offer: he would construct the fourth bay for approximately £560 and wait twelve months for payment.[33] When the council dallied, Perry pushed harder and addressed the parish council himself. He would reduce the price to £510 and, if the bank would not agree to the extra loan, he would build it at his own expense, giving 'the committee as much time as they needed to repay him'.

The council members finally agreed, provided that the twelve guarantors consented to the extra cost and St Paul's congregation requested it. The council's decision was made a little easier as members realised that the Department of the Interior had already agreed to four bays and that Jim Perry had quietly excavated the site for the extra bay.[34] While the 'council was in a pleasant mood', Weale mentioned without notice that St Paul's would have no organ and that St John's had a spare one in the gallery; perhaps it could be used by the new church on a temporary basis if restored. He moved a motion to that effect and the council unanimously agreed.

The enthusiasm to build and furnish the church did not disguise the financial liability that was steadily mounting. The mortgage stood at £2,374 in October 1939 and St Paul's was required to repay £256 a year, more than half of which was interest. The church had acquired the old organ on loan but had to pay £118 for its restoration together with other costs and £238 was owed on new pews, despite the donations already received. Carpets and other furnishings required maintenance, a church cleaning fee had to be paid and ongoing accounts for utilities, ground rent, advertising, printing and postage had to be met. At the diocesan level, the assessment fee had been set at £350 a year but the council had successfully argued for its reduction to £300, payable in monthly instalments. There were major costs that loomed in the near future for a rectory, tennis court and beautification of the church grounds. While the old hall at Kingston was still being used, there were also bills for electricity, general maintenance and weekly cleaning.[35]

In the meantime Weale pursued two of his own aspirations. He wrote to the Dean and Chapter of St Paul's Cathedral in London, explained the efforts of the parishioners in Canberra and enquired whether a block of sandstone might be donated to the new building 'for incorporation in its fabric in the west end of the church'. His quest was successful, the block arrived and he was congratulated on his initiative. He also wrote to Cecil Faulkner (the former assistant priest), then in Leicester, about the need for a 'worthy and historic lectern'. The parish church of St Denys in Leicester had an 'unused wrought-iron lectern' and Cecil approached the church on behalf of St Paul's. St Denys agreed and the refurbished lectern 'came with the blessing and good wishes of the Vicar and Church Council'. Few understood, however, how a bulky parcel was delivered to 'Captain

St Paul's Church 1939 © *St Paul's Archives*

Weale c/o Department of Naval Stores, Sydney', to be transferred to Canberra. Another inspirational gift was the altar frontal donated by Lady Whiskard who sent to England for material samples. When these arrived, a suitable material was chosen, the Royal Needlework Society of England was asked to perform the sewing of the frontal and the orphreys and the finished product was 'brought to Canberra in the official packages of the High Commissioner.'[36]

As the building fund reached £1,670 in August 1939, the church was virtually completed and parishioners arrived to clean the interior. 'Dust, dirt, wood chips and noise pervaded the atmosphere, but the sight of Lady Whiskard working diligently on her knees at the foot of the Altar ... inspired all to do their best.' The church was prepared for opening day on Sunday 6 August 1939, the 25th anniversary of the church's commencement. The church grounds were levelled with truckloads of soil donated by the Kingston Hotel and graded by the authorities with Weale's influence but the site turned into a quagmire when it rained, requiring loads of ashes to be spread with the voluntary assistance of Ossie Byrne from St Christopher's Church. Tom Whiting arrived back at the church a few weeks before the ceremony, following a period of leave for his marriage to Isabel in Dubbo.

The opening was timed for 3pm, midway between a drenching that started at noon and lasted until 6pm. Huge pools formed in the red mud and a beach umbrella sheltered Bishop Burgmann from the downpour as his procession walked solemnly around the church. All waited for him to knock on the door seeking entry. After the words, 'Reverend Father-in-God, we pray you to dedicate this church', the bishop proceeded to bless and dedicate the prayer desk, the lectern, the pulpit, the chancel step, the chancel and the altar before addressing the people and praising them for their efforts.[37]

When church members purchased *The Canberra Times* the next day, they were dismayed to find that Adolf Hitler had made alarming demands on Poland. By the end of the month, German troops had bombed five Polish towns and three days later the people of Canberra read the sombre news that war had been declared between Great Britain and Germany.[38] As a consequence, Prime Minister Robert Menzies said, Australia was also at war. St Paul's Manuka had been opened only four weeks before open hostilities began, disconcertingly reminiscent of events in 1914 when the mission hall had been opened days prior to the outbreak of the Great War. [39]

The Sunday on which Britain declared war on Germany was not a pleasant day in Canberra with rain squalls keeping many inside. Those who ventured out to Evensong returned home and heard, through the static of short-wave radio, the BBC announcement of the declaration of war. The reaction was muted and far different from 1914. The scars of the Great War still lingered, the effects of the Depression were not completely erased and the threat of involvement in another conflict on a far-distant continent produced a dulled reaction. As the historian Michael McKernan concluded, Australians 'remembered with some horror and even guilt how joyously they had welcomed the war in 1914,' and the 'dominant passion in 1939 was not bellicose excitement but rather regret tinged with disappointment that war must come again'. Subdued reactions were reinforced by the absence of any real danger to Australia before Easter 1940.[40]

Some did enlist, pilots left for Britain, a contract was let for the construction of buildings at the RAAF Base at Canberra and recruitment drives began in March 1940 for an army corps for home duties. Then, throughout 1940, the population slowly came to understand the threat when the Netherlands was invaded and Paris fell. Petrol prices rose and fuel rationing commenced, local recruiting began, train services from Sydney to Canberra were reduced and paper for newspapers was rationed. The city felt an immediate impact when all public servants agreed to work additional time on Wednesday nights without pay.[41] Robertson lamented the horror that war entailed and counselled his parishioners to keep their 'faith in God's purpose for the world'. Like many other clergy, he believed that 'the triumph of evil is short-lived and good must win'. The rector underlined the importance of prayer, Bible reading and the sacraments. He ensured that the church bell at St John's was rung at noon each day to remind people to pray that the 'hearts of all would be filled 'with the spirit of our Lord Jesus Christ'.[42]

With a different approach, Burgmann sought to pinpoint the factors that had led to hostility, those aspects that might be redressed. 'Selfish nationalism and the spirit of isolation are the evils which have brought disaster to us all', he contended as he explored the origins of unrest – injustice, financial greed, a harsh Treaty of Versailles in 1919, secret deals between nations and the unwillingness of world leaders to support the League of Nations. The church, he acknowledged, had to carry on 'her work of pastoral ministry and the proclamation of her Gospel' but must do more by looking through the conflict 'to the issues involved' and steadily set them 'before the people'. He preached that because God is a God of love, God will respect our freedom 'even

to the point of allowing us to destroy ourselves and our civilisation'
and, hence, we must do our part to transform society in the service
of God as we strive for 'truth, justice, love and freedom'.[43] The bishop
received accolades for his general analysis but his long-term solution
for church involvement was general and bypassed the strategies by
which resolution might be achieved. Moreover, he remained vague
about 'the ways in which the Gospel spoke uniquely to the problems
facing the world'.[44] Nevertheless, with hindsight, one might refer to
a bishop who was willing to take a stance and to speak out on issues
on which other church leaders were mute.

Between 1939 and 1941, there were two sides to Canberra's existence, one centred on political decisions, the war effort and overseas
events and the other on normal daily life in the scattered suburbs.
August 1940, for instance, was a stressful time as Germany prepared
for an invasion of Britain, Mussolini maintained war operations in
North Africa and the Japanese demands on Indo–China continued to
escalate. In response the Australian Government imposed resource
restrictions and foreshadowed a 'tightening of the belt'.[45] At the local
level, however, life continued with a seeming disregard of conflict and
hostility. A flag bridge party was arranged at the Kingston Hotel to
raise funds for the St Paul's Building Fund,' the St John's Ladies Guild
held 'a pleasant afternoon' for its members, Catholic youth groups
enjoyed a ball at Queanbeyan and 400 people attended the Radio
2CA Women's Club Dance. The Canberra high school arranged a
school ball, the croquet club continued its Wednesday afternoon
competitions and the YMCA outlined a range of activities for the
young people of the city. When St Paul's Church marked its first
anniversary in August 1940, celebrations included a bright program
arranged by the Women's Guild in the lounge of the Civic Hotel and
a speaker addressed the audience on the social and religious life of
women in India.[46]

With the war far away, Whiting was keen to build the proposed
tennis court next to the church, organising 'an eager band of young
people' to work for months preparing the foundations.[47] The court
surface was completed by June 1941 and all looked forward to the installation of lights and the completion of the club's pavilion.[48] Officially
opened on 13 November 1941 in front of a crowd of 200 spectators,
it was the only court in Canberra at which night tennis was possible.

Bookings each weeknight helped to defray 'all expenses incurred' and the members devoted 'all surplus moneys to the Building Fund.' Then at the annual bazaar a few weeks later, a 'merry night' allowed the crowd to enjoy the produce on sale and buy gifts from the Christmas tree, contributing £105 to the Building Fund in the process.[49]

In the same week as the fete, however, the situation became very grave when the light cruiser HMAS *Sydney* was lost with 645 on board and HMAS *Parramatta* was torpedoed. Pearl Harbor was attacked by Japanese forces a few days later. Australians realised that invasion was now possible – some said imminent – and the country scrambled to defend itself. The new Curtin Government imposed further restrictions, regulated the work force, redirected production and steadfastly concentrated on the war effort. To save electricity the Prime Minister required evening lights to be reduced.The new tennis court lights at St Paul's were turned off for over three years, depriving the church of a source of income.[50] It was a difficult time for St Paul's parishioners as funds dried up and petrol rationing curtailed the Archdeacon's visits to outlying centres, hospital patients and the elderly.[51] Tom Whiting rode his bicycle as usual but was hampered after lengthy periods of illness in hospital.

Evening meetings were difficult as car owners had to screen their headlamps, resulting in road accidents. Inspectors went 'around to ensure there was no light seeping through [torn] blackout window paper' and even the sanctuary lamp in the church was extinguished each evening.[52]

Air-raid trenches at Parliament House 1942
© *Australian War Memorial ID 136211*

The nation's fears were galvanised into action when Japanese raids on New Guinea were reported and Darwin suffered the first bombing attack in February 1942. Three midget submarines entered Sydney Harbour in late May, the eastern suburbs were shelled a week later and 20 submarines were reported off the coast, resulting in further attacks on Sydney and Newcastle and the sinking of merchant ships off the coast.[53] Many believed that the capital was a possible target because it housed the seat of government, an air base and HMAS *Harman* – the

RAN Wireless-Transmitting Station opened in 1939. Street signs were removed to confuse any invader although, as some persons waggishly conceded, Canberra's circular streets were enough to bamboozle any enemy. The government decreed that 'the owner of every building which at any one time in any one day accommodates 20 or more persons' must construct an approved air raid shelter, forcing St Paul's council to excavate a zig-zag slit trench in the church grounds.[54] Regular drills were essential when alarms were sounded, requiring children and adults to evacuate the church and enter the trenches, resulting in disruption and very dirty shoes.

Severe rationing was introduced and coupons were issued to purchase limited amounts of food, petrol and clothing. Families turned once again to Canberra's plentiful rabbit supply for meat. Old clothes were repaired and recycled. Cars were put up on blocks because of the absence of fuel.[55] The restrictions affected the ability of St Paul's Women's Guild to collect items for jumble sales and to provide for stalls, resulting in reduced fund-raising efforts. Fortunately they overcame some restrictions by growing and selling vegetables, fresh fruits and preserved fruits. Manuka became livelier, however, when the Services Club was opened near St Christopher's Cathedral in 1941 and extended in August 1942, providing dances, concerts and other forms of recreation for service personnel.[56] St Paul's Church was eventually permitted to hire the club for its own activities.

The war years were difficult for St Paul's but the zeal of the people was strong and church numbers increased. By April 1940, there were about 38 communicants at regular services and 70 at Easter, a total of 190 for a month, the figure rising to 249 by August and 302 a month during 1941.[57] The annual number of communicants rose to 4,082 (340 a month) in 1943, to 5,300 (442 a month) in 1944, and 5,400 (450 a month) in 1945.[58] The clergy welcomed the increase but were disappointed at the number of nominal Anglicans who rarely attended church except for rites of passage (baptism, marriage and burial). Services were also increased from five each week (two Communions on Sunday, a children's service, Evensong and a service on Wednesday) when another Sunday service was added in July 1940 and six extra Evensongs were scheduled during the week – a total of twelve services each week.

The pressure on Tommy Whiting was too severe and by July 1941 the weekly Evensongs were mercifully discontinued and Sunday services were reduced to four although the midweek service was continued. Finally, because of blackout restrictions, Sunday Evensong was rescheduled to 4pm in 1942.[59] It was too late, however, and, like Canon Ward before him, the young priest's health deteriorated, leading to his hospitalisation on four occasions and a lengthy period of recuperation at the end of 1942. The lack of a car and the need to ride his bicycle in all weathers contributed to his health problems, leading the Archdeacon to comment rather coldly that Whiting 'has had a rather weakening time and will have to *go slow* for a while'.[60]

Church financial difficulties also contributed to Whiting's anxieties. Continuing commitments in 1939 were close to £350 a year but income was £248, a shortfall of 30 per cent.[61] The bank required a repayment of £125 every six months and, when this could not be covered from regular sources, it was supplemented by the sale of 'needlework, cakes, produce, dolls, novelties, sweets, ice-cream, soft drinks and flowers', and by desperate appeals for an additional £50.[62] Despite these efforts, the debt on the building was still 'over £2,000' in 1944 notwithstanding five years of repayments. St Paul's annual assessment fee was £350 in 1940 but the church was unable to meet its obligation of £29 a month when there were no funds available and 'the treasurer was authorised to make payment [only] as money came to hand'.[63] The church once again resorted to dances, games evenings, sales and choir recitals to raise cash. The Archdeacon, however, was less than impressed, informing parishioners that some other centres had met their assessments and that 'if St Paul's, Ainslie and Sutton had met theirs, there would have been a credit instead of a debt balance for 1941. All three could have done better'.[64] An empty coffer at St Paul's was not an isolated instance and there were occasions during 1942, 1943 and 1944 when special appeals were desperately launched.

By continued hard work, St Paul's raised over £750 during 1944–1945 and met its assessment target of £400, finishing with a credit balance of £22 after years of exhaustive effort. Again, however, Robertson appeared unsympathetic, indicating that it was time the debt on the church 'was completely wiped off'. St Paul's would 'ultimately be a very beautiful building' but only one-third had been erected and the parishioners should 'put every effort into its completion.'[65] Two years later the Archdeacon required St Paul's to accept full financial responsibility for its operation without any assistance from St John's. This was a natural development, of course, but it meant that the church had to meet the total cost of stipends, car allowance, rent for the priest's house, full assessment fees of £460, maintenance of the church and grounds and contributions to missions, while still paying off its mortgage.

The church would probably have defaulted in its repayments had it not been for the extraordinary efforts of the St Paul's Women's Guild and the tireless efforts of twelve to fifteen women – Mesdames Mollison, Rowley, Jackson, Roach, Harding, Whiting and their team. The guild organised the annual bazaar, often making a profit equivalent to a six-monthly mortgage repayment, while the annual ball in the Albert Hall drew a responsive crowd of up to 650 and proved a major fund-raising event.[66] Unfortunately the ball had to be discontinued during the worst years of the war, resulting in an even greater need for day-to-day fund-raising activities at Manuka, Kingston and the Causeway.

The lounge of the Kingston Hotel was a constant meeting room for lectures, games afternoons and bridge parties and the proprietor offered the lounge and kitchen facilities to the church without cost, while others donated food.[67] The Guild met other needs, however, as the majority of women were not in paid employment despite the increasing numbers involved in wartime tasks and membership provided an opportunity for fellowship and service. They held regular Communion services, arranged addresses, contributed to missions and sought to enhance the beauty of the church with kneelers. In wider ventures, they forwarded gifts to parishioners on active service and arranged food parcels for England.[68] At the same time, the men's committee held regular working bees, helped build the tennis court and pavilion, installed the lighting system, dug drains, planted trees and shrubs and spread gravel on the site. Working in teams of fifteen in summer 1943, they met on Friday nights from 6pm to 8pm to maintain the grounds.[69]

One of the difficulties at Manuka was the absence of a church hall, forcing parishioners to use the Wellington, Civic and Kingston Hotels for gatherings and social events. When the council enquired in 1940 'into the practicality of removing the church hall' from Kingston to the Manuka site, the Department of the Interior refused permission as it was unclear who had actually paid for the original building.[70] Eventually the authorities clarified the issue in June 1942:

> ... this Hall [at Kingston] was erected by members of the Church of England with the permission of the Commonwealth ... No form of tenancy appears to have been granted to your Church Authorities in respect of the site and whilst your ownership of the building is recognised, the site is held, rent free, at the will of the Commonwealth. It is thought that your position ... should be more clearly defined and ... it is proposed to recommend that your Church Authorities be granted a Permissive Occupancy of the site, at a peppercorn rental, under conditions reserving to you the right of removal of the building.[71]

With legal hurdles removed, Whiting again stressed the 'urgent need for a hall', advising council that Mr Lowes had offered to dismantle, remove and re-erect the Kingston hall in the Manuka church grounds for £100.[72] The offer was accepted but its removal caused Whiting considerable embarrassment. Seeking permission for the building's removal, Whiting approached Charles Daley, the Secretary of the Department of the Interior, but his request was declined as the old hall would spoil the Manuka environment. By a little surreptitious manoeuvring, the priest then obtained permission from Senator Collings, the Minister for the Interior. Reading only the first paragraph of the senator's approval letter, Whiting had the building removed and re-erected at Manuka but, because 'it looked so dilapidated and unsightly', he 'decided to place it out of sight behind the church'. A rather explosive letter soon arrived from the senator's secretary, accusing the priest of disobedience and threatening litigation. When Whiting retrieved the original letter of approval, he found a stipulation that the church should be located 'in the open on the hillside so that it would prove [to be] an eyesore that the church people would have to remove'. Mortified, Whiting offered humiliating apologies which were fortunately accepted, and the church was granted two years to remove the building.[73] It was eventually removed 42 years later, proving the willingness of St Paul's Manuka to submit to a secular authority over time.

Youth work was vital for Thomas and Isabel Whiting. The cramped conditions were not conducive to teaching young children in the back of the church and it was with relief that the kindergarten moved into the relocated hall in February 1944 'with space for children to move'.[74] Between 1939 to 1944, there was no separate Sunday school for the primary-aged group but the children's service continued uninterrupted with a common worship period, after which the kindergarten children retired and the older children were instructed together in the church. Whiting revitalised the 'Younger Set' in 1937 and saw its vision broaden when a branch of the Young Anglicans (YA) was formed and 25 young people were admitted to membership in 1940.[75] They enjoyed social and religious activities but were constantly reminded of war as eight of their number joined the forces and served overseas in the army and air force.[76] Between 40 and 50 young people were confirmed each year, the Archdeacon making it clear that *all* young Anglicans should attend confirmation classes over lengthy periods of time.[77]

In the public schools, religious instruction continued to occupy much of the priest's time and it was fortunate that Whiting had the assistance of a group of women who assisted at Telopea Park Public School, including Phyllis Bullock, a committed instructor and gifted musician.

While music was important at Kingston, the move to Manuka resulted in new opportunities after the church obtained St John's disused organ, paid the £118 restoration fee (with another two-year loan at 6 per cent interest), and met the annual maintenance cost of £6.[78] The organ was located at the front of the church on the left wall and served for 20 years with Mrs 'Mim' Wrigley acting as the main organist. Music appreciation was enhanced by Whiting, an enthusiastic musician, who helped to organise choir recitals and afternoon presentations of sacred music and eventually prompted the choir to plan a Christmas cantata.[79] For the anniversary services in 1941, the council invited James Hardman to return from Queensland and, as he preached at one of the services, he recalled the first donation to the proposed church in 1933, marvelled with gratitude at the new building, enjoyed the music and thought back to the small organ in St Paul's-in-the-tin-shed. He was then asked to present 'a supper set' to Mrs Holmes who had been the organist during his tenure.

By December 1941, the choir commenced what was later to become a tradition when they sang a selection of Christmas carols ('the first time we have been able to muster the choir for Christmas'). They included the Girls' Grammar School in a joint program in 1943. At Easter the choristers presented Charles Wood's devotional oratorio, *The Passion according to St Mark*.[80] Separately, Phyllis Bullock trained the Children's Choir, a group of 'twenty-four young people' who, by the end of 1944, were regarded as 'part of the Sunday School' for attendance purposes, allowing them to attain stamps in their books and compete for annual attendance prizes.[81] Hence, the move to the new church, the acquisition of the 5-stop positif organ from St John's and the encouragement of the rector helped to maintain the earlier emphasis on music, while enhancing congregational singing and choir involvement, both classical and sacred.

It was then that Whiting received an invitation to work in Tanganyika, a prospect that appealed to the 35-year-old priest. When members of the council heard the news they asked to meet the bishop so that they might discuss a replacement with him.[82] They quickly received a letter from Robertson 'expressing his indignation that the council should have contemplated approaching the Bishop on a matter concerning St Paul's without first consulting him'. Not only had Tom Whiting and the council been discourteous by neglecting appropriate protocol but they had also forgotten the rector's swift and indignant response when he felt his position and prestige were offended. Attending the next meeting of the council, he 'explained in detail the privileges and authority of an incumbent [and] the correct procedure for bringing a matter to the notice of the Bishop'.[83] The private meeting between Robertson and Whiting was not minuted.

Reverend Thomas Whiting c. 1943
© St Paul's Archives

Unfortunately for Whiting his health deteriorated further, 'partly from mental strain and partly from his excessive perambulations on his bicycle ... no less than 4,000 miles in seven years'.[84] Hospitalisation ensued, he was forced to forego the opportunity to work overseas and he contacted Bishop Burgmann, indicating his willingness to minister 'wherever he was needed most in the work of the diocese'. The bishop understandingly appointed him to Binda 'to give him some relief from his heavy duties'. Archbishop Sir Marcus Loane, a close friend of Whiting, later referred to the 'strenuous years' that the priest endured in the 'pioneer church' of St Paul's and to the assistance that Bishop Burgmann provided for him, even requesting him to write and publish *The Priest in Society* and to continue his studies at a higher level.

Robertson did not attend Whiting's farewell, sending a message to 'say he was too occupied to be present'. He allowed the gathering to be chaired by the Presbyterian Minister, the Reverend Hector Harrison, a member of the local Minister's Fraternal.[85] The Archdeacon later informed parishioners through *Parish Notes* that:

> Mr Whiting has done a good piece of work in connection with St Paul's and he will always be able to look back and feel that he played no little part in the building of the fabric and spiritual life of St Paul's. He came to Canberra at a time when St Paul's people were endeavouring to put together sufficient money to enable them to begin the work of building. And his keenness and co-operation with those who were pushing that project gave the urge that resulted in the building of the present portion of the Church. He has been a loyal colleague and we will miss him.[86]

Tom Whiting preached his last sermon at St Paul's on 5 February 1944, after which he, Isabel and the children left for Dubbo for a vacation before commencing at Binda.[87] He was later transferred to Bega in 1950, was made a Canon of St Saviour's Cathedral, went to England in 1965–1966 to pursue research into the history of the priesthood in ancient societies, accepted a position as rector of Boorowa on his return and retired to Bathurst where he continued his priestly office when his health permitted. He died in June 1986 before submitting his doctoral dissertation.[88]

The Canberra Times referred in 1944 to his seven years at St Paul's, where the church life had grown 'in an amazing way' and where the first portion of the new church had been opened, dedicated and 'largely paid for'; where the church tennis club was flourishing with a court and pavilion constructed during his time; and where the removal of the old church hall was taking place.[89] Almost 50 years later, Jacynth Woolven could still write, 'as children of ten and eleven, I shall always remember his arriving at that little church in Kingston on his bicycle and taking off his cycle clips' to walk into the church. 'He always kept our interest in the church.'[90] But it was probably St Paul's parishioners who provided the words that he appreciated most, 'It has been a happy ministry' and 'it has given Mr Whiting an experience vouchsafed to few young priests in the early years of their ministry.' He leaves 'with fond memories of his work here and with an assurance that he gives his work to one [Canon McKeown] who will ably carry it on.'[91]

Notes

1. Robertson to Burgmann, 4 and 15 April 1937, NLA, Burgmann Correspondence, MS1998, Box 34.
2. St John's, Clergy Superannuation Cards, StJ Archives; also *Western Advocate*, 4 July 1986.
3. PN, April 1937; StJ Register of Services; and CT for April–May 1937.
4. Whiting's handwritten 'Pastoral Report', 1937, StPCC, 1937.
5. Robertson to Burgmann, 7 May 1938, NLA, Burgmann Papers MS1998, Box 34.
6. PN, February 1938.
7. 'Pastoral Report', 1937.
8. 'Pastoral Report', 1938, NLA, AGM, StPCC, 1938.
9. CT, 22 May 1937.
10. PN, June 1937.
11. T Whiting, 'The Story of St Paul's Church, Canberra South from the Day of its Inauguration, 4th August 1914 to the Establishment of the Church at Manuka between the Years 1937–1944', NLA, MS3085, Box 1.
12. Headline news in CT between 21 January and 2 June 1937.
13. CT, 14 April 1937; Whiting, 'The Story of St Paul's'; PN, August 1937.
14. First Meeting, St Paul's Men's Committee, 11 August 1937, NLA, MS 3085, Box 1.
15. Whiting, 'The Story of St Paul's'.
16. In 2008 Gwen Jackson recalled the antagonism felt by some of the congregation, Personal communication, 2008.
17. *Yearbook of Australia*, 1937, Government Printer, Canberra, p. 364.
18. PN, February 1938.
19. StJPC, 17 June and 19 August 1937; and Whiting, 'The Story of St Paul's'.
20. PN, March, April and July 1938.

21. PN, October 1938. Also StP's Annual Bazaar proceeds, attached to the Pastoral Report, 1938, NLA, StPCC, 1938, MS3805, Box 34.

22. StJPC, 21 July and 11 August 1938 (Supplement to StJPC, October 1938); 25 September 1938.

23. Whiting, 'The Story of St Paul's'.

24. StJPC, 24 November 1938; and Whiting, 'The Story of St Paul's'.

25. The loan was negotiated through the Bank of Australasia. See: Acting-Manager to Robertson, 28 June 1938, NLA, St Paul's Church Kingston, MS3805, Box 4; and StPPC 24 August 1938.

26. The 12 guarantors were: WJ (Jim) Perry (builder of St Paul's Church); JH Starling (Secretary to the Prime Minister's Department, Public Service Board and churchwarden St John's 1928–1939); O Woodger (Real Estate Agency and manager of the Manuka Swimming Pool; parishioner of St John's); EA Jensen (jeweller in Kingston); G Crease (accountant with the Department of the Interior); AE (Bert) Jackson (Captain in WWI; served in Gallipoli and the Somme; won the MC; prominent in the RSL; tradesman; works supervisor); EW (Bill) Parkes (Clerk to the House of Representatives); Les F Johnson (Government Printer at Kingston); Henry Warwick; H Johnson (licensee of the Hotel Civic); and Miss I New (proprietor of a Kingston café).

27. Whiting, 'The Story of St Paul's'.

28. StPPC, November 30, 1938.

29. A Bolitho and M Hutchinson (eds), *Stories of the Inner South: from a Day of Memories at Manuka Pool* (pp. 20–21), Arts Council of the ACT, 1992.

30. CT, 24 September 1937.

31. PN, June 1939.

32. PN, February 1939.

33. StPPC, 16 March 1939.

34. StPPC, 3 April 1939.

35. StPPC, 9 October 1939.

36. Whiting, 'The Story of St Paul's'.

37. Whiting, 'The Story of St Paul's'. CT, 7 August 1939.

38. CT, 7 August 1939; 4 September 1939.

39. StPPC, 23 November 1939.

40. M McKernan, *All in! Australia during the second world war*, Nelson, Melbourne, 1983, pp. 1, 35.

41. These events and restrictions were reported in CT from February to June 1940.

42. Rector's letter to the parishioners, PN, November 1939.

43. Bishop Burgmann's Charge to the Synod of the Diocese, PN, October 1939.

44. Frame, *A Church for a Nation*, p. 204.

45. CT, 20 August 1940.

46. CT, 7 and 8 August 1940.

47. PN, July 1940; StPCC, October 14, 1940.

48. PN, June 1941; StPCC, 8 September 1941.
49. StPCC 10 November 1941; CT, 26 November and 16 December 1941.
50. PN, January 1942.
51. CT, 20 June 1942.
52. A Bagnall in J Baskin, *Wartime in Canberra: An Oral History of Canberra in the Second World War*, National Trust of Australia (ACT), 2005, p. 4.
53. These events were reported in the CT between February and July 1942.
54. CT, 9 and 30 April 1942; 26 May 1942.
55. See: Justice Rae Else-Mitchell in Baskin, *Wartime in Canberra*, pp. 86–91.
56. CT, 27 August 1942.
57. PN, May 1940; February 1941.
58. StPCC, 8 February 1943; 1 February 1944; 27 February 1945; 26 February 1946.
59. Services and times are recorded in each edition of PN from 1940 to 1945.
60. PN, January 1943.
61. Statements attached to StPCC, 9 October 1939 and 6 March 1940.
62. PN, March 1941; October 1942; June 1943.
63. PN, March 1940; PN, June 1941; StPCC, 8 December 1941.
64. PN, March 1942.
65. PN, March 1945.
66. PN, March 1941; PN, August 1942.
67. StPPC, 13 May 1940.
68. PN, October 1941; October 1942; November–December. 1943. CT, 8 December 1943. Also a letter from Reverend F Ward in PN, November 1947.
69. PN, May 1940; June 1940; July 1940; September 1940; November–December. 1943.
70. StPCC, 13 May 1940; 10 June 1940.
71. Surveyor-General and Chief Property Officer, Property & Survey Branch, to Archdeacon Robertson, 23 June 1942, NAA, Series A414 (A414) Control # 64. (41/1/3451)
72. StPCC, 12 July 1943. StJPC entries, 14 December 1943, indicate that Mr Lowes was to move the church but when Whiting wrote his version he indicated that the builder, Mr Perry, agreed to remove and re-erect the hall for the price of labour. See Whiting, 'The Story of St Paul's, p. 25.
73. Whiting, 'The Story of St Paul's, pp. 25–26.
74. PN, November–December. 1944.
75. PN, May 1940; December 1940.
76. PN, August 1943 (Len Maugher, Norman Fulton, Frank Colwell, Ron Hill, Jack Marshall, Keith Harding, Dick Grey and Jim Chapman)
77. StPCC, 11 August 1941.
78. StJCC, 1 February 1939.
79. PN, October and December 1940.
80. PN, January and February 1942.

81. PN, November–December. 1943, November-December. 1944.

82. StPCC, 12 July 1943.

83. StPCC, 9 August 1943.

84. Whiting, 'The Story of St Paul's', p. 28.

85. *The Western Advocate*, 4 July 1986.

86. PN, January 1944.

87. CT, 5 February 1944.

88. T Whiting, 'The Priest in Society', (a family production), 1988.

89. CT, 3 February 1944.

90. Letter from Jacynth Woolven to Mrs Whiting, 12 March 1988, StP Archives. File: Obituaries Canon Whiting.

91. PN, January 1944.

9 An era concludes, 1945–1949

Conflict continued in Europe and the Pacific during 1944 and eventually came to a welcome end in 1945, ushering in a period of postwar reconstruction and development. Another series of events also emerged to change the social and religious history of Canberra, some unravelling quietly from as far back as 1937 but all culminating by 1949. St Paul's Manuka ended 33 years under the guidance of St John's Church and anticipated its own emerging leadership role in a new parish; three Anglican centres closed, a result of the city's demographic changes; services at HMAS *Harman* peaked before declining in importance; the two denominational schools attained enrolment viability and entered a new growth phase; and Archdeacon Robertson resigned his incumbency after leading the parish for two eventful decades. All five events contributed to the close of an era and the emergence of another.

The first of these developments concerned St Paul's Church itself. Canon Kenneth McKeown assumed responsibility for the south, Robertson remarking that they had been ordained together as deacons at Bathurst 31 years before.[1] They had become 'great pals' through the Brotherhood of the Good Shepherd and had met up again after McKeown had spent five years in North Queensland, eventually joining the Goulburn Diocese. In 1941 he had resigned as Vice-Dean and Canon of St Saviour's to take up chaplaincy work with the army but had now returned to parish work. Robertson was enthusiastic, 'Well, he is coming to take up Mr Whiting's work in St Paul's [and] Canberra will realise their good fortune when they meet this loveable man'.[2]

The year after McKeown's arrival, war hostilities drew to a conclusion when Germany signed unconditional surrender terms and the Japanese capitulated following the frightful carnage of atomic attacks on two cities.[3] *The Canberra Times* reported that peaceful Canberra 'has never known such scenes as were witnessed after the announcement of peace'. 'Shops shut their doors, office workers downed their tools and the children made for the shopping centres.' Papers were showered on the roadway, people sang and yelled and 'a great din' was made by an amazing number of cans and tins that vied 'with the screech of air-raid sirens'. Revellers converged on Manuka Oval where the shopkeepers distributed free fruit, vegetables, bottles of soft drink, meat pies and cigarettes, and a carnival throng of 2,000 attended organised celebrations, dancing and children's games on the oval near St Paul's.

At the same time, 'the floodlit pile of the Australian War Memorial gave solemn reminder of the suffering and sacrifice through which peace' had come. A national service of thanksgiving was held at the

Archdeacon Robertson, Canon McKeown and Reverend Pyke 1946
© *St John's Schoolhouse Museum*

War Memorial with a parade of ex-servicemen 'in larger numbers than ever before'. Uniformed school children, volunteer war workers and all branches of the fighting services gathered together 'under the flags of the Allied Nations which fluttered bravely in the breeze'.[4] St John's and St Paul's held their own thanksgiving services to celebrate the peace, McKeown rejoicing at the allied success 'which meant keeping back the evil which threatened the world' and thanked Britain for the role it had assumed.[5]

McKeown was quite critical of the Anglican Church's plans for postwar development, however, and expressed his views forcibly from the pulpit. Whereas the Presbyterian Church had 'a big plan of development and work,' he believed that this vision was 'sadly lacking in the Church of England in this country'.

Nominally the Church has an enrolment of approximately 45 per cent of the population. It is because 35 of the 45 per cent are inert or spiritually inept that the Church is unable to renew its strength and make a bold forward movement. The aliveness of the Church at this time is the thing that matters so far as the future is concerned and the imagination of the young people. Deadness must bring other unpleasant conditions around it.[6]

McKeown quietly set about rejuvenating the church after the deleterious years of war and turned his attention to those returning from active service during 1945 and 1946. 'Welcome Home' evenings were organised by St Paul's 'to make the returning boys and girls feel that there is a definite place for them in the life of the Church and the community' – a series of informal socials that provided opportunities for old friends to meet again, for new acquaintances to be made and for 'the newest dances' to be learned.[7] The air-raid shelter in the grounds of St Paul's was filled in despite the prohibitive cost of £6 10s charged by the Works and Services Branch.[8] Working bees were held to improve the church landscape, shrubs were planted and the church council recommended the creation of a 'Memorial Garden' 'to all who gave their lives in the War'.[9] Hoping to raise the £200 required without holding dances for the purpose, the church commenced work on the reconstruction in April 1946 and finished the task nine months later under Don Youngman's supervision.[10]

McKeown's term as priest-in-charge was relatively short as the bishop appointed him to Cooma in April 1947, replacing him with Gordon Armstrong, a younger but equally friendly priest who had once been a server for McKeown in Young. Together they discussed the ministry at St Paul's, Armstrong accepting and following the broad policies developed and pursued by his predecessor. As their combined ministries lasted only the six years between 1944 and early 1950, the issues faced by the two clergymen were very similar.

They both concentrated on youth work, especially the all-important Sunday school. McKeown was perturbed by the lack of religious teaching in public schools, believing that half an hour of instruction each week was 'inadequate to teach the children the faith'. Fortunately, the old tin church had just been moved to Manuka and he had a hall for youth activities, allowing him to focus on the Sunday school. He encouraged the work of Reg Coombe under whose leadership more than 150 youngsters attended each week during 1946.[11] The combined children's service–Sunday school was so successful that the four teachers in the senior school under Coombe and the three in the kindergarten (Betty Jackson, Pat Andrews and Joyce Shannon) had to recruit seven additional teachers as the number of children climbed to almost 200 early in 1948, a result that gave considerable satisfaction to Gordon Armstrong.[12] The children collected funds for a baptismal font, held concerts and plays and were involved in Christmas-tree socials, Christmas parties and annual picnics during the summer months, so that Armstrong could report in 1949 that the number of children attending each Sunday was climbing even higher.[13]

The Young Anglicans began to expand once again after the war, relieved that all who had served on active service had returned safely home. The 20 members met each fortnight, alternating their meetings between the church hall and the homes of members and, by Armstrong's time, occasionally gathered at the rectory at 90 Canberra Avenue, where the priest and his wife hosted debates and chaired animated discussions. A bus trip was organised to Kosciuszko, social events were frequently held and a monthly corporate Communion service was held as an established part of their witness.[14]

Turning to the choirs whose numbers had suffered during the war years, McKeown acknowledged that 'the senior choir is not a large body' but it 'has done very well' and the singing of the services 'has depended' on it. By the end of 1946 the choir was 'strengthening', Mrs Wrigley had returned as organist after a period of absence, anthems were being sung once again and there were plans for special music at Easter.[15] Unfortunately, the resurgence did not continue and Armstrong reported in 1948 that, except for a special dedication festival or anniversary, 'choir work does not appeal to many'. Consequently, 'I have taken the step of cancelling choir practice and replacing it with a Congregational Hymn Singing Session, beginning at 7pm each Sunday night', the service at which the adult choir normally performed.[16] The junior choir, however, was reorganised under Mim Wrigley and Mr Blackman and received due acknowledgement for its contribution to the morning services.

Adult group activities had been affected during the war but the Women's Guild revived the annual dance in the Albert Hall in July 1947, increased the number of social events, continued to organise the annual fete and was delighted to see the 'financial burden becoming lighter each year'.[17] The Archdeacon commented on the 'small number of women' involved but acknowledged their continuing efforts to raise funds and to help 'the church meet the [annual] quota assessment.'[18] Younger mothers usually joined the Mothers' Union that met each month. Women were elected for the first time to the church council in 1944 when Mrs Harding and Mrs Jackson attended meetings, encouraged by Whiting and McKeown.[19] The Church of England Men's Society no longer operated in 1946 and it was not until 1948 that there was talk of its relaunch. The men carried their share of church life, however, by involvement in administrative duties and by improving the church buildings and grounds. They organised the senior Sunday school, assisted in staging children's pageants, organised annual picnics and contributed to fund-raising activities such as fetes, dances and special events. There were some, however, who missed the additional fellowship and intellectual stimulus that had been provided by the CEMS in former years.[20]

Hence, the postwar period was one of rejuvenation as the church and the community gradually returned to a semblance of normality. McKeown provided a gentle spiritual guidance for the congregation, welcoming home the men and women from active service, encouraging the youth of the church, revitalising some of the adult groups and exemplifying the love of his God whom he served with humility. He died in September 1948, eighteen months after his move to Cooma, but he knew that his efforts would be continued and developed by his protégé, Gordon Armstrong.

The Reverend Gordon Armstrong
© St Paul's Archives

In turn, Armstrong steered the church through three important years as wartime restrictions were gradually eased and as parishioners planned for the future. Significantly, he realised and accepted that the needs of the south were changing rapidly, requiring the former relationship with St John's to be concluded and a new parish formed with St Paul's as its centre. When he expressed these thoughts at the annual general meeting in March 1949, one chaired by the Archdeacon himself, he virtually sealed the swell of opinion favouring separation and foreshadowed the end of an era in the development of the church south of the Molonglo.

The second major development concerned three Anglican ventures at Molonglo, Causeway and Westlake – settlements originally designed as temporary housing areas. As they declined in population, fell into disrepair and eventually closed – their demise often prolonged by wartime conditions – the church came to realise that the three had been stagnating and losing population over a twelve-year period.

The settlement at Molonglo had continued to provide low-cost accommodation for Canberra residents after 1937, many using it as a stepping-stone to better housing elsewhere. While the government policy had been for the tenements 'to be demolished as they became vacant or as other homes were found for the occupiers', the settlement had lingered with a minimum of care and maintenance.[21] Whiting had ridden his bicycle to the decaying centre in all weathers during February and March 1938 and talked to the residents after Evensong but the numbers had been low – between 16 and 30 – and had declined soon after with only two services being held during 1939.

Consequently, with the projected opening of St Paul's at Manuka in August, it had been decided to discontinue services at Molonglo, the last service being held in June 1939.[22] Thereafter the small congregation had been required to walk to the newly commenced service at the Causeway, find their way to Christ Church Queanbeyan or travel to St Paul's. The children likewise could attend the Sunday school at the Causeway or transfer to the new kindergarten in the old mission hall at Kingston in October under the direction of Isabel Whiting.[23] As the population had declined further, there had been one more attempt to revive the Anglican centre during 1941 when a volunteer gathered the young people together for a children's service–Sunday school, a venture that lasted from February to June but eventually it had also ceased and the old Molonglo School building had closed in 1942.[24] After serving as an internment camp and a low-cost housing centre for Canberra's workers, Molonglo faded away and by 1948 there were only ten families living in the area. It gradually changed character and merged into present-day Fyshwick.[25]

The demise of the Causeway ministry took a little longer as the settlement had maintained a relatively constant population between 1937 and 1940 even though the physical condition of the area had deteriorated due to the absence of 40 Causeway men on active service, some of whom were tragically killed in action. The inhabitants had then been spurred to redevelop the settlement, opening a baby welfare clinic and refurbishing the Causeway Hall. Over 600 people had attended the opening of the reconditioned building in 1941, causing a correspondent to claim that the Causeway had not known such enthusiasm since 'the boom days of 1926'.[26] Throughout the year, footpaths, stormwater drains, fences and gates had been constructed and the houses progressively painted. The local association conducted concerts, dances and suppers 'to raise funds for the comforts of Causeway men in the forces'. A tablet with the names of the enlisted men had been mounted in the hall.[27]

One of the last original Causeway homes.
© ACT Heritage Library, DCT Collection.

Whiting had resumed services in November 1937 with a 'children's service' under the control of a volunteer from St Paul's at Kingston. Not successful, it had ceased in July 1940, whereupon St Paul's Women's Guild used the hall for jumble sales, children's events and sales of produce during the war time years.[28] While Robertson and Whiting had desired a presence at Causeway, they had found it impossible to do so with limited resources and it was left to the Ministers' Fraternal, in a spirit of cooperation, to organise united services in the Causeway Hall, seemingly from the start of 1942 and continuing every few months until 1945.[29] With victory in Europe assured in June 1945, McKeown indicated that he would withdraw from the united church services and begin a weekly Anglican service in July. This was the final venture by the Anglican Church at the centre as the small attendances (only 6 to 14 communicants) caused McKeown to express his disappointment and withdraw on 2 December 1945.[30]

In retrospect, Anglicanism had endured 20 chequered years at the Causeway. Services had been held from 1926 until 1929, were discontinued for eight years and were recommenced by Whiting from 1938 to 1940 until united services had been introduced. McKeown's attempt at revitalisation in 1945 was the last to occur and by the end of the year the Anglican Church withdrew and concentrated on areas and suburbs of greater population.

The fate of Anglican services at Westlake followed a completely different pattern as the settlement of 61 wooden cottages continued to provide low-cost accommodation for a population not destined for an early removal. The 'ice-man, greengrocer, butcher and baker' still visited on a regular basis, 'the Rawleigh's man (who sold patent medicines) and the seller of material, sheets, tablecloths and other linens' made fortnightly calls and the milkman filled the billy-can on the top step every night.[31] The gardens continued to flourish and the fruit trees and grape vines helped people to cope during the bleak days of war. Canberra did not advertise the Westlake settlement (a similar fate to that of Molonglo) because a temporary settlement or camp did not improve the city's desired status. While there was little reference to the locality in the newspapers, except when it achieved sporting success, the Westlake inhabitants were a closely knit group and possessed pride in their own community.

Anglican services had been revived in 1938 when Bishop Burgmann had founded the Young Anglicans (YA) for people between the ages of 15 and 35, a group pledged to 'fight against injustice and oppression' and to seek strength in the 'Teaching and Sacraments of the Church, in prayer and meditation, in study and thought.'[32] At the suggestion of the bishop and the clergy, the YA had commenced monthly church gatherings in the Westlake Hall opposite the tennis court on Sunday evenings. The first service had been held in September 1938, the young people not only conducting the service but also visiting the local homes from time to time and later thanking many friends who 'assisted us in building up a congregation'.

As their plans had widened the YA had arranged an 'audacious undertaking for a group of inexperienced and imperfect young Anglicans', organising a three-day mission at the centre with Communion services at 6am each day.[33] Then, in a vigorous burst of activity, the members had continued monthly church services, commenced a weekly Sunday school, organised a boys' club, arranged and trained a choir for the church service, organised a weekend camp for 18 youngsters at the Cotter River and developed a plan to present the bishop with a consecration gown. Sunday school numbers had risen from 9 in February 1940 to 23 in April as the young people had continued to visit homes and encourage attendance.[34] It had been difficult to maintain the motivation during the war years, however, when some of the Young

Anglicans had enlisted and served overseas, resulting in the loss of services during 1941 and 1942.[35] Perhaps the local folk were too absorbed in other developments that were occurring nearby.

Until 1940 the United States had conducted its consular representation through the government of Great Britain but official diplomatic representations commenced between the Americans and Australia in January 1940, leading to the establishment of the American Embassy, the first in Canberra. The foundation stone of the ambassador's residence was laid jointly by Prime Minister Curtin, Senator Collings and America's minister, Mr Nelson Johnson, on 4 July 1942. Wartime restrictions delayed the construction but the building was finally occupied by Christmas 1943. In its publicity material the United States proclaimed that the building had 'a commanding site with panoramic views of the city and mountains' but it did not mention that it overlooked and encroached on the Westlake settlement of 61 homes, nor could it envisage the eventual closure of the settlement as the area gradually developed as a diplomatic precinct.[36]

A few weeks after the opening of the American Embassy, the residents of Westlake received word that afternoon Anglican services would resume in the Recreation Hall each fortnight commencing on 21 February 1943. Those who attended met Frederick Bastian who had been studying for Holy Orders for some years but had interrupted his studies to enter service with the Merchant Navy on the outbreak of hostilities. Arriving in Canberra to continue his studies at the Canberra University College and to serve part-time as a stipendiary lay reader,[37] Bastian faithfully ministered in the parish at a time when there was a shortage of priests. He conducted fortnightly services at Westlake, carried responsibility for much of the ministry at the new Ainslie centre and developed youth work for almost two years before he left in August 1944 to work with the Missions to Seamen in Melbourne. (In his later years, Bastian became Archdeacon and Diocesan Registrar of the Diocese of Willochra.)

Despite the construction of the American Embassy, the Westlake area was still isolated and depressed. The residents had applied for the extension of the bus service from State Circle to Westlake in 1941 but approval was considered unlikely in wartime when no extra buses were available and because of the 'narrow state of the road' into the settlement.[38] By 1944 a Sydney newspaper claimed that Westlake was 'a slum', leading to a quick reaction from those 'who had lived at Westlake and made the best of difficult conditions for 20 years'. It was asserted that people 'were compelled to live in sub-standard homes by the inability of the Government to provide better homes' but that the residents kept their properties 'habitable' and that the area was always clean.[39]

The local parishioners were certainly loyal to the church, sustaining fortnightly Anglican services from February 1943 until April 1949. During this time, a young man left the Department of External Affairs, trained for the ministry and served as a curate at Young. Made a priest in 1944 at the age of 25, Laurence Maxwell Murchison joined the parish as a fourth priest in 1946 and was made responsible for northside Anglican centres by the Archdeacon.[40] Additionally he ministered to the Westlake community, building up the youth work, meeting the people in their homes and conducting services from March 1946 until June 1947 when he introduced his successor, Gordon Armstrong. Murchison left to become 'the Parish Organist in the Parish of Christ Church, South Yarra in the Diocese of Melbourne'.[41]

During Armstrong's ministry Westlake residents were progressively moved to other areas resulting in declining Anglican attendances at the Westlake Recreation Hall during 1948. It was not long before fortnightly services were reduced to monthly gatherings and collections were no longer sought. The Anglican ministry ceased altogether in April 1949.[42] Thereafter, the old 'temporary' homes were progressively demolished, the area of Westlake slipped into gradual oblivion as more diplomatic residences and embassies were planned and constructed in the 1950s and 1960s, and Lake Burley Griffin was formed and filled in 1963.[43] And so, a ministry begun in 1927 and conducted intermittently but faithfully over a 22-year period, came to an inevitable conclusion. It was left to a revitalised Westridge (Yarralumla) suburb from late 1949 to meet the needs of the remaining people at Westlake and the adjoining areas.

A third development affecting the church centred on naval activities at HMAS *Harman*. With the development of radio communication during the 1930s, the Australian Commonwealth Naval Board had recommended the establishment of a strategic wireless station in Canberra because of its secure location 120 kms from the coast. Opened on Commonwealth land near the New South Wales border and Queanbeyan in April 1939, *Harman* provided communication services for ships of the allied navies in the Pacific region during the war. As hostilities intensified in 1941, the first servicewomen began as telegraphers, forming the WRANS (the Women's Royal Australian Naval Service) in 1941. Some of the WRANS occupied the Molonglo School after its closure in 1942.[44]

During August 1941, representatives of *Harman* had visited St Paul's during its anniversary services, after which the Commanding

Aerial view of HMAS *Harman* 1951.
© *ACT Heritage Library – Department of Capital Territory's Pictorial Record of Canberra 1951-53*

Officer had telephoned Whiting and asked if the curate would 'conduct Divine service on one Sunday morning in each month in accordance with Naval routine'. Whiting had agreed (with Robertson's concurrence) and found to his bliss that his bicycle was not required:

> From that time onwards, on the first Sunday of the month, the Naval limousine arrived at the curate's home at 9.15am, conveyed him to *Harman*, where he was received ceremoniously by the Commander and other ranks and escorted into the hall for Divine service.

The young priest later confessed that 'the reception, the singing and the participation of all who assembled for worship and the official farewell after each service, made a lasting impression on one who had never had any association with such naval discipline'. He enjoyed the experience and appreciated the disciplined services in the Recreation Hall for up to 250 naval men and women but the inclusion of a chauffeured car contributed equally to his pleasure.[45]

With his padre's background, McKeown was less surprised by naval protocol but equally impressed when he took over from Whiting in 1944 and ministered twice each month until 1946. Perhaps the Archdeacon also appreciated chauffeured transport for he assumed responsibility for the church parades in May 1946 and conducted weekly services for the next three years until his departure from the parish.[46] In this way the ministry at *Harman* was transferred from St Paul's to St John's in 1946 but ultimate responsibility for the chaplaincy was not resolved until 1950. While services continued beyond 1949, numbers attending services began to decline and the form of the chaplaincy became problematic, causing the strong Anglican influence to wane during the 1950s.

A fourth issue affecting the Anglican Church up to 1949 entailed the two denominational schools. The exigencies of war brought both challenges and benefits to the schools and resulted in changes of relationship with the diocese. For the Canberra Grammar School, the period 1934 to 1939 had constituted 'the first great era of growth and development', leading to building extensions in 1938 and a further mortgage of £21,500. According to the headmaster's daughter, 'Our 20 acres on the hill, surrounded by its boundary trees, became an antbed of activity ... [as] the air was split by a cacophony of banging and hammering that drowned the voices of children at play and masters at work'. The Governor-General, Lord Gowrie, had opened the new buildings in February 1939 as enrolments had reached 145, increasing to 154 in 1944 and 200 in 1945 when the school was 'filled to capacity'.[47]

The war had negative effects, however, causing the small number of teachers to endure very high teaching loads. To strengthen the staff, the Reverend Kenneth Clements was appointed Director of Studies. Clements was destined to serve as bishop of the diocese from 1961– 1972. Almost inevitably, the school's motto, *Deo, Ecclesiae, Patriae* (For God, for Church, for Country) had become starkly meaningful when the first 'old boy' was killed in France at the end of 1939. The headmaster was shocked, the staff distressed and the school went into mourning, but much worse was to follow as 27 old boys were killed before the end of the war. It was a 'massive sacrifice' made more poignant as Canon Edwards sadly read the names of casualties and prisoners of war at the speech day each year.[48] During 1943 the students raised funds, contacted those on active service and provided them with a copy of the school magazine, while, to allay their own fears, the pupils built crude air-raid shelters appropriately named 'Hurricane Way' and 'Spitfire Alley' near a dry creek close to the present Monaro Crescent.[49] By November 1945 there were plans to erect a large modern gymnasium and sports pavilion as a memorial to the old boys killed in the war.[50]

The school emerged from the war years and entered a new phase. Day students began to outnumber boarders. By 1947 the headmaster and the bishop had different ideas on the future administration of the school, leading Canon Edwards to resign and accept a United Nations post with UNICEF in Greece where the University of Athens conferred an honorary doctorate on him for his services two years later. Edwards had maintained the independence of the Canberra Grammar School, preserving its Anglican orientation and participating in parish and diocesan events but fiercely resisting attempts to ally it closely with the Canberra parish or its politics. On Edwards' departure, Bishop Burgmann decided that the Diocese of Goulburn 'should take over the school' and relieve it of its large debt and its inability to re-equip its facilities.[51] The Reverend David Garnsey (a future bishop of Gippsland) was appointed headmaster and Canberra Grammar School could later claim to have had two future bishops on its staff after the war. Hence, by 1949 the school had achieved enrolment viability but its financial position had reached a desperate position.

The relationship between the Canberra Grammar School and the parish varied from time to time, clouded partly by the personalities involved. While Robertson and Edwards were life-long friends, differences were apparent in their ministries. Robertson accepted that the school was 'an extra parochial organisation' but was peeved that it was not more intimately involved in parish affairs.[52] Territorial in his approach, he had informed the bishop in 1939 that the school 'carries no prestige and is looked upon as the citadel of Snobocracy', a 'hindrance and not a help to Church life in the Parish … [while] any help that we have had has been dragged out of the place'. Robertson claimed that his own children 'would have had a far better education and a more sound Christian instruction at the [Telopea Park] High School.' For his part Edwards was equally intent on maintaining the independence of the school without its entanglement in parish concerns.

While it was maintained that a number of Telopea Park School students became strong members of the Young Anglicans and that 'only one ex-pupil [of Canberra Grammar School] has shown any inclination for religion', one must understand the differing stances of the two men. Robertson was offended by any taint of Protestantism while Edwards was more liberal in his approach and preached in the Baptist Church when invited. Robertson chastised 'his friend Bill', objected strongly to the bishop over the matter and claimed that Edwards displayed 'bad manners and unpardonable discourtesy' as an Anglican priest when he came 'within the precincts of my parish' to perform religious services 'without first obtaining my consent'.[53] It was a territorial dispute, a doctrinal difference of opinion and a determination on the part of both parties to uphold differing principles – one sought to integrate the school more fully into parish life under the Archdeacon's control and the other aimed to maintain its independence. Anglicanism on the south side of the Molonglo was not divorced from theological dispute, personal aspiration or political overture.

Up the hill at the Girls' Grammar School (CCEGGS), enrolments had virtually doubled in the early 1940s when fathers were on active service and Canberra was considered a 'safe' city for young daughters. By 1943 the total enrolment stood at 160 and reached 214 in 1945 requiring additional accommodation and a new wing. Even this was insufficient to cope with the number of young children attending.[54] Consequently a junior kindergarten was added in 1944 when the administration acquired a disused classroom. The new facility was opened by Lady Gowrie in March 1944 and enabled the separation of the Junior School into two age groups and then to three the following year.

Despite these advances, the Girls' Grammar School faced even greater fiscal stress than the boys' school when the council experienced severe difficulties, losing £2,000 between 1935 and 1943. It was unable to pay 'either the principal or the interest on £2,500 owing to the Church Extension Society' until 1946, a problem accentuated by the war.[55] Increased fees were offset by the financial outlay on air-raid precautions and on spiralling food costs. The school also experienced difficulties finding qualified teaching and domestic staff and meeting the 'necessity for school repairs and the replacement' of resources. The school's income came entirely from fees and it struggled to remain viable during difficult times.

There was a closer relationship between the parish and the girls' school than with the boys' school. Archdeacon Robertson, as chaplain, continued to conduct a school Communion service each week and took a personal interest in the social and spiritual interest of the girls, some of whom attended services at St John's and visited the rectory for morning tea. Religious instruction classes continued through the war years, even though petrol rationing made visits more problematic and the Archdeacon prepared many of the girls for confirmation.[56] 'Robbie' and Olive Robertson probably felt a degree of pride when their daughter, Helen, was Captain of Forrest House in 1939, little knowing that it would eventually be renamed 'Robertson House' in honour of the Archdeacon himself. [57]

Both the Canberra Grammar School and CCEGGS received the continuing support of Bishop Burgmann who attended functions, addressed annual speech days, took an interest in the curriculum and supported the staff and students. Additionally, both schools received the support of influential community members who served on the school councils and contributed to fund-raising activities. By 1949 both schools were well established and exerting an important influence on the Canberra community, both able to claim that their pioneering days were over. Nevertheless, both still faced financial difficulties as they expanded to meet enrolment pressures.

The fifth issue that brought the era to a close was Robertson's resignation. It was late in 1948 that close friends began to notice that the Archdeacon was evidently unsettled. He had been rector of St John's for almost 20 years and Archdeacon of Monaro or Canberra since 1935, guiding the Anglican Church through the years of Depression, war and postwar rehabilitation. In May he would turn 60 and was questioning whether additional years at St John's were warranted. Robertson's relationship with Burgmann was quite testy and the bishop's move to Canberra in 1947 had meant that his own position as church spokesman had been diminished, some claiming that the bishop's 'coming' meant his 'going'.[58] Perhaps this was the opportunity to explore new endeavours.

There were rumblings at St Paul's that the *Parish Notes* centred too much on St John's, leading the Manuka congregation to commence a monthly roneoed circular in November 1948 devoted to their own affairs.[59] Ken Wright increasingly proposed the formation of a new parish, indicating that there was little incentive for St Paul's parishioners to work for their own church. Others who had previously acknowledged the support of St John's now believed that 'obstacles were being put in the way of their progress'.[60] Some even asserted that, because of the demands of the entire parish, Robertson had 'little time for parochial work' at St Paul's, a claim the Archdeacon realised was partly true as there were periods when he knew he was 'away too much'.[61]

Moreover, his own interests were modifying as he became increasingly attracted to the Australian Board of Missions (ABM). He had recently been elected to the board and the centenary committee of ABM and had been voted onto the NSW committee with numerous positions of importance. In Canberra he had stressed missionary activities and invited speakers to assist in attracting 50 additional missionaries and raising £100,000.[62] He was offered the position of Chairman of ABM in October 1948. In February 1949, after discussing the matter with Olive, Robertson eventually informed the parishioners of his resignation, adding that 'I was unanimously elected to the position and accepted it'.[63] In Hempenstall's judgment, the Archdeacon 'sought to climb out from under Burgmann's control' and finally left Canberra for the ABM 'where he could wield his executive skills comparatively unhindered'.[64]

At farewell gatherings, the Archdeacon received the highest accolade from the Governor-General, Mr McKell, who had known him before he had come to Canberra. 'Robertson had not confined his activities to the church alone but was a real citizen' who had 'exercised a tremendous influence on the community'. McKell referred to the 'intense sincerity and affection' felt by the people as Canberra had 'grown from an Empire outpost to the capital of a great nation', and highlighted the contribution that Robertson and his wife had made. The Prime Minister, Mr Chifley, sent a laudatory letter 'expressing his admiration for the splendid work the Archdeacon had carried out in Canberra'. Father Wellington spoke on behalf of the Roman Catholic Church, referring to the close relationship that had existed between

Robertson and Monsignor Haydon (who had died three weeks before), indicating that the Archdeacon's departure would be 'a loss not only to the religious life of this city' but also in matters 'social and political'. James Colwell expressed the pride felt by the parishioners of St John's at the Archdeacon's 'promotion' while representatives of Hall and St Paul's Manuka (Don Youngman) 'thanked Archdeacon Robertson for assistance in establishing their churches'.

In response, Roberson alluded to nineteen and a half years during which he had come in contact with Canberra people and had developed 'the highest respect and affection for them'. He referred to 'the spirit of fellowship between ministers of other churches' and paid a special tribute to Monsignor Haydon 'whom he had learned to admire and love'. The Archdeacon was sorry to leave but glad to be undertaking the work before him. His responsibility was 'to provide men and women for his new parish, the Pacific'. At the end of proceedings, Bishop Burgmann bade farewell to the Archdeacon and introduced the new rector of St John's. A few days later Charles Robertson and his wife, Olive, left for Sydney.[65]

Robertson had a profound influence on Canberra and on the development of Anglicanism in the parish, although his incumbency was not without tension. As he moved the liturgy at St John's away from the 'middle-of-the-road' approach of Frederick Ward, his orientation was not accepted by all parishioners. After each Communion service, the rector reserved any unused consecrated elements for urgent occasions or for sick visitations, but when he indicated his intention of reserving the sacraments in an aumbry or steel tabernacle on the altar itself, dissension escalated and this led to a split in the congregation.[66] Bishop Burgmann received correspondence about the 'worshippers who have been driven away from St John's' – the latest being Mr and Mrs Starling – and who have found 'comfort at St Paul's which they could not find, or had lost, at St John's'. Under Whiting, St Paul's continued the 'middle road path' that Ward and Fletcher had professed and did not embrace the full extent of Robertson's Anglo-Catholicism.

Fearing that the Archdeacon would introduce Anglo-Catholic 'innovations' at St Paul's that were 'palpably against the teachings of the Church of England', Captain Weale appealed to the bishop that 'we may be permitted to continue' as we are at St Paul's 'without disturbance' to 'our services, fabric, etc'. He suggested that Burgmann 'create us a Parochial Mission' and that the bishop himself 'be the Curer of our Souls with Mr Whiting as your representative', with all parts south of the Molonglo River to be included in the Mission district of St Paul's'.[67] Burgmann wrote privately to Robertson: 'I take it for granted that you can carry your people with you in the matter of Reservation for the sick, [but remember that] you have Churchmen of every kind in Canberra and we must hold them all'.[68] Robertson did not carry all the people with him and did not proceed with installing an aumbry on the altar, advising the bishop that he would wait until the objectors were 'sufficiently educated'.[69]

While he enjoyed his ministry and the position it afforded him, Robertson was often impelled by the intensity of his own emotions when his principles were involved, chief of which was the 'catholicity' of the church that stood sacrosanct and overshadowed other denominations. He established the Clergy Fraternal Group in Canberra and professed oneness of spirit with his colleagues but confessed to Burgmann that 'I cannot bring myself to look upon Non-conformists as brother Christians. They are to me schismatics ... I cannot really love them ... The Lord can probably get on alright with them but I can't'. He soundly condemned Edwards for conducting services in the Baptist Church and complained to the bishop about his friend but was quickly informed that 'Edwards (or any incumbent) is answerable to me [as bishop] alone'. A year later Robertson chastised Burgmann himself 'for preaching in a Church not in communion with the Catholic Church' and protested that the bishop had not consulted him as rector first, something he felt embodied a lack of 'courtesy'.[70]

When righteously roused, the Archdeacon could be formidable. On one occasion he heard of a man drinking in the hotel while his wife was suffering in hospital, causing Robertson to visit the bar, invite the man to visit his wife and, when he refused, take him by the collar, march him home and reprimand him the entire way.[71] A parishioner later recalled how he 'helped the wives and children who were badly treated by their husbands. He 'would go to the men and talk to them, even helping a few to change'.[72] He even had to defend his own pugilistic actions in court.[73] The Archdeacon's strong social conscience together with his equally strong temperament assisted many of Canberra's depressed families to find help and solace but at times the mixture proved a liability. The great majority, however, knew and respected him for his friendliness, enthusiasm and interest and for the energy he expended on the church, the parishioners and those in need. To his closest friends he was simply 'Robbie' while to most others he was 'the Archdeacon', 'a man of God' and a man of the people.

Robertson's concern for the southside was expressed from the first days of his incumbency when he sanctioned the extension of the mission hall and appointed James Hardman as the first unofficial priest-in-charge of southside centres. He encouraged money-raising efforts and publicised the efforts of those who sought to swell the Building Fund coffers. After the appointment of Tom Whiting as priest-in-charge, the Archdeacon was required to balance the enthusiasm of the parishioners as they raised funds for their own church against the wider demands of the developing parish. He restricted the construction of the first stage of the new church to a manageable mortgage, a judicious action in view of the constricting economy and the restrictions of World War II. While accused of 'dictatorial methods' by Weale and others, a claim not without some justification, he was true to his own spiritual predilections, considered the needs of the entire parish and based his economic decisions on a caution borne out of extensive experience. By 1949 he had prepared the way for a new parish south of the Molonglo.

He could leave Canberra knowing that his contribution to the entire parish, including the south, was lasting and that the Anglican faith had been consolidated. It was true that the Anglican centres at Molonglo, Causeway and Westlake had declined and closed and that the Anglican presence at *Harman* appeared to have peaked. But the first stirrings of Westridge's resurrection were apparent, the two denominational schools had become well established and St Paul's had become the strong centre of Anglican witness in the south. The debt on the Manuka church building had been reduced to £995,[74] church numbers were strong, youth work was burgeoning and there was optimism about the future. As the era closed, the 1950s loomed with cascading confidence.

Notes

1. CT, 12 February 1944. Kenneth McKeown had been a Canon of St Saviour's Cathedral and had forfeited the title when he left the cathedral to become an army chaplain. The title was restored in 1944, PN, June 1944.
2. PN, January 1944.
3. CT, 8 May and 8 August 1945.
4. CT, 16 and 17 August 1945.
5. CT, 9 May 1945.
6. CT, 26 November 1944.
7. PN, January, April and October 1946.
8. StPCC, 13 February 1945; 4 June 1945.
9. PN, April-May 1945, January and March 1946.
10. PN, April, August, September and October 1946; January and September–October. 1947.
11. PN, April 1946; May 1946.
12. PN, December 1946; February–March 1948.
13. PN, November–January. 1949 and January 1950.
14. PN, May 1946; June and July 1947; April–May 1948.
15. PN, January and December 1946.
16. PN, August 1948.
17. PN, April–May 1948.
18. PN, January 1948.
19. StPCC, 14 February 1944; 11 April 1944.
20. Frank Colwell was one who recalled the wonderful friendship of CEMS and referred to others who expressed the same opinion, Personal communication, 2008.
21. CT, 28 November 1940.
22. StJ Register of Services, 1937–1939.
23. PN, September 1939.
24. StJ Register of Services 1941. As these services were recorded in the Register of Services for St John's, not St Paul's, it is likely that the volunteer with initials A McG was a parishioner at St John's.
25. Foskett, *The Molonglo Mystery*, p. 105.
26. CT, 27 and 28 June 1941.
27. CT, 13 August 1941.
28. StP Register of Services, 1937–1938; CT, October 1938. The time of service varied between 10am and 11am.
29. There is a reference to the United Services in PN, June-July 1945, p. 5. The StP Register of Services records five or six services each year during 1943 and 1944.
30. CT, 30 June 1945; PN, August–September 1945.
31. Gugler, *Westlake*, p. 118.

32. PN, May 1938.

33. PN, December 1938.

34. PN, September 1939 and May 1940; StJ Register of Services, 1939–1941; CT, 17 and 24 February 1940.

35. The StJ Register of Services indicates no services between 15 December 1940 and 21 February 1943.

36. 'History of the US Embassy', *http://canberra.usembassy.gov/history.html*

37. CT, 6 and 20 February 1943.

38. CT, 19 July 1941.

39. CT, 4 August 1944.

40. PN, March 1946; Body, *Firm Still You Stand*, p. 204.

41. PN, June 1947.

42. StJ Register of Services, 1948–1949; PN, April 1949.

43. A Gugler, *True Tales from Canberra's Vanished Suburbs of Westlake, Westbridge and Acton*, CPN Publications, Canberra, 1999, p. 6.

44. 'HMAS *Harman*', *http://www.navy.gov.au/HMAS_Harman*

45. Whiting, 'The Story of St Paul's; PN, November 1946; A Nelson, HMAS *Harman 1943–1993*, DC-C Publications PPUBS 4308/93, Canberra, pp. 3–4.

46. StJ Register of Services, 1946–1949.

47. J Pulford, 'Deo, Ecclesiae, Patriae' (pp. 18–48), in P McKeown (ed.), *Deo, Ecclesiae, Patriae. Fifty Years of Canberra Grammar School*, Australian National University Press, 1979, p. 40; also CT, 10 December 1945.

48. For example, CT, 12 July 1941; 16 and 27 December 16 1941; 11 December 1943; 10 December 1945.

49. Pulford, *Deo, Ecclesiae, Patriae*, pp. 44–45.

50. CT, 1 November 1945.

51. D Garnsey, 'Struggle and development, 1948 to 1958' in McKeown, *Deo, Ecclesiae, Patriae*, p. 104.

52. M Robertson, 'The Ven. Charles Shearer Robertson: Some memories'. *Anglican Historical Society Journal*, Diocese of Canberra & Goulburn, No. 19, 1995, p. 5.

53. Robertson to Burgmann, 30 May 1939; Robertson to Edwards, 6 May 1939, NLA, Burgmann Papers, MS1998, Box 34.

54. CT, 14 December 1943; 12 December 1944; 10 December 1945.

55. Waterhouse, *A Light in the Bush*, pp. 74; 99; 192–193; and CT, 19 December 1945.

56. The StJ Register of Services records the weekly visits of the archdeacon between 1930 and 1949.

57. Much of the information on CCEGGS is from Waterhouse, *A Light in the Bush*, Chapter 6 and pp. 192–193.

58. The frosty relationship is borne out in the correspondence between Robertson and the bishop in the Burgmann Papers in NLA at MS1998, Box 34. See also: Frame, *A Church for a Nation*, p. 209.

59. StPCC, 6 September 1948; 1 November 1948.

60. StPCC, 8 August 1949. Gwen Jackson and Frank Colwell indicated that this was a feeling widely held in 1948 and 1949, Personal communications, June 2008.

61. StPCC, 8 August 1949. The archdeacon had agreed with this in PN, April 1947.

62. See PN, March, April, May and July 1947; June and August 1948.

63. PN, March 1949.

64. P Hempenstall, *The Meddlesome Priest. A Life of Ernest Burgmann*, Allen & Unwin, Sydney, 1993, p. 263.

65. CT, 13 May 1949.

66. PN, May 1939.

67. W Weale to Bishop Burgmann, 10 March 1940, StJ Archives, First Series 1913–1947, P.14/10–P14/14.

68. Bishop Burgmann to Archdeacon Robertson, 23 May 1939, NLA, Papers of Bishop Burgmann, MS1998, Box 34.

69. Robertson to Bishop Burgmann, 30 May 1939, NLA, MS1998, Box 34.

70. Robertson, 'The Ven. Charles Shearer Robertson: Some Memories', p. 3. Also Correspondence between Robertson and Burgmann, 6 May 1939; 23 May 1939; and November 1940, NLA, Papers of Bishop Burgmann, MS1998, Box 34.

71. Joan Thurlow, Personal communication, August 2008.

72. Bill Thurlow, Personal communication, August 2008.

73. CT, 9 November 1941.

74. PN, March 1949.

10   'A vital Anglican centre', 1949–1959

The early 1950s were a 'turning point' in Canberra's development, bolstered by Prime Minister Menzies' decision to expedite the transfer of the Public Service, to encourage the expansion of the city and to 'draw Canberra out of the doldrums'.[1] Parliament set up a Senate Select Committee on the Development of Canberra late in 1954 and its influential report paved the way for the creation of the National Capital Development Commission (NCDC) in 1957. This body planned new residential areas, established local centres with shops, schools and recreational facilities, linked existing suburbs by appropriate roads and created the lake that was appropriately named after Walter Burley Griffin. The Church of England was caught up in the euphoria, opening new churches and creating new parishes north and south of the river. The two denominational schools accepted increasing enrolments and planned new buildings and St Mark's Memorial Library offered theological resources to clergy and laity alike. The initial expansion, however, occurred at St Paul's Manuka from the end of 1949.

Before leaving Canberra, Archdeacon Robertson chaired a meeting to investigate 'the desirability of establishing a separate Parish with St Paul's as its centre'. The 29 parishioners agreed to the proposal, Gordon Armstrong added 'his warm support', and a five-person committee was appointed to confer with the bishop and St John's council.[2] By August 1949, the committee reported that Burgmann was not averse to the concept. Archdeacon Robert Davies, the new rector of St John's, thought that it 'might be given a trial' and that St John's council, although 'not enthusiastic about the separation,' would 'not raise any serious opposition' if the matter were pressed.[3]

There were two issues of concern. The first was the attitude of Robertson who, according to Reg Coombe, had seen Canberra South as a 'poor relation of Canberra North'. He had sketched a map of the proposed parish with a 'dividing line' that wandered 'about the district selecting the cottage of a parishioner here and rejecting one there', a proposition that was 'wholly preposterous' and designed 'to attach about half the settled area of the southside to St John's'. In a private letter, Coombe urged Burgmann to see through Robertson's intentions.[4] The second issue concerned finance. Realising that St Paul's had not even met its assessment target for 1948, the committee members prepared a budget 'for a minimum expenditure of approximately £1,250 per annum', a conservative estimate that did not include provision for a curate whose input would soon be required.[5]

When the parishioners met in October 1949, they accepted the report but realised that the committee was divided over the time of its implementation. Some wished to take 'immediate steps' to form a new parish while others desired to defer it for two years. Two meetings and four or five hours later, the parishioners decided to recommend immediate implementation by a vote of fifteen to eight.[6] The bishop, however, had already determined to make changes pending the probable creation of a new parish – Gordon Armstrong would be transferred to Adelong as rector on 1 March 1950 and Ross Border would take his place at St Paul's.[7] Border, considered to be financially adept, was travelling around the diocese seeking funds for the Canberra Grammar School, having already transformed 'a huge debt' at Barmedman into a 'considerable credit balance' in four years while simultaneously completing his own studies for a degree in law.[8]

A few months later the bishop invited the Reverend JT Ross Border – a hard worker, academic, fund-raiser and inspirer of people – to accept the position of priest-in-charge at Manuka. Davies and Border met, discussed issues and pondered how to overcome the differences between the two 'factions' at St Paul's, suggesting the creation of a parochial district as an intermediate step. This would assist all parties, 'test the financial strength of St Paul's' and give the parishioners 'an opportunity to *prove* that they can pay' their way.[9] The bishop was more optimistic, however and, after waiting for St John's council to indicate its approval, authorised the creation of a parish to include 'that part of the city and suburbs of Canberra to the south of the Molonglo' and

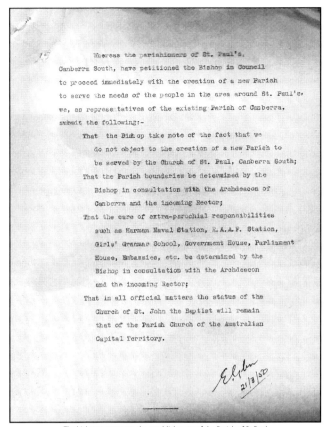

Whereas the parishioners of St. Paul's,
Canberra South, have petitioned the Bishop in Council
to proceed immediately with the creation of a new Parish
to serve the needs of the people in the area around St. Paul's,
we, as representatives of the existing Parish of Canberra,
submit the following:-

    That the Bishop take note of the fact that we
    do not object to the creation of a new Parish to
    be served by the Church of St. Paul, Canberra South;
    That the Parish boundaries be determined by the
    Bishop in consultation with the Archdeacon of
    Canberra and the incoming Rector;
    That the care of extra-parochial responsibilities
    such as Harman Naval Station, R.A.A.F. Station,
    Girls' Grammar School, Government House, Parliament
    House, Embassies, etc. be determined by the
    Bishop in consultation with the Archdeacon
    and the incoming Rector;
    That in all official matters the status of the
    Church of St. John the Baptist will remain
    that of the Parish Church of the Australian
    Capital Territory.

The bishop consents to the establishment of the Parish of St Paul
E Gbn = Ernest, Goulburn   © *St Paul's Archives*

proclaimed the Parish of St Paul, disregarding Robertson's former boundary suggestions.[10]

At 45 years of age, Border had an impressive academic background, a Licentiate in Theology, bachelors and masters degrees in Arts (Syd.) and a Bachelor of Laws (Qld). He had served in Armidale, Tamworth, Binalong and Tarcutta before his appointment as an RAAF chaplain. Following uniformed service he was appointed rector of Barmedman.[11] Described as friendly and organised, 'a man's man' who was said to incur the bishop's irritation when he played rugby union on Saturdays, he could exhibit a slight aloofness when he wished.[12] After meeting Davies, Border wrote that he was 'looking forward' to working with him 'more than I have ever looked forward to anything'. 'The challenge has gripped me most intensely and I am straining at the leash to get cracking on the job'. He said he would be 'most deeply disappointed' if anything went awry 'with the bishop's plans', and concluded, 'I'm sure we can work as a team there and make Canberra really a live and vital Anglican centre.'[13] Three months later, he was to be the rector of the new parish, an appointment that opened up new and exciting possibilities while posing demanding challenges.

As a large congregation assembled at St Paul's for his induction on 26 March 1950, the participants robed themselves in the old hall, the choir boys marshalled in the grounds and the procession moved into the church. Canon Garnsey, headmaster of Canberra Grammar School, proclaimed the existence of the parish and the bishop inducted Border as rector, handing him the keys of the church 'with all rights, profits and appurtenances thereto belonging'. The *Te Deum* was sung, addresses were delivered, the choir led the singing and the procession eventually filed out with due 'solemnity and pageantry'.[14]

The procession, 26 March 1950. The tennis court and clubhouse are in the background.   © *St Paul's Archives*

The parish was created in troubled times. World tensions existed as the Cold War escalated and Russia exploded an atomic device, causing consternation in the west. Fears of communism were further raised with the proclamation of the Peoples' Republic of China. In Australia there were disorderly strikes, with coal mine closures and interruption to production resulting in claims that communists were trying 'to wreck the country' and prompting the new Menzies government to promise legislation to outlaw the Communist Party.[15] While rationing had been lifted on some goods, petrol rationing was reimposed late in 1949. Electricity was still rationed in Canberra and there was a scarcity of building materials. Additionally, there was an epidemic of poliomyelitis across Australia, but especially rampant across the south-east areas of New South Wales, causing anxiety among young parents and dismay to the medical fraternity.[16]

In Canberra itself, the population had jumped to almost 19,000 with 'more than 1,200 migrants from European countries' arriving in the city during 1949, the intake being 'too fast' and the existing machinery unable 'to cope with it'. Over 300 houses were constructed during the year but there were 'more than 2,300 families' awaiting homes. Public servants were told 'they must wait 33 months from the time of their application', while those who worked in private enterprise were simply 'left hoping'. New shops were needed to serve over 8,000 people on the northside while only five hotels served the entire city, resulting in deplorable drinking conditions at the 5pm rush hour. On a positive note, Canberra elected its first member to the House of Representatives (Jim Fraser, a parishioner of St Paul's) and the commencement of buildings for the Australian National University (ANU) 'pushed the National Capital a step further ahead'. The administrative block opposite Parliament House was taking shape, temporary administrative offices were completed near the Hotel Kurrajong and extensions were proceeding to the Cotter Dam. Overall, the 'dreams of 25 years' began to spiral to fruition and it was hoped that the Department of the Interior would develop the city into 'the promised land' pledged 'in the days of long ago'.[17]

Moreover, it was reported that a religious revival was taking place with increased church attendances, 'a greater number of younger

1951 Powerhouse facing Wentworth Avenue; the Causeway (top left); Narrabundah (top right); Kingston (right of Wentworth Avenue).   © ACT Heritage Library, DCT Collection

people taking part in church activities', and the growing strength of organisations affiliated with the churches. Davies believed that the reawakening 'had become most noticeable over the last few months' as young people looked for leadership and found hope in religion. An Anglican Men's Movement had been commenced in Canberra with strong membership, the Young Anglicans and Junior Anglicans were 'receiving a steady flow of members', and the Women's Guilds were playing 'a great part in a reawakening of the affairs of the church'. While Armstrong, still at St Paul's, suggested it was too early to judge the long-term effects, the churches of other denominations reported similar increases in attendance and interest.[18]

In a flurry of activity, Border enthused the church council with a widened vision. Church organisations were rostered to provide refreshments after Evensong and parish parties were commenced so that people could enjoy fellowship together. The rector began a systematic visitation of the parish, calling on 250 homes in eight months but found that he could not keep pace with growth and had to 'retrace his steps in certain streets'. Inside the church he accepted Arthur Bird's offer to train an adult choir and 24 members soon appeared in colourful robes, transforming the Evening Service with 'special music of a high standard'. Realising that assistance might be required in other centres, he appointed Don Youngman and Henry Speagle as the first two lay readers in the parish and the council authorised the commencement of a quarterly magazine, *The Pauline,* devoted to south-side activities and sponsored by local businesses.[19]

Like Robertson before, Border continued weekly religious instruction at the Girls' Grammar School and visited Telopea Park and Canberra High School to instruct all grades from kindergarten to Leaving Certificate level, commenting on the amount of preparation required in the older classes which 'have as many as 80 pupils in them'. Being an ex-RAAF chaplain himself, he was appointed reserve chaplain at HMAS *Harman* and conducted services every Friday afternoon as well as 'other duties of a compassionate nature'. As time went by, he delegated this responsibility to the assistant clergy, Lawson James and Bill Pryce.

Within a year, there was 'a vast improvement in Evensong attendances' and a 'steady improvement in the 8am Eucharist', although the 11am service continued small in numbers. A dedication festival was well attended and the service was broadcast over ABC radio, the first from St Paul's.[20] Five of the clergy from Canberra Grammar School assisted the church, while Bishop Burgmann, Kenneth Clements (the assistant bishop of the diocese) and other dignitaries attended on special occasions. The first year of the new parish was characterised by energy and assiduous enterprise.

Border knew, however, that a daunting building program lay before the parishioners, one that would tax their faith and their ability to pay. They had worked for eleven years to repay the original church debt, one now reduced to a mere £59, but were they prepared to incur further heavy debt?[21] He believed they would if given appropriate leadership and he set out to provide the direction. The parish was divided into sections and parcelled out to councillors who called at every house 'enquiring for Church of England people' and endeavouring to persuade them to contribute through the envelope system or 'to provide a bank order' as a contribution. With extra money available and with the help of the Women's Guild, the existing debt was liquidated and the church was no longer encumbered by August 1950.

The Building Committee recommended that the church site be enlarged 'by an additional frontage of 100 feet [33 metres] on Captain Cook Crescent', approval being granted by the end of 1950. An application to construct a rectory in the church grounds was successful and tenders called, a new loan was negotiated and the men of the parish organised working bees to dig the foundations and assist the contractors during 1951.[22] By August the bishop dedicated the rectory, the Border family 'took up residence' in November and the parishioners gratefully erected a plaque to Mrs Wright who had contributed more than £500 to the project.[23]

With the rector no longer leasing a cottage, some thought that money would be saved but they soon learned otherwise. The rented house would also be retained, possibly for a curate, the first to be appointed at St Paul's. Moreover, overall costs increased as the rector's salary was raised to £526 a year with a transport allowance of £200, insurance was taken out to cover the rectory for £7,200 and funds were set aside to assist a fledgling 'daughter church' at Yarralumla. Moreover, a new church hall was required, a second tennis court was being mooted and there were serious moves to extend the church, even to increase the proposed height of the church tower which had previously been modified to save funds.[24] With all this in mind, the church treasurer presented his report in March 1953, informing the council that the general balance was in debt by £22 while the Building Fund had only £42 in account. In short, there were grandiose plans but the church had no money. The aim to raise £500 by the end of the year for the Yarralumla community raised further anxiety.[25]

Undeterred, Border urged the council to support Reg Coombe's offer to establish a new Church Building Fund, one eventually created in July 1952 with Reg as secretary. For added measure, funds were committed to enclose the tennis pavilion as a classroom for the burgeoning Sunday school. So much was happening that the council took out a public risk insurance policy for £1,000 to cover the work of the rector, the new curate (25-year-old Edgar Rolfe[26]) and the Reverend Harold Hunter who had been appointed to the staff of the Canberra Grammar School and gave unstinted support to the work at St Paul's over a five-year period.[27] In May 1953 the rector outlined proposals to complete the church building and presented cost estimates for survey work and potential alterations. He advised that guarantors for a bank loan had been arranged and asked council to agree to his actions, 'provided the bank is agreeable to advancing the loan and the diocese consents to the contracting of the debt'.[28] Events moved rapidly and the council formulated the wording of the inscription on the foundation stone to be set by the Governor-General on 22 November 1953, a week after foundations had been poured.

In an open air ceremony, during which 'heavy thunder rolled across the sky' and 800 spectators 'sought shelter under umbrellas, trees or in cars during the singing of hymns', a massed choir of 200 from St John's, St Paul's and the two Anglican schools provided choral items, supported by the Canberra City Band. Bishop Moyes of Armidale welcomed Sir William Slim and requested the Governor-General to set the stone, watched by Anglican clergy, the high commissioners for Ceylon and New Zealand, Aubrey Martensz (Head of the Diplomatic Corps) and the Leader of the Opposition, Dr HV Evatt. His Excellency set the stone 'in the name of God the Father, God the Son and God the Holy Ghost'. When wicker baskets were handed around, £750 was collected for the church extensions while 'pluvius insurance' (for rain) returned an extra £100.[29]

Completing the church was not easy. The quality of the bricks was poor and replacements were required. Labour was short, additional fund-raising activities were needed and normal maintenance was still necessary on the church buildings and grounds. Moreover, stipends were increasing, children's services were hampered by the lack of suitable accommodation and increasing populations at Yarralumla and Narrabundah required new ventures. There were constant com-

The temporary wall at the front of the church before extensions in 1955. © *St Paul's Archives*

plaints that the church was cold in winter and the organ needed constant repairs. By September 1955 the tower was completed and parishioners were optimistic until the treasurer revealed that the overdraft of £6,000 was exhausted and that further funds were required. The bank fortunately raised the overdraft to £12,000 'to meet increased costs and a larger project than was originally intended.'[30] Eventually, by June 1956, with 'tiles still on the ground and scaffolding in place', the bulldozer was readied for ground works, while volunteers sanded and treated the church floor.[31]

The rector later acknowledged the work of 206 volunteers who had dug foundations, tied the steel, poured the concrete and saved over £900. Volunteer carpenters had put the roof on the vestries and laid the bearers and joists while plumbers had worked on the ambulatories. Electricians had installed the electrical systems, painters had primed all timbers and engineers had surveyed the land for drainage. In fact, an open invitation had been extended 'to every tradesman who called himself an Anglican' to volunteer for Saturday work on the building, thereby saving hundreds of pounds. Then, realising that more would be required inside the church, Border sought a few gifts:

> Seven pews for the nave; four pews for the choir; a Bishop's chair; a Bishop's desk; a lectern to match the pulpit; altar frontals; new carpeting; an organ; a pulpit lectern and light; an organ seat; a table for the priest's vestry; chairs for the priest's vestry; cupboards for the choir vestry and priest's vestry; stained glass windows [and] rear choir screens.[32]

The weather was kind and the 'sun shone brightly' for the early Eucharist on 18 November 1956 when the rector was the celebrant to a packed church, 'the Dean of Sydney [the Very Reverend Stuart Barton Babbage] preached and the Bishop of Armidale [Moyes] pontificated'. At the children's service, the Scouts, Cubs and Guides presented their colours in the church, the children from Yarralumla and Narrabundah Sunday schools attended and all heard a 'captivating talk by Bishop Moyes'. The 2pm service of dedication was one of pageantry and colour with a guard of honour for His Excellency the Governor-General and Lady Slim and for the assembled bishops and other dignitaries. The servers and cross-bearers were robed in white albs and wore coloured apparels of red, green, gold and floral designs, while the choir added to the occasion – the boys in black cassocks and white surplices, the girls in white frocks and veils and the men and women in red cassocks, white surplices and red Canterbury caps. Visiting priests wore colourful academic dress and the robes and mitres of Bishops Burgmann, Moyes and Gordon Arthur (the assistant bishop of the diocese) added splashes of green and gold to the ceremony. Then quietness descended as the choir, trained by Mim Wrigley, sang the anthem, 'Behold the Tabernacle of God' and the sentence of dedication was read by Arthur and signed by Burgmann.[33]

All viewed with pride the chancel and sanctuary, the tower and vestries and a new section of the nave, the total building capable of seating 320 people and being 'longer than the floor of Albert Hall'. The old 'St John's' organ was placed in the tower loft, although its tone was more muffled in its new location. At the back of the church a piece of fabric stone from Westminster Abbey had been placed in the wall, a gift from the dean and chapter of the great abbey. The pioneer ladies of the church were not forgotten as the congregation gazed at the 'magnificent stained glass window' – 'The Ascension of our Lord' – a gift of the St Paul's Women's Guild to the parish church at a cost of £1,500. It was believed that this window 'being placed in the largest Anglican Church in the Capital Territory' should pay homage to 'the countless women throughout the Commonwealth who have worked for the Glory of God in His Church'. At the conclusion of the service, all were introduced to Charles Gumley who had 'supervised the work throughout for no profit at all,' saving the church over £2,000. The rector, the council and the congregation presented him with a silver tea and coffee service and tray 'as a mark of appreciation for all his services'.[34]

With the extensions completed, the accounts were finalised. The council had commenced the extension project with 'virtually nothing in hand' and had borrowed £12,000, but the parishioners had also contributed £7,250 by volunteering their labour and donating £2,400 for furnishings and £1,500 for the stained glass window.[35] During the remainder of Border's incumbency, it was not possible to pursue further construction projects and the old tin hall, said to be in 'fair condition' in 1957, still played a vital part in the day-to-day life of the church. The rector, however, was more critical of the hall describing it 'as out of date as a T-model Ford'.[36]

The financial challenges facing the parishioners during the 1950s were acute. Canberra's population jumped from 15,156 in 1947 to

Extensions to St Paul's 1955 © St Paul's Archives

28,277 in 1955, during the period in which St Paul's parish was created and coinciding with a postwar baby boom, the development of new suburbs and the spiralling effects of inflation. With church and rectory debts to repay, the council emphasised weekly giving, members again knocked on doors to find new sources of income and Border and the curates visited homes to urge church participation. Fetes were held, including one at the Prime Minister's Lodge when, with the blessing of Mrs Pattie Menzies, stalls were erected in the grounds and 600 people enjoyed pony rides, hoop-la competitions, lucky dips and copious quantities of food. Over £1,000 was raised, allowing the Ladies' Guild to meet the final cost of the memorial windows.[37] Additionally, the St Paul's ball was recommenced in the Albert Hall in 1949, an annual event that helped to publicise the church and provide a useful source of income.

It was a losing battle, however, as the church found it impossible to cover its costs which were compounded by rising inflation. The rector's salary, only £500 early in 1950, rose to £1,500 in 1955 plus £600 for travelling allowances, while the stipends and allowances of all staff reached £3,700 in 1956. A church secretary was employed in 1955 (mercifully relieving the rector's wife of much of the parish organisation), holiday and sick leave provisions were introduced for the clergy and insurances on church property escalated. Additional funds were needed to meet youth programs and to provide 31 weekly classes of religious instruction by the clergy and their eight lay helpers – a total of 1,116 school lessons during 1955. The addition of extra classes at Yarralumla and Telopea Park in 1956 required fourteen lay teachers. At the church, special provision had to be made for 109 baptisms in a year.[38]

The task was beyond the church's resources and the parish turned to the Wells Scheme, a USA-based fund-raising system that was introduced to Australia in the 1950s. The parish council paid a fee to this organisation to explain the scheme and to tutor selected church members in its procedures. A list of every Anglican member in the parish was prepared (whether church attender or not), the region was divided into zones to which canvassers were appointed and every home was visited. Each canvasser was trained to gain an invitation into homes ('never on the doorstep') to outline the work of the church, to emphasise the joys of sacrificial giving and to seek definite pledges of financial support 'commensurate' with each family's income. Small pledges were considered demeaning and generous givers were deemed to be those who pledged 5 per cent of their income over three years. The rector believed that this 'veritable revolution in Australian church financing' could mean 'the disappearance of bazaars and such things as means of raising money'. Bishop Burgmann considered that the Wells Scheme 'jolted many congregations' to take seriously 'the sacrificial giving on which the church should live and grow'.[39] Many church members were uneasy and some objected outright but most accepted, often with reluctance, and went from door-to-door gaining pledges. By August 1955 the council paid almost £3,000 to the Wells organisation in fees but had received 500 pledges for almost £36,000 from the parish, including Yarralumla and Narrabundah. Mrs Border was thankful that the new church secretary overviewed the organisation from the tin shed and that the rectory dining room table was spared. A 'Loyalty Dinner' was organised to remind faithful parishioners of their obligations and to gain further pledges over time, a function deemed to host 'the biggest crowd to be served at one sitting at any function in Canberra'. A supplementary loyalty dinner for newcomers to the church increased pledges by £2,000 in 1956 and a further £4,500 in 1957, £2,000 of which was earmarked for the 'new parish of St Luke at Yarralumla'[40] (see chapter 15).

The first pledging session was an unqualified success as the church repaid more than £9,000 to the bank, leaving a capital debt of £10,000 to be repaid at the rate of £2,000 a year plus interest. The council provided £8,000 for the stipends and living costs of the rector, two assistant priests and a secretary over three years and another £1,000 for a parish car and travel for the assistant clergy. A total of £600 was allocated for teaching materials – projectors, daylight screens, film strips, prayer books, choir hymn books and psalters, £950 on utility payments and organ repairs, £750 on diocesan commitments and £2,000 on 'charitable causes' including missions. Little wonder that the rector and the council were enthusiastic and espoused the Wells Scheme with zeal. The bishop was likewise impressed and no-one expressed surprise when Border was made a canon of St Saviour's Cathedral at the synod early in 1957.

By 1958 pledging began again, this time over a two-year cycle without the input of Wells. The rector sought in excess of £20,000, his expansive plans including additional clergy, a kindergarten room, a youth centre, a women's club room and church hall, 'an adequate organ', heating for the church and a chapel and hall at Narrabundah. While the church was required to maintain repayments on the rectory at £300 a year plus interest, he also wished to extend 'missionary giving and charitable undertakings'. Border's message was uncompromising: 'Our need is for sacrificial giving – giving that really costs us something, giving that is planned and deliberate'.[41]

The new canvass moved more slowly as pledges inched toward £16,000 but Border asserted 'that the prospects for the year ahead were equally as bright' as in past years. It would be a year 'of consolidation' with some expansion, particularly at Red Hill and along the Cooma Road at Narrabundah.[42] Secretly, however, he wished for a greater response and persuaded the council to approach the bank to relax repayments on the church to £1,000 a year, not £2,000, and requiting a lower figure of £500 to the diocese off the rectory account.[43]

These adjustments allowed more flexibility while the church still met its commitment to the Yarralumla Church, planned for a new church hall and opened a fund for a new church organ. Hence the 1955 and 1958 canvasses were crucial to the expansionary plans of the parish and without them sustained growth would not have been possible. It was the commencement of a business approach to budgeting and to fund-raising.

Border's continuing quest for funds arose from his own spirituality and his commitment to spread the word of God. St Paul's School of Christian Knowledge was developed in 1953 for those who sought 'to discuss the basis of their religious faith in an intelligent and informed manner'. A midweek study program over seven weeks was provided by the bishop, the local clergy and by Christian academics from the ANU.[44] Special Lent services attracted 'big crowds', harvest festivals were reintroduced, transport was provided for the elderly and crèche facilities were developed. Border's sermons were particularly dynamic. He wrote them out in longhand, read them to himself repeatedly and then delivered them forcefully without notes, a beautifully crafted presentation aided by his legal and 'photographic' memory. Adept also at writing, he contributed to the spiritual growth of the parish through articles in *The Pauline* over a ten-year period. Combining with the Church Army during 1956–57, he organised children's missions at Yarralumla, Narrabundah and St Paul's to maintain the interest of the youth and encourage their full church participation. While it was hard work conducting confirmation sessions spread over months, classes were considered crucial to spiritual growth and the priests emphasised their importance, all being heartened when the bishop confirmed large numbers each year.[45]

The rector maintained a middle-of-the-road approach to Anglicanism, combined with an evangelistic style suited to an increasing population. He encouraged music, a robed choir, the 1950 revision of *Hymns Ancient & Modern* and moderate ritual. When a number of priests were ordained at St Paul's in 1956, he commented that 'the spacious chancel and sanctuary' of the church made 'ancient and lovely old English procedures' possible.[46] His

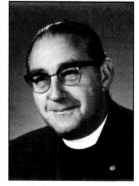

The Reverend Ross Border
© Framing Matters, Manuka

sense of 'English procedures' was undoubtedly heightened during February 1954 when Queen Elizabeth II and the Duke of Edinburgh worshipped at St John's and Border acted as one of the bishop's chaplains. On that day, 240 selected parishioners packed the small church, 2,000 people listened to the amplified service outside and 3,000 lined the approaches to the lych gate, while the choirs from St Paul's Manuka and St Clement's Yass led *al fresco* singing in the church grounds.[47]

Continuing the church's developing musical tradition, the adult choir under Arthur Bird led Evensong and branched out to present carols and excerpts from 'The Messiah' in combination with choristers from St Clement's, Yass.[48] After Ted Le Mesurier conducted the choir for a short period, Mrs Mim Wrigley became choirmistress and was sponsored by the parish council to attend the summer school of the Royal School of Church Music in 1956. Inspired by its message, she taught the choir and the congregation 'how to sing the chants and music recommended' at the school and invited Dr Gerald Knight, the Director of the Royal School of Church Music in London, to visit St Paul's and instruct the choirs from St John's, St Clements Yass and St Paul's. The following year the choir presented a festival of music with anthems, quartets, duets and solos and performed at both the 11am service and Evensong, delighting all with the high standard attained.[49] When John Barrett, the organist and choirmaster of St Andrew's, Brighton, Victoria, visited St Paul's in 1959, choirs from Canberra, Cooma, Goulburn, Temora and Queanbeyan descended on St Paul's for another festival.

In the meantime the antiquated organ from St John's – dismantled, repaired and removed to the loft at a cost of £73 in 1956 – met the requirements of the church despite a mounting desire for something better.[50] Reg Coombe had already sought to initiate 'a fund for the purchase of a larger organ' in 1958 and the festivals of music highlighted the need for something more appropriate. It was left to the rector to find a solution in 1959 when he heard that Taralga parish was disposing of an organ. The Women's Guild paid £110 for the organ, Mr Roach installed it and the old organ went to St Luke's at Deakin. Mim Wrigley enjoyed playing the new instrument although she was concerned that she extracted more volume but less quality. Nevertheless, she promptly organised another festival of music for 1960.[51]

The Women's Guild, with Mrs Border as president, devoted its activities to the spiritual and social needs of its members and ran the annual ball and church fete to pay off the church's mortgages. The guild aided the Mothers' Union, a related support group for mothers with small children. Ladies were elected to the parish council although, at the diocesan level, their influence was limited and it was not until 1957 that synod 'unanimously agreed that women should be eligible for membership' and urged that the constitution be altered in order to permit the change.[52] The men organised working bees to maintain the church, rectory and grounds, planting shrubs and tending lawns. They repaired the old tin church, covered the floor with masonite, helped repair the church roof, enclosed the tennis club pavilion and resurfaced the court itself. The Anglican Men's Movement, so strong in 1950–1951, declined however and required resuscitation by Jim Monro early in 1959 with the prompting of the rector.[53]

Effective programs for children and youth were thwarted by the lack of accommodation and, as Sunday school teachers 'valiantly [tried] to cope with a situation which was impossible', the church altered the Sunday school to a children's service in 1950. This allowed 50 kindergarten children to meet in the old hall while 200 others met in the church for opening worship, after which those of secondary school age retired to the tennis pavilion for Bible study. Harold Hunter, formerly headmaster of Mittagong School, taught the primary-age children in the church as one group with the aid of flannelgraph boards and pictures painted by gifted children. The children 'learnt to sing the Eucharist' and completed a simple study of Matins 'including the singing of the Responses, the Venite, Te Deum, Jubilate and selected Psalms'. There was no lack of volunteers from the children when invited to assist as junior servers and sidesmen and all were encouraged to go on to the Junior Anglicans and Young Anglicans at a later stage.[54] When the church extensions were completed in 1956, the rector was thankful that 'we are now able to accommodate another 100 extra children' but it was 'quite obvious that we need a further building' in which those 'of primary school age can be taught'. By the end of the year, some of the older children were diverted to the 8am service.[55] Religious instruction in schools was no less demanding, 1,400 classes being taught each year by three ladies at Yarralumla, three at Narrabundah, three at Telopea Park and five at

Griffith Primary Schools. There were constant appeals for additional support as the clergy sought to confine their own ministrations to 4,200 home visits in three years, 354 church services each year and extended classes for about 75 confirmees.[56]

The Young Anglicans were involved in barbeques, community singing, parties, dances and camps, sometimes combining with other church groups across Canberra. In addition to their bi-monthly meetings, they attended a regular corporate Communion, were assisted in their studies by the curates and often provided refreshments for the congregation after Evensong. Moreover, with a wide range of trade skills among their members, they helped to renovate the hall and paint the interior.[57] A younger group (fifteen to eighteen years) was not well provided for, prompting the church to revitalise a Junior Anglican Group in 1959 with an average attendance of 40 at dances, games, films, barbeques and tennis matches.[58] The Scout and Cub troops catered for another 40 boys who sought to be self-supporting through the Bob-a-Job program but were happy to take time off for Sunday school picnics at Acton Park and to join in planned 'frolics'. The boys organised a fete in the church grounds with 'stalls, mini-golf, Aunt Sally, hoop-la and what not with great gusto' and equalled their organisational skills 'by the energy and determination with which they consumed toffee apples, hot dogs and bags of sweets.'[59]

St Paul's reached out into the community to a degree not seen in previous years. Special services were arranged, the bishop visited more often and annual reports listed the names of influential clergy, academics, politicians and community persons who visited the parish. ABC radio broadcasts were requested on a regular basis and St Paul's became a centre at which recently ordained deacons and priests were introduced to parish life. One of Border's curates later recalled the precision with which the rector worked – well-prepared staff meetings, weekly reports on activities and help for new clergy. Border was a dynamic and visionary leader.[60] Eventually clergy were ordained at the church with appropriate ritual, two choirs, good music and an enthusiastic congregation.

On a personal level Border continued his own studies and published a 56-page book in 1956 entitled *The Founding of the See of Goulburn.* As he reflected on the problem of disparate diocesan synods, the fractured General Synod and the need for a clear and workable constitution, his research resulted in the publication of a major constitutional study on the Church of England in Australia in 1962.[61] Later in life he wrote an authoritative article on Thomas Hobbes Scott, the first archdeacon in New South Wales.[62] No-one ever accused Border of leisurely inactivity. His scholarship and approach encouraged parishioners to believe he would soon be offered an episcopal appointment. To the surprise of many and to Border's own disappointment, the invitation never came.

Border's ten-year contribution to St Paul's was highly significant but the Manuka church was only one aspect of his legacy and other suburbs also benefited from his leadership. With a rapid increase in Canberra's population, the government announced in July 1946 that a site at Narrabundah would be surveyed and tenders called for the erection of houses.[63] Almost overnight this flat and dusty region turned into a feverish building site as a sewerage system was put down, stormwater drains were constructed, tenders were let for 68 houses in Narrabundah and Griffith and prefabricated homes were ordered from Britain. A plan to complete twelve homes each month was quickly exceeded – 525 were under construction in September 1947 and another 130 planned.[64] Fibro dwellings sprouted as the first 196 residents arrived in 1947, a school bus service was commenced to

Narrabundah's prefabricated housing, 1951.
© ACT Heritage Library, Department of Capital Territory's Pictorial Record of Canberra, 1951-53.

Telopea Park and St Christopher's Catholic School, a shopping centre developed in Boolimba Street, roads were formed at a rapid pace and trees and shrubs were planted to enhance the environment and reduce its starkness. A community hall, mothercraft centre, pre-school and tennis court were constructed but difficulties were still experienced in providing sufficient shops, schools and recreational facilities as the Narrabundah population reached 3,382 in 1954.[65]

By mid-1951 the Salvation Army had commenced a witness in the new suburb and Border accepted that it would be necessary to provide a residence and stipend for an Anglican priest as well.[66] At that time, however, Border had no assistant priest, had already discontinued the 11am service at St Paul's to provide a presence at Yarralumla and could do little more than visit homes during the week and invite the new arrivals to services at St Paul's. Then he saw an opportunity at the Narrabundah Infants School in 1952 (although it was not officially opened until March 1953) and arranged for a parishioner to conduct religious instruction for Anglican children.

While the council negotiated a suitable church site with the Department of the Interior in 1953, financial restrictions prevented further progress.[67] Nevertheless, something had to be done and it forced Reg Coombe to act. Working virtually alone, he secured the use of the Narrabundah Community Hall, invited local children to a Sunday school on 1 August 1954 and was rewarded when 44 children attended, followed by 43 the following week and 51 the next. For the remainder of the year he led the group but asked Border, Harold Hunter and the assistant priest, Stanley Ford, to provide some assistance. This was a prudent move as they became aware of the challenges involved.[68]

Eventually the rector wrote to the department in October 1954 indicating that the Narrabundah Hall was 'too small for our purposes' and applying for a block of land for a 'hall-chapel combined structure and a [priest's] residence'. His request was successful and the church was granted a 99-year lease on land at an annual rent of £40 (10 per cent of the land value), provided it submitted a plan of proposed buildings, their purposes and the times at which they would be constructed.[69] Border then advised parishioners that the 'Sunday school and kindergarten would be held in the Narrabundah Infants School' from February 1955, a venture that continued under the direction of Reg Coombe for a further three years until his resignation in September 1957.[70]

Coombe's retirement forced the church to further action and the rector was fortunate to have the
assistance of Lawson James, who was ordained at St
Paul's in December 1956. James assumed responsibility for the Sunday school, worked closely with the
superintendent, Mr W Evans, from late 1957 until
1959 and appointed three new teachers as numbers
increased. On James' departure, the rector asked the

The Reverend W Pryce
© Bertram Family Album

new curate, Bill Pryce, to replace him and requested his own secretary,
Deidre Baldwin, a graduate of St Christopher's College in Melbourne,
to train the teachers in 'up-to-date teaching methods'. Fortunately,
accommodation was not a difficulty as the venture continued in the
Narrabundah School until early 1960 when difficult decisions were
required about the future of the centre.[71]

Education in a wider sense was destined to provoke considerable
controversy during the 1950s as increasing numbers of public servants arrived from Melbourne with the expectation of enrolling their
children in independent schools. The Canberra Grammar School
was now the legal responsibility of the diocese and Canon Garnsey
had replaced Canon Edwards as headmaster. As enrolments climbed
beyond 200 in 1951 and bordered on 300 in 1960, the Department of
the Interior granted an extra 20 acres of land, the grounds eventually
reaching Flinders Way and Mugga Way.[72] This allowed the school to
erect a war memorial gymnasium and invite Prime Minister Menzies
to set the foundation stone in July 1954. With additional classrooms
required in 1954–1955, Bishop Burgmann predicted that 'we can
reasonably expect to have 500 or 600 boys at the school within the
next five years', necessitating 'a large additional building program'.[73]
The sum of £30,000 was advanced through bank overdrafts by 1952
but the school required more to meet its future expansion.

The government was aware that the two Catholic secondary
schools and the two Anglican schools were in financial trouble and
in 1956 approached Bishop Burgmann and the Catholic Archbishop,
Eris O'Brien, offering to meet the cost of interest (up to 5 per cent)
on new non-residential secondary school buildings for 20 years.
When the news reached the press, state aid to education was fiercely

debated on radio, in newspapers, in churches and in parliament itself. Protestants accused the Roman Catholic Church of seeking aid for all its church schools. Many Anglicans believed that the necessary separation of church and state was being violated. There was a widespread fear that the funding of independent schools in Canberra would be the wedge that would ultimately lead to state aid to non-government schools throughout the Commonwealth. Burgmann, however, took the issue to synod in 1956 and argued strongly for government assistance. A motion was put that 'this council accepts the offer of the Commonwealth Government'.[74] The bishop carried the synod with him and the diocese accepted the government's proposal.

The reaction was strong as the divisive issue rippled across the diocese, involving both the clergy and their congregations. After Burgmann explained the basis of his decision to Bishop Moyes in Armidale, his colleague argued that it was 'quite idle of [Deputy Prime Minister] Fadden to suggest that what is done in Canberra does not affect the rest of Australia' and he accused Burgmann of going 'alone so often that it does not make the rest of Australia feel that you are a member of the team'. With the Anglican Primate, Archbishop Howard Mowll, 'speaking with one voice and you with another, [you have] made us a laughing stock in [Roman Catholic] eyes and I regret that with all my heart'.[75] The councillors of St John's protested against state aid. Canon Edwards asked whether this was 'part of the price demanded by Eris [O'Brien] for past and promised support'. Mowll stressed his opposition hoping that Burgmann would finally reject the offer. One postcard contained only two words, 'Judas Iscariot'.[76]

Among the diocesan clergy, Tom Whiting objected at first but was later convinced of the bishop's wisdom, while the legal-minded Ross Border penned three pages of argument in favour of the synod's decision and addressed them to Moyes.[77] 'Seldom has an important matter of a controversial nature been so affirmatively decided,' he declared, with the government's offer being 'overwhelmingly' accepted.[78] Burgmann's own muted response was pragmatic: 'If the Canberra Grammar School is arrested in its development, its future is grim' but 'if it is enabled to go forward,' it will 'become, along with the Girls' Grammar School, one of the great schools of the Commonwealth'. Burgmann, the 'meddlesome priest', quietly stated his conviction 'that the Diocesan Council made a wise and statesmanlike decision'.[79]

The board of management at Canberra Grammar School decided on a two-storey building under the new government provisions in 1956, watched construction the following year and made plans for further development. By the end of 1959 a separate Infants School had been opened on the northside in conjunction with the Girls' Grammar School, headmaster McKeown reminding parents that further debt would be involved as the school struggled to house new enrolments.[80]

The Girls' Grammar School was not the responsibility of the diocese but Burgmann was adamant that the diocese 'has always had a moral responsibility and an affiliation' with the school, a close relationship that should continue.[81] The school had serious debts but new primary classrooms were constructed or acquired in 1951 and 1953, office space was extended in 1954 and the grounds were constantly improved.[82] The school combined with Canberra Grammar School to provide joint Leaving Certificate classes in mathematics and French, a move that was educationally successful but proved impracticable because of the time involved in movement between the schools.[83] By 1956, with numbers expanding each year, the school was acclaimed to be operating most successfully but its debt was debilitating, especially when a new secondary block was contemplated.[84] In desperation it turned to synod for assistance but legalities prevented the diocese from providing funds 'for bodies outside the Church organisation'. As a last resort, the school board offered to sell the school to the diocese, an overture that was successful and the school's assets and liabilities were transferred to the Diocesan Property Trust. The school's enrolment climbed to 320 soon after.

A major diocesan initiative affecting the southside was the development of the cathedral site on Rottenberry Hill, overlooking the proposed lake and the future King's Avenue Bridge. The local clergy vaguely referred to a 'proposed cathedral' to be erected when the mood became more propitious but 'propitious times' did not eventuate and it was left to Burgmann to take the first major step in the use of the site. After observing collegiate libraries in Wales and London in 1948, Burgmann became obsessed with the creation of a theological library in Canberra and fixed his gaze steadfastly on Rottenberry Hill.[85] He was successful and over 1,000 people 'gathered in spite of uncertain weather' in 1955 when the Governor-General Sir William Slim set the foundation stone of the Anglican National Memorial Library, which became known as St Mark's Library, 'a memorial to chaplains, doctors, dentists, nurses and missionaries who gave their lives in Australia's wars'. Two years later, at the opening of the library in February 1957, 'the most colourful and impressive Anglican ceremony ever held in the National Capital' took place with 3,000 people involved. 'Bathed in warm sunshine', the Royal Military College band provided music as 800 lay Anglican officers and representatives preceded a robed procession of 200 clergy, choirs, servers and religious sisters, a prelude to 'the arrival of the Episcopal Procession of two Archbishops and 22 bishops'. 'We have come together to open and dedicate these buildings for the advancement of Christian learning,' Burgmann announced, making sure to request tax-free donations of books to the library in the process.[86]

'It is the privilege of old men to dream dreams,' said the ageing Burgmann as he and his wife, Edna, moved into a flat attached to St Mark's when he became warden of the library. The dreams did not materialise quickly, however, as funds were limited but programs began and were advertised throughout the local parishes. Lunch-hour and evening lectures were provided by the bishop and organised by a committee that included Ross Border.[87] During 1958 a Japanese priest, the Reverend Daniel Uemura, studied part-time at St Mark's Library and was attached to the staff of St Paul's Manuka.[88] The ecumenical influence of St Mark's spread slowly. When Burgmann retired as bishop in 1960 and then as warden in 1964, he left an important but mostly unfulfilled vision for others to further. In retrospect, his influence was profound.

The decade of the 1950s was clearly a golden age for St Paul's parish, headed by Ross Border who in 1950 had been 'straining at the leash' to make Canberra 'a live and vital Anglican centre'. Arriving at an opportune time as the parish was created and challenged by an ever-increasing population in the south, Border built up the congregations, the number of communicants rising from 3,410 during 1950 to 7,976 in 1957 and then to 9,571 in 1959 (including Yarralumla

The Right Reverend Ernest Henry Burgmann
© St Mark's National Memorial Library Archives

and Narrabundah).[89] The work was demanding and constant, parish organisation often difficult and financial worries ever present but the positive result was evident for all to see.

Late in 1959, Border recognised the bishop's characteristic voice on the telephone and agreed to call on him for a chat. He was told that he had done his work faithfully and was invited to become the Archdeacon of Albury. According to some, the rector was disappointed that he had not previously been called to a bishopric, a feeling made more acute when his old friend ('My Dear Bob Davies') was named Coadjutor-Bishop of Newcastle. In October 1959 Border informed the parish of his intended departure early in 1960 and advised that the Reverend Lawrence Murchison would be the new rector. The council acknowledged 'its appreciation of the long, untiring and devoted service of its first rector ... in the development of the Parish of Saint Paul', expressed its regret at his departure and extended its genuine good wishes 'on his appointment as Archdeacon of Albury'.[90] The rector spoke at all three services on Sunday 7 February 1960, his last at St Paul's, with many people being forced to remain outside 'because of limited space in the church'. Bishop Gordon Arthur, mindful of the rector's continuing contribution, paid tribute to 'the amazing work done by Canon Border in the parish and in the life of Canberra generally'.[91]

Hence, after a highly effective incumbency of ten years, Ross Border left 'a live and vital Anglican centre'. As rector he had nurtured the development of St Paul's Manuka, commenced worship centres at Yarralumla and Narrabundah and looked to the day when ministry would be required at Red Hill. Involved in educational ventures, he had staunchly supported religious instruction in public schools, contributed to the development of the two Anglican schools and enthusiastically encouraged St Mark's Memorial Library. As first rector, he had developed the parish and it was fitting that Bishop Arthur acknowledged his significant contribution to the city of Canberra as well.

Notes

1. E Sparke, *Canberra 1954–1980*, Australian Government Publishing Service, Canberra, 1988, p. 38.
2. StPCC, 1 March 1949.
3. StPCC, 8 August 1949.
4. Coombe to Burgmann, 12 March 1949, NLA, Burgmann Papers MS1998, Box 36, 'Canberra' file.
5. PN, March 1949; StPCC, 8 August 1949. The report indicated a total of £1250 but this was wrong as it totalled £1275. Evidently an item for £25 was added after the total was calculated.
6. StPCC, 10 and 25 October 1949. The speeches, for and against the motion, are recorded in StP Archives.
7. PN, January 1950.
8. SC, 1 October 1949; 1 February 1950.
9. Border to Davies, 21 December 1949. (A seven page letter in StP Archives).
10. The bishop consented to the parish, 21 March 1950. StP Archives.
11. JTR Border Superannuation Card, StJ Archives.
12. Frank Colwell, Personal communication, 2008.
13. Border to Davies, 21 December 1949.
14. PN, April 1950.
15. CT, 29 July 1949.
16. These events were reported in the CT from June 1949 to February 1950.
17. CT, 30 December 1949.
18. CT, 1 October 1949.
19. *The Pauline*, 1(4), 1951.
20. Bill Pryce, Personal communication, 2009.
21. StPPC, 8 May 1950.
22. StJPC, 3 April 1950; 12 February 1951.
23. StPPC, 3 April 1950; 14 August 1950; 9 October 1950; 13 August 1951; 12 November 1951
24. StPPC, 14 June 1951; 2 March 1952.
25. StPPC, 9 March 1953.
26. The first assistant was Edgar Rolfe (1953), followed by Stanley Ford (1954), Lawson James (1956), William Wright (1957), Daniel Uemura (1958) and William Pryce (1959).
27. StPPC, 14 July 1952; 8 September 1952; 13 October 1952.
28. StPPC, 8 June 1953.
29. CT, 23 November 1953; *The Pauline*, Christmas 1953.
30. StJPC, 28 September 1962.
31. StPPC, 18 June 1956; 20 August 1956.
32. *The Pauline*, Trinity 1956 and Christmas 1956.
33. This account is based on the report in *The Pauline*, Christmas 1956.

34. StPPC, 22 October 1956; *The Pauline*, Christmas 1956.
35. StPPC, 22 September 1962.
36. *The Pauline*, February 1957.
37. CT, 9 April 1951.
38. StPPC, 15 August 1955; 21 November 1955.
39. *The Pauline*, June 1955; Lent 1956.
40. *The Pauline*, June 1955 and September 1957; StPPC 15 August 1955.
41. *The Pauline*, April 1958.
42. StPPC, 15 February 1959.
43. StPPC, 18 August 1958.
44. *The Pauline*, March 1953.
45. *The Pauline*, February 1957. There were 18 and 64 confirmees during 1957 and, while 64 was a high number, it was not unusual for 20, 30 or 40 to be confirmed.
46. *The Pauline*, Christmas 1956.
47. SC, 52(2), 1 March 1954.
48. *The Pauline*, March 1953.
49. *The Pauline*, Trinity 1956; Christmas 1957.
50. StPPC, 17 September 1956.
51. StPPC, 20 April, 18 May and 15 June 1959.
52. *The Pauline*, June 1957.
53. *The Pauline*, n.d. (next after April, 1959). *The Pauline* and the StPPC minutes reported the group's activities from 1950 to 1958. StPPC, 17 February 1959, reported the revitalisation of the Group.
54. *The Pauline*, June 1954.
55. *The Pauline*, February 1957; StPPC, February 1957.
56. *The Pauline*, Lent 1956; April 1958.
57. *The Pauline*, June 1950; Christmas 1955; February 1957.
58. *The Pauline*, September 1959.
59. *The Pauline*, Trinity 1956.
60. Bill Pryce, Personal communication, 2009.
61. JTR Border, *Church and State in Australia 1788–1872: A Constitutional Study of the Church of England in Australia*, SPCK, London, 1962.
62. JTR Border, 'Thomas Hobbes Scott (1783–1860)', *Australian Dictionary of Biography*, vol. 2. (pp. 431–433), Melbourne University Press, Melbourne 1967.
63. Greig, 'The Accommodation of Growth: Canberra's growing pains 1945–1955', *Canberra Historical Journal*, New Series, no. 57, 2006, p. 13–14.
64. CT, 2 April 1946; 2 December 1946; 17 September 1947.
65. Greig, *The Accommodation of Growth*; CT, 30 January 1945 and 25 August 1949.
66. CT, 31 October 1951; *The Pauline*, Michaelmas 1951.
67. StPPC 8 June 1953.

68. *The Pauline,* Trinity 1952 and September 1954; StPPC 16 August 1954; StP Register of Services, 1954.

69. Secretary Department of the Interior to Border, 7 December 1954, StPPC, 20 December 1954.

70. StPPC 13 February 1955; 21 February 1955; 22 March 1955; StP Register of Services, 1954 to 1957.

71. *The Pauline,* September 1959.

72. Speech Day reports in CT, 8 December 1950; 6 December 1951; 5 December 1952.

73. Speech Day reports in CT, 10 December 1953; 13 July 1954; 10 December 1954.

74. This is the original wording proposed by Burgmann. A few words were later added for clarification, NLA, MS 1998, Box 24.

75. Moyes to Burgmann, 16 August 1956, NLA, Burgmann Papers, MS 1998, Box 24.

76. All letters are filed in NLA, MS1998, Box 24.

77. Border to Moyes, 16 August 1956, NLA, Burgmann Papers, MS1998, Box 24.

78. *The Pauline,* June 1957.

79. Burgmann's notes for SC, September 1956.

80. Headmaster's annual reports, CGS, 1956–1959.

81. SC, 1 May 1950.

82. Speech Day reports in CT, 8 December 1950; 7 December 1951.

83. Speech Day reports in CT, 4 December 1952; 11 December 1953; 9 December 1954.

84. Waterhouse, *A Light in the Bush,* p. 117.

85. Hempenstall, *The Meddlesome Priest,* pp. 311ff.

86. SC, 1 March 1957.

87. *The Pauline,* September 1957.

88. *The Pauline,* Christmas 1957.

89. StP Register of Services, 1937 to 1958.

90. StPPC 20 December 1959.

91. CT, 8 February 1960.

11   The Murchison and Munro years, the 1960s

Within a few days of Laurie Murchison's arrival, the congregation realised that it had acquired a 'package deal' – a highly spiritual man, a brilliant organist, an acclaimed academic, a Volkswagen, one or two dogs, a pipe and one 'who could live in another world'. One of his choir members once chided him with the words, 'You passed me in the street without saying hello.' Murchison replied, 'Yes I know, but I was thinking of something important.'[1]

Canon Laurence Murchison with his dog, Skipper.
© Bertram Family Album

After his earlier time in Canberra, he had served in Victorian churches, St Saviour's Cathedral, Goulburn and Bombala as well as furthering his musical studies in Britain. Now 41 years old and unmarried, Murchison was a recognised academic, a graduate of the University of Sydney with First Class Honours in English, Latin and Greek, the University Medal in Classics and two overseas diplomas in organ music. He could enjoy Greek poetry in the original text and immerse himself in Byzantine history in which he was an acknowledged authority. Gentle and spiritual by nature but eccentric in ways, he was inducted as rector of St Paul's on 22 March 1960.[2]

Since Murchison had left Canberra in 1947, the population had jumped from 15,000 to 50,000, new suburbs had been created, heavy machinery was stripping the bed of the future Lake Burley Griffin and King's Avenue Bridge was taking shape over a dry river plain.

Tenders had been called for the construction of Scrivener Dam, a new water storage facility on the Upper Cotter River was under way and tractors were levelling the site for the ANU library. The decision to expedite the transfer of the Department of Defence to Canberra resulted in a ferment of office construction at Russell Hill as well as a scramble to construct sufficient housing for the staff on its removal from Melbourne.[3]

Expansion was also rapid in Murchison's new parish where flats were being constructed near the church, the Manuka shopping precinct was being extended and developers were eyeing the hockey grounds and parklands between the church and the shops. Houses were covering Red Hill where a new primary school had been opened a few weeks before and another school at Griffith was about to open. Moreover, it was predicted that Canberra's population would reach 100,000 by 1974 and top 250,000 by the turn of the century.[4]

With Murchison's arrival, the council considered its agenda. Eight priorities had been outlined by Canon Border in 1958: pay off the church and rectory debts; increase the number of clergy; provide for an increasing population and the needs of young people; build a new hall; heat St Paul's church; develop the work at Narrabundah; provide for Red Hill when required; and maintain adequate sources of funding.[5] Murchison talked with the curate, Bill Pryce, who had carried the parish for three months, about the intensity of the work, the operation of the parish council and the inordinate effort involved in school religious instruction. Don Youngman and Jim Monro reviewed the parish finances with him, noting total receipts of £8,686 during 1959; expenditure of £7,000 (half of which was marked for stipends, salaries and allowances); the debt on the church of £6,500 and another of £2,971 on the rectory; the recent renegotiation of the bank loan to make smaller annual repayments; and a gift of £65 to start a pipe organ fund for the church.[6]

Murchison – who was installed as a canon of St Saviour's Cathedral early in 1960 – was not an administrator and the council soon provided major input into detailed planning, administrative assistance and fund-raising activities. Within eighteen months the church introduced an additional Communion Service each Sunday, arranged three confirmation services in one year for a record number of candidates, organised special 'welcome services' in May and December 1961 for parish newcomers, reintroduced crèche facilities and coordinated 100 street representatives (one person in each street) 'to act as the eyes and ears of the rector'.[7] Bill Pryce worked at a relentless pace and visited 800 homes in six months (over 30 each week) in addition to his other duties.[8]

As one of his first projects Murchison assessed the new Taralga organ and recommended the purchase of 'an electronic organ' in its place. When council voted to acquire 'an organ in three months' time, Murchison took a hasty trip to Sydney', decided on a Compton organ and had Palings deliver it 'on a sale or rejection basis'.[9] To cover the cost of £1,870, a loan of £1,100 was required after the sale of the old instrument for £100.[10] Then, following the rector's further requests, the choir boys were paid 'by attendance' instead of by prizes and dozens of hymn books were purchased for congregational use.[11] A new organist and choirmaster, John Barrett, was appointed in February 1962 and immediately proclaimed the new Compton organ to be inferior and hoped for a 'real pipe organ'. Organists, church organs and organ preferences proved to be expensive.

One of the most crucial needs was a church hall and Don Youngman crafted a letter to the church's bank, hoping that it 'might be willing to grant a loan' of £27,000.[12] When it declined, the church turned to another institution, secured the loan and accepted a tender of £20,525 for the hall, the finished building being promised in 20 weeks.[13] The grounds were readied, the fences repaired and a telephone installed in the hall in preparation for the dedication by the bishop. Keith Archer (the Commonwealth Statistician and parishioner) ceremonially opened the hall on 2 May 1964. The treasurer insured the complex for £21,000 (adding an additional £2,000 for contents) and left a few problems to be solved at a later date – the acoustic properties of the basement, the sealing of the basement floor, inadequate drainage and the allocation of space to church organisations.[14]

In the meantime, Youngman recommended that 'the outstanding debt' of £1,500 on the church be paid off and, with a sense of relief, the last payment was made, allowing Bishop Clements (by now the diocesan bishop) to consecrate St Paul's on 16 November 1963, eight years after extensions had been completed. Canon Tom Whiting appreciated a special invitation to preach and smiled wryly as he observed the old tin shed that he had promised to remove by 1946. Happily he was no longer responsible for its destiny.

As Border had predicted, the number of clergy increased and Murchison was fortunate to have the assistance of five devoted men. Bill Pryce assisted him to settle into the parish, discerning his brilliant academic scholarship, musical ability and piety but noticing that the new rector was 'one not too concerned with everyday practicalities'. In addition to normal parish duties, Pryce conducted two services a week at HMAS *Harman* where he was appointed chaplain. A loyal colleague to Murchison, Pryce was appointed rector of Warialda in 1962.[15]

Pryce was succeeded by Peter Bertram, a former local government clerk. After he was priested and appointed to St Paul's, he assumed a wide range of duties, ministering beside a rector 'who was not easy to work with'. With Laurie, 'you had one day off each year,' he recalled and were sometimes put in awkward situations. 'He ordered me to get up on the church roof and, when I declined, he demanded: "Are you defying me?" I answered that I was but that I also wished to preserve my safety. We clashed over three years but Laurie

The Reverend Peter Bertram
© *Bertram Family Album*

didn't hold resentments.' He was 'a brilliant man with a big heart' but one who could 'get people's backs up because of his own personality'. Murchison once demanded from the pulpit that a misbehaving child be removed from the church. On another occasion – after pronouncing the benediction – he required the congregation to remain standing and practise the creed with due veneration, as they had not done it 'properly' during the service. Living at Narrabundah and assuming responsibility for the fledgling Narrabundah congregation, Bertram was called upon to provide increasing assistance to the rector towards the end of 1964.

Frederick Dau was appointed to St Paul's in 1962 at the age of 51 after having served in a number of Victorian and NSW parishes. He found some difficulty moving from rector in charge of his own parishes to that of curate under Murchison 'who could be autocratic at times and always unpredictable'. Fred's sermons, always 20 minutes in length, were not necessarily inspiring but he was responsible for a number of men entering the ministry. He served in all capacities across the parish, taking charge of the Young Anglicans and assuming major responsibilities at St David's in Red Hill and HMAS *Harman*.[16]

Two others provided valuable input from 1964. One was a Canadian, Anthony Waterman, who studied at the ANU for his doctorate over three years and joined the staff of St Paul's as an honorary priest.[17] The other was Graeme MacRobb, an officer with the Church Army, who took up residence in the Stuart Flats in February 1965 to assist the rector while continuing his Church Army work. Known as Captain MacRobb, Graeme was heavily involved in youth activities, Sunday school teaching and school religious instruction.[18]

St Paul's was basically a local church during the 1960s, concentrating on residents who lived within a 25-minute walk from the church and believing that additional centres were required for those who resided farther away. Hence, the rector and his assistants turned their attention to the two developing areas, Narrabundah and Red Hill. On Murchison's arrival, it was decided to continue the Sunday school at Narrabundah, first under Pryce and then under Dau, and to defer the construction of a church.[19] Peter Bertram moved into the parish-provided home in Boolimba Crescent, Narrabundah and held the first Anglican service of Communion on 3 March 1963 in the Salvation Army Hall.[20]

Conducting weekly services for 20 to 40 people, he commenced the Junior Anglicans, a junior choir, fellowship groups at Narrabundah High School and a joint Causeway–Narrabundah youth group that met during the week. A Churchwomen's Union was formed, providing a spiritual home for the ladies and a basis for fund-raising activities. By the end of 1965 the Narrabundah Building Fund had reached £470. The locals were pleased when a plan for a church hall was prepared and the Building Committee sought the 'voluntary labour of bricklayers, carpenters and other tradesmen' to construct a building at a cost of £3,000 to £4,000. When Bertram left the parish for the incumbency of Bribbaree in January 1966, he reflected on three hectic years of parish expansion and the development of a vibrant group at Narrabundah. According to Murchison, the curate's 'success with the High School Fellowships was outstanding and the people of Narrabundah' would 'long remember his pastoral ministry'.[21] Over 40 years later, Peter

Narrabundah House-Church (left unit); 6 Boolimbah
Crescent   © *Bertram Family Album*

Anglican services in the Narrabundah Salvation Army Hall
© *Bertram Family Album*

Junior Anglicans in the Narrabundah House-Church with
the Reverend Peter Bertram.   © *Bertram Family Album*

Narrabundah Junior Choir   © *Bertram Family Album*

Bertram still had fond memories of Narrabundah, including the day
he took a group of boys to Cooma by bus. On the return trip, the
police stopped the vehicle, boarded the bus and asked all the boys to
open their pockets. The officers then retrieved the stolen goods that
the boys had taken from a café. Services continued at Narrabundah
after Bertram's departure, shared by Murchison, MacRobb, Dau and
another curate, John Bunyan.[22]

The second region requiring Murchison's attention was Red Hill, a
quiet area that sloped up to La Perouse Street where there were a few
homes and a piggery. While some future streets had been pencilled
on a map, Mugga Way stopped at Flinders Way in 1954, the Canberra
Grammar School stood on the edge of settlement[23] and the rise was
reserved for children's play and for the rabbits that were snared in
large numbers. The suburb became a reality during 1959 and a school
was well advanced by the end of that year. Three bedroom homes were
built for £5,000 in an area that was 'kerbed, guttered and tar sealed',
supplied with electricity, water and sewerage and located close to
'schools and shopping centres'. There were plans for a preschool, a
mothercraft centre and recreational facilities and it was expected that
the 'whole of the Red Hill district' would be developed by the end of
1964.[24] Sites for churches had not been determined early in 1960 but

this did not prevent Bishop Burgmann – prompted by Border and Murchison – to apply for a site for an Anglican church.[25]

Laurie Murchison, accompanied by Bill Pryce, found a buoyant, young community served by the school which opened in February 1960 with an enrolment of 330. Another 100 children arrived within two weeks. Workmen were struggling to complete the Infants Block as six additional children were enrolled each week, a result of the compulsory transfer of government departments from interstate.[26] Suzanne Curtis described the scene as 'nappy valley' filled with young families and an air of excitement.[27] Jim Monro collected a small group of helpers and held the first Sunday school at the local school on 19 June 1960, only to find the room too small. And so an Anglican presence was extended to the Red Hill area, a successful venture that continued for 21 months until additional services were required.[28] The need was accentuated in August when 407 blocks of land were auctioned at Red Hill, Griffith and Ainslie and another burst of building construction took place.[29]

The parish council prepared a notice of intention to erect a church and by February 1961 a 'site had been reserved'. Murchison obtained approval to hold church services in the Red Hill Primary School and the rector and Fred Dau conducted the first service there for over 100 people on 18 March 1962. Bishop Clements, a resident in nearby Mugga Way, was invited to attend Matins the following month and a pattern was established in which Communion and Matins were alternated every four weeks. In 1964 fortnightly services were introduced.[30]

The church conducted a needs-survey and reported that, in 1964, the Red Hill region contained over 1,550 blocks of land of which 'only 140 were uninhabited' and that it was 'already 90 per cent built-up'. When 27 men and women from the church visited each of the 1,411 homes, they discovered 444 Anglican or part-Anglican households with 800 adults and 773 children. The average age of the children was seven and there were 100 between the ages of fourteen and eighteen. The potential for the Anglican Church was exciting, although it was debatable whether the area 'tentatively demarcated for a future parish' and with no room for expansion, could be self-supporting – the diocesan average was 600 households per parish, not 444.[31]

The Department of the Interior was asked to allocate a clergyman's residence at Red Hill. The local parishioners were invited to St Paul's in May 1963 to form 'a Committee with a view to building a church'. Bishop Clements agreed to the name, 'St David's Red Hill'. The parish council set aside £2,500 for a proposed building and determined that 80 per cent of the income from the Red Hill area in excess of £1,500 each year be set aside for the future structure.[32] It was a satisfactory milestone when over 60 people met at the school on 23 February 1964, walked in procession to the site on the corner or La Perouse and Fortitude Streets and dedicated the large block of two acres (0.84 hectares).

Fortnightly services continued in the school during 1964 and 1965 led mainly by Fred Dau but there was mounting frustration as the community sought to solve a mesh of financial and administrative challenges. Was it prudent to build a traditional church building or was a smaller hall a better option? Would it be preferable to have a structure that could also serve as a local community centre? Would the Methodist Church join in a joint venture? Would the Presbyterian Church share its land in a collaborative endeavour?[33] Additionally, the community's financial viability was questionable and prevented a ready solution. Little assistance could be offered by St Paul's which encountered difficulty in honouring its own diocesan obligations, let alone provide continued financial assistance to St David's. The debate continued unresolved.

Financial restrictions not only delayed the construction of St David's Church but also dictated much of the development across the entire parish during Murchison's incumbency. While St Paul's was able to liquidate the debt on the church extensions by April 1963 – repaying £6,500 in three years – the construction of a church hall plunged the church into debt by over £20,000, with extra costs for fitting out the building. Added expenditure was incurred as assistant clergy, honorary priests and office staff were employed, inflating the amount budgeted for 'stipends and other allowances' from £3,700 in 1956 to over $13,600 in 1966.[34]

Continuing expenditure – not to mention discomfort and complaint – stemmed from the coldness of St Paul's church in winter and attempts to install adequate forms of heating. The council was involved in ineffectual but costly efforts to raise the temperature inside the building so as to reduce the pain of arthritic sufferers. Heaters were placed at floor level, blowers purchased, carpets laid and costly under-carpet heating installed – all to no avail. (The defective under-carpet heating needed to be disconnected in 1969 before fire broke out.)[35] Heavy coats and thick socks proved cheaper and more practical and were to continue in vogue. Moreover, pigeons added to the expenditure causing such a distasteful smell on the carpet that Murchison ordered the wardens to wash and disinfect the floor. When this was ineffective, the rector used incense for the morning services – one of the few times that he used incense in six years.[36]

The need for building funds for the new centres at Red Hill and Narrabundah stretched the parish budget. In 1966, for instance, over $1,100 was transferred to the Red Hill Building Fund to increase it to $7,100. A similar fund at Narrabundah held almost $1,800.[37] It was the diocesan payment, however, that caused the greatest concern as the parish struggled to meet its annual 'Diocesan pledge' (formerly known as an assessment). The amount of the pledge rose from £663 in 1960 to £1,103 in 1961 and to £2,000 in 1965.[38] In the meantime, the treasurer reported parish deficits of £1,100 ($2,200) in 1965 and $2,300 in 1966, the figure appearing considerably more when decimal currency was introduced in 1966.

To meet these ever-increasing costs the parish required a corresponding increase in giving. Family pledging continued but, in a story all too familiar, the 1960 canvass was not 'particularly successful' when only £16,000 was promised over two years. When the parish was unable to pay its diocesan pledge because of its financial obligations 'in the creation of the Yarralumla Parish' the canvassers returned to door-knocking to raise funds.[39] An analysis of the pledges made in the 1964 canvass reveals that, of the 440 pledges (including 110 in the Red Hill area), 202 or 46 per cent of families contributed between 1 shilling and 5 shillings a week, while only 7 per cent gave more than £1.[40]

While financial viability was important, it was only one factor in the development of a strong church and the promotion of healthy fellowship. Worship patterns were strongly influenced by the bishops who steered St Paul's along a middle-of-the-road form of Anglicanism. Murchison fitted into this broad Anglican approach and was parochial rather than diocesan-oriented. Described as 'a somewhat liberal theologian' and a 'churchman of the old school', Murchison was often observed praying alone in the church. With his knowledge of Byzantine philosophy and culture, together with his mastery of Greek, he was drawn towards a Greek form of Orthodoxy that was reflected in his preaching. Although not dynamic, he was sincere and reflected an academic approach in his sermons which were said to be somewhat above the understanding of young people. Monday mornings were set aside to review the sermons of his curates and to assess their content and spirituality.

The rector was not averse to change, however and often experimented with new approaches. On one occasion he and the curate moved the altar out from the wall to a central position in the sanctuary – 'a half hour of puff and pant' – but when Murchison found the result aesthetically disappointing, they lugged it back to its original position. On other occasions, Murchison would disconcertingly whisper to the curate as they walked towards the altar during morning service, 'Let's change things and do something different.' Consequently, the rector was not particularly perturbed when alternative forms of the liturgy were considered. In reality, both Border and Murchison had already modified the liturgy at St Paul's – a church meeting simply requested the bishop 'to approve the deviations from the Prayer Book that have been used habitually in the Parish.'[41] Bishops Burgmann and Clements were well aware of the 'deviations'.

The music liturgy was particularly important to both Murchison and John Barrett, although it resulted in some friction between them as they both had definite views on its form and place. The senior choir, numbering about twenty, received acclaim for its radio and television broadcasts, its special performances on Palm Sunday, Dedication Sunday and Holy Week services and its liturgical music often performed to well-known international settings. The junior choir was given personal tuition by the rector who became something of a father-figure to the boys. Choral and organ recitals attracted gratifying attendances and the choir often combined with visiting artists and societies such as the Canberra Society of Singers and the Canberra School of Music. John Barrett's association with the Royal School of Church Music attracted many artists to perform at the church, while his and Laurie Murchison's expertise at the organ console won widespread acclaim.

St Paul's was a busy church with a range of organisations including the Men's Group that had been resuscitated in 1959. The men met each month with attendances varying from fifteen to 25. They had informative speakers, held dinner dances, arranged working bees and attended corporate Communion services.[42] The Churchwomen's Union (CU) engaged in both spiritual and social activities. They raised money for the church, conducted fetes and assisted a range of missions, religious groups and community causes. Affiliated with the CU was the Family Life Group which held daytime meetings for about fifteen women and evening gatherings for up to 25. The number of communicants rose from 9,379 in 1960 (an average of 180 each week) to 13,916 in 1963 (weekly average 268) and 15,806 in 1964 (weekly average 304).[43] Together with the work at Narrabundah and Red Hill, St Paul's required the input of assistant priests and curates, the help of honorary priests and strong support from committed parishioners.

Despite the positive signs, there were some worrying trends that emerged between 1960 and 1965 in the work with children and youth groups. The Young Anglicans were not a dynamic group until the church hall was built and it was most difficult to find adult leaders to assist other youth fellowships. The same trend became apparent in the kindergarten and Sunday school. There had been 80 children in the Sunday school in 1965 in addition to large numbers in the kindergarten but enrolments fell and 'there was an unexpected loss of teachers', after which 'there were never sufficient teachers to enable the school to operate effectively.'[44]

Unfortunately, amid the vibrancy of the church and the increased activity, Laurie Murchison began to show signs of reserve and stress. Not equipped to deal with administrative duties or with challenging interpersonal relationships, he neglected his own welfare and, on one occasion, was forced by the curate to call for medical assistance when suffering pneumonia. The rector went for long walks with his dog, found it more difficult to cope with normal duties and relied increasingly on his mother who visited the rectory to provide domestic assistance. The continual misbehaviour of the older boys in his religious education classes at Telopea Park School led to a scene where he threw the blackboard duster, stormed out of the room and never returned to the school. He finally buckled under the weight of leadership for which he was not equipped and the rigours of a society into which he did not easily fit. Burnt out emotionally and quite ill by the start of 1965, he was forced to take three months off, admitting, 'This is a killer parish.' Eventually, he returned to duties for a year but never administered Holy Communion again, a duty he left to others.[45] It was not a spiritual relapse – his faith remained strong but it was a withdrawal from a harsh world into his own sensitive sphere of devotion, scholarship and learning.

Fortunately for Murchison – indeed for the parish and the diocese – the episode had a relatively satisfying and fulfilling conclusion. A few kilometres away, St Mark's Memorial Library employed tutors such as the Reverend Hayden McCallum and the Reverend Douglas Kemsley (1963–1964) and, after Bishop Clements intervened and appointed another priest to St Paul's, Canon Murchison was made a full-time tutor at St Mark's Library in March 1966. It was there that his profound talents and expertise were appropriately channelled into the education and training of others, a world for which he was manifestly better suited.

The diocesan assistant bishop, Cecil Warren, became the acting rector. It was he who informed St Paul's congregation of the appointment of their new rector, Dr John Munro, who was 49 years of age with qualifications that were listed as LTh, BA(Melb.), MTheol, PhD(Lond.). After his ordination in 1943 he had served a curacy in Warnambool, Bishop's Chaplain to the University of London, Dean of Christ Church Cathedral in Ballarat, Supervisor and Federal Director-General of Religious Broadcasting with the ABC and rector of Dee Why. In his personal life, the new rector had already suffered deep sadness when his wife had died, leaving him with three children to rear. He was, however, accompanied by his mother who would care for the family. (Mrs Munro was to be affectionately known as 'grandma' by the congregation.)[46]

Munro was aware of the changing society in which the church was operating – protests against the Vietnamese war, a movement to 'Ban the Bomb', legal claims by indigenous people, challenges by the feminist movement, a move to relax censorship laws and a desire for greater sexual and artistic freedom. The emergence of an anti-establishment culture had seen young people rejecting traditional values, experimenting instead with drugs, Eastern religions, different forms of art, music and literature and community-living styles. There was resentment against 'the monotonous routine of getting up, going to work, coming back home to the suburbs and attending church on Sunday.'[47]

The rector was surprised at the 'considerable turnover' of the population in his new parish, the 'ebb and flow of families to overseas and other appointments' and 'the wide diversity of incomes, occupations, education and cultural conditions' among his congregation.[48] His challenges differed from those of his predecessors, however, in that St Paul's had already been built, extended and consecrated; the debt on the rectory was small; and the church hall was well used by church organisations. Nevertheless, there was a frightening debt on the hall and church maintenance was required.

He quickly discerned that 'some people, resident fairly close by', did not know of the church's existence, prompting him to commence a monthly periodical, *Cross-Way*, in which the activities of the parish were advertised.[48] Nevertheless, he was puzzled 'why a church with so many graces as St Paul's – fine music, good site and intelligent and sensitive liturgical tradition – should be so undervalued by the bulk of those' who claimed to be Church of England. In his opinion, the parishioners needed to care more, attend church more frequently, turn to biblical and doctrinal study and learn the meaning of obedience to God.[50]

In response to Munro's challenging message, the number of communicants rose and peaked at 16,029 in 1967, an average of 308 each week (including St David's and St Barnabas'). John Bunyan recalled that 'the parish was flourishing', the Sunday morning services 'were packed' and John Munro was 'a very fine leader, intellectually very able, pastorally very experienced, a somewhat reserved but outstandingly professional parish priest'.[51] After 1967, however, the numbers fell to 13,496 in 1969 as the social revolution affected the parish and church attendance declined in importance.[52] Gone were the days when a clergyman could insist that attendance was 'an obligation' on every Anglican adherent. The newspapers no longer reported sermons and pronouncements from the pulpit received less coverage. By 1970 *The Canberra Times* discontinued its 43-year-old policy of providing a weekly 'Church Services' column free of charge and imposed a fee on those that wished to advertise their activities.[53]

Munro sought ways to reach nominal Anglicans – those who claimed 'Church of Everything' adherence – those who were among the 700 communicants at Easter and 780 at Christmas but who showed indifference to the church for the rest of the year.[54] He commenced

'The Learning Church', requiring those preparing for confirmation to attend 5pm classes each Sunday at a 'colourful, participatory young people's Eucharist' where he experimented with 'commentary, catechetical question and answer and film-strips' to deepen their spirituality.[55] Adults seeking confirmation and the recently confirmed were invited to explore church life more deeply and he visited the homes of those whom he believed to be less sincere about confirmation, speaking to parents about their obligations.[56]

Despite his efforts, numbers continued to drift, church finances fell and Munro asked regular parishioners 'to take a long hard look' at how they might 'cooperate with the clergy'. The council organised 'Operation Deep Think' in October 1969 when 32 parishioners held a conference at the Anglican Youth Centre at Tathra to consider how the parish might operate more effectively. The participants concluded that church-going Anglicans were 'a minority group' and that 'the church had ceased to be a focal point of social activity', particularly in Canberra where there was 'a wealth of social activity, service clubs and opportunities for intellectual stimulus'.[57] 'The Anglican Church, despite some examples to the contrary, had a reputation for coldness' and St Paul's was no exception. Its mission required reorientation; lay people needed to be involved more often; and 'religious instruction in schools' demanded review. 'How to interest and hold young people was almost a universal problem' and St Paul's needed to tackle the issue.

Six church groups were formed to strengthen parish finances, welcome newcomers, assist new confirmees, encourage and assist young people, develop fellowship and social activities and examine parish council procedures. Name tags were introduced, a coffee and tea hour was commenced after the 10am service, visits to the homes of newcomers were arranged, activities were planned around the 'Learning Church for Confirmees' program and a questionnaire was developed to tap the interests of youth. Progressive dinners and afternoon teas were arranged for older groups, barbeques held to welcome newcomers and parishioners invited others to their homes. This soul-searching produced positive results. Parishioners became better acquainted, attendances increased and innovation was introduced. Receipts rose, construction of a chapel at Red Hill inched ever closer, attempts were made to incorporate the struggling group at

Narrabundah more effectively and the church grounds were replanned.

Believing that wider community involvement was required, the rector goaded his denominational colleagues to form the Guild of St Martin. This lay group of 30 parishioners, rostered on one day a month, assisted those in difficult situations waiting for 'regular social service agencies to take over' – the provision of food, short-term accommodation, legal assistance, counselling and encouragement. An inter-church venture, the guild was commenced in 1969 and operated well with lay direction until impoverished folk sought more direct intervention and longer-term support.[58]

Within St Paul's parish, Munro encouraged the two outreach centres, knowing that the arrival of the new curate would assist the work at Narrabundah. Gerald Farleigh[59] was described as 'a moderate evangelical in a gentle way' when deaconed at the end of 1965.[60] After being the only 'ordained supervisor' on the staff of David Jones in

The Reverend Gerald Farleigh
© Farleigh Family Album

Sydney, he came to Canberra in 1967 at Bishop Clements' invitation and became an integral member of St Paul's team. When Anglican services were discontinued in the Narrabundah Salvation Army Temple, it was decided that Farleigh – unmarried at the time – should occupy the top floor of the two-storey house in Boolimba Crescent, allowing church services and the kindergarten to meet in the lounge room downstairs. The senior Sunday school moved to the Narrabundah Primary School.[61] As the curate built up the work at St Barnabas', the rector acknowledged the 'thoroughness of his work, both in preaching and ministering ... a most dependable asset in all we attempt together'.[62] Farleigh married in 1968 and moved out of the house, allowing the upstairs flat to be rented and the senior Sunday school to meet downstairs, thus saving weekly rent at the school.

The Narrabundah congregation did not increase in numbers and the clergy sought the reasons. In effect, Narrabundah had developed as a working-class suburb and St Paul's was unable to determine the role it should adopt. Would it simply provide a meeting place, a 'presence', and try to attract those who were 'presently uninterested' or would it launch into social work activities 'in which the church presence would be little more than enabling?'[63] Ruth Frappell's contention that the strength of Anglicanism 'lay in its middle-class suburban parishes' appeared justified and St Paul's found difficulty in coping with a population that was uninterested (perhaps disinterested) in its message.[64] When the authorities asked for a definite commitment on the church's leased land near the Narrabundah shops, Munro contacted the Archbishops of Sydney and Melbourne, seeking their advice on dealing with similar inner-city suburbs in the state capitals. He was forced to concede in February 1971 that 'our continuing debate' about the Narrabundah area 'is by no means resolved'.[65] He was spared further involvement when invited to move to Albury and, with a sigh of relief, bequeathed the problem to his successor, Neville Chynoweth.

Meanwhile, there were different pressures at Red Hill where the Department of the Interior sought action and hinted that the church site might be lost. The rector painstakingly analysed the *raison d'être* for a local church, typing seven foolscap pages of notes for the parish council and concluding:

> I turn away categorically from the idea of creating little parishes on the fringe of St Paul's – either at Narrabundah or Red Hill. Both are missionary areas and as such are still ... the responsibility of ... St Paul's ... [At Red Hill] we ought to build an aesthetically pleasing but reasonably modest hall-cum-chapel or chapel-cum-hall (call it what you like) well adapted to providing variable spaces with perhaps a couple of separate rooms. Then the next and not too delayed, step is to build a reasonable residence alongside. St Paul's can still be the main church [and] St David's chapel can be small or large according to demand.[66]

With this firm decision, St David's committee began a tortuous four-year exercise involving designs, sketches, disputes and escalating costs. In September 1969 tender envelopes were opened for a building projected to cost $25,000 but all quotes ranged from $36,000 to $38,000. The tenders were rejected and the committee fell glum, the council minutes referring to 'the long and sad history' of the enterprise and consequent 'shock and dismay'.

Finally, Jack Firth, a St Paul's parishioner, came to the rescue and, with input from the Reverend Geoff Sibly, devised plans for the future structure. At the same time, the parish council considered a paper entitled 'The Development of St David's at Red Hill', one that suggested 'up to 20 Housing Commission style retirement units' on the land. By the time the rector closed the meeting just before midnight, it was agreed that St David's committee should make final modifications to the plans for a multi-purpose building and submit them to the firm of Lopez and Sons. The cost was not to exceed $25,000 and the proposal for retirement units was to be further explored.[67]

After years of disappointment and frustration, Sibly witnessed signatures on a contract for the construction of the church in October 1971. Munro had moved to Albury a few months before but, prior to his departure, had received a letter indicating the estimated cost of the design to be $27,605. Moreover, the Diocesan Responsibilities Committee would inspect the Red Hill site to consider the future construction of Aged Persons' Units in conjunction with St David's.[68] With the planning work virtually completed, Munro had handed over the construction phase and substantial financial commitment to his successor.

The new debt on St David's was only one of the challenges facing St Paul's treasurer. He reported annual deficits of $2,300 in 1966 and approximately $4,000 in 1967 but the situation would have been worse if the stewardship campaign had not been linked with the screening of a film, *A Man called Peter.* A crowd of 750 came to see it at the Canberra Theatre, leading to new financial pledges and church commitments.[69] To curtail expenditure, the parishioners rostered themselves to clean St Paul's church and hall to save $750 a year, the Red Hill plans were modified and the three churchwomen's guilds arranged extra fund-raising activities. By the end of 1968 Don Youngman reported that the income exceeded outgoings by $600, a 'considerable relief' after three years of crisis.[70]

Financial clouds descended again during 1969 when the parish council considered the need to reduce the number of clergymen to two, lowered the diocesan pledge by $500 and sought desperately to rally parishioner support. The efforts of the council, aided by the challenge of the rector's 'Operation Deep Think' program, finally counteracted the financial slide. By 1970, an accumulated debt of $3,050 had been reversed. By the time that Neville Chynoweth was installed as incumbent, the general balance was a mere $26, but there was $20,000 set aside in the building funds of Red Hill and Narrabundah, a further $2,000 in St Paul's furnishing fund and almost $1,300 in the organ fund. There was no chance of complacency, however, as the debt on the church hall still stood above $34,800.[71]

Apart from financial tensions, St Paul's maintained a pleasant, friendly fellowship during Munro's incumbency with the church continuing its middle-of-the-road form of Anglicanism. When Gerald Farleigh was appointed, Bishop Clements told him that 'we don't go in for any of that Anglo-Catholic nonsense here' while Bishop Warren indicated that the wearing of vestments 'was not a doctrinal statement' at all. Farleigh later agreed that 'we were not fussed about churchmanship' at St Paul's.[72] Munro was 'an old fashioned modernist, an intellectual, a rationalist Christian' who was unhappy with the portrayal of Jesus in the New Testament, believing that one had to 'peel away the layers' of mythology to find 'the historical Jesus'.[73] One of his curates referred to Munro's 'intellectual honesty' and his 'desire to seek the truth wherever that search led' as he explored the field of 'philosophical theology'.[74] Accepting that the worship of Jesus had supplanted the worship of

The Reverend J Munro
© Framing Matters, Manuka

God, the rector stated, 'I am a Theist, not a Jesusist.' Nevertheless, this was not readily apparent in his preaching. His sermons at Christmas on the Christ-child and at Easter on the Resurrection were inspiring and fitted well into a traditional Christian message.[75]

Soon after Munro's arrival in 1967, the Liturgical Commission recommended changes to the Prayer Book and provided revised materials for new liturgies. The rector introduced 'two of the new liturgies' for appraisal and by February 1969 the 'majority of parishioners' were 'reasonably happy with the [Second Series] Alternative Rite' used in England.[76] His own predilections were quite apparent in 1970, however, when he agreed that, while the church had benefited from changes, he was in no hurry to launch into further experiments while there were more pressing issues – meaningful fellowship, efficient pastoral care and relevant religious instruction.[77]

In musical liturgy, the two choirs maintained busy schedules and often raised money to swell the organ fund.[78] Their striking robes and

Canterbury caps were well known throughout the diocese as they sang at the Canberra Theatre to welcome the Archbishop of York, at the Royal School of Church Music and at St Saviour's Cathedral to welcome the Primate of Australia. Short recitals were performed at other churches as well as a 'chamber music version' of Handel's *Messiah*.[79] In 1970 the activities of the choirs included: six national broadcasts; cutting an L.P. record of hymns; recording the background music for the Canberra Repertory Society's play, *Murder in the Cathedral*; and performances at the annual law service, St Saviour's dedication anniversary service and the National Eisteddfod in Canberra.

The 1961 electric organ was meant to satisfy requirements until a pipe organ could be acquired and, in December 1967, Barrett raised the issue again. He was informed that 'if money could be specially raised' without recourse to parish funds 'there was no objection' to the acquisition of a pipe organ.[80] With only $117 in the organ fund, the organist embarked on his quest. Twelve months later the fund stood at $2,070, the result of donations, broadcasting fees, recitals and bank interest. By December 1970, it had reached almost $6,200, allowing Barrett and the Reverend Owen Dowling to investigate possibilities.[81] When the pipe organ from Wangaratta Cathedral would not fit in the organ loft at St Paul's and one from Sydney was too expensive, the council considered a new organ built specifically for the church. The departure of Munro in 1971 meant the matter was left to his successor.

Among other organisations at St Paul's, the Men's Group organised excursions, films, debates and working bees and invited ambassadors, high commissioners, parliamentarians, members of the judiciary and international visitors to address them.[82] The Churchwomen's Union assisted the formation of CU groups at Red Hill and Narrabundah, arranged 'Quiet Days', Bible readings and Communion services for members, provided transport for the elderly, remained heavily engaged in fund-raising activities and contributed to missions.[83] The Family Life Group visited the hospital's obstetric ward each week, contacted new mothers and supplied assistance when required, their most effective work being done quietly 'behind the scenes'.[84]

The Young Anglicans became more active from 1965 enjoying picnics, barbeques, snow trips and camps and participating in the parish ball and Christmas party. However, in a sequel repeated across the diocese, the movement lost direction, interest fell away and – in the words of Munro – the YAs 'decided not to go on' during 1968.[85] Moreover, the involvement of adults in youth leadership activities collapsed, with Captain MacRobb claiming in 1967 that 'during the past two years not one adult' had offered to share in youth ventures or assist the clergy in this work.[86] The church was quickly losing the ability to engage its youth.

The same trend was apparent in the Sunday school where the number of children regularly dropped despite the efforts of the teachers. Picnics were held, Christmas plays arranged, teaching methods analysed and teaching aids purchased but the numbers continued to decline.[87] There was little mention of the Sunday school in *Cross-Way* in the late 1960s with Munro stressing instead the activities of St Paul's Youth Group for those between 13 and 17 years.[88] The attitudes of young people to church attendance and church social life were changing markedly and, by the end of Munro's incumbency, 'holding the interest' of the adolescent and youth groups in the parish had passed the crisis point.

There were similar concerns about religious instruction in the public schools which had grown exponentially as the school population had increased. Canon Border's team had taught 1,400 lessons a year but, by 1966, Munro, the curates and lay helpers provided over 80 lessons each week in relatively large classes and often to unresponsive youngsters. Fred Dau was so distressed by the misbehaviour in his Telopea Park classes that he could not perform other duties for some hours after religious instruction.[89] Despite the 'enormous' task involved Munro declined an invitation to provide religious instruction on an 'inter-denominational basis', determined that St Paul's would 'not default' in teaching the faith, but his frustration boiled over when he contemplated the 'great odds':

> … an educational system which leads young people in the upper reaches of the secondary school to spend up to nine periods each per week on science and mathematics and makes do with an all too short period of 'Scripture', inevitably unrelated to the rest of the curriculum, non-examinable and lacking the kudos of professional teaching and recognition.[90]

While he believed that the Anglican Church would be compelled to 'set up small modest parish schools outside of the secularist system', he opposed a unilateral Anglican withdrawal from religious instruction 'as we'd have no position left from which to negotiate a better way'.[91] Soon after expressing this statement, Munro transferred to Albury but, before his departure, he and the incoming incumbent discussed religious instruction in schools, a conversation that eventually led to a partial resolution.

Religious instruction in the independent sector, however, caused no difficulties. Canberra Grammar School enjoyed a time of rapid expansion after 1960, its enrolments jumping from 426 to almost 1,000 in a decade. The first part of a new junior school was opened in 1964 and a second stage planned and new buildings for a library, boarding school and science block were constructed. As the secondary course was extended from five to six years, the numbers seeking tertiary education jumped and the percentage of scholarship winners increased. Bishop Clements dedicated the Chapel of Christ the King in 1965 amid signs that the spirituality of the boys was being enhanced through the school's closer ties to the diocese, their assistance for diocesan homes, the entry of two 'Old Boys' into the priesthood and the leadership of ex-students in a number of parishes. The school choir also established links with the Manuka church, participating in joint Christmas carol services and other special events.[92]

Moreover, there was a growing list of school staff who were noted within the wider Anglican Church: Harold Hunter provided voluntary assistance at St Paul's, Kenneth Clements had been installed as the Bishop of Canberra & Goulburn and Canon Garnsey became Bishop of Gippsland. The senior history master, the Reverend John Bunyan, was awarded an overseas scholarship after which he was appointed as assistant priest of St Paul's and tutor at St Mark's. The English master, the Reverend David Durie, was appointed to St Mark's in 1969. In time, the 1960 school captain, John Gibson, would also enter the priesthood and would later become Archdeacon in the Riverina Diocese. Bishop Radford's earlier hopes were fulfilled as the school grew and its influence in the community matured and flourished.

The Canberra Girls' Grammar School likewise enjoyed a period of expansion as enrolments jumped, Higher School Certificate numbers rose, associations were formed with the *Alliance Française* and Goethe Society and new laboratories, classrooms and a library were opened. Extensive renovations were made to the boarding house and a separate cottage for the head teacher was built. During the 1960s some of the girls attended Sunday services at St Paul's and combined with St Paul's choir on special occasions. After the chaplain, Guy Harrison, was appointed, most girls attended chapel in the boarding house until a new chapel was set up in the back of the assembly hall. Harrison conducted Sunday services and weekly prayers, prepared confirmees, arranged services for foundation day, the Old Girls' Reunion and prefects' induction and organised Lenten addresses. By the end of the decade a separate junior school was required. It was commenced in 1970, completed in 1971 and opened in 1972.[93]

A few kilometres away, St Mark's Memorial Library was involved in its own form of ecumenical education. During Bishop Burgmann's wardenship (1960–1964), tutors were appointed. Canon Murchison was accepted as a full-time tutor in March 1966. The library collection rose to 25,000 volumes by 1967. Murchison and Bunyan tutored in theology subjects, discussion groups met in the library and lunch-hour lectures were given 'by some of Australia's ablest leaders'.[94] Murchison accepted a leading role, organising and chairing meetings and directing courses of study. Evening lectures attracted up to 70 people.[95] In the judgement of the Reverend Dr Robert Withycombe, later Warden of St Mark's, 'St Mark's became a place where clergy remedied the deficiencies of their pre-ordination training' by studying for higher qualifications. It provided 'a haven for dislodged theological educators' who were able 'to write and teach in greater freedom' and opened its doors to the general public to hear 'eminent Australian and overseas speakers'.[96]

By 1967 Bishop Clements believed that St Mark's should have its own council and proposed a new entity named 'St Mark's Institute of Theology' with the library forming part. Dr John Nurser was appointed warden in 1968. The Institute was developed as an in-service centre for the clergy, readership of St Mark's Review was expanded and plans were made for the library 'to serve as a catalyst for the growth in the next decade of an Australasian Union School of Theology in Canberra'. After Bishop-in-Council resolved that the diocese undertake 'the training of men for the ministry' in Canberra, the Reverend David Durie was appointed the Supervisor of Training and a new program was 'tried out with a handful of students' in 1972. A professor was appointed as Visiting Fellow and four of the first five students moved into residence at the new Burgmann College at the ANU where the College of Ministry was initially located. In the view of Dr Munro, the 'new venture of training clergy in Canberra has got away to a good start.'[97]

In retrospect, the Parish of Manuka grappled with the expansion of Canberra during the 1960s and the changing society in which the church operated. While the population continued to increase and new areas were opened, church attendances rose, levelled out and began to wane, the decline leading to financial difficulties as the council sought to fund new centres, meet debt repayments and raise money to cover diocesan pledges.[98] The diocese, in turn, canvassed strongly for funds, an appeal that further pressured fund-raising activities in the parish.[99] While St Paul's continued vibrant for most of the decade, there were ominous signs of change as the 'baby boomers' reached secondary school and moved into the workforce, experiencing relatively prosperous times and a more liberal society fed by newspapers, radio and television. Young people reacted with increasing difficulty to imposed authority, an attitude reflected in the secondary schools and particularly in religious instruction classes. Coupled with the unwillingness of adults to participate in children's and youth activities, the Sunday school declined in importance, the Young Anglican movement ceased and young people increasingly looked outside the church for recreation and entertainment. When 'Operation Deep Think' determined in 1969 that the youth problem 'needed to be tackled', the congregation did not realise that it was virtually too late and that a whole generation was passing them by.

John Munro was appointed Archdeacon of Albury and left Canberra in May 1971. At a large gathering in the church hall, it was recalled 'that the Parish had grieved with Dr Munro in his sorrows and rejoiced with him' in the joy 'of his recent marriage'. Tribute was paid to his daughter, Deborah, for her constant work at the Narrabundah centre and Sunday school and to his son, Howard, for his work at every working-bee at St Paul's. After an incumbency lasting six years, John Munro departed for Albury, ultimately accepting the position of Chairman of the Australian Board of Missions and a greater involvement in religious programs through the Australian Broadcasting Commission.

Notes

1. 'A recollection of Bishop D Garnsey', *Anglican Historical Society Journal*, October 1994, p. 35.
2. CT, 12 March 1960.
3. CT, 19 December 1959; 23 January 1960.
4. CT, 13 and 14 January 1960; 12 March 1960.
5. The needs were outlined in a brochure on pledging, April 1958.
6. StPPC, AGM, 20 March 1960.
7. StPPC, 18 February 1962.
8. *Our parish and our church. St Paul's Canberra*, St Paul's Publication, 1960.
9. StPPC, 19 June and 17 August 1961; D Youngman, 'Organs and organists', in H Taylor-Rogers, 'St Paul's Parish', Canberra, StPPC 1991, p. 82.
10. StPPC, 20 November 1961; and AGM, 18 February 1962.
11. StPPC, 8 July 1960; 18 February 1963.
12. Youngman to the Manager, Commercial Banking Co. of Sydney, 28 September 1962.
13. StPPC, 27 September and 19 November 1962; 16 September 1963.
14. StPPC, 20 April, 20 July, 17 August 1964.
15. Bill Pryce, Personal communication, 2009.
16. Peter Bertram, Personal communication, 2009.
17. *Cross-Way*, July 1967
18. StPPC, 17 August 1964; 15 February 1965; StP Register of Services for 1965.
19. Murchison discontinued records for the Narrabundah Sunday school in the Register of Services but its continuation was recorded in the weekly 'Church Services' column of the CT from March 1960 to 26 October 1962.
20. StPPC, 17 September 1962; StP Register of Services, 1962–1963.
21. StPPC, 1966 annual report.
22. John Bunyan, a graduate of the University of Sydney, was ordained in 1959 and appointed Senior History Master at Canberra Grammar School until the end of 1962 when he went to the UK as Lucas Tooth Scholar and studied postgraduate theological courses at the universities of London and Durham. Appointed to St Paul's in 1966 for a short term, he became a tutor at St Mark's from 1967 to 1969 before leaving for parish work in England (*Cross-Way*, August 1967).
23. Official map of Canberra, 1954.
24. CT, 14 January and 8 April 1960.
25. Memorandum from the Reverend J Munro, StPPC, 19 September 1966.
26. CT, 4 and 19 February 1960.
27. Suzanne Curtis, Personal communication, 2009.
28. StPPC, 1960; F Hawkins, 'St David's, Red Hill. The planning decade 1962–1972', *Anglican Historical Society Journal*, 5, April 1988, p. 13.

29. CT, 5 August 1960.
30. StP Register of Services 1961–1964.
31. Report of a survey, February 1964, NLA, MS3085, Box 4, 'St David's'.
32. StPPC, 20 August 1962; 22 April 1963; StPPC, 15 July 1963 and 21 December 1964.
33. StPPC, 1963 to 1966 and Hawkins, 'St David's Red Hill'.
34. Treasurer's report, StP 1966, NLA, MS 3085 Box 2.
35. StPPC, 15 September 1969.
36. Gerald Farleigh, Personal communication, 2009.
37. Treasurer's report, StP 1966, NLA, MS 3085, Box 2.
38. Treasurer's report 1961, StPPC, February 1962; Treasurer's report 1965, StP NLA, MS 3085, Box. 3.
39. Warden's report 1960, StPPC, 12 February, 1961.
40. StPPC, 22 June 1964.
41. StPPC, 18 May and 18 June 1962.
42. Activities were outlined in *Cross-Way* and in StP annual reports.
43. StP Register of Services, 1960 to 1971.
44. StPPC, 1967 annual report.
45. Remarks by former curates and other clergy.
46. Gerald Farleigh, Personal communication, 2009.
47. G Sorgi, A Russell and K Powell, *World events and Australia*, Longman Cheshire, Melbourne, 1985, chapter 12 and p. 271.
48. StPPC, 1966 annual report.
49. StPPC, 17 April 1967.
50. StPPC, 1966 annual report.
51. John Bunyan, Personal communication, 2009.
52. StP Register of Services.
53. StPPC, 18 May 1970.
54. Figures are extracted from StP Register of Services, 1967 to 1971
55. *Cross-Way*, December 1967–January 1968.
56. Recollection of Joan and Bill Thurlow, Personal communication, 2008.
57. A 22 page report, 'Operation Deep-Think' in StPPC, 11–12 October 1969.
58. *Cross-Way*, October 1969.
59. Other assistant priests (including honorary positions) during Dr Munro's incumbency were: R Fowler (1969–1970); A Batley (1969–1970); H Cox (1969–1971); G Sibley (1970–1972).
60. John Bunyan, Personal communication, 2009.
61. StPPC, 15 May 1967; Report on St Barnabas', Narrabundah, Jim Monro, StPPC, 1 August 1984.
62. Rector's 1967 report, StPPC, 18 February 1968.
63. 'Committee report to explore the future of St Barnabas' Narrabundah, StPPC, August 1975.
64. Frappell, 'Imperial Fervour and Anglican Loyalty' in Kaye et al (eds), p. 98.

65. Rector's 1970 report, StPPC, February 1970.
66. Memorandum from the rector to St Paul's parish council, 19 September, 1966, NLA, MS3085, 'St David's'.
67. StPPC, 17 November 1969; 20 July 1970.
68. StPPC, 11 May 1971. 'Future use of Red Hill site'. Memorandum from Munro to the Council.
69. StPPC, annual reports for 1965, 1966 and 1967; *Cross-Way*, October 1967.
70. StPPC, 1968 annual report, NLA, MS 3085, Box 3.
71. Figures are extracted from the annual reports.
72. Gerald Farleigh, Personal communication, 2009.
73. Neville Chynoweth, Personal communication, 2009.
74. John Bunyan, Personal communication, 2009.
75. Gerald Farleigh, Personal communication, 2009. Two of Munro's sermons were printed in *Cross-Way*, February and May 1971.
76. *Cross-Way*, November 1967 and March 1969.
77. StPPC, 1969 annual report
78. StPPC, 1970 annual report.
79. StPPC, annual reports for 1965 to 1971.
80. StPPC, 18 December 1967.
81. Treasurer's reports in StPPC, annual reports 1967 to 1971.
82. Activities were advertised in *Cross-Way* and in StPPC, annual reports.
83. CU 1967 annual report. See: CU activities in St Paul's annual reports 1965 -1971.
84. See StPPC, annual reports for 1965, 1966, 1967 and 1971.
85. StPPC, 1968 annual report.
86. *Cross-Way*, May 1967.
87. StPPC, 1967 annual report.
88. *Cross-Way*, February 1971.
89. Peter Bertram, Personal communication, 2009.
90. StPPC, 1967 annual report.
91. StPPC, annual reports 1969 and 1970.
92. See the headmasters' and a/headmasters' Annual Speech Day reports during the 1960s, CGS Archives.
93. This history is based on *Burrawi* 1960–1961 (NLA, N373.947 BUR); and the reports of the headmistress/headmaster 1966–1971 (NLA, N373.222 CAN).
94. *Cross-Way*, July 1967.
95. John Bunyan, Personal communication, 2009; St Mark's Library Newsletter, No. 7, March 1965.
96. Robert Withycombe, 'St Mark's at fifty: A brief history'. In *St Mark's turns fifty*. St Mark's National Theological Centre, Canberra, 2007, p. 33.
97. *Cross-Way*, February and April 1970; February and April 1971.

98. The numbers of communicants were recorded in the Register of Services: 1963 (13,916); 1964 (15,806); 1965 (13,704); 1966 (14,998); 1967 (16,029); 1968 (13,947); 1969 (13,496); 1970 (15,140).

99. Cecil Warren, *A Little Foolishness: An Autobiographical History,* Church Archivist Press, Toowoomba, 1993, p. 55.

12   Grappling with change, 1971–1982

Australian society experienced considerable turmoil in 1971 with anti-Vietnam war demonstrations across Australia, anti-apartheid demonstrations against the South African Springboks, challenges to save Lake Pedder in Tasmania, a growing demand for the relaxation of abortion laws in the ACT and a move to decriminalise homosexual acts between consenting adults. With the surprise victory of the Democratic Labor Party in the Senate and the growing disenchantment with the McMahon Liberal government, there were clear signs of a society in upheaval.[1]

The new rector of St Paul's, Neville Chynoweth, had witnessed many shifts in society since serving with the 2nd AIF in the Middle East and New Guinea and then as musical director of an army entertainment unit. At the age of 24 he had entered Moore College, completed his theological training to licentiate level in 1949 and later graduated from the University of Sydney with bachelor and master degrees in Arts. (For his Master's thesis he studied the influence of the Oxford Movement on church music.) After serving in rural areas and city parishes and with a background in printing, the armed forces, music, hospital chaplaincy and pastoral work, he had moved to All Saints' Ainslie at the invitation of Bishop Clements in 1966. During his incumbency ('the hardest five years of my life'), he had to cope with a spiralling population in Canberra's north and a crippling church debt (which was successfully liquidated) while gaining another degree through the Melbourne College of Divinity.[2]

Neville Chynoweth was inducted into St Paul's on 20 June 1971 and settled into the parish with his wife, Joan, and children. The rectory became a hub of activity activated by a 'pastor who did not spare himself' and Mrs Chynoweth 'who combined charm and graciousness

with abounding energy'. There was always hot water on the fuel stove
and a pot of soup for those who dropped in. The Churchwomen's
Union frequently met with Joan in the rectory and the parish council conducted some of its meetings in the sitting room. It was the
commencement of a rewarding period for the church despite the
challenges of the time.[3]

The immediate agenda was largely set by circumstances already
forged. John Barrett's insistent push for a pipe organ required sensitive direction. Parish concerns included school religious instruction,
a building at Red Hill, the future of St Barnabas' house church and the
need for financial prudence. Moreover, Bishop Clements had foreshadowed contentious changes at the next diocesan synod. Underlining
all these issues was the rector's desire to harness the strengths of the
parish, promote worship and develop the spirituality of the congregations amid the growing signs of renewal in the Anglican diocese.

He appreciated the leadership of the organist/choirmaster and accepted Barrett's inherent conservatism in the 'singing of canticles and
psalms' and 'choral settings of the Eucharist'. Choral and instrumental
recitals were frequent and a close connection with the Royal School of
Church Music was maintained. The two church choirs participated in
annual eisteddfods, performed at church and diocesan functions and
recorded 'Community Hymn Singing' for the ABC.[4] Special music was
provided at the dedication of the two windows installed in memory
of the first rector, Ross Border, and there was rarely a month in which
the choirs were not involved in some special event. The choirmaster
regularly played the new Canberra Carillon.[5]

It was the installation of a pipe organ, however, that was of immediate concern. With $5,677 in the organ fund in 1971, the council
decided to install a custom-built pipe organ at a cost of between
$8,000 and $9,000. The instrument was designed with two manuals of
six ranks on the Great and four ranks on the Swell with an extended
rank on the Pedal, while the Console would have provision for a third
manual 'when money was in hand to add a Choir Organ'. To be located
in the loft above the sanctuary, it would eliminate the 'crackles' of the
electronic organ, have greater clarity and volume and produce 'pleasant softer tones'. As it was being built, an extra rank of pipes was added
'as a memorial to Sir Kenneth Bailey', and its range was extended with
two donations by Dr and Mrs Walter Cliff and the Wheat family. Then

the church received 'a substantial gift' from John Munro in memory of his son Robert who had died in the rectory and 'whose musical gifts and contribution to parochial life' were well remembered. Tony Welby installed the organ in August and a dedication service was conducted on 24 September 1972. Archdeacon Munro gave the address and the choirmaster of St James' Sydney, Walter Sutcliffe, was the visiting organist.[6]

Unfortunately, the council did not heed Barrett's warning that roosting pigeons shared the organ loft and that problems would result. It was not long before bird feathers, rubbish and heavy rains flooded the loft and drenched the organ. Wistfully, the council estimated the damage at $200 but Welby, who was hastily summoned from Sydney, quoted $1,000 plus $60 'for an emergency visit' and an additional $50 each quarter for tuning.[7] Despite some repairs to the tower, the problem was not overcome and, in the words of some parishioners, the organ was 'virtually drowned' during 1974 and 1975, causing alarm to the insurance company and suggestions that compensation might be forfeited.

Three issues required resolution at a wider parish level. First, Chynoweth tackled the issue of school religious instruction, wrote a paper on secondary school involvement and highlighted the 'ineffectiveness of what has been done in the past on almost every level' – didactic, moral and religious affiliation. 'If our presence is *right,*' he concluded, then 'our methods are plainly *wrong.*' He urged council to withdraw from Narrabundah and Telopea Park High Schools 'as soon as convenient to them'. Council accepted his recommendations, withdrew and introduced voluntary lunch-time lectures 'on religious, ethical and social matters'. The response was 'surprisingly good' with some lectures 'attracting over 100 students as well as teachers'. Thirty years later, Neville Chynoweth still referred to the 'withering' of religious instruction in secondary schools and the suspect nature of well-meaning lessons provided by many of the laity.[8]

A second issue, building a church at Red Hill, was inching toward resolution, assisted by the curate, Geoff Sibly. Stemming from the earlier work of John Munro, the bishop approved the plans, a bank loan was secured and final approval was granted by the authorities for the construction of a building at a cost of $28,615.[9] Thankful parishioners watched as the foundations were poured in January 1972 and

the steel frames and buttresses erected, allowing Bishop Warren (by
now the diocesan bishop) to lay the foundation stone on St David's
Day, 1 March. It was a proud moment for Bill Curtis and his team as
they recalled the parishioners 'who had served the church well in their
sacrificial giving and work.'[10]

The bishop returned to open 'the crowded chapel and hall' on 16
July 1972. In front of 250 people, the rector expressed gratitude to Jack
Firth, the architect and Derek Wrigley, the design consultant, who 'had
given their services freely.' Spurred on by Geoff Sibly, the furnishing
appeal reached almost $7,000 aided by the Churchwomen's Union
which contributed $2,000 for floor coverings and the profit from an art
and pottery exhibition in the church hall. When Sibly was appointed
to the Parish of Braidwood in October, Chynoweth acknowledged his
three-year contribution to the parish:

> His vision and concern for all ... the building of St David's
> and its furnishing have contributed very much to its success
> in completion, not least in the virtual payment in full of the
> furnishings so far. As well, his musical gifts gave him a leading
> part in the installation of the organ at St Paul's.[11]

Neville and Joan Chynoweth did not realise how much St David's – the
'little gem of a building' and the garden dedicated to Bill Curtis – would
figure in their lives for more than 40 years.

Up to 50 people attended weekly services conducted by the three
clergy, Geoff Sibly, David Hill and John Bowen, and the rector conducted worship on a regular basis. Chynoweth maintained close
contact with the wardens. He lamented the unexpected death of Bill
Curtis in 1972 and relied increasingly on the assistance of warden,
Alan Benson. Between 25 and 30 children attended Sunday school
with Dorothy Anderson but at-
tendances fell as the 'baby boom'
declined and as many youngsters
found interests outside church
life.[12] Sunday school teaching
itself became less attractive and
the rector regretted the 'lack
of people who were willing to
teach.'[13] There was discussion on

St David's Red Hill   © St Paul's Archives

a retirement village behind the church but nothing eventuated during the 1970s apart from cutting the long grass to discourage snakes. The small church had made a promising beginning by 1973 although it could not foresee the economic strife immediately ahead.

The third issue concerned the Narrabundah problem: was a separate church really viable for thirteen people and, if so, in what form?[14] There was little progress until September 1972 when, following Sibly's appointment to Braidwood, the number of parish clergy was reduced to two and the Narrabundah Churchwomen's Union proposed that Sunday services cease. Consequently, council discontinued services from December, encouraged the parishioners to worship at St Paul's and provided car transport for those in need.[15] Nevertheless, the Boolimba Crescent property was retained and the women continued to meet and conduct stalls at the Fyshwick Markets. By February 1974, the parish council surrendered the land originally allocated for church purposes but the ultimate resolution of St Barnabas' future was to wait for some years.

Apart from these parish concerns, diocesan issues assumed greater significance during Chynoweth's incumbency. The General Synod had appointed a number of commissions during the 1960s and their valuable reports began to influence church thinking. A softening relationship with the Roman Catholic Church after Vatican II, a widened sense of ecumenism, a greater concern with society's disadvantaged and an emphasis on justice and compassion were apparent by the early 1970s. Hence, when Jim Monro, Reg Coombe, Don Youngman, the two curates and the rector set off for the 1971 synod at Goulburn, they realised that they too would discuss 'matters of public interest' on which decisions had not been previously possible.

One issue was the sensitive topic of abortion, especially when the mother's health was in jeopardy, in cases of rape and incest and where serious deformity of the child was likely. After numerous amendments, a motion accepting abortion in these cases was passed, the vote of 95 to 37 indicating that the synod 'did not express approval' of those who sought abortion in different circumstances. On the issue of homosexuality, it was accepted by 128 to 17 that 'an understanding society' was more likely 'to help homosexuals' than one that rejected and punished them. Consequently, the synod informed the Attorneys-General that, while the 'church's traditional teaching and history does not condone homosexual practice', Christian faith 'does not ask the civil power to treat homosexual acts between consenting adults as criminal offences'.

As it deliberated the issue of racism, the synod was distressed 'at the violence and division' caused by segregated South African sporting teams and believed that 'it would be unhelpful' if Australia were to 'engage in official sporting contests' with teams 'as at present selected'. Such condemnation forced the synod to admit that 'we Australians are also guilty of racism' particularly in relation to the indigenous population in a coastal parish of the diocese. According to Jim Monro, synod members caught some of Bishop Clements' vision 'to enable them to think their way through difficult problems and face them with courage'.[16] In turn, the bishop believed that the decisions were 'indicative of the main stream of Christian conscience', the then Primate (Archbishop Frank Woods) expressed his approbation and *The Canberra Times* gave its approval to the church's more liberal attitude.[17]

A few days later the government announced that Australian forces would be withdrawn from Vietnam by Christmas. Within months, the McMahon government was defeated at the polls, the first Labor government in 23 years was elected, the end of national service was decreed, an 'Aboriginal tent embassy' stood on the lawns outside Parliament House, Australian servicemen began leaving Vietnam and the Reverend Sir Douglas Nicholls was knighted – the first indigenous person to be so recognised. Australian society was undergoing profound change – a form of renewal – as it became more liberal and more inclusive. The synod's decisions reflected a similar change, a movement towards revitalisation and incorporation.

Many young people sought renewal through less traditional forms of worship more relevant to their needs – greater freedom, modern music, heightened emotion and spontaneity of expression. The 'Jesus Movement' of the late 1960s and early 1970s spread to Australia as 'a major hippie element within some strands of Protestantism', while the charismatic and Pentecostal movements emerged within the historic churches. Emphasising the Holy Spirit and the gifts of the Spirit, the charismatic movement grew in Canberra in the 'cell church movement' (home gatherings) and in the prayer groups of the Catholic Archdiocese of Canberra & Goulburn.[18] Its influence on the Anglican Church was not uniform, was generally more subdued and was seen as part of a wider movement known as 'revival' or 'renewal'. Bishop Warren agreed that 'the charismatic movement was making its mark and there was much talk of *renewal*' but he steered away from the idea of 'charismatic renewal' (baptism in the Spirit) and sought 'more temperate ways of achieving the desired result'.[19]

Chynoweth believed that the 'rock operas' *Jesus Christ (Superstar)* and *Godspell* and 'religious themes in popular music' indicated a 'reawakening interest in the Christian faith' and, while cautioning against 'vague and woolly thinking', agreed to a youth service with rock music, pop songs and special lighting in the church. The 'Love Mass' emphasised 'an act of worship rather than a spectacle or concert' but 500 people 'young in years and heart' packed the church. Repeated again in 1973 on the theme of 'Hope', its popularity among young people indicated the appeal of a less traditional approach to worship.[20]

On one occasion, Malcolm Williamson conducted a 'jazz mass' at St Paul's with the assistance of a choir that was attending a local music course. He explained to a bemused congregation that:

> this is the last night of the pre-Christian era. You are all slaves … you are all shackled together. Join arms with the person next to you and sway with the music. Now the sun is rising… Bend down, DOWN under the pews if you can. Raise your arm horizontal. That is the horizon. Lift your arm slowly above it. That is the sun, the light of the world, coming now into the world. But keep singing! Stamp your feet too, if you can! Make your whole body take part in the Mass …

As the congregation relaxed and participated, they were divided into two parts to sing 'Jesus lover of my soul' and told:

> Make it SOUND like a love song! Wave your arms towards the altar. Show your desperate longing for truth and salvation and holy things. Christ is coming! Wave your hands and handkerchiefs. You're in a ticker-tape procession for the Christ, down Broadway or somewhere …

Then, as the congregation moved to take Communion, the voices 'of the choir rose to the panelled ceiling in a jazz setting' of 'The Lord is My Shepherd' and the communicants responded 'five beats to the bar, Alleluia, Alleluia'. The effect on the congregation was dramatic and exciting.[21]

The rector was aware, however, that renewal implied something lasting and was gratified when Fred Dau occupied the pulpit while he and Joan were on long-service leave. Dau explored 'the Meaning of Renewal' in his sermons and continued the theme after the rector returned with a wider vision to deepen the faith of the parish. Recalling the success of 'Operation Deep Think' during Munro's incumbency, Chynoweth prompted council to plan another retreat, 'Deep Think II'. His wartime involvement, attendance at Moore College, his expansive theological views and his love of Anglicanism and its Prayer Book, had fashioned his concepts of spirituality and liturgy. The evangelically-oriented Moore College had instilled in him the importance of biblical knowledge and personal commitment; his views on biblical interpretation and Christian living had ensured his acceptance of a *via-media* form of Anglicanism. He did not embrace 'extreme High Churchmanship' and did not confess to be 'an Anglo-Catholic with prayers to saints and the virgin', but saw himself as a 'Prayer Book Catholic' who accepted the conservative ritual of the church to enhance a sense of holiness and beauty.[22]

The rector hoped that 'Deep Think II' would revitalise faith, deepen parish life and 'recreate the enthusiasm and initiative' of the previous conference. Directed by John Livermore (the Permanent Head of the Department of the Army), the weekend at Tathra in 1973 attracted 48 parishioners who examined Christian education, outreach programs, ecumenism, forms of worship and family life. The conference

The Reverend Neville Chynoweth
(family album)

concluded that the Sunday school needed attention while children's church services should be simplified. Traditional worship patterns needed to be varied, more adult involvement introduced, seating rearranged and a greater involvement 'of women within all aspects' of church administration, worship and service 'should be initiated'. Moreover, 'the effect of the charismatic experience might be studied' because 'the spontaneity of such worship has rewards in many ways'.

The conference also decided that greater effort was required to contact families in hostels, cater for 'latch-key' children, provide emergency accommodation for the needy and 'adopt' children at the Grammar Schools, with less emphasis on correct dress in church. It was proposed that the 7am service be combined with the 8am service and that breakfast be provided in the hall to develop a sense of fellowship. The recommendations were referred to five parish council committees with suggestions for another conference, 'Deep Think III', in October 1975.[23] While the participants realised that parish congregations were falling during 1973, they were not to know that numbers would decline even more over the next two years (see Table 12.2).

Within the diocese, Bishop Warren – aware that the appeal of Anglicanism was waning and that church life was viewed as routine and sterile in the minds of many – led a diocesan renewal program known as 'Impact 74'. It advocated 'simultaneous programs of financial stewardship and pastoral care' over successive phases: parishioners would make financial pledges for the year and teams of lay people would systematically visit fellow parishioners, supporting each other and encouraging church involvement. This would 'cancel out the complaint that parishioners were visited only for money' while enhancing the importance of pastoral care in the parish.[24]

In the first phase, parishioners took a pilgrimage to St Saviour's Cathedral in Goulburn, a joint expression of faith, shared experience and common goals. Special trains were run, buses hired and a crowd of 4,000 to 5,000 'gathered on the grassy paddock to the north of the cathedral'. They listened to contemporary religious music led by a guitar group from Tumbarumba and enjoyed 'just the right balance of gaiety and earnestness' to the launching of 'Impact 74'. The train from Canberra was 'filled to overflowing and the good fellowship engendered on the journey' put the crowd 'in the right mind' for the inspiring rally.[25]

This was followed by a parish training program for those involved in the visitation phase, preparing each person to call on five families to explain 'Impact 74'. The families were then invited to thanksgiving services at which they were asked to offer their lives to God and make a 'weekly financial commitment' to the church. Following these services, 'a program of pastoral care and outreach' was developed as contact was maintained with the families on a regular basis. In St Paul's parish, 65 visitors called on 'well over 350 parish families' and followed up with repeat visits to those who could not attend the thanksgiving services.

> By the end of the day, over 200 families had completed cards promising a total of about $700 per week – $36,000 per year. There were 53 new pledges and 64 increases ... the estimated total of pledges was about $41,000, with open plate collections expected to bring the total to about $45,000 ... [compared] with total expenditure last year of about $33,000.

The rector was impressed but stressed that visitors should continue their pastoral visits 'and gradually spread out to others as well'.[26]

In the meantime, Neville Chynoweth had acquired a raft of new responsibilities after Bishop Warren's installation as diocesan bishop in November 1971. When the bishop rearranged the archdeaconry boundaries at the end of 1972, he appointed the rector of Manuka as Archdeacon of Canberra from January 1973 and later as Bishop's Commissary to act during the bishop's 'temporary absence from the province or during any temporary incapacity'. With 'Impact 74' well underway, Chynoweth was nominated for the vacant see of Bendigo and, when he confided in Bishop Warren, was asked if he wished to leave Canberra. The rector replied that 'he would prefer to stop in Canberra' whereupon Warren quickly nominated him as the assistant bishop of the diocese. Carried away by the news, St Paul's newspaper, *Cross-Way*, congratulated the new 'Assistant *Archbishop*'.[27]

After his consecration and commissioning, a special service was held at St Paul's – 'a joyous occasion' – where Eleanor Scott-Findlay referred to the rector's concern for others, his ability to display sympathy, empathy and understanding and his capacity to discuss 'things spiritual' that are 'not quite as cut and dried as we would wish them' to be. Joan Chynoweth's support and personal contribution were acknowledged and the congregation hoped that the new bishop and his wife would 'find lots of good episcopal reasons' to return to St Paul's. Within days Bishop Chynoweth had responsibility for work in the new areas of Canberra, collaborating with other clergy and the NCDC and participating in confirmations, parochial visitation and pastoral support for his colleagues.[28]

As he concluded his last service, the rector recorded his feelings in the Register of Services: 'The close of a very happy and all too short ministry in this wonderful parish. N.J.C, 23 February, 1975.' He had stressed spiritual renewal, watched the commencement of St David's Red Hill, grappled with the problem of religious education in secondary schools and brought a nurturing warmth to the pastoral care of the parish. While the register recorded a decline in the number of St Paul's communicants over three years (14,877 (1972); 12,600 (1973); 11,211 (1974)[29]), this was partly balanced by the number who transferred to and worshipped at, St David's (see Table 12.2). Nevertheless, despite the rector's efforts, the overall parish decline was over 17 per cent during the same period, a trend that was to continue across the nation throughout the 1970s.

As Bishop Warren searched for a replacement – one neither 'charismatic' nor stridently evangelical – he remembered John Falkingham, the Dean of Newcastle Cathedral, who had an intimate understanding of liturgy, was well organised and theologically moderate – a safe appointment for St Paul's.[30] After his ordination and completing an Arts honours degree in history and ThL(Hons), he had spent seven years as chaplain to Trinity College (Melbourne) and eleven years as Vicar of Malvern where he was also the Examining Chaplain for the Archbishop of Melbourne and a canon of St Paul's Cathedral. On his move to Newcastle, he lectured at St John's College in Morpeth and served as a member of both the Liturgical Commission and the executive of the Church Army in Australia. Described as a 'scholarly English gentleman', he was gentle in nature with a keen and analytical mind.[31] His subtle sense of humour was exemplified in Newcastle when an escapee from a psychiatric hospital entered the cathedral and Falkingham asked him who he was. The poor man proclaimed, 'I am God's Son.' 'Well,' responded Dean Falkingham, 'your father said to go and sit down on the seat and be quiet.'

Falkingham's incumbency coincided with a time of crippling inflation, an expansion of diocesan influence vis-à-vis the parish and the modification of the church's liturgy. Inducted at Manuka on 2 March 1975, he and his wife, Joan, met members of the council, many of whom were influential community members or held highly responsible government positions. The rector noted that stewardship and pastoral care figured strongly under Lieutenant-Colonel Des Ireland and that Michael Game's financial report indicated debts on the parish hall ($36,000) and St David's church ($15,000). The council was concerned with the Narrabundah church, youth work, fellowship, music and the all-important subject of 'Australia 73' – the revision of the church liturgy.[32]

Like his predecessor, the rector realised that the faith of the congregation was his prime concern and sought ways to enhance the parish spirituality. He encouraged the 'Deep Think III' Conference in Cooma late in 1975 and stressed that pastoral care, education and missionary activity were all part of evangelism although he did not think that 'the parish as a whole was doing this very successfully'. He promoted weekend parish retreats at St David's and at Bishopthorpe (Goulburn) to develop prayer, fellowship and spirituality, hoping that they would 'become part of our parish program', and emphasised the development of small groups to promote adult Christian education.[33]

Four major trends were evident during Falkingham's incumbency. First, the rector followed international trends closely, explored church union and became actively involved in ecumenical movements. He promoted the efforts of the World Council of Churches and prayed for Christian consensus, lamenting 'the apparent lack of interest in Canberra in the matter of unity' and the 'poor results of previous endeavours'. When the Archbishop of Canterbury met Pope Paul VI in 1977, the rector ensured that the occasion featured on the front page of *Cross-Way* and was gratified when the Archbishop of Canterbury, Dr Donald Coggan, preached 'at a great ecumenical service at St Christopher's Roman Catholic Cathedral' at Manuka. Moreover, he was greatly encouraged by the formation of the Uniting Church in Australia (by the union of the Methodist, Presbyterian and Congregational churches) in the same year.

By 1978 the local clergy of 'various Christian groups' met regularly 'to discuss common problems and possible joint activities', and lay representatives hoped to join 'in combined action on matters of mutual concern'. Ecumenical services were held in the Baptist and Uniting Churches during 1979 and reciprocated at St Paul's under the auspices of the Canberra Ministers' Fraternal.[34] From 1980, however, the impetus for combined ventures waned. The rector was still involved in ecumenical activities in 1981 but they were 'poorly attended' and little contact was made with Presbyterian or Roman Catholic parishioners.[35] According to Bishop Chynoweth, ecumenical interest declined as it was realised that the goal of organic church union was not really possible at the time. One practical venture involved Kingston Baptist, Wesley Uniting and St Paul's Manuka, a project to support a Christian community in the Kingston-Narrabundah area for young people not attracted to church. Called the 'Daifullah Community' under the guidance of the ANU Ecumenical Chaplain, it held monthly bush dances, met informally each week, provided help and support in times of crisis and offered Christian training. Within a year, it developed outdoor programs for high school students and planned a centre for 'latch-key' primary school children each afternoon.[36] When it faced a financial crisis in 1980, St Paul's Council donated $100 in addition to its annual contribution.[37]

A second issue during Falkingham's incumbency was the liturgy of the Anglican Church and the attempts to revise the 1662 Prayer Book. The *Book of Common Prayer* was venerated because of 'the beauty of its language, the spiritual sensitivities of its liturgy and the fact that it formed a bond of unity for Anglicans'.[38] While minor changes had been introduced over time, including a modified form of Communion in 1928 (the so-called 'Diocesan Rite'), it was accepted as the authority that governed liturgy and worship in Australia throughout the 1950s. Despite these virtues, its language was archaic – not the vernacular of a modern society – and revision was long overdue.

Cautiously accepting the need for change, the 1950 General Synod had appointed a Prayer Book Commission to examine possible changes, a decision made easier by the passage of an Australian Constitution in 1962. Following the commission's favourable report in 1966, a Liturgical Commission had been formed to 'test the water' and provide draft services for trial.[39] It was in this context that Dr Munro had experimented with different forms of the liturgy at St Paul's between 1968 and 1970. By 1973 St Paul's had received another experimental liturgy, 'Sunday Services Revised' (SSR) and Chynoweth had applied to the bishop for permission to use it at Manuka and Red Hill. To allow parishioners to express their feelings, a questionnaire had been distributed, with 43 per cent of the 105 respondents giving the 1662 form their first preference, 30 per cent the SSR, 14 per cent the Revised Services Series 2 and 8 per cent the 1928 Diocesan Rite. Sixteen indicated that they had 'changed their attendance habits to avoid SSR and six had said they would worship elsewhere' if it were introduced, prompting the rector to roster different liturgical forms during the month and notify the congregation in advance.

The next experimental form, 'Australia 73', introduced the most change, leading Chynoweth to affirm that, while some 'felt unable to accept change at all', there was a 'general approval and even enthusiastic acceptance' of the liturgy. He had convened meetings to discuss its continuation, frequency of use, ritual, lay participation, preferred practices and any other matters of moment to parishioners. The 'other matters' included kneeling, the writer in *Cross-Way* decreeing that when the words (Kneel), (Sit) or (Stand) were written in brackets, one did not have to obey, but when KNEEL, SIT or STAND were 'printed without brackets, that is what you do'. The introduction of change did not always pass without opposition.[40]

One period of experimentation ended in March 1975, when Bishop Warren judged that many worshippers 'were tired of the booklets, pamphlets and sheets of paper' used in trial services. He knew, however, that the 'enormous amount of work' that had been done would assist acceptance of the new prayer book when published.[41] John Falkingham had performed much of this work himself as secretary of the Liturgical Commission and he now observed positive reactions by the parishioners. In 1976 he informed the congregation that a new form of the Communion service entitled 'Australia 77' had been issued with modern versions of Morning and Evening Prayer and alternative versions of marriage, baptism and confirmation services. Finally, parishioners learned that the General Synod had accepted the new prayer book, 'a fitting finale to more than ten years of sustained and devoted consultation'.[42]

It was left to the wardens to provide a fitting accolade in February 1979:

The introduction of the Australian Prayer Book to the whole country is of great personal satisfaction to our Rector, who has given many years of devoted work to the project as Secretary of the Liturgical Commission; and it is a source of pride to us all that he has been awarded the degree of Doctor of Theology as a recognition of this effort.[43]

The Reverend J Falkingham
© *Framing Matters, Manuka*

The 1978 prayer book was not meant to replace the 1662 version and both were expected to continue in use. The council introduced *An Australian Prayer Book* as the basis of the liturgy at St Paul's and St David's.[44] Nevertheless, devotion to the 1662 liturgy and the conservatism of sections of the congregation ensured its continuation at the 7am service at St Paul's.

It was fitting that the *Australian Hymn Book*, an ecumenical venture, was published around the same time. Both the Reverend Owen Dowling (former organist at St Saviour's Cathedral, Goulburn) and Bishop Chynoweth made considerable inputs into its publication which John Barrett described as a 'further enrichment of our worship'. Nevertheless, Barrett and the adult choir found difficulty in accepting changes to the choral liturgy. They took some time to become accustomed 'to the new psalm translations at Evensong' and retained 'some well known musical settings for the 1662 Prayer Book' for one service each month.[45] Hence, while Bishop Warren claimed that both the new prayer book and the hymnal were part of the church's wider renewal process during the 1970s, unanimity at St Paul's was not possible and the rectors were aware of traditional attitudes present among sections of the congregation.

A third trend was the combination of stewardship and pastoral care under the rubric of renewal – a push to enhance the influence of the diocese, increase the church's income and significantly extend parish visitations by members of the congregation. 'Impact 74', the program of 'simultaneous financial stewardship and pastoral care' that had been commenced during Chynoweth's time, became an annual event and it was anticipated that the church would extend its influence and receive additional funds.

These plans were thrown into confusion when the Australian political scene became unstable and the Whitlam Labor government was dismissed by the Governor-General in November 1975.

The national economy had earlier faltered when growth stalled in 1973 and inflation accelerated. During the 1960s the inflation rate had stabilised at about 4 per cent, increased to 7 per cent about the time Chynoweth became rector and then accelerated exponentially to 18 per cent (21.6 per cent by one economic indicator) by 1975, the first year of Falkingham's incumbency.[46]

Table 12.1
St Paul's finances: 1971–1981[47]

Year	Income $	Surplus (Deficit)	Stipends Rent Travel	Parish Pledge	Other Extra Parochial Costs
1971	31,459	167	16,700	4,888	2,050
1973	36,390	204	19,616	5,230	3,482
1974	46,031	34	25,045	7,706	5161a
1975	58,204b	1,053	30,088	9,273	3,427
1976	58,453	2,008	29,508	10,464	9,744c
1977	59,397	3,055	32,460	11,087	6,042
1978	71,706	46	42,908	12,772	4,962
1979	75.099	(3,132)	47,115	13,571	5,741
1980	78,946	(140)	45,626	14,004	9,565
1981	81,600	288	47,785	14,407	6,618

a Includes $1,931 not paid. b Includes a special diocesan appeal.
c Includes $6,326 for 1975–76 special appeals.

The economic effect on both the parish and diocese was devastating as the church sought to keep up with rampant prices, salary increases and escalating interest payments. As shown in Table 12.1, the annual expenditure on stipends, rents and travel at St Paul's rose 286 per cent over a decade ($16,700 to $47,785) even though the number of curates dropped from time to time and it was acknowledged that clerical stipends were lower than other professional groups. The rise in interest rates was most devastating at St David's where the bank debt was usually repaid at $1,200 a year but the interest alone in 1974 amounted to $1,326. In fact, St David's total debt increased from $14,438 to $15,105 over three years, despite the repayment of $3,600. It forced the parish council to increase the amount of repayments and turn hurriedly to St David's Churchwomen's Union – led by Joan Chynoweth, Elizabeth Brown and Joan Falkingham – for a dedicated and sustained fund-raising program.[48]

The diocese suffered similar financial crises and approached the parishes for support. The synod had abolished 'parish assessments' in 1959 and had introduced a pledge system whereby each parish promised or pledged a specified amount each year. The St Paul's and St David's pledge of $4,888 in 1971 rose to $14,407 by 1981, a rise of almost 250 per cent, as the church sought to maintain a contribution equal to 20 per cent of its total income. Eventually the situation became critical. At the end of 1975 the council considered reducing the parish staff or lowering its pledge to the diocese which faced a deficit of $60,000 itself. Fortunately, when a special appeal was launched, it activated an immediate response and St Paul's parish forwarded over $9,500 to the diocese within two months with a further $1,300 promised. The church finished the year without a deficit, over $5,500 was contributed to the diocese as a gift and the 1975 diocesan pledge of $9,270 was met.[49] Not all appeals were successful, however, although the council still managed to repay the instalments on St Paul's hall, a liability that was reduced to $27,700 by the end of 1981.

The parish was also responsible for so-called 'hidden costs' in their budgets. As part of their 'extra-parochial donations' each year, parishioners contributed to St Mark's Library, the College of Ministry, Anglican Women of Australia, Church Army, World Vision, Dr Barnardo's Homes, a range of missions and Bible societies, Christmas Bowl collections and the Daifullah Community at Narrabundah. And then, the diocese canvassed for additional funds for the chaplaincies at the Canberra and Woden hospitals. Times of inflation were indeed harsh and their effects had a ripple effect through the entire community.[50]

It was quite remarkable, therefore, that the pipe organ at St Paul's was installed, maintained and further developed over ten years without cost to the parish and that an extensive music program was virtually self-funded under Barrett's direction. Through concerts, recitals, television and radio broadcasts, weddings, organ tuition and periodic donations, the organ fund was topped up each year, permitting the completion of both the Great Manual and the Choir Organ. By 1981 the Pedal Organ was strengthened and the Great Organ was given better balance, finally achieving Barrett's goal. The junior choir with 20 members sang at the 10am service, the senior choir with similar numbers at the evening service and the two combined for special events. They participated in parliamentary and law society services, functions at Duntroon, Evensong at St Mark's Library, recitals at neighbouring churches, ceremonies at St Saviour's Cathedral, regional eisteddfods and at choir festivals with the Royal School of Church Music.

By 1981, John Barrett had completed two decades as organist and choirmaster at St Paul's, adding his traditional approach to its musical life. He was responsible not only for the installation of the pipe organ but also for a musical tradition that he clearly nurtured. Moreover, he took a close interest in the music at St David's, encouraged the organist, Dr John Bellhouse, and advised the wardens on the choice of organs.[51] During 1981 and 1982 he suffered from ill health and retired at the end of 1982. His 'farewell' was the 'magnificent service of Nine Lessons and Carols on Christmas evening', a fitting tribute to his devotion and inexhaustible energy. When the 1982 annual report was issued, John Barrett's yearly summary was missing – he died two weeks after retiring, his work finished.[52]

The move for increased stewardship and pastoral care naturally extended to St David's and St Barnabas', two centres in contrasting socio-economic neighbourhoods. Falkingham delegated major responsibilities to the clergy at St David's, although he conducted services himself and worked closely with the wardens while Canon Dau returned occasionly in an acting capacity. The women ensured the viability of the centre by extricating the church from its desperate financial position, purchasing items for worship, contributing to missions and assisting the College of Ministry at St Mark's. They organised social activities, arranged and coordinated an annual art and pottery exhibition and took part in prayer and Bible study groups. Some taught in the Sunday school that catered for 15 to 25 children in 1975–1977 but only nine in 1981.[53] An external cross was erected to the memory of Bill Curtis in 1975 and the grounds were improved. Plans were considered for an eventual retirement village, a residence for the assistant bishop and a separate dwelling for the curate. Despite these plans, no construction had begun when Falkingham retired from the parish in mid-1982.

Down the hill at Narrabundah, a completely different scenario unravelled. After services had ceased at St Barnabas' in December 1972, a small group of women calling themselves the 'mission group' continued to raise funds through hobby exhibitions and the sale of produce. Raising $860 in 1975, $600 in 1976 and $1,100 in 1977, they made annual donations to missions, children's homes and individuals in need. Falkingham praised their 'great vigour' and 'amazing financial results for missionary work'. While it was generally agreed that 'the worshipping population at Narrabundah' did not 'seem viable', a newly ordained priest, Dr Jim McPherson, recommenced monthly services during 1978, first in the home of Mrs Alice Wheat and then at the Narrabundah Primary School but, 'in spite of careful visiting', the numbers were 'very small indeed'.

The council could not resolve the future of Narrabundah, 'the most difficult pastoral problem in the parish'. While the work of the assistant priests was well known in the district, particularly among South-East Asian refugee families, the disconcerting mobility of the population and their seeming indifference to Anglicanism meant that the total attending St Barnabas' over eleven months was 56 and the largest number at a service was only 10. When Jim McPherson moved from the parish, services at the school were discontinued. A church warden summed up the situation in blunt terms, 'Our impact on and ministry to the area ... is negligible. We remain pretty much an upper-middle-class community; and we have failed and continue to fail, that part of the parish.'[54] At the end of 1980, the women's 'mission group' contributed another $640 to diocesan projects and then disbanded, Hilda Blewett and Eva Ives thanking 'all who have supported St Barnabas' over the years'. While it appeared that the Narrabundah program had finished, no-one understood the legalities of disbursing the $11,600 in the building fund or the yearly interest that was accruing.[55]

Another venture that was phased out was the chaplaincy at HMAS *Harman*. As society's attitudes to 'enforced' religion changed, it was decided to abolish compulsory church parades by the early 1970s and the last mandatory Anglican services were most likely conducted by Fred Dau. During the 1980s, any part-time chaplaincy was provided by representatives of the Anglican, Roman Catholic and 'other Protestant' denominations. *Harman* increasingly became an administrative support centre for Navy Office at Russell Hill. The Principal Chaplain, John Jones, who worked at Navy Office, held Communion services for small numbers at *Harman* 'a few times a year' and conducted an occasional wedding or baptism in the chapel. His main responsibility was the provision of counselling when approached by officers and sailors attached to the establishment.[56]

The two denominational schools likewise reached a significant stage in their development when the direct input of the diocese was constitutionally reduced. While the grammar schools were independent in their daily management, the bishop was still 'heavily involved' as chairperson of both boards of management and was required to maintain a close working knowledge of policy and fiscal concerns. By February 1972, however, the chairperson's role was assumed by a lay person and the bishop became the official Visitor. Bishop Warren then considered whether the schools could be '*set free* by incorporation' and, after a decade of constitutional negotiation and amendment, the schools were established as corporate bodies from January 1981.[57]

A fourth trend was the changing pattern of worship in the parish. Over time, there had been a predictable pattern to church life involving Sunday morning services, Evensong and a midweek gathering, with additional services on saints' days. While some parishioners had been drawn from outside the immediate confines of the church, most lived within the parish and their social life was frequently centred on church activities. These patterns had started to break down during the 1960s, the result of changing attitudes, television, cars and Sunday sport, so that by the late 1970s most parishioners attended services only once on Sunday. While Neville Chynoweth had presented his annual report to a large Evensong congregation in 1972, this was no longer possible in 1979 when the senior choir of 20 usually 'outnumbered the congregation' at St Paul's.[58]

The Sunday school – numbering 250 to 300 in Border's time – collapsed as the baby boom ended and non-churchgoing families no longer sent their children. Average weekly attendances at St Paul's Sunday school plummeted to nine in 1981 with another nine at St David's as the church-like format of the school provided little motivation for the majority of youngsters to attend.[59] Changing its emphasis to youth activities, St Paul's introduced the Wednesday Club for 11–14-year-olds (emphasising sport and social activities), the Monday Club for the 14–16-year-olds (accenting social and religious interests) and the Young Adults group (providing social, community-oriented and devotional pursuits).[60] Religious instruction in schools likewise suffered reverses. Having discontinued traditional instruction classes in secondary schools in 1971, the church concentrated on primary school instruction but the clergy were not able to meet their commitments every week because of other duties and the inability to find a band of teachers on a full-time basis. Falkingham warned that if any of the clergy were transferred, it might 'be necessary to withdraw altogether' from the primary schools.[61]

While the overall population of Canberra climbed from 155,000 in 1972 to almost 225,000 in 1980, numbers in the older parts of the inner-south actually declined. The population of the parish dropped by 2,500 between 1971 and 1975 – Narrabundah by 830, Red Hill by 500 and Griffith by 440 – a change that not only reduced the number of Anglicans but also contracted the financial base of the parish.[62] The number of communicants at St Paul's dropped from 15,540 in 1971 to 9,637 in 1975, some transferring to St David's (see Table 12.2). Even so, the combined numbers at both centres saw a drop of more than 25 per cent over five years. From 1977 the annual number of morning-service communicants at St Paul's stabilised at about 9,000 and St David's achieved an average of 1,750 each year, while numbers at each Evensong plunged to less than 30 including the choir.[63]

Table 12.2
Number of communicants
St Paul's and St David's 1971 – 1982[64]

Year	St Paul's Church	Outside St Paul's[a]	St Paul's Total	St David's Church	Overall Total
1971			15,540	-	15,540
1972	13,825	1,052	14,877	839b	15,716
1973	11,919	681	12,600	1,460	14,060
1974	9,080	2,131	11,211	1,639	12,850
1975	9,049	588	9,637	1,973	11,610
1976	8,730	897	9,627	1,683	11,310
1977	9,162	1,251	10,413	1,687	12,100
1978	9,201	1,858	11,059	1,927	12,986
1979	9,064	2,042	11,106	1,964	13,070
1980	9,701c	1,733	11,434	1,795	13,229
1981	9,089	1,947	11,036	1,598	12,634
1982	9,433	1,985	11.418	1,613	13,031

a Communion in aged-care facilities and hospitals   b Part-year only
c Includes 407 communicants at Bishop Chynoweth's farewell (16 November)

The decline in communicants would have been even more marked had the church not provided a strong ministry to aged-care facilities within the parish. As indicated in the column 'Outside St Paul's', the

number of these communicants in 1982 comprised a sizeable proportion of the total figure – 530 at the Upper Jindalee Home, a further
283 at Lower Jindalee, 172 at Morling Lodge, 77 at Karingal, 614 at the
Woden Valley Hospital and 309 in their own homes, a total of 1,985
persons.[65] Moreover, 'about 20 per cent' of regular parishioners – and
an even greater percentage of younger families – lived 'outside the
parish' in 1981. This seriously affected church organisations when
evening meetings were scheduled or young people were involved.
Consequently, much of the parish life, particularly its specifically
spiritual aspects, became increasingly focused on Sunday services as
parishioners avoided travel or participation in midweek activities'.[66]

Such changes to worship patterns were obvious but few realised
the long-term effects of changing attitudes to women's involvement
in the church. For 50 years the Churchwomen's Union had been 'a
workhorse', raising money and supporting the work of missions. It
had ensured the financial viability of St Paul's and St David's thus
contributing to new programs and enhancing the beauty of buildings and grounds.[67] Bishop Warren believed, however, that 'in the
prevailing mood of renewal, many women felt the CU to be out of
balance', more intent on fund-raising than on complementary spiritual
development. The attitudes and interests of women were changing
as more entered paid employment and so had less time, making the
movement irrelevant or simply crowded out of busy schedules. The
older members were finding CU activities too arduous. The decline
in numbers placed an undue burden on those remaining. A new approach, perhaps a different organisation, was required.

Consequently, an umbrella organisation called Anglican Women
was formed in 1975 to encourage women 'to participate fully and
confidently in the Church's liturgy, government and community life'.
The first president, Joan Chynoweth, watched the development of the
movement that, by 1983, saw women 'doing everything but priestly
duties'.[68] Even the possibility of ordination to the priesthood had been
raised at the General Synod in 1977 and two years later a long 'discussion of this controversial topic' had resulted in 'a Bill for a Canon to
alter the Church's constitution, one that would ultimately remove any
constitutional barrier to the ordination of women to the three Orders
of bishop, priest and deacon'.[69] While that development lay in the
future, the diocesan synod accepted the first women delegates in 1976.

The training of ordinands at St Mark's in the Canberra College of Ministry required that theological students be attached to a parish and be actively involved in a pastoral ministry with supervision. Consequently, theological students became involved in the ministry at St Paul's and St David's, often taking a role in youth work and instruction. When the Reverend Dr Robert Withycombe became Warden of St Mark's in 1975, he stressed the wider mission of 'promoting Christian influence', not concentrating solely on clergy training.[70]

Despite these advances and the devoted efforts of loyal parishioners, St Paul's found a decade of changes difficult. Financial restrictions, the ageing of the congregation, a lack of people volunteering for youth leadership and religious instruction and the collapse of the Sunday school movement, all contributed to a sense of uncertainty and disquiet. The church magazine, *Cross-Way*, lost its local focus and printed more articles of a general nature. At the end of 1980 it changed from a professional monthly production to a duplicated quarterly overview without a permanent editor. The parish council attempted to do too much and could not keep up with its own aspirations.[71] Consternation grew as the tennis court fell into disrepair, and the floor of the church near the baptistry rotted and caved in. The tower continued to leak, affecting the organ and disrupting services.[72] Even a major parish conference in 1980 that canvassed the themes of spirituality, pastoral care, lay involvement, finances, parish administration and Christian education lacked energy and failed to grapple fully with the issues involved.

When the annual report was read in February 1982, the two wardens 'regretfully' concluded that 1981 had not been 'a particularly successful year for St Paul's parish' and that support for the church had fallen despite the efforts of 'the faithful few'. They sincerely hoped that 1982 would 'show a new intensity of interest among other parishioners' so that the church might regain the vision and vigour of past years.[73] As society changed, the church lost its evangelistic fervour and settled into an inward-looking, prosaic attitude, somewhat listless and stolid in approach. The 'safe appointment' of a traditional scholarly rector at a time when the parish required a more dynamic and creative approach also worked against parochial expansion.

The rector felt the seriousness of the situation, knowing that he had lost some of his motivation since completing his work on liturgical reform and and the introduction of new forms of worship in the parish. Another of his dreams – an ecumenical spirit and Christian unity – was also fading in Canberra as joint ventures were discontinued. He had been honoured by his appointment as archdeacon in April 1981 but his extended duties had placed further pressure on him and he knew he should retire. After discussing the situation with wife, Joan, and members of the council in October, he resigned, suggesting to the bishop that his resignation take effect from 30 June 1982.[74] He retired to the Canberra suburb of Weston.

It is only by considering the previous fifteen years that one may understand fully the decline of the parish in the late 1970s and early 1980s. There had been a revolution in societal attitudes and behaviour, a profound change detected by John Munro when he was rector. He had understood the likely effects on the church and had sought with some success to arrest the drift. By their positive attitudes, both he and Neville Chynoweth helped to delay the worst effects of this decline until the mid-1970s, although the trend was clearly obvious and accelerating. Not even the diocesan renewal program and the revised liturgy stemmed the decline, exacerbated by the financial downturn, the parish's diminishing population and the negative attitudes of young people to church life. Neither John Falkingham nor the parish council could fully prevent the loss of belief and the deterioration in the church's position, even though a more dynamic input might have had a stronger outcome. As Tom Frame pointed out, it was a wider crisis in believing, belonging and behaving, a time when an 'all-week church for the entire community' fast became a 'confined Sunday morning church for the eucharistic faithful'.[75] Was it hoping too much that John Griffiths, the next rector, would reverse this major trend?

Notes

1. CT, 20 June to 3 August 1971.
2. Neville Chynoweth, Interview tape, NLA, Oral History Section, 1995; Neville Chynoweth, Personal communication, 2009.
3. *Cross-Way*, June and July 1971; and Eleanor Scott-Findlay, Personal communication, 2009.
4. John Barrett provided a choirmaster's report in each edition of *Cross-Way*.
5. *Cross-Way*, August 1971; January 1972.
6. *Cross-Way*, June and October 1972.
7. StPPC, 17 September; 15 October 1973.
8. 'Religious Education in Secondary Schools', NLA, MS 3085 Box 2; StPPC, 19 July 1971; *Cross-Way*, June 1973; and Neville Chynoweth, Personal communication, 2009.
9. StPPC, 19 July and 18 October 1971.
10. *Cross-Way*, April 1972.
11. *Cross-Way*, July, August and October 1972.
12. StD, Register of Services, 1972–1974; StD Sunday School Report, 1973.
13. StD, Register of Services, July 1972 – 1975; StPPC, 22 November 1971.
14. Report on St Barnabas' Narrabundah, StPPC, 12 August 1975.
15. StPPC, 22 November 1971; *Cross-Way*, February and April 1973.
16. 1971 Synod Report in *Cross-Way*, October 1971.
17. CT, 3, 4, 10 and 19 August 1971.
18. *http://www.rnc.org.au/CellNetAustralia/ozmovement.htm* and *http://canberra.disciplesofjesus.org/display_page.cfm?cid=310213165B500F7555*
19. Warren, *A Little Foolishness*, pp. 99–100.
20. *Cross-Way*, May 1972; August 1973.
21. M Williamson, *Malcolm Williamson: A Mischievous Muse*, Omnibus Press, London, 2007, pp. 263–264. I am indebted to Bishop Chynoweth for this reference.
22. Neville Chynoweth, Personal communication, 2009; and Neville Chynoweth, Interview tape.
23. *Operation Deep Think II*, Report of StPPC, 19 November 1973.
24. Warren, *A Little Foolishness*, pp. 107–111.
25. *Cross-Way*, April 1974; Warren, *A Little Foolishness*, p. 108.
26. *Cross-Way*, June 1974.
27. *Cross-Way*, February and October 1973; August 1974; Neville Chynoweth, Interview tape; Neville Chynoweth, Personal communication, 2009.
28. *Cross-Way*, August and November, 1974.
29. StP, Register of Services, 1972 - 1974.
30. Warren, *A Little Foolishness*, pp. 147–148, 181.
31. *Cross-Way*, February 1975; the author's own recollections.
32. StPPC, 18 March 1975.

33. *Cross-Way*, October 1975, December 1975–January 1976, July 1980; StPPC, 1977 annual report.
34. *Cross-Way*, July 1976, August 1977, September 1978, June 1979; StPPC, 1977 annual report.
35. StPPC, 10 November 1981.
36. *Cross-Way*, February, March, June and September 1979; August 1980.
37. StPPC, 9 September 1980.
38. Fletcher, *The Place of Anglicanism in Australia*, p. 195.
39. Fletcher, *The Place of Anglicanism in Australia*, p. 195.
40. The different experimental liturgies, the reactions of the congregations, the results of questionnaires and the judgments of the rector are recorded in monthly issues of *Cross-Way* between June 1973 and February 1975.
41. Warren, *A Little Foolishness*, p. 149.
42. *Cross-Way*, July 1976 to October 1977.
43. StPPC, 1978 annual report.
44. *An Australian Prayer Book*, The Standing Committee of the General Synod of the Church of England in Australia, Anglican Information Office, Sydney, 1978.
45. *Cross-Way*, May 1978; Fletcher, *The Place of Anglicanism in Australia*, pp.197–201.
46. P Kriesler, *The Australian Economy* (3rd ed.), Allen & Unwin, Sydney, Chapters 2 and 3.
47. The figures are collated from StPPC, annual reports from 1971 to 1981.
48. StPPC, 18 February 1975.
49. *Cross-Way*, December 1975–January 1976; February 1976.
50. All extra-parochial payments were recorded in the treasurer's annual reports that formed part of StPPC, annual reports.
51. See John Barrett's annual reports to StPPC, 1971 to 1981.
52. John Barrett's annual reports in StPPC, annual reports 1971–1981.
53. The wardens of StD included annual reports in StPPC, annual reports.
54. StPPC, 1977 annual report.
55. Details relating to St Barnabas' are found in the rector's annual reports and in the reports submitted by the 'mission group' in StPPC, 1975 to 1980.
56. John Jones, Personal communication, 2009.
57. Warren, *A Little Foolishness*, pp. 83–86.
58. Choirmaster's report, StPPC, 1979 annual report.
59. Sunday School report, StPPC, 1981 annual report.
60. Youth Group reports, StPPC, 1975 to 1980.
61. StPPC, 1979 annual report.
62. *Cross-Way*, September 1975.
63. StPPC, Register of Services 1979–1980.
64. Collated from StP Register of Services, 1971 to 1977 and StD Register of Services, 1972 to 1977.

65. The figures are collated from StPPC, Register of Services 1982.
66. Warden's report, StPPC, 1977 annual report.
67. See the reports of the Churchwomen's Unions (StP and StD) in each of the annual reports, including 1977.
68. Warren, *A Little Foolishness*, p. 106.
69. *Cross-Way*, October 1981.
70. Robert Withycombe, Personal communication, 2009.
71. Report of J Monro to parish council, StPPC, 1 February 1982.
72. StPPC, annual reports 1979–1981.
73. Warden's report, StPPC, 1981 annual report.
74. StPPC, 10 November 1981.
75. Frame, *Anglicans in Australia*, chapters 4, 5 and 6.

13   The Griffiths era, 1982–1997

John Griffiths arrived as rector amid the fervent hopes of St Paul's for rapid rejuvenation. Born in Cairns, trained at St Francis' College and ordained in Brisbane when 26, he had moved south to Young in the Diocese of Canberra & Goulburn in 1972 and then to Turvey Park in Wagga Wagga in 1976. Now, six years later, he accepted the incumbency of St Paul's at the age of 46 and arrived in Canberra in October 1982. Both he and his wife, Barbara, were described as 'lively and hospitable' and 'able to produce a sense of buzz'. John was not an academic but had 'flair, energy and passion', 'generated life', and was willing to take a risk. In his personal life he could relax, 'appreciate finer things' and turn his skill to furniture restoration.[1]

While his training had been in the Catholic tradition and he had retained such elements as incense, candles, cope and chasuble, he 'was open to spiritual renewal and a good dose of evangelical fervour' as a result of 'a renewal experience' while in Young. Described as 'competent, controversial and somewhat provocative', the new rector was 'a man of faith', a person of prayer and one who 'preached with a sense of urgency'.[2] When asked to outline his own strengths in 1982, Griffiths mentioned 'enthusiasm, creativity, positive approach and perseverance', together with 'worship, preaching' and adaptability. He saw his own weaknesses as 'impatience with minor details', being job-orientated rather than people-orientated at times and insensitivity to the real issue on occasions.[3]

To the casual observer Canberra was a vibrant city in 1982. The Queen had opened the National Gallery of Australia two weeks before, the High Court of Australia had been completed, a costly complex for the Australian Archives had been inaugurated and the Australian Defence Force Academy was being built adjacent to the

Royal Military College at Duntroon with affiliation to the University
of New South Wales. Massive site preparations were progressing for
the new Parliament House expected to be completed by 1988 and
the NCDC had formulated plans to link the old and new parliament
buildings by a land bridge over the roads that encircled Capital Hill.
Canberra had evolved into a national capital under the guidance of
the NCDC and national governments, a city that embraced the High
Court, the National Gallery of Australia, the Royal Australian Mint,
the National Archives of Australia, the Australian War Memorial, the
National Library of Australia, the Australian Institute of Sport and
the seat of national government.[4]

Under the lustre of these advances, however, were the lingering
effects of economic recession. The Fraser government had let no local
contracts for four years and provided no funds for land-servicing since
1980. The projected population of Canberra–Queanbeyan had been
downgraded from 500,000 to 400,000 and the development of the
Tuggeranong Valley had slowed. The downturn, first pronounced in
1973, continued into the 1980s and was marked by volatile inflation
rates that peaked again in 1982, causing distress to those with family
mortgages and commercial loans. Reflecting a fall in demand and
an increase in real wages, the unemployment rate that had averaged
2.9 per cent during the late 1970s increased to 6.7 per cent in 1982
and to 9.9 per cent in 1983 while the 'money wage growth' increased
from single-digit figures to 15.8 per cent in 1981–82.[5] It was a difficult
period for the parishioners, the parish and the diocese.

After he met the two assistant clergy, Andrew Constance and
Edwin Byford, the new rector surveyed the church buildings that were
outwardly pleasant but required costly maintenance and repair. He
judged the rectory to be noisy and 'requiring relocation'.[6] Over the
next week he counted the communicants: 12 at the 7am service; 35 at
8am; 74 at 10am; up to 20 at Evensong; and a dozen at the Wednesday
service. Andrew Constance reported another 35 at St David's, together
with a demand for Communion in aged-care facilities and private
homes.[7] There were many empty seats and the rector pondered an
appropriate course of action.

He had assistance, however, as 40 parishioners had listed the
strengths and weaknesses of the parish and itemised 'the things we
would like to see happen'. They appreciated the music and choirs, the

support of 'the clergy team', the ordered and predictable pattern of worship, the good fellowship that prevailed and the dedication of a 'faithful core' of worshippers. Weaknesses included the absence of youth, the small Sunday school and an ageing population with a 'disinclination to become involved'. The 'falling congregations' stemmed in part from a lack of communication, the presence of an 'exclusive club' comprising 'old originals', a resistance to change and 'a lack of faith to step out' and 'cope with difference'. A 'lack of warmth in the fellowship', little 'variety *within* services' and 'the absence of outreach programs' had resulted in a church that was inward-looking without faith to 'witness, testify or share'.[8] There were different expectations within the congregation and a potential for inter-group tension.

When parishioners listed their first priority, they hoped for 'young people in the congregation', 'youth-aligned services' and 'outreach programs for youth', together with fewer services, varied church music, 'songs that we know', more 'spontaneity in church' and community-based programs. A number sought a deeper spiritual life, a procession of witness, more prayer groups, a less conservative parish and a 'fearless and faithful ministry of word and Sacrament'.[9] Griffiths noted the challenges, not fully comprehending the harrowing time that lay ahead with depleted funds, rampant inflation and a declining financial base to the parish. To add to the complexity, his suspicions of tensions between groups were confirmed.

The rector turned his attention to finances. The small deficit of $584 in 1981 jumped to $4,024 by the end of 1982 and caused real distress when it reached $17,000 with an accumulated deficit of $21,000. At the same time, the diocese, which had previously rented homes to the church for the use of curates, now sold its properties, requiring St Paul's to pay rent of $600 each month for a curate's residence. The parish debt became 'depressing', working bees were not well attended and the wardens believed that there was a lack of 'responsibility by many parishioners to the life of the parish'. Even with severe cutbacks, the annual debt was still $19,600 at the start of 1985 with an immediate need 'for expenditure well in excess of $100,000 on major maintenance, renovation and clergy housing'.[10]

When the two curates left in 1983, council replaced only one to save a salary, leaving Griffiths and the new appointee, Lindsay Troth, with more onerous responsibilities. Visits to aged-care homes were reduced or discontinued, the church secretary was not reappointed, major maintenance projects were deferred and special fund-raising efforts were initiated. Despite the grave situation, the council planned to purchase a home in Narrabundah as a curate's residence at a cost of $66,000 (partly offset from funds in the Narrabundah Church Fund). This led to some disapproval, the withdrawal of parishioner pledges and criticism of the rector and the council. Increasingly concerned, Griffiths made a difficult decision.[11]

St Paul's contributed 20 per cent of its income to the diocese each year, an amount that had reached $14,000 in 1981 (see Table 12.1). When this jumped to almost $21,000 in 1984, the rector alluded to the inferior rectory, the 'pitiful' parish cars, the huge debt remaining on the hall and the excessive rent for a curate's residence. He argued that the diocesan contribution was not 'in keeping with our reduced income' and privately claimed that 'the diocese was *milking* the parish'.[12] 'The time has come,' he argued, 'to look to ourselves.' He proposed that the payment be reduced to $10,000. The council was divided. The honorary priest, Pat Haldane-Stevenson, upset the council by referring to its 'superficial attention' to the rector's plans. Jim Monro resigned and, after animated debate, the diocesan pledge was set at $14,950, a decision taken 'reluctantly' but totally 'justified by the parish's own [reduced] income'.[13]

Throughout 1986 the financial situation gradually improved, a result of fiscal 'pruning' and aided by $2,200 from a dinner at the Zambian High Commission, $5,400 from a parish fete and increases to the pledges of the parishioners. By the start of 1987 the surplus in the bank was $27,500, partly due to the replacement of an assistant priest by an officer of the Church Army (Captain Evan Cocker) at a lower salary. And so, despite mortgages of $24,600 on the church hall and $52,000 on the Narrabundah residence, the initial financial crisis had been overcome after an exhausting period of cutbacks and restraint. However there was little respite as the organ required a complete restoration and relocation.[14]

A contentious issue facing the congregation was the form of service the rector espoused. This constituted no difficulty at St David's under the direction of the curate and the honorary priests. Lindsay Troth and the youth group introduced a 'contemporary Eucharist' once a month for more than 40 communicants and services using

An Australian Prayer Book were easily accepted. At St Paul's, however, there were differences of opinion, especially when Griffiths stated that he did not want 'bottoms on seats' but people who were eagerly involved – doers and not just listeners.[15] Desiring the congregation to be involved, he moved the altar to different locations, much closer to the worshippers. Some accepted, others objected and he was forced to accept a three-month trial and seek written reactions to the changes. While the support was not unanimous, the rector was encouraged to proceed and 'make the rearrangement more workable' by relocating the choir. Council then requested him to 'preach a series of sermons' to 'explain fully the deliberation and reasons' for the new prayer book. In particular they asked why the 'Peace' was included in the service – should such individual involvement really be encouraged?

Twelve months after his induction, the rector admitted that 'there was some discontent' in relation to his 'attitude to worship' which promoted gathering around the altar and children taking an active part in the service.[16] He sought approval to admit children to Communion 'at an early age (about seven)' so that they could 'take their place in the Family, develop in it and be confirmed' when they reached maturity. He wished 'to attract and build up teenagers' with 'the type of music and singing that appeals to them – and [perhaps] others also'.[17] He hoped to 'broaden the music at St Paul's to the extent of directing a musical', one that would involve the congregation, be 'fun for all the choir' and 'attract new members' to its ranks. Dissension soon arose when music was involved.

The Reverend John Griffiths
© *Framing Matters, Manuka*

Music at Evensong had traditionally been a major event at St Paul's under John Barrett's direction. The choir had established a reputation for leading the chants and psalms and providing a traditional Church of England musical liturgy. But the evening congregation had dwindled and Griffiths believed that it was a waste of resources for the choir to concentrate on Evensong when he wished to build up the Sunday morning services. The rector then made an error of judgment by consulting the wardens but not the rest of the council, the congregation nor, more importantly the choir itself prior to announcing that the adult choir would be amalgamated with the junior choir and sing at morning services.

The word went out that the rector had 'sacked' the choir, strong letters were forwarded to the council and one person objected to the 'high-handed, discourteous and philistine action' on the part of a clergyman 'who has shown since his arrival ... that he will brook no opposition to any project he has determined on'. The repercussions lingered as Canon Laurie Murchison was asked to be the organist and choirmaster at traditional Evensong services until Les Davy took over and 'faithfully' maintained 'the tradition of Choral Evensong'. While music was the ostensible reason for the dispute, the underlying causes were the conflict between the conservative and the innovative, the desire by the choristers to maintain a traditional approach and the lack of consultation on the part of the rector and wardens.

When the evening choir refused to participate at morning services, Griffiths informed the council that he required 'a balance of traditional and contemporary music' at 10am to cater for families and to attract 'new people to the parish'. It 'must reflect a much broader musical tradition and speak to today's society', perhaps including a 'small group of instrumentalists and singers' led by 'someone experienced in the field of contemporary church music'.[18] Introducing ensemble music, he asked the congregation to sing to the music of strummed guitars. Many responded, some frowned and small numbers rebuked him but he replied that 'pruning' is 'usually a painful' affair. Nevertheless, strumming was a little too charismatic for St Paul's and that idea was gradually dropped.

During 1986 the type of music and the location of the choir caused further dissension. Joe Johnson, the director of music, acknowledged the 'increase in the amount of contemporary music' at the morning service but still hoped to train the morning choir in 'sight reading, chanting and some appropriate anthems by the classical masters'.[19] When he opposed moving the choir from the sanctuary to the back of the church it was too much for Griffiths who offered the director's position to another person. An ardent traditionalist, Johnson resigned, arguing that the new arrangement would be unworkable and that the musical traditions of St Paul's would collapse.[20] It was the last attempt by the conservative group to dictate the music at St Paul's. San Ky Kim took over the 10am junior choir and late in 1986 the evening choristers agreed to sing at the 8am Communion service on the fourth Sunday of each month. The following year, the main choir led the 10am service during Lent while the junior choir, under Betty Erskine's direction, contributed one of the hymns.

The poor condition of the pipe organ was an even more pressing issue during the 1980s. Despite being tuned every three months, the organ became so badly 'drowned' by water that the organ builder refused to carry out further repairs until it was moved to a different position. Consequently, the church debated whether to arrange the organ pipes on both sides of the sanctuary above the choir or to construct a loft for the choir and place the console at the back of the church. During this debate, the position of organist for the 10am service was openly advertised, Griffiths deciding to split the positions of organist and director of music and to create an organ committee to explore the options for the restoration, upgrade or replacement of the organ itself.[21]

Of the two applicants for the new position, Griffiths favoured Christopher Erskine who had moved to Canberra in 1974 at the age of 19. Erskine had practised organ at the Wesley Uniting Church in Forrest, had been associated with music at St Clare's College and, since 1981, had been the organist at the chapel of John XXIII College at the ANU. Though he mentioned his association with John Barrett and the Royal College of Church Music in Canberra, Erskine emphasised more strongly his ability to arrange and rewrite music, to use 'trumpets and timpani to augment the musical resources at great festivals of the church', to lead congregational singing and to incorporate other musical styles when appropriate. He captured the rector's approbation when he stressed that 'a bit of imagination can transform a [musical] piece into an exciting arrangement for organ and other instruments'. As 1986 drew to a close, Griffiths announced that 'St Paul's is most fortunate in having Mr Chris Erskine as Organist at the 10am Sung Eucharist and Mr San Ky Kim as Choir Master'.[22]

For more than two years, Erskine advised parishioners that the location of the organ in the sanctuary was 'an acoustic disaster', its sound choked and muffled by the time it reached the body of the church and compounded by the brick arch that prevented the travel of sound between the sanctuary and the nave. He advised that, to be heard with clarity, the organ needed to be in a gallery in the nave, one that was 'big enough to hold the choir and any other instrumentalists' on special occasions.[23] When agreement was reached and approval granted to proceed with the building of a loft, council called tenders, hoping that the final cost might be about $24,000 but, when completed and dedicated by Bishop Dowling on 18 February 1988, the figure topped $34,000 and the parish applied for a faculty 'for an overdraft of up to $30,000'. Moreover, there would be additional costs if the organ were to be moved and restored, resulting in fears about the ability of the parish to meet its liabilities.[24]

Actually, there was no room to manoeuvre as fifteen years 'of relentless water flows' had reached 'every corner of the instrument, including the console', with 263 of the 1,269 pipes not working and a further 240 'fairly unreliable'. Erskine disavowed responsibility for most of the 'strange noises' coming from the organ and believed that 'the whole instrument would soon collapse' if not dismantled and taken to Sydney for a complete repair, a costly undertaking but one that could not be avoided. The council agreed and the console was moved to the back of the church as an interim measure, reuniting the choir and the organist.

Opening of the new loft and its dedication by Bishop Owen Dowling, February 1988   © St Paul's Archives

The dismantled organ was taken to Sydney, gradually restored by Peter Jewkes over a period of eighteen months and installed in the loft in August 1990. The pipes were arranged in an aesthetically pleasing fashion in a wooden casing, helping the projection of sound but limiting the floor space for the choir and instrumentalists. The total cost of $103,000 was partly offset by an insurance payment of $13,100, a bequest of $20,000 from the estate of a devoted parishioner, Ruby Josland, a donation in memory of Mim Wrigley and from fund-raising activities. After a loan was negotiated the church paid $77,000 to the creditors, leaving a shortfall of $26,000. The organ was rededicated at 'a marvellous service' in September and had an immediate effect on the congregation who sang 'more lustily'. The effect was even more pronounced when the Archbishop-designate of Canterbury, Dr George Carey, visited St Paul's in February 1991 and the organ was accompanied by trumpets and timpani to the delight and inspiration of all.[25]

Betty Erskine then assumed responsibility for both choirs. A virtual 'new adult choir was formed' and the junior choir concentrated once again on the 10am service. The choir moved 'upstairs' and sat 'on the smallest chairs from the hall, with the tenors and basses on risers between the two halves of the organ case' because of the limited space available. Nevertheless, the choirs flourished, singing at special services, the presentation of *Son et Lumière*, the dedication of St David's Close and the children's carol service where 'the church was packed and the spontaneous response of the crowds of children was delightful'. It seemed odd, however, when Chris Erskine mentioned that the organ was incomplete and that more stops were required to 'add incomparable grandeur and snarl' to the music.[26]

Apart from finances and music, Griffiths gave particular attention to the myriad aspects of spiritual development, pastoral care and fellowship. He urged parishioners to join Bible study and prayer groups and encouraged them to meet regularly for discussions. He and his wife fostered dinner groups, the casserole bank and morning teas – any activity that brought people together. Social activities, theatre parties and drama festivals were considered an integral aspect of fellowship, helping to bond the participants in unity and 'love for one another'. This became even more important after it was decided to cease Evensong and other Sunday evening services in 1988.

One of the major outreach programs was the Kids Club (or Thursday Club), commenced in 1985 to attract primary-aged children to the church. Meeting in the hall each week during school terms and for two years in the home of Judith and Bob Webb, the children enjoyed games, singing, craft activities and a meal. After the rector visited Griffiths Public School and advertised the program, 96 children turned up, each paying $3 a session to keep the project self-funded. The Kids Club proved to be a continuing success and, after children from Red Hill and Forrest joined in 1989, the organisers tried to limit attendance to a 'comfortable number of 60,' requiring new children to be placed on a waiting list. Judith Webb, the mainstay of the group, was assisted by Rosemary Huff-Johnson, Robyn Simkus, Judi Gilchrist and Beth Bennett as well as the two curates, Steve Simkus and Nick

Hearnshaw. It was only the lack of adult leaders that prevented the commencement of a parallel group each Tuesday.[27]

Programs for teenagers varied over time but reflected the declining interest of young people in church affairs. While part-time leaders found difficulty in maintaining continuity, Simkus and Hearnshaw became involved and achieved some success with a 'small but loyal and enthusiastic bunch of teenagers' who met each Sunday evening for 'activity, singing and learning, followed by the highlight of the evening, pizza and chips'. Four young people represented the parish at the Diocesan Youth Synod and youth services were organised in an attempt to swell numbers. In a related activity, Hearnshaw developed contacts with juvenile offenders at the Quamby Detention Centre, an extremely difficult chaplaincy.[28]

The Sunday school, which had declined to only nine in 1981, began to rejuvenate in 1984. Janie McOmish was asked by Barbara Griffiths to lead the 10am school and told by the rector to buy teaching materials at the Catholic Bookshop. Average attendances rose to 30 and followed a predictable yearly pattern – numbers rose in summer, fell in winter and were down at Christmas. The routine varied but included a short period in church, withdrawal for Sunday school in the hall and return to church for the Communion. The children participated in the Spring and Music Festival and prepared assiduously for a nativity presentation at Christmas.[29] A crèche existed intermittently, requiring parents to attend and supervise their own children.

Religious instruction in schools was rationalised when a weekly program at Forrest Primary School was jointly serviced by St Paul's and St Luke's, Deakin. An inter-denominational program was begun at Narrabundah and Red Hill in 1983, involving teachers from the Anglican, Uniting, Catholic, Baptist and Presbyterian Churches and the Salvation Army. By 1988, 550 children in two schools received ecumenical instruction in concentrated blocks of teaching (one lesson each day for a week in each term), encouraging the clergy to expand the scheme to three schools when Griffith Primary joined in 1988–1989.[30]

Fellowship for women revolved around the Churchwomen's Union under the direction of Margaret Roberts and Joan Bruce. They organised regular functions, annual fetes, balls and floral festivals, and raised funds for the parish. They contributed to St Mark's Library, the Brindabella Gardens retirement homes, housing for the assistant clergy, the organ fund and church maintenance. Some were involved in the tapestry club that provided kneelers for the church under the leadership of Betty Erskine. The umbrella organisation, Anglican Women, was more concerned with wider diocesan issues and, under Barbara Griffiths, embarked on meetings and the discussion of issues facing the Anglican Church. It was not averse, however, to 'mulled wine, hot plum pudding and brandy sauce' at Diana Colman's home on a cold winter's night.[31] As the men's group declined during the 1980s, they were sometimes invited to join the women.

Barbara Griffiths saw the need for the 'casserole bank', a type of 'wheels on meals' which distributed food to the needy. Constantly on the telephone from early morning, she spurred others to be involved and to contribute their time and energy to other parish activities. Another venture, commenced by Anne Maybanks in February 1988, was a second-hand clothing exchange that operated from the renovated tennis court pavilion. It provided for 'pensioners, single parents, students and large ethnic families' who used the exchange as an alternative to charity hand-outs. Renamed 'Jonah's Place' in 1990 and relocated in the hall, the shop was closed temporarily and reopened in January 1991 as St Paul's Op Shop under the control of Robin Gordon and a group of ten volunteer women.[32]

The outreach program at Narrabundah was less successful. While services at Narrabundah had been discontinued in 1972, there were always those who believed that Anglican services should be recommenced when resources became available. The issue resurfaced in 1985 when the council purchased a home at Narrabundah for the assistant priest and Captain Evan Cocker moved in, allowing him and his wife to act as counsellors and recommence Sunday services in the primary school. It was always a tenuous enterprise, however, attracting only seventeen communicants each Sunday in 1986, eight in 1987 and seven in 1988, causing continuing debate about the venture's viability and the inability of the local church to make meaningful progress.

The rector and the council received criticism over the removal of the old tin hall from the Manuka site in 1985. Historians from St John's Schoolhouse Museum board of management urged the preservation of the building 'as part of the National Capital's heritage'; the National

Trust of Australia (ACT) sought its conservation having listed it on the Trust's Register of Classified Places; and the Canberra and District Historical Society wrote to Bishop Dowling offering to preserve and relocate the building because of its significance.[33] The parish council argued, however, that the 'old iron church building' should be 're-moved' and Bishop Dowling indicated that the building was of little historical importance.[34] The structure was dismantled and taken to Caloola Farm in the ACT in 1985, the parishioners believing that it would be used as a chapel or craft centre for the boys at the centre. In effect, however, the building could not be reassembled and was broken up, being used around the farm for fences and animal enclosures.[35]

It is evident that the first four years of Griffiths' incumbency were difficult. Those who prized 'the ordered and predictable pattern of worship' – the so-called 'faithful core' of worshippers in 1982 – were seen as 'old originals' who resisted change and were unable 'to cope with difference.' Termed the 'exclusive club', they had developed the church over years, paid off the original building and the 1955 extensions, enjoyed the ritual of the liturgy and its music and experienced a justifiable pride in their hard-won accomplishments. John Falkingham's traditional form of Anglicanism and his relatively conservative approach had suited this group and reinforced their attitudes. On the other hand, a larger group of parishioners wished for less '1662 traditionalism', greater 'variety *within* services', a liturgy involving the congregation, wider musical forms and greater emphasis on youth and social fellowship. Most of the congregation agreed with the rector when he introduced changes but his self-acknowledged 'impatience with minor details', his enthusiasm for particular projects and his occasional insensitivity 'to the *real* issue' added to tensions. It was the episode with the choir that brought matters to a climax and eventually led to resolution. After that, opposition waned as he concentrated on – and enjoyed – his pastoral duties, helping to bond the church and enhance the fellowship for which he and Barbara were to be remembered. He was quick, however, to appoint new members of the church to positions on the council, some only three months after their arrival in Manuka, and found a confidante in Chris Erskine who provided strong support not only as organist but also as Chairperson of the Jubilee Committee during 1988 and 1989.[36]

St Paul's Jubilee Ball in the Albert Hall, 1989   © *St Paul's Archives*

Following the 1988 bi-centennial celebrations in Canberra, the church's jubilee year (the fiftieth anniversary of the Manuka church) in 1989 proved to be memorable. The parishioners danced well into the night at the Jubilee Ball in the Albert Hall, enjoyed the church production of *Murder in the Cathedral*, participated in a Jubilee Service and luncheon at 'Back to St Paul's Weekend' at the National Convention Centre and were involved in the opening of St David's Close by Bishop Dowling. A sanctuary chair was dedicated, the gift of Don Smith and his wife, while a further five chairs were presented and dedicated to the memory of Lieutenant-Colonel Sir Charles Anderson by his family and friends. To mark 50 years of witness, stained-glass memorial windows were installed behind the gallery, although partly hidden by the organ.

As he reflected on the progress of the church between 1982 and 1990, John Griffiths was heartened by the increasing attendances. There had been 11,418 communicants when he arrived, followed by a 20 per cent fall between 1983 and 1985 as clergy numbers were reduced, services combined, visits curtailed and economies effected. Thereafter, there had been a steady annual increase (see Table 13.1), reaching a recorded peak of 12,606 and an estimated actual attendance well over 17,000. Moreover, St Paul's was increasingly viewed as a city church for important gatherings with more than 500 attending the Royal Commonwealth Service in 1988 in the presence of Her Majesty Queen Elizabeth II and the Duke of Edinburgh and over 200 at the annual service to mark the opening of the parliamentary year.

The rector was even more gratified to note the sustained increase in numbers at the Sunday 10am service where communicants rose from a weekly average of 67 in 1982 to 122 in 1988.[37]

Table 13.1

Communicants – Attendances at St Paul's 1982–1990[38]

1982	1983	1984	1985	1986	1987	1988	1989	1990
11,418	11,035	9,711	9,054	9,943	10,853 *(14,104)	11,535 *(14,688)	11,771 *(14,835)	12,606 *(17,611)

* Actual attendances including communicants and non-communicants.

Griffiths was fortunate to have the assistance of curates and assistant priests who gave loyal support, assumed a leading role at St David's and St Barnabas', visited aged-care homes and hospitals and led youth programs across the parish.[39] Additionally he received the invaluable input of a group of non-stipendiary deacons, priests and lay workers who offered their time unselfishly to the work of St Paul's and St David's, including John McKellar, Graham Bishop, Dean Barker, Pat Haldane-Stevenson, Dennis Johnson, Lyn Mattingley, Gloria Oliver and Ken Batterham. The early years had been arduous but Griffiths believed that, with assistance, the future was promising.

As the rector commenced the second phase of his incumbency, the wardens declared that the parish was 'exceptionally fortunate in having the unstinting time and care' of John and Barbara who were 'unceasing in their efforts' for the church and its people. Parishioners responded to the couple who were spiritual in outlook and outgoing in approach, despite John's 'ethereal' qualities and his inattention to fine detail from which he was often rescued by Barbara. With such a positive attitude, the parish launched into the next six and a half years, concentrating on three main areas: the material progress of the church; the worship and pastoral care of the parishioners; and the expansion of evangelism and outreach programs in the neighbourhood. It was a stage that coincided with the ordination of women to the priesthood in the diocese in December 1992.[40]

Material progress was assisted when the inflation rate levelled off at 6.6 per cent by 1989 and dropped to about 2 per cent in 1991. However, unemployment climbed sharply, peaking at just under 11 per cent and the economy dived into a short but distressing recession

in 1991.[41] Building opportunities were much better
with lower interest rates
and the church decided to
proceed with two develop-
mental plans, the first at
Red Hill where St David's
Close was constructed, incorporating a residence for
a curate or assistant priest.

The tennis pavilion is demolished on the site of the new rectory.
© St Paul's Archives

(The Close was ultimately constructed by the diocese). When a third
member of staff was required, however, the council decided to sell
the Narrabundah property that was 'sub-standard' and costing about
$800 interest a month and build a new rectory at St Paul's.[42]

In 1990, the building committee examined the feasibility of constructing 'Aged Persons Units' on the St Paul's site but concluded
that there would be few benefits as a new hall and a rectory were
more urgent. Another proposal was to upgrade the hall and rent out
the basement for commercial purposes. A third proposition was to
'construct a Professional Centre' on site, refurbish the church hall,
demolish the existing rectory, construct a new residence and provide
a 'new entry canopy' to the church – a major redevelopment.[43] None
of these alternatives came to fruition
and a less costly proposal to demolish
the tennis court and pavilion and erect a
second rectory was accepted.

When it was discovered that the
church would need to pay an ACT bet-
terment tax of $40,000 plus a $1,000
administration fee, plans were put on
hold and the three wardens entered
into lengthy and frustrating negotiations with the authorities. Six months
later a compromise was reached and
the church paid a reduced tax of $2,000
and an administration fee of $650. In
March 1992 the first sod on the rectory
site was turned by three long-serving

Bishop Neville Chynoweth watches as the
foundation stone is set for the new rectory, 1992.
© St Paul's Archives

parishioners – Doreen Myers, Gwen Jackson and Frank Colwell – and the foundation stone was blessed in June by Bishop Chynoweth who returned in November to dedicate the completed building. The rector described it as 'a comfortable home' and 'a place for hospitality and fellowship'. The assistant priest, Nick Hearnshaw, was content to move into the old rectory and reduce his travel costs.[44] The church's income (excluding St David's) reached $250,000 for the first time in 1992 but the expenditure was almost $476,000 leaving a deficit of $226,000 mainly accrued from the construction of the rectory which cost $221,000.

The financial outlook appeared quite bleak when parishioner pledges were not 'up to expectations' in 1992 and the wardens were compelled to intervene by selling a parish car, introducing a debt reduction program and paying off the debt on the hall to avoid further interest payments.[45] By the end of the year, the loan liabilities had fallen to $199,000 and the budget balance was $31,000. A major contribution to this positive position was achieved by reducing the salary bill. Ian Wright, the Warden of St David's Close and priest with special responsibility for St David's, departed and Bishop Chynoweth assumed the same positions. In the words of the wardens, the bishop offered 'his great ministry talent in an honorary capacity', contributing considerably to 'budget savings'.[46] By the end of 1996 the budget was still in surplus by $13,000, helped by proceeds from the fete ($11,000), the hire of the church hall ($14,000) and the dedication of those who ran the Op Shop ($3,000). The annual diocesan pledge had risen to $32,500 and an additional item had been added to the budget – assistance for the new Parish of St Mary-in-the-Valley.[47]

As a second area of concentration, Griffiths sought to enhance the worship of the parishioners and their sense of fellowship, asking that it be 'lively' so as 'to express the presence of the risen Christ in our midst'. He added wryly, with tongue in cheek, that it should be done 'decently and in order' because 'it is Anglican'.[48] Worship and fellowship were extended when breakfast was introduced after the 8am service in 1994 to supplement the 'coffee bar' for the 10am worshippers. The 7am service provided for a small group who preferred the 1662 *Book of Common Prayer*, while the 8am service was attended by 30 to 40 communicants, rising to 50 during 1995–1996. The 10am Eucharist attracted a growing congregation that swelled from 95 in 1986 to 141 in 1992. When added to the 50 who did not take Communion, attendances of 200 became usual, the nave 'reached maximum comfortable seating capacity' and an evening service was commenced to ease the situation.[49] While the number of communicants remained relatively constant between 1992 and 1996, annual attendances rose to more than 22,000 (see Table 13.2), prompting Griffiths to comment that the parish was 'in the best of health' in 1996 and 'probably the best' in his fifteen years of incumbency.[50] Moreover, the introduction of *A Prayer Book for Australia* in 1995 presented few difficulties.

Table 13.2
St Paul's communicants–attendances[51]
1990–1996

	1990	1991	1992	1993	1994	1995	1996
Comm's	12,606	12,506	11,480	11,664	11,072	12,119	12,743
Attend's	17,611	*20,538	19,895	18,674	18,009	19,175	22,199

* Inflated by special events.

Music played a greater role in the worship after the relocation of the organ. There were two choirs under Betty Erskine's direction, one consisting of a dozen who sang at the 10am service each week and another that comprised this group together with additional numbers co-opted from outside the church. This broader group, known as 'St Paul's Singers', performed at special occasions – liturgical welcomes, diocesan farewells, the annual Festival of Nine Lessons and Carols and *Faure's Requiem* on ANZAC Day. By the end of 1993, the rector asked Oliver Raymond to direct the 10am choir. This left Betty Erskine in charge of the overall music program with more time to concentrate on the larger group whose activities extended far beyond the parish. A third smaller choir was established in 1995 to sing at the 8am service.[52]

As the music program expanded under Raymond's leadership, the choir sang the psalm pointed to an Anglican chant and provided two anthems during Communion. It presented the Good Friday performance of 'Crucifixion' by John Stainer and combined in a Christmas venture with the choir of St Christopher's Cathedral. The combined services – one at St Paul's and the other at St Christopher's – made 'a splended contribution to the celebration of Christmas in Manuka' and established an ecumenical tradition in music. The following year the choir, with the assistance of music scholars at the church, presented special performances by Mendelssohn and Handel and chorales from Bach's 'St Matthew Passion'. The St Paul's Singers took part in the law service, the ANZAC Requiem and the graduation service at St Mark's National Theological Centre.[53]

Pastoral care was seen as an extension of worship and concentrated on particular groups and individual needs – Lenten studies, 'small groups' in the homes of the parishioners, flower arrangers and the tapestry group.[54] Hospitality Sundays encouraged parishioners to visit one another's homes for relaxed meals and home Communions were given to the sick and infirm. The Warden of St David's Close provided for the pastoral needs of the Red Hill parishioners. Cursillo, a Christian formation program first introduced by Bishop Warren in the late 1970s and promoted by Alan Vickers, gathered people from across the diocese to deepen their spirituality and quicken their Christian commitment.

Age began to weary the ladies of the Churchwomen's Union who decided in 1992 to rename their group the St Paul's Senior Women's Fellowship. They reduced their activities but still continued 'to assist with parish functions and activities'. The Anglican Women were strongly involved in parish activities: they attended spiritual gatherings, arranged cultural evenings at the rectory, assumed an increasing role in the fete and the parish ball and catered for suppers after services, parish plays and ANZAC Day performances.

Youth work did not advance significantly between 1990 and 1996, despite the continuing efforts of the curates and a small number of dedicated leaders. Nick Hearnshaw's analysis in 1991 was applicable throughout the 1990s:

> Unlike the younger children's ministries, teenagers attract virtually no support ... Most teenagers at St Paul's are already overcommitted to other things: school, sport, other cultural groups, etc and a church youth group has either a low priority or simply doesn't figure at all. There is nobody at the church who is either able or willing to be involved with children of high school age.[55]

When theological students from St Mark's were involved as leaders, the problem was accentuated as they were unable to provide continuity because of their other commitments and their frequent moves. In short, there was always a small band of young people at St Paul's who were actively involved in church affairs but their numbers were small and no long-term plan of activities could be made for them.

The Sunday school, which had been revitalised in 1984, continued with about 50 children on the roll in 1991 and an actual attendance of between 25 and 30. Encouraging the children to return to the service after Sunday school, the rector asked them to sing or to display their activity sheet from the day's lesson, giving them a sense of achievement and reminding the congregation of the dedicated work of the teachers. The attendance dropped to twelve during 1995 but children continued to be involved in nativity performances. A 'party at Mr and Mrs McOmish's home' was a highlight for the group.

The third area on which Griffiths concentrated was evangelism and outreach programs. When the Anglican Church ushered in a Decade of Evangelism in 1990, the rector quickly agreed with Dr George Carey that evangelism does 'not mean confronting people with a large floppy, black Bible' but represented 'everything we do with conscious motivation' to win people for God's Kingdom.[56] Outreach included the casserole bank and food hamper distribution, the chaplaincy services at the Quamby Detention Centre and the Op Shop which opened every Friday afternoon and Saturday morning, providing assistance to those in need, friendship among the helpers and a source of income for the church.[57] The Thursday Club continued as a major activity, needing to be divided into two sections – one for those between five and ten years of age and another for the BKs (Big Kids) ten and over. In a program described in 1993 as 'probably the greatest success in outreach to the St Paul's community', it continued to reach up to 60 children each week, most from outside the church. The provision of Christian education in public schools was continued on an ecumenical basis, involving 600 to 700 children and 24 teachers at Red Hill and Narrabundah schools, a program that had operated most successfully since 1983. Ecumenism extended also to the exchange of pulpits with the clergy preaching in other churches two or three times a year.

Other outreach programs began during this period in response to social needs. St Paul's was a large parish with many parishioners living outside the parish boundaries and most were 'not at home during the day', even if the clergy had time to visit. With the majority of women in paid employment, most families owning one or two cars and with money available for outside interests, substantial daytime contact between the clergy and the parishioners evaporated. Consequently, it was decided to commence a Telecare program in 1993 under the supervision of Trish Levick, whereby a number of trained parishioners kept in touch by telephone with those on the church roll and passed on to the clergy the names of those who required support. By 1996 Telecare was an integral aspect of the pastoral care program, concentrating on those who were 'ill or in distress', 'frail or homebound' and newcomers to the church.[58]

Next door to the church was a series of multi-storey apartment blocks known as the Stuart Flats. Catering for a wide range of inhabitants, the flats were home to some disadvantaged people who needed assistance and continued support. When the Baptist Church was allocated the use of a flat (with a verandah) as a 'drop-in-centre', it approached St Paul's with the possibility of a joint venture. In 1993 a committee was formed to explore the possibilities. This developed into The Verandah, an outreach program that offered food packages and bread donated by local firms, as well as a casual room, a friendly face and informal support contacts.

Another venture saw the revitalisation and extension of the aged-care program. Visits to nursing homes did not cease entirely after the exacting years of the 1970s and early 1980s but it was mainly at Jindalee in Narrabundah that contacts were maintained. When the Reverend Ken Batterham assumed the chaplaincy of the Jindalee Nursing Home in 1989, he provided 25 bedside Communions each week and held short services for a similar number and assisted the families of the residents and the nurses. Others involved in visitation programs were Gloria Oliver, Sue Youngman and Lynette Reeve. After her ordination as deacon in February 1995, Jill Elliott concentrated on the aged-care ministry at Morling Lodge, Jindalee and Carey Gardens. Such ministries extended the earlier work of the Reverend Thory Bonsey, the Reverend Rob Lamerton and Bishop Neville Chynoweth.[59]

St Paul's became particularly well known for an outreach program centred on John Wallis and his love of directing dramatic productions. Following an advertisement in the press that sought the involvement of local talent in staging *Murder in the Cathedral* at the church, a group of singers and actors (the 'Saints and Sinners') achieved renown for their performances in 1989. This was followed by further productions including *Everyman* (1991), *Riverbend* (1992 – based on Sydney Nolan's paintings), *A Man for all Seasons* (1993), *St Joan* (1994) and *The Diary of Anne Frank* (1995). A major presentation in 1990 was *Son et Lumière* based on Leonard French's paintings 'Seven Days of Creation'. Usually combining actors, singers, instrumentalists and organ, these productions not only created sustained interest but also brought many outsiders to the church, including some from the grammar schools.

Relationships between St Paul's and the two grammar schools became 'personal rather than formal' after the schools were incorporated in 1981.[60] Hartley Hansford, chaplain of Canberra Grammar School from 1983, conducted services at St Paul's and, according to Griffiths, helped 'to cement links' between the school and the parish. As a result of Adrian Keenan's influence, the boys' choir sang at St Paul's on a regular basis and the school's cadet unit assisted at the annual fetes. The school also donated a spotlight to illuminate the stained glass windows in the eastern wall of the church. The Girls' Grammar School developed closer ties to St Luke's when John Bowen was chaplain of the Junior School for some years but, after the chapel was built, Robert Willson (chaplain from 1985) conducted services and confirmations at the school itself. He recalled that there was not a close formal relationship with the local churches although St Paul's requested the school choir to perform each term.[61]

St David's at Red Hill, once an outreach program itself, had developed into a mainstream suburban church. On Griffiths' arrival in 1982, he found a church building in pristine condition, newly painted, with hedges cut and grass mowed for the annual Art and Pottery Exhibition in October. After opening the exhibition, he met the parishioners, inspected the new Yamaha electric organ (replacing the original Wurlitzer) and learned of the plans for an annual giant garage sale. There was a pleasant working relationship between St David's and St Paul's, although a degree of uncertainty existed as to whether Red Hill should assume an identity of its own. Two wardens were responsible for the daily administration of the centre, a fellowship committee organised the church's social activities, including an annual cricket match between St David's and St Paul's, and an active women's organisation arranged fund-raising activities. During 1982, over $2,300 was raised by the parishioners, allowing them to pay $1,300 off the building mortgage and $700 off the organ. St David's played an important role in the life of the parish.[62]

Within a year the rector confirmed that St David's was 'endeavouring to maintain its own identity' and delegated major responsibility for its oversight to Lindsay Troth and Dean Barker.[63] Some Red Hill parishioners wanted him to attend more regularly and he explained that his absence was not 'a neglect of duty' at the centre. Andrew Constance and Lindsay Troth led the church between 1982 and 1984 after which it relied on the voluntary assistance of John McKellar, Dean Barker, Pat Stevenson, Dennis Johnson (a diocesan youth officer) and occasional assistance from theological students in training.

The lack of a regular priest-in-charge resulted in a sense of discontinuity and the number of weekly communicants fell from 42 in 1984 to 31 in 1988. One of the advantages of the small congregation, however, was the cohesiveness and active involvement of parishioners in church life. Duties were rostered and most of the congregation were fully occupied in fund-raising activities including the annual garage sale. Theatre nights were organised (41 returning on one occasion to the Gay–Curtis home for supper), 'soup, pie and hymn nights' were held, dinner and restaurant parties arranged and the parishioners walked the streets of Red Hill singing carols at Christmas time. The small Sunday school was amalgamated with St Paul's for twelve months in 1986 but, even when it recommenced in June 1987, it was restricted by the lack of space. The building contained only the church itself, toilets and a kitchen area. The teachers requested an additional room and lamented the constraints on children's activities. There were raised expectations, therefore, when

St David's Close opened in December 1990
© St Paul's Archives

site developments were planned and a possible extension to the church was mooted.

There had always been a belief that some form of aged-care facility would be constructed at St David's after Neville Chynoweth mentioned it in 1973 but it was not until 1988 that Carefree's plans for 27 units, a clergy residence and a separate meeting room came to fruition. Despite frustrating delays, the concept was approved and Bishop Dowling dedicated the beginning of construction of St David's Close on 7 September 1989. Fifteen months later, on 2 December 1990, the Close was opened, two months after the commissioning of the Reverend Neal Salan as warden with regular duties at St David's Church. As the units were occupied, attendance at St David's rose from 35 in 1990 to 49 the following year, one of new members being the retired priest, Thory Bonsey, who was 'to provide regular relief' for Salan and his successors. When Salan left the parish, Ian Wright took over as warden and was assisted by a property officer who attended to issues of maintenance.

During 1993, John Griffiths was appointed an archdeacon, resulting in a reassessment of clergy duties at the end of Wright's term as warden. Bishop Chynoweth had acted as consultant to Ian Wright during the rector's absence on long-service leave and had accepted increasing duties in the parish, and, hence, it seemed fitting when Griffiths announced:

> I still cannot believe my good fortune in securing as my associate in ministry, the Reverend Rob Lamerton and as the Warden at St David's, Bishop Neville Chynoweth. We commissioned them and officially welcomed them and their families ... on 29 January [1995] ... We are already experiencing the graciousness and experience in ministry that Rob and Bishop Neville bring to us and give thanks.[64]

As he settled in as warden of the Close and priest with special responsibility for St David's, Neville Chynoweth, with Joan, returned to the world of Sunday services, midweek Communions, prayer groups, music and special Christmas events. Their 'warmth and friendship' were 'key factors in setting the tone and direction of the St David community'. Predictably, the parish and the diocese were quick to call upon him for wider duties. Joan became fully engaged once again in

Anglican Women and the spiritual and social activities of St David's, bringing an irrepressible commitment to fund-raising activities for the church. By 1996 the average weekly numbers at Red Hill rose to 60 (45 communicants), gas heating was installed and a spire erected in memory of Jack Firth who designed the building in 1970–71. To allow some time for reflection, Bishop Chynoweth had the timely assistance of Thory Bonsey and Edgar Rolfe (the first curate appointed to St Paul's in 1953).

During the 1990s, John Griffiths' wife, Barbara, became seriously ill, spending time in hospital during 1995 and never fully recovering her health. As the months passed, it became obvious that medical assistance was increasingly required and in 1997 the rector informed the council of his intention to retire and move to Melbourne. In farewelling them, the congregation expressed their deep appreciation to the couple who together had revitalised the church during a sixteen-year incumbency. In that time they had built up numbers, stressed joyful worship, fostered fellowship among parishioners and promoted a vibrant church life. They left Canberra in September 1997. Barbara passed away two years later.

Notes

1. These are the judgments of parishioners 25 years later and of Griffiths' previous curate, Eric Burton.
2. Eric Burton, Personal communication, 2009.
3. Report, StPPC, 9 November 1982.
4. Sparke, *Canberra 1954–1980*, Chapters 14 and 15; *http://www.defence.gov.au*; *http://www.hcourt.gov.au*; *http://nga.gov.au*.
5. Kriesler, *The Australian Economy*, Chapters 2 and 3.
6. StPPC, 9 November 1982.
7. StP Register of Services, 1982.
8. StPPC, 9 November 1982.
9. StPPC, 9 November 1982.
10. StPPC, annual reports 1982 to 1984.
11. StPPC, annual reports 1983 to 1985.
12. Lachie McOmish, Personal communication, 2010.

13. StPPC, 1982 and 1984 to 1986; StPPC, rector's report and council papers, 11 September 1984; Letter from the Reverend Pat Stevenson 21 September 1984.

14. StPPC, 1986 annual report.

15. StPPC, 1983 annual report.

16. StPPC, rector's report 13 December 1983.

17. StPPC, rector's report 8 March 1984.

18. StPPC, rector's report 13 August 1985.

19. StPPC, 1985 annual report.

20. D Johnson to council, StPPC, 10 June 1986.

21. StPPC, annual reports 1984 to 1987; rector's report 8 July 1986; Council Minutes 10 June 1986.

22. C Erskine, Application for the position of organist, StPPC, Attachment to the rector's report, 9 September 1986; 1986 rector's report.

23. StPPC, 'A Gallery for St Paul's', 1986 annual report.

24. StPPC, 1987 treasurer's report.

25. StPPC, 28 May 1988 and 9 September 1990; 1990 annual report.

26. StPPC, choir reports in 1989 and 1990 annual reports; organ report 1990.

27. Judith and Bob Webb, Personal communications, 2010; StPPC, 1988 annual report.

28. StPPC, annual reports 1983 to 1990.

29. StPPC, annual reports 1983 to 1990; Janie McOmish, Personal communication, 2009; Rosemary Greaves, Personal communication, 2008.

30. StPPC, annual reports 1982 to 1990; Beverley Butterfield, Personal communication, 2010.

31. StPPC, annual reports 1983 to 1990; Diana Colman, Personal communication, 2008.

32. StPPC, annual reports 1989 to 1991; Joan Boston, Personal communication, 2009; Judith Webb, Personal communication, 2010.

33. Letters in StPPC, 14 August and 11 September 1984; and 12 February 1985.

34. Correspondence, Bishop Dowling to R Winch, 24 August 1984. File: "St Paul's Manuka", Canberra & District Historical Society.

35. This information came from the Reverend R Hensen, clergyman at the farm, Personal communication, 2008

36. Bob Webb, Personal communication, 2010.

37. StPPC, 1988 annual report.

38. Figures calculated from StP Register of Services, 1982 to 2000.

39. Curates and assistant priests included Edwin Byford, Andrew Constance, Lindsay Troth, (Capt.) Evan Cocker, Colin Place, Steve Simkus and Nick Hearnshaw.

40. Fletcher, *The Place of Anglicanism in Australia*, chapter 8; and Frame, *A Church for a Nation*, chapter 17.

41. Kriesler, *The Australian Economy*, pp. 9, 43, 57.

42. StPPC, 6 May, 2 June and 26 October 1990; 24 February 1991.
43. StPPC, Letter from Concrete Constructions 21 March 1989; Council minutes 21 November 1989 and 26 October 1990.
44. StPPC, rector's report and Building Committee's Report, 1992 annual report.
45. StPPC, annual reports 1989 to 1993.
46. StPPC, annual reports 1994 and 1995.
47. StPPC, 1996 annual report.
48. StPPC, 1991 annual report.
49. StPPC, 1992 annual report.
50. StPPC, 1996 annual report.
51. These figures are calculated from StP Register of Services 1990 to 1996.
52. StPPC, annual reports 1991 to 1995.
53. Oliver Raymond, Personal communication, 2010. Betty Erskine provided reports on the music program from 1990 to 1996 and Oliver Raymond between 1994 and 1996.
54. The following sections on pastoral care, the Senior Women's Fellowship, youth work and Sunday school are based on StPPC, annual reports 1990 to 1996.
55. StPPC, rAeport from Nick Hearnshaw, 1991.
56. StPPC, 1990 annual report.
57. The sections on evangelism and outreach programs are based on StPPC, annual reports 1990 to 1996.
58. Trish Levick, Personal communication, 2009 and StPPC, annual reports 1993 to 1996.
59. StPPC, annual reports for 1989 and 1995.
60. Hartley Hansford, Personal communication, 2010.
61. Robert Willson, Personal communication, 2010.
62. StPPC, (St David's), 1982 annual report.
63. StPCC, annual reports include specific reports by the wardens of St David's, the fellowship committee and the superintendent of the Sunday school. The following section on St David's is based on those reports each year.
64. StP, 1994 annual report.

14   A city church, 1997–2010

The departure of the Griffiths 'brought a sense of loss' to many parishioners – a predictable reaction after a long and fruitful incumbency – but it also provided an opportunity for the parish to evaluate critically its strengths and weaknesses and to plan for the future. The new diocesan bishop, George Browning, attended a meeting at St Paul's, listened to the views expressed and assisted parishioners as they considered 'changes and improvements that could be made to the life of the parish'.[1] As the bishop contemplated a possible replacement, his thoughts turned to Archdeacon Jeffrey Driver and St Mark's, a few kilometres away.

Driver had been a cadet journalist in New Zealand and subsequently sub-edited a number of newspapers in New Zealand, regional Australia and suburban Sydney. After studying at Ridley College in Melbourne, he was appointed to the mid-Richmond parish, Woodburn, in the Diocese of Grafton. He also wrote articles for the national Anglican paper, *Church Scene*. With his wife, Lindy, and two children, he came to the Parish of Holy Covenant at Jamison in November 1985, writing this time for the diocesan newspaper, *Anglican News*. During his four years at Holy Covenant, he reorganised parish groups, reconstituted finances, encouraged fellowship in the homes of parishioners, supported the ordination of women as priests and was involved in an array of ecumenical ventures.[2] Then, after spending five years as rector and as Archdeacon of Young (1990–1995), he was appointed Executive Director of St Mark's National Theological Centre.

The bishop recalled the significant changes that had occurred at St Mark's – the departure of the warden, the Reverend Dr Robert Withycombe, the appointment of Bishop Bruce Wilson as principal of the Canberra College of Ministry and the amalgamation of

304 Camps, settlements and churches

the Institute of Theology, the library and the college into St Mark's National Theological Centre in 1989. An agreement had been forged between the newly-formed centre and Charles Sturt University whereby, in 1995, St Mark's became the seat of the School of Theology in the Faculty of Arts. Driver's contract as director was short-term and Bishop Browning knew that the archdeacon was 'missing parish life'. He had helped establish links with the university, had increased student numbers at St Mark's and given it a 'more vital and sustainable future'. Browning offered Driver the incumbency of St Paul's.[3]

A few days before Christmas 1997, Driver was inducted into the Parish of Manuka and was welcomed a week later to St David's at an evening carol service. Thanking Rob Lamerton, who had carried the parish in the changeover period, Driver was aware of the pastoral needs of the parish and the challenge 'of getting to know people' after the previous incumbency. He quickly acknowledged the energy that John and Barbara had displayed and the 'enhanced tradition of worship' and the 'diversity of ministries' they had bequeathed to the church and the city.[4] He suspected, however, that it would not be an easy task to follow a couple who had won loyalty and a degree of personal allegiance. His suspicions were correct.

Jeffery Driver arrived at the church 'totally exhausted from his work at St Mark's'. A different personality from Griffiths, he kept a low profile as he discerned the ethos of the parish and was perceived as friendly although 'somewhat distant' and 'a little difficult to get to know'. Additionally, the rector was a member of three wider bodies – General Synod, the interim board of the Australian Centre for Christianity and Culture and Bishop-in-Council – and he was not always available when casually sought. A measure of resentment arose when he mentioned the possibility of change to established practice and modified the 'family-orientated liturgy' developed by the previous rector. There was even a hint of disapproval that Lindy Driver had her own full-time career as a nurse, could not be involved in every aspect of church life and would not fulfil the stereotype of the 'rector's wife'.[5]

What the parish did recognise, however, was a businessman who was well-organised and capable of leading others, one who understood finance and who could promote a vision while marshalling others to assist. Spiritually knowledgeable and dedicated, Driver was 'accepted but not necessarily adopted' by some of the parishioners. And then adversity struck. He was taken to hospital, operated on for cancer and began an enforced convalescence. Parishioners softened and expressed genuine concern for his welfare. The rector unbent more and appreciated their acceptance. He later wrote, 'The care of the parish for Lindy and me through this time deepened our bonds to its people and has assured that the people of St Paul's and St David's will always have a special place in our hearts.'[6] A new stage emerged as the church warmed to his vision. Parishioners also realised that Lindy had her own mission among the elderly and frail, that she would rush from the Brindabella Gardens Retirement Home to Manuka to be involved in children's work and that her contribution to the church was dedicated and loyal.

Council members soon noticed that the rector moved away from debates on daily issues and 'administrative trivia' towards 'larger

The Reverend Jeffrey Driver
© Framing Matters, Manuka

issues' involving 'creative strategies and initiatives'. Delegating routine matters wherever possible, he asked the council to create teams with specific responsibilities such as pastoral care, worship, administration, buildings and grounds and site development. In one sense this was a return to the 1970s but it was successful in the main as the sub-groups worked alongside the clergy 'with genuine responsibility' for a shared ministry.[7] By 2001 most of the groups were operating effectively with those involved in building and fund-raising assuming added importance. The wealth of talent in the parish unfortunately created its own problems as many parishioners operated 'at high levels of professional commitment' and found that 'continuing church commitments' were difficult, prompting Driver to encourage short-term project involvements.[8]

As emphasis was placed on pastoral care, the church was fortunate to have the assistance of Eric Wright who had been ordained by Bishop Chynoweth in 1978. With a background in law, he had served for 32 years with the Office of Parliamentary Counsel and the Attorney General's Department, retiring as 2nd Parliamentary Counsel in 1996 after a distinguished career. Arriving at Manuka late in 1997, he became involved in regular Sunday work and other duties, teaming closely with Driver and inspiring over 50 people to be active participants in pastoral work.[9] The parish was divided into areas, each allocated a leader and a team of home visitors and quarterly visits were introduced to maintain interest in the church and provide support for individual families. In 1999, Eric said of the workers, 'I have never encountered a parish with such a large proportion of its lay people willing to roll up the sleeves and get to work.'[10] In the meantime, Pam Wright provided secretarial assistance for the church and became an organist for the 8am service.

As the pastoral work developed and Wright assumed a different role, a pastoral care coordinating group took over responsibility with Les Bohm as convenor. It implemented a wide-ranging program that included lunches to enthuse people and broaden their skills. At the same time, existing programs were expanded. The Verandah included the provision of children's toys and the Kids Club maintained popularity until 1999 when it declined through a lack of adult leaders. The welcomer program was stressed, a 'Welcomer Kit' was developed and a church paper, *The Clarion*, was distributed as part of the visiting program. Hospitality lunches allowed parishioners to meet in each other's homes, a book club started and the Op Shop extended its mission by opening on some weekdays. Unfortunately Telecare was wound back when it was wrongly believed that home visits would make telephone contact and support redundant.

A walking group was commenced by Eric Wright and attracted continuing support as about 20 people enjoyed Saturday walks varying from pleasant rambles to challenging hikes. The topic of 'flat walks' (regardless of the hills or mountains involved) became a source of gibe as Wright was 'vilified' by his friends for his understatements, eliciting comments such as, 'I should like to go on one of the walks, but the trouble is, you can't believe a word that the reverend gentleman says.' Wright's pleasant manner and humour were an asset to the entire pastoral care program.[11]

Meanwhile, worship was stressed, the sanctuary team encouraged and the liturgy developed the ritual expected of a 'city church'. A service 'of a contemporary nature' known as 'St Paul's at 7' was also introduced and generated its own following, one that involved the young people of the church. This venture ran successfully for about two years but was closed owing to the difficulty of maintaining sufficient leaders. At the same time, Bishop Dowling was involved in a monthly service with a healing emphasis.

Taking up the rector's theme, a 'Church in the City – Church in the Village', St Paul's gradually adopted the role of Canberra's substitute cathedral in that the diocesan cathedral was situated over 100 km away. Early in 2000, visits by the Primate-elect, Archbishop Carnley, and Queen Elizabeth II underlined the notion that St Paul's was a place 'where major celebrations and gatherings' could 'focus faith in the life of a maturing *bush capital*'. The regular liturgy was clearly middle-road Anglicanism, although some said it edged 'a little higher with more ritual' causing some muted comments about churchmanship. This did not prevent the rector from referring to 'the tensions and fragilities in Australian Anglicanism', particularly the differences in sympathy apparent in the Diocese of Sydney.[12]

Music under the direction of Betty Erskine continued as a vital aspect of the church's liturgy. The three choirs accepted different roles – the main church choir at the 10am service, the smaller choir (rejuvenated with the title 'Phoenix Choir') on a less-regular basis at 8am and the St Paul's Singers at performances across the city, annual law services, Easter Eve performances, ANZAC Day commemorations and graduation day ceremonies. Choristers granted scholarships by the church gave valuable assistance to the regular choir. During this period, Betty reduced her involvement in all choirs. Oliver Raymond eventually assumed the directorship in 2000, having already directed the 10am choir since 1994. In a tribute, Raymond wrote:

> [Betty Erskine] came to the musical life of the parish at probably its lowest ebb in decades. In 1988 we lost our major choir [and she] took on the job of building from scratch and trying to maintain as far as possible the musical tradition of St Paul's. By the early 1990s she had built the choir to the point where it could ... take on major works such as the highly acclaimed successful ANZAC Requiems.[13]

Special musical occasions continued to cause discomfort for choir members, however, as choristers, the organ, a bank of trumpeters and timpani 'crammed into the gallery' and jostled for space. It was hoped that church extensions would overcome the problem.

The large number attending the 10am service during the latter years of John Griffiths' incumbency continued during Driver's time. A few months after his arrival, the rector discussed the 'provision of additional seating to cope with congregational growth'. When numbers continued to grow at both the 8am and 10am services, he indicated that the church 'should set its goal' of increasing congregational seating by '30 per cent within the next twelve months'. A masterplan for site renewal was developed, an architect's report commissioned and John Griffiths was invited back to launch the building development program in 2000.[14] A new lectern in the pulpit was dedicated to Barbara Griffiths' memory during this visit. With the aim of commencing the construction of two additional bays on the western end of the church after Easter 2001, plans were finalised, the original bricks were matched in colour and texture and appeals launched to raise almost one million dollars. As the music gallery was also involved in the extensions, the loft was removed and the organ dismantled for the second time in ten years. Building began with the early onset of winter.

As the excavations were dug, the foundations poured, the walls constructed and the roof erected, parishioners inspected the progress week by week. They were pleased when the additions were completed by late 2001. The church was filled to capacity on 9 December when

St Paul's Manuka 2010

Bishop Browning dedicated the extensions and the Governor-General, Dr Peter Hollingworth, unveiled a dedication stone on the exterior of the building. The extended gallery provided additional space for both the organ and the choristers but the organ music 'struggled to fill' the entire church. Plans for the installation of bells in the church tower were not completed in time and awaited additional finance.

Development naturally came at a cost and parish finances were again stretched to cope with maintenance, new projects and heavy interest payments. While income rose from $307,000 in 1987 to $630,000 in 2001, the figures masked $77,000 of interest payments on the rectory (with more still owing), an annual diocesan contribution that had risen to over $38,000, donations to St Mary-in-the-Valley and clergy stipends of over $85,000 a year. Moreover, $281,000 of the receipts in 2001 comprised donations to the building fund (only 30 per cent of what would be required) and the church realised that it had plunged into substantial debt as invoices from the builders were received. Even the cost of utilities rose to over $20,000, prompting the wardens to turn off the lights more quickly after services. The creation of an Arts Foundation stimulated additional donations and assisted the music program.[15]

With his additional duties as diocesan archdeacon including the Anglicare Council and Retirement Community Services, the rector was fortunate to have the assistance of Elaine Farmer and Eric Wright, together with the input of Pat Haldane-Stevenson until 1999. The ministry team was augmented in 1998 with the part-time appointment of Caroline Campbell until her move to Gundagai in 1999; the full-time services of Lynda McMinn in 2000–2001; and the valuable input of Robin Lewis-Quinn. Jill Elliott and Gloria Dowling continued their faithful ministry as chaplains to the aged-care communities and many other parishioners were committed to the fellowship, educational and outreach programs of the parish. Moreover, the clergy used the St Paul's website to record their sermons and other items of interest.

Parish programs included 'Alpha', a course involving a series of videos and the discussion of issues in small groups, followed by a shared meal, and 'Cursillo', the twenty-year-old program aimed at individual spiritual development. Pot-luck dinners, together with dessert-and-coffee nights, allowed fellowship in informal groups; Lenten series and Sunday night programs provided teaching and discussion opportunities; and Credo and the Education for Ministry (EFM) course catered for deeper study needs. The Senior Women's Fellowship, Anglican Women, the Tapestry Guild and prayer and Bible study groups met specific interests and contributed to the life of the church. A chaplaincy was supported at the Narrabundah College and John Wallis' production of *Antigone* fostered fellowship and promoted church outreach.

Considerable effort went into the provision of educational programs but with only limited success in terms of numbers involved. Janie McOmish and her team had learned that Sunday school attendances would rarely exceed 20 and that they would often fall, depending on the time of the year. Nevertheless, some children continued to attend Sunday school and joined the rector each week on the steps of the sanctuary for story time. Sometimes the rector's fly fishing rod illustrated his message. Youth workers were appointed, small youth groups commenced and recommenced, a dozen teenagers were included in a worship roster, children's church was developed and youth education lunches were arranged – all of which achieved some success but were hampered by relatively small numbers and the lack of continuity as leaders moved to other ministries.[16]

During the period 1997 to 2001, Bishop Neville continued to minister at Red Hill with twin duties. He had special responsibilities for St David's Church and was also the warden of St David's Close until December 1999 when he relinquished the position to Judy Taylor. While the debt on the church had been liquidated in 1984, it was not until 1997 – the 25th anniversary of the church's opening – that St David's was consecrated by Bishop Browning. Over 100 sang to the sound of a new organ purchased at a cost of over $10,000.

With attendances varying between 50 and 60, the parishioners continued to be a close cohesive group involved in dinners, fashion parades, musical afternoons and garage sales to raise money for Anglicare, World Vision, St Mark's National Theological Centre, the extensions to St Paul's Church and an array of missionary activities. Additional funds were derived from catering for the parent-teacher evenings at the Girls' Grammar School, from weddings and from stalls at the annual garage sales. The gardens were tended, the Sunday School attracted small numbers, Lenten studies were held, the tapestry group provided church kneelers and the healing group met on a regular basis. Much was owed to the loyalty of parishioners such as Glad Curtis, Dorothy Anderson, Bill Thorn, Helen Cameron, Bruce Wilson and Duncan Anderson. Moreover, Archdeacon Driver exchanged pulpits, maintaining an interest in Red Hill and working cooperatively with Bishop Neville and the two honorary assistants, Edgar Rolfe and Thory Bonsey.[17]

By 2001, Jeff Driver had been archdeacon for over twelve years, had gained wide experience in many aspects of church life at diocesan and national levels and believed that it was time for a change. Nevertheless, he was surprised when approached and nominated for the See of Gippsland, leading to his consecration as bishop in St Paul's Cathedral at Melbourne in November 2001.[18] Returning to Manuka until December, he participated in the dedication of the additions to St Paul's by Bishop Browning. He also attended a parish council meeting where Chris Erskine, the presiding officer, referred to 'the changes and innovations that the rector had made', in a parish 'remarkably blessed' by his incumbency. In return, Driver commented on the way that the parish had changed – 'there has been a shift' – and he asked the council to consider whether it desired future rectors to continue the direction.[19]

The new Bishop of Gippsland was installed three days before Christmas 2001, wearing a bishop's ring that was a gift of the people of St Paul's and bearing a pectoral cross from St David's. Four years later, Driver was elected Archbishop of Adelaide. His legacy to Canberra included a close liaison between theological education and a university, an extended vision for the parishioners of St Paul's and a major step in the creation of a 'city church' in the national capital.

With Driver's departure, the search for a new rector began again, a seemingly routine procedure refined over time. It was not widely understood, however, that, beneath the seemingly benign nature of church life at Manuka, St Paul's was not an easy parish to administer. Each of the past two rectors had experienced difficulty as they contended with early opposition to their policies and the parishioners were generally highly educated, often with strong views of their own. Moreover, the Clergy Appointment Board had to keep in mind that

> St Paul's is a large parish and the pastoral needs are great … with acknowledged gaps in the extent and coverage … The way into full participation and service [in the church] is not obvious … The parish has not been able to successfully integrate youth … The focus on children is very limited. Sunday school is run with insufficient support from the congregation. The parish has not yet been successful in integrating contemporary expressions of worship and spirituality.[20]

A middle-of-the-road form of Anglicanism was deeply rooted in the church's culture so that any sustained displays of evangelicalism were looked on with disapproval and any major move towards high church ritualism was equally viewed with suspicion. Even John Griffiths had found it prudent to drop the term 'Father John' and his use of incense had been strongly opposed and discontinued by request.

At that time, the Reverend Dr Scott Cowdell had accepted a redundancy from the principalship of St Barnabas' Theological College in Adelaide after a diocesan restructure. He had already been in contact with Bishop Browning who had raised the possibility of his coming to Canberra. When Archdeacon John Parkes contacted Cowdell and asked if his name could go forward to Manuka, he consented. He was called for interview in November, promptly offered the incumbency and requested to begin work at the start of January 2002. He was subsequently informed by one of the parish nominators that the committee had sought an intellectual, a person with pastoral experience and someone with past involvement in major building projects. Because he was unable to take up duties for three months, the new rector detected a resulting degree of 'ill feeling' in the parish. He was also aware of tension and anxiety 'about the just-completed building project and the huge debt' incurred. Scott Cowdell and his wife, Lisa Carley, a government lawyer, arrived after Easter and settled into the rectory, glad to come to a 'major, well-resourced parish with a national pulpit'.[21]

Born in 1960, Cowdell was a theologian with an impressive academic record which included a first degree in science, further degrees in theology and arts and a doctorate from the University of Queensland in 1994. Trained for the priesthood for five years at St Francis' Theological College in Brisbane, his three published works indicated wide scholarship and a deep knowledge of Christology and other areas of theology. His most recent work, *A God for this World*, illustrated his concern for relating faith to contemporary issues in modern society. As a tutor at the University of Queensland, lecturer at Trinity College, Melbourne, senior lecturer in theology at Flinders University and principal of a theological college in Adelaide, his academic experience was extensive and unquestioned. Moreover, it was during his time as rector of All Saints', Chermside, in Brisbane that a new church and rectory had been built, giving him valuable insights into the recent developments at St Paul's and the need for financial consolidation.[22]

Parishioners soon learned that they had acquired a forceful preacher, whose well-crafted sermons aimed to influence and teach. While his academic background was apparent, Cowdell had the added ability to relate biblical teaching to contemporary issues in society and to stimulate thought and discussion on a range of sensitive and controversial matters. These included issues of human sexuality, one result of which was that a number of gay men and couples joined St Paul's during those years. When parishioners in 2010 recalled his sermons, they mentioned his capacity to question, sometimes to provoke and usually to challenge. Viewing his role as a 'public intellectual', the rector connected the gospel to social issues, interpreted worship and discipleship in countercultural terms, stressed the need for Christian inclusivity and related film to his message. Over the five years of his incumbency, he spoke publicly on issues that confronted the Christian community, including lectures entitled, 'What can we learn from *The Da Vinci Code?*' and 'Who's afraid of Richard Dawkins?' In short, Cowdell saw the pulpit as a means of promoting social justice, chastising exclusivity within society and the church and extending the embrace of the Christian message.

Acknowledging the importance of the catholic tradition in worship, the rector stressed the importance of the liturgy. He introduced changes to the 10am service by reducing and streamlining the sanctuary team and ending lay deacon roles. This led a small group of 'laity who saw their roles as more senior in the sanctuary' to abandon sanctuary involvement, as the ordained deacon assumed 'the deacon's role for the first time'. The use of bound prayer books in services was replaced by a high-quality weekly worship booklet containing the text of the liturgy, readings and hymns; the 'Peace' was declared from the altar rather than from the steps of the sanctuary; a director of liturgy was appointed as an experiment; and the worship edged higher although never really departing from the broad spectrum of traditional Anglicanism. One small incident, however, proved a focus for some disquiet when the rector kissed the altar during the Eucharist, a practice that some felt was more Roman than Anglican. Other liturgical changes were thoroughly explained and often canvassed in advance, while several marks of advanced Anglo-Catholic churchmanship were not reintroduced during Cowdell's incumbency, such as incense and a robed choir. The rector later 'rejoiced in achieving the consolidation of a modern catholic feel to the worship', one that was broadly accepted by the parishioners, although some unease remained.[23]

Like his predecessors, Cowdell emphasised the place of music in the liturgy. After the extension of the church building in 2001 and the consequent dismantling and reconstruction of the organ during the process, the rebuilt instrument was not sufficiently powerful, a fault that was rectified within days when it was doubled in size with the use of digital technology. With a hybrid organ – part-pipe and part-electronic – greater power was achieved as well as a greater range of stops from very quiet to loud and with more versatility across the range of sound. In the opinion of Chris Erskine, the new sound not only filled the building but also led to louder congregational singing and enjoyment.[24]

The 10am choir continued under Oliver Raymond's direction until the end of 2005 providing anthems, psalms and canticles; singing at law services, graduation ceremonies, ecumenical services and weddings; and combining with the choir of St Christopher's Roman Catholic Cathedral to present Christmas carol services each year. A harp, brass sextet, timpani and organ, together with two choirs, readers and clergy, resulted in a strong popular appeal as well as a highly valued means of outreach. Musical scholars, sponsored by the church, added to the liturgy through the trumpet, harp and organ, while choristers from the grammar schools contributed to a number of services, the Christmas Pageant and the 11.30pm service on Christmas Eve. Bishop Dowling's small vocal ensemble often sang at the 8am services at which he was the organist.[25] When it was felt that the extensive musical program was unsustainable, a review resulted and Dr Peter Pocock, who had recently returned from the United States, was appointed to 'move the musical culture towards that of 'a lively Episcopal American parish' rather than 'that of an English Cathedral'.[26] Pocock was subsequently ordained deacon and relinquished his music ministry at St Paul's in 2008.

On his first visit to St Paul's, the rector had discerned 'tension' relating to the debt on the church extensions, a perception that proved to be correct as ways were sought to liquidate the liability. The redevelopment had not only involved the extension of the church itself but had also included variations to the church, the hall and the surrounds, rebuilding and digitally upgrading the organ, installing a new public address system and payments for professional fees. Excluding $23,300 paid for work already completed in 2000, the cost, without projected interest payments, was $750,000 of which $325,500 had been donated by the end of 2001. The difference had to be met from diocesan loans, pledges by parishioners and sizeable interest-free loans for specified (and usually short-term) periods. Moreover, the debt on the rectory was still $47,000 and church expenditure exceeded income in 2002. The situation caused the rector to press for a financial strategy to cover $110,000 owed to the Anglican Development Fund and $450,000 on the interest-free loans.[27]

The next few years witnessed a remarkable effort to pay off the debts, although it occasioned frank exchanges of opinion in council, different expectations and rival financial policies. As there appeared no strategy in place for repayment of the debt except for what the rector saw as an 'indefinite perpetuation' of 'impecunity', Cowdell proposed to 'democratise the debt' by stretching it over a long-term mortgage and moving on to other priorities.[28]

The Reverend Dr Scott Cowdell
© Framing Matters, Manuka

Spurred on by this challenge, the development committee argued that a mortgage of $225,000 over 15 or 25 years would amount to unnecessary interest payments, a scenario to be avoided. 'Detecting a groundswell of similar opinion' among parishioners, council determined to make additional appeals to the parish in 2003 and 2005 and was gratified as generous donations and commitments were increasingly received. It was announced on 3 November 2006 that the debt of $770,538 had been cleared, less than five years after the completion of the extensions.[29] This included tax-deductible donations made to the Arts Foundation over the same period. The sustained work of the development committee was duly lauded and the parishioners were relieved. The rector said he was happy to be proved wrong about the best strategy to employ, later expressing his delight that the 'huge monkey on the back of the parish' had been removed. He believed that 'the atmosphere' of tension had been cleared, allowing the parish to move on positively without overwhelming fiscal anxieties.

Three other achievements were significant during this period, the first being the installation of bells in the church tower. Planned over years, the project demanded consultations with the ACT Government, structural assessments of the church and tower and an impact minimisation on surrounding residential areas. All eight bells were donated, four new and four used, with the oldest bell cast in London in 1876. The bellringers, with impetus from Ian Sykes, raised most of the $180,000 required to finalise the project. Alan Christie contributed much to the detailed planning and the project was carried through to completion with the rector's encouragement. The bells, together with major siteworks, were dedicated on 15 June 2003 by the Administrator of the Commonwealth, Sir Guy Green. The oldest bell was named 'Queen Nelly Hamilton' in memory of a nineteenth-century leader of the Ngunnawal people and others were named after those dear to the donors. Henceforth, the bells welcomed parishioners each Sunday and heralded special occasions.

The second major achievement was the redevelopment of the church grounds facing Captain Cook Crescent and Canberra Avenue, made possible by a generous gift of the Snow and Byron families. Terry Snow, manager of Canberra Airport and a major supporter of diocesan welfare initiatives, had been the head chorister at St Paul's and had come to lament the state of the grounds. Landscaping the site involved the establishment of lawns down to the streets, construction of a reflective pool and the building of a much-needed car park. This was made easier by the positive pastoral relationships developed by the curate, Lynda McMinn, aided by the rector. At the same time the Garsia Garden in front of the church hall was developed to include a wall for plaques in memory of the deceased. As this disturbed previous memorials to loved ones in the garden, there was an understandable degree of distress experienced by some of the parishioners but the end result was dignified and judged to enhance revered memories.[30] A smaller rose garden, developed with the help of Joan and Neville Boston, using rose bushes from the Griffiths era and resited from the refurbished rectory garden, was dedicated to the memory of John and Barbara Griffiths.

The third achievement was realised in 2007 when the church paid off the debt on the rectory. Constructed at a cost of $220,589 in 1992 and expected 'to serve the parish for at least 50 years', the new rectory had been financed by a loan at a relatively low rate of interest but there were some years in which no repayments off the principal were made at all. Consequently, $47,000 was still owed at the start of 2003 with the possibility that the liability would continue for many years. However, from 2005, annual payments were increased and the debt was liquidated to the relief of the rector, council and parishioners. By the end of 2007, St Paul's annual receipts amounted to $349,500, expenditure stood at $342,500 and there was an operating surplus of $7,000. During the Cowdell's incumbency, the budget rose by over 26 per cent, while the diocesan contribution rose from $35,500 to $42,900.[31]

During the worst financial periods, the staff had been reduced and the rector was fortunate to have the input of honorary priests and assistants. During 2002 Eric and Pam Wright departed to serve in Bungendore and Lynda McMinn was appointed to the incumbency of Holy Covenant in September. Lynda, with the assistance of Eric Wright and Elaine Farmer, had been responsible for St Paul's before the rector's arrival and the wardens agreed that her ministry had been 'exceptional'. Bronwyn Suptut was appointed as curate in December 2002 and contributed to 'an effective team ministry', subsequently becoming rector of St Barnabas', Charnwood, in December 2004. Robin Lewis-Quinn, who had acted in a non-stipendiary capacity over some years, accepted responsibility for the 7am service. She was made an honorary associate priest, lived in the old rectory in 2005 and served as stipendiary associate priest during 2006 and 2007. The parish benefited from the continuing support of Bishop Owen Dowling, Tony Parkinson, Dean Griffiths, Elaine Farmer, Susanna Pain, John Moses and Jill Elliott. Attendances averaged around seventeen at 7am, about 40 at 8am and about 125 at 10am. Smaller numbers attended healing services and midweek Communions.[32]

As in previous incumbencies, fellowship groups continued and outreach programs were maintained and developed. The ecumenical Verandah venture, involving the Anglican, Baptist and Uniting Churches, continued to open three times a week, the Op Shop earned over $5,000 a year thus providing a significant personal ministry, the chaplains ministered to old people in the Retirement Homes, the Trading Table earned money for chaplaincy at Narrabundah College, a marriage preparation team was set up to conduct workshops and individual sessions for couples, and welcoming committees extended greetings and invited newcomers to Sunday breakfasts and morning teas each week. The captain of the bellringers, Ian Sykes, handed over the captaincy to Julie Doyle in 2005. Fellowship and education were nurtured through the Senior Women's Group, Tapestry Group, Walking Club, Cursillo, the EFM, flower arrangers, Movie Group and the newly formed 'Discovery @ St Paul's' led by Pam Bongers. Annual fetes meant hard work for a team leader and numerous assistants but netted between $9,000 and $11,000 by 2006–2007, helping to maintain the church's financial viability.

The Sunday school closed in 2005 as numbers declined following an accident to Janie McOmish that left her unable to continue. Janie had helped revitalise the Sunday school from 1984 and her 20 years of devoted service were enjoyed by hundreds of children and appreciated by their parents. Apart from a small team of helpers, parishioners gave little physical assistance to the Sunday school movement at St Paul's. The young people's ministry suffered a similar outcome, influenced by small numbers and the lack of continuity among leaders. Nikolai Blaskow and Susanna Pain were able to lead a group for some time but it disbanded after the two leaders moved to Holy Covenant, Jamison.[33] Believing that the era of the Sunday school was over, the rector discussed the issue with parents and then discontinued the school, replacing it with a children's liturgy run by Robin Lewis-Quinn between the two Sunday services.[34]

'Young Adults' proved to be a successful venture, a group that met weekly at the rectory for a meal and a wide-ranging discussion of faith and life issues. Enthused by their participation, the group commented on the 'challenges they received from Scott Cowdell' to explore issues in depth and to confront prejudices, an enthusiasm that still prevailed in 2010 when members of the group recalled their meetings six years before. Over a dozen young adults became active members of the 10am service.

The rector's responsibility included St David's where he had the regular assistance of Bishop Chynoweth, Edgar Rolfe, Jill Elliott and Thory Bonsey (until the end of 2002) and the occasional input of Robert Willson and Eric Wright (until his sudden death in 2005). While Cowdell presided and preached occasionally at Red Hill, he left pastoral care in the hands of Neville Chynoweth whom he designated as Pastor at St David's and who, by 2003, had ministered for ten years, 'the longest single period in any one place [for the bishop] in almost 50 years'. Pursuing a 'prayer book tradition' – middle-of-the-road Anglicanism – the bishop drolly maintained that he could not complain about the churchmanship as he had helped develop it, 'reaching back to the 1970s'. With about 60 communicants each Sunday, the congregation was cohesive and involved in services. The people donated to the church and contributed funds to disaster appeals, the Verandah, World Vision, Anglicare, the Red Hill Primary School Connections Program, other missions and the Narrabundah College chaplaincy. Joan Chynoweth remained a driving force, organising two garage sales which returned between $12,000 and $18,000 annually. Memorial windows were installed, 'a handsome font' was donated by the Curtis–Gay family in memory of Glad Curtis, a paschal candle stand was donated by the Rolfes and the parking lot was asphalted. Particular attention was placed on pastoral care among the elderly and a spirit of fellowship was maintained with the continuing input of Duncan Anderson, Bill Thorn, Helen Cameron, Bruce Wilson, Mollie Burton and Heather Schmitzer.[35]

Despite the progress that had been made, Cowdell did not find it an easy incumbency. He wrote in 2005 of the fragility of Anglican churches that require 'so much energy' to keep them going, significantly referring to:

> the tenuousness of attachment to the Church, the high expectations of lay people, the enormous scope for disappointment they demonstrate and the amount of effort necessary to fulfil the diverse expectations of a congregation – let alone to lead it![36]

Some of the difficulties resulted from the size of the Manuka parish, the extent of the debt to be liquidated and the financial constraints that prevented the appointment of additional staff. Some believed that the time devoted to the rector's academic interests, the writing of *God's Next Big Thing: Discovering the Future Church*, his work on the Doctrine Commission of the General Synod of the Anglican Church of Australia and his lecturing commitments at St Mark's contributed to a self-imposed tension. However, this is most unlikely. He was highly motivated as a pastor and theologian, thoroughly enjoying his academic pursuits.

There was a complex interaction of events that combined to raise misgivings on both sides throughout the rector's tenure. First, there was the disapproval of events that heightened a perception of advanced Catholic tendencies, even though these were not extreme nor ventured beyond a relatively middle-of-the–road form of Anglican liturgy. Nevertheless, they heightened feelings and led to reproval from some with contrary leanings. Second, there was a small minority that was offended by the rector's refusal to avoid controversial themes, an emphasis that could incorrectly be viewed as a socialist-directed philosophy. Third, there was an old-fashioned conservative resistance to any departure from prevailing practice, from the comfort of the known to the new and unfamiliar. It was a combination of all three that led to a degree of negativity towards some of the rector's policies. On the rector's part, he was determined to effect change despite resistance to the introduction of a managerial style that placed more importance on convictions than unquestioned acceptance. As one member of the congregation contended, he brought a spiritual rather than a social-club agenda which caused distress to some and brought applause from others. His critics claimed that he lacked 'people skills' and that this affected the harmony of the parish. Others emphasised his forceful preaching, his youth work encouragement and his ministry of comfort to the sick.

Disinterested analysis points to difficulties on both sides. Some parishioners had difficulty in coping with an intellectual rector with social, financial and liturgical agendas that challenged those who sought a placid status quo. Cowdell admitted that he did not always cope well with negativity from a small group who felt aggrieved. There were many parishioners who were convinced of the need for reasoned change at St Paul's and supported most of the rector's initiatives, although some were undoubtedly concerned when people's feelings were perceived (rightly or wrongly) to be of less importance than a principle at stake.

There was one agenda to which the rector unswervingly adhered over five years – the transition of St Paul's from the village-type, social-group-oriented church of the Griffiths era towards a city-church appropriate to the national capital. On his arrival, he referred to his incumbency as a 'transitional stage' during which 'unfinished business must be seen through' – site works, bells, repayment of parish debts – in order to reach a stage where the parish could settle into 'a renewed sense of mission and purpose'.[37] Not long before his departure, he wrote that 'we have now negotiated a period of transition' beginning with the Griffiths ministry, 'extending through Jeff's significant ministry' and reaching a point where 'the parish today is taking shape in a new way'. The parish now embraced a deepened liturgy, an extended vision, a capacity to meet new challenges and the ability to be a city church in the national capital. As national leaders attended special events at St Paul's and memorial services were conducted following international tragedies, the church attained the status to which Jeffrey Driver and Scott Cowdell aspired.

With much achieved, Dr Cowdell felt the increasing attraction of full-time theological work and when offered an appointment in the Public and Contextual Theology Strategic Research Centre of Charles Sturt University, he accepted. His incumbency ended on 3 June 2007. He was to continue his vocation in research and writing as Canon Theologian of the Diocese of Canberra and Goulburn.

Notes

1. StP, 1997 annual report.
2. B Barnes, *A Noble Experiment: A History of Holy Covenant Anglican Parish, Jamison ACT, 1968–1992*, Holy Covenant Anglican Church, 1992.
3. Jeffrey Driver, Personal communication, 2008; Frame, *A Church for a Nation*, p. 282.
4. StP, 1997 annual report.
5. Views recalled by parishioners in 2009–2010.
6. Jeffrey Driver, Personal communication, 2008.
7. StP, 1998 annual report.
8. StP, 2001 annual report.
9. Pamela Wright, Personal communication, 2009.
10. E Wright, 'Pastoral Report', StP, 1999 annual report.
11. E Wright, 'Pastoral Care', StP, 1998 annual report.
12. StP, 2000 annual report.
13. Oliver Raymond, Personal communication, 2010; StP, 2001 annual report.
14. StP, annual reports 1997–2001.
15. Financial reports, StP, 1997–2001.
16. StP, annual reports 1997–2001.
17. StD, annual reports 1997–2001.
18. Jeffrey Driver, Personal communication, 2010.
19. StPPC, 11 November 2001.
20. Parish Profile (Diocesan Clergy Appointment Board), StPPC, November–December 2001.

21. Scott Cowdell, Personal communication, 2008–2010.
22. Based on discussions with Scott Cowdell and notes he provided.
23. Scott Cowdell, Personal communication, 2008–2010.
24. Appendix to music report, StP, 2001 annual report.
25. StP, annual reports of the Director of Music, Dr O Raymond, 2001–2005.
26. Scott Cowdell, Personal communication, 2008–2010.
27. See: 'St Paul's Development Appeal Committee' report and general financial report in StP, 2002 annual report; and 'Towards a Financial Strategy for the Parish,' StPPC, 2 February 2003.
28. Scott Cowdell, Personal communication, 2010.
29. Development Committee Reports, StP, annual reports 2003–2006.
30. StP, annual reports, 2002–2004; and remarks by parishioners.
31. StP, annual reports for 1992 and 2007.
32. StP, annual reports 2005–2007.
33. StP, annual reports 2002–2007.
34. Scott Cowdell, Personal communication, 2008–2010.
35. StP, annual reports 2002–2007 contain the yearly reports on St David's Church.
36. Scott Cowdell, 'On Loving the Church' in T Frame and G Treloar (eds), *Agendas for Australian Anglicanism*, ATF Press, Adelaide, 2006, p. 253.
37. StP, 2002 annual report.

15   St Luke's Deakin–Yarralumla

The Parish of St Luke can trace its origin to the commencement of Anglican services at the Brickworks (Westridge) in May 1914 and later at Westlake in July 1923. As outlined in previous chapters, the growth of Westridge was largely dependent on the continued demand for bricks, tiles and pipes to supply Canberra's development while Westlake's existence stemmed from the need for temporary camps and settlements to house the builders of the city's public buildings.

When Archdeacon Bob Davies arrived at St John's in 1949, he found that Anglican services had ceased at Westridge thirteen years before and that parishioners had been required to walk two miles to the Westlake Hall. When services had ceased there also in April 1949, an even longer trek had been required to St John's, Reid, or St Paul's, Manuka. Davies realised that the Westlake settlement was doomed to eventual closure but was immediately interested in the Westridge area where the population – 320 in 1947 – was projected to increase quite substantially.[1] A deputation of 25 residents had met with the Minister for the Interior in February 1949 seeking additional bus services, improvements to the oval, removal of the Westridge Hall, the appointment of a resident police officer and the tarring of roads 'to eradicate dust from bus and garbage traffic'.[2]

The entrance to Novar Street was considered dangerous because of fast traffic on the Cotter Road but speeding was impossible in Yarralumla itself where paths and roads had received little attention since they had been laid 20 years before and where people had to ne-gotiate 'bog-holes' instead of paths.[3] There was only one shop, situated on the corner of Bentham and Hutchins Streets and shoppers were required to take the long trek to Manuka for many goods.[4] Two buses serviced the area each day, one for workers and the other for children who attended the schools at Telopea Park and St Christopher's at Manuka. Most of the ten telephone lines were taken by the Forestry School and departmental undertakings, leaving only two lines for private residents.[5] There was just cause for complaint.

Archdeacon Davies and the Reverend Gordon Armstrong drove to this 'outer suburb' in September 1949 and organised a house-to-house visitation, distributing an invitation which read:

> ... we would like to provide an opportunity for the Church of England people to meet together for fellowship and worship ... On Sunday, October 9 [1949], at 3 pm, in the Westridge Hall, we intend to hold a Family Service [and then] discuss plans for the future of the Church of England in Westridge. We look forward to you and your family being present at this service.[6]

The clergymen were met with 'genuine welcome and goodwill' and there was sufficient interest for them to organise regular gatherings in the old Westridge Hall with the Brickworks on one side and open fields and slopes on the other.[7] Davies conducted the first 'Family Service and Sunday school' on Sunday 22 October 1949 and scheduled a regular monthly family service and a weekly Sunday school thereafter. Then, thinking of future needs, the archdeacon applied for 'land for a church, hall, rectory and tennis court' in October.[8]

The Westridge Church lay within the new Parish of St Paul from March 1950 and when Ross Border, as new rector, asked why there were so few from Yarralumla who attended St Paul's Manuka, he was told, 'We don't have cars and there are no buses and it's too far to walk'. He answered, 'Well we had better build a church out there.'[9] His conviction was strengthened in June 1950 when he heard of a proposed housing program for 1,800 new homes in three years 'with dwellings stretching to within a short distance of the Swedish and American embassies'. A community centre, shopping block, hall and four pre-school play centres were envisaged, together with two sports ovals and a primary school.[10]

Moving quickly, Border urged St Paul's council to apply to the Department of the Interior for a cottage at Westridge for a priest 'when the need arose'.[11] It took seven years before one was available but, in the meantime, the earlier application for church land was successful. During 1952 a map of the proposed church site became available – an open paddock on elevated land on a major circular road, a prime position later to be known as 'Section 30 Newdegate Street'. As Adelaide Avenue had not been constructed at the time, the suburb of Yarralumla included the Newdegate area that later became the suburb of Deakin.

Aerial view of Yarralumla 1953. The Brickworks and Forestry Department are on the far right.
© ACT Heritage Library, DCT Collection

The Yarralumla congregation and Sunday school met in the Westridge Hall from October 1949 until February 1956 but the hall was inadequate for the increasing numbers. Homes were being constructed, people were moving into the area, academics from the recently founded Australian National University were arriving and shops were being planned, causing the rector to comment that 'we must ... build either a church or a hall or both at Yarralumla in the not too distant future'. By Easter 1952, an 'Open Letter to all Anglicans at Yarralumla' indicated that the children's service provided for 50 each Sunday, Morning Prayer or Communion was held each week, a Women's Guild had been formed under the direction of Mrs Tarrant, Mrs Stretton and Mrs Reid and information about the guild could be obtained from Mrs Dyer 'at the Store'.[12]

The women at Yarralumla soon launched into fund-raising activities for the proposed church. Cake stalls and jumble sales were held, competitions for poultry dinners were conducted, cakes were decorated and raffled, card parties were organised and the church entered the rag trade when *The Canberra Times* informed its readers that collectors would call for rags to be sold for profit. Plans were made for the first fete to be held on the Yarralumla sports ground in February 1953 where 'a baby minding centre' was available to allow parents to visit the stalls, purchase goods and 'indulge in side-show activities'. Such events would guarantee 'a great occasion for all visitors and a substantial boost to the building fund'.

Growth was rapid as 'prefab' houses were erected and a pharmacy, butcher's shop, bank and dental surgery were constructed.[13] During 1954 the Sunday school expanded as 'new faces appeared each week'. The parishioners of St Paul's and Yarralumla began to talk of a future separate parish and St Paul's agreed to bear the cost of expenses and stipends for the area.[14] Border was aware, however, of the need for a more appropriate building and, when a modern brick primary school was being constructed in Loftus Street during 1955, he applied to the Department of the Interior for permission to transfer church services to the school.

By early 1956 the 'folk at Yarralumla' were very pleased that they

could hold church and Sunday school services 'each Sunday in the beautiful new Yarralumla Primary School'. Charles and Elizabeth Price, who had just returned from Magdalen College Chapel and St Mary's in the High at Oxford, felt like 'pioneers' when they attended services at the school – a 'primary school

The Reverend R Border conducts a service in the Yarralumla Primary School.
© St Luke's Archives

hall, kindergarten chairs, piano, make-shift altar' – but 'it was orderly and very friendly and we soon felt we belonged'.[15] (When Governor-General Sir William Slim and his wife attended services, they were provided with 'proper chairs'.) With the opening of the school, religious instruction classes were provided for the children each week by Mrs Loomes and Mrs Pentecost.[16]

Nevertheless, the rector was uneasy about the response from Yarralumla. Despite the consensus to build 'a hall with a chapel attached' at a cost restricted to £6,000, the progress was slow,[17] and Border indicated that 'a great deal more interest will need to be shown

by those living in that area if successful development is to be made.'
He became more critical as he considered financial obligations.

> The Parish Council has diverted 75 per cent of all Yarralumla
> income to the … building project there and people at Yarralumla
> do not pay one penny towards stipends and wages or towards
> the payment of the debt on their Parish Church of St Paul or
> on their rectory … The rest of the Parish is carrying this weight
> and it is up to the large majority of Anglicans at Yarralumla
> to show some appreciation of what others are doing for them.
> They cannot expect to be spoon-fed all the time.[18]

His pointed words were not aimed at the small band of faithful parishioners who worked constantly and had collected over £900 towards
their new church but at those whose membership was little more than
nominal, many sending their children to the Sunday school but not
attending or contributing themselves.[19] Action resulted within weeks
when a working committee was set up 'to investigate the desirability of
the creation of the Yarralumla Parish and the prospect of commencing
a building by the end of the calendar year [1957]'.[20]

When 35 parishioners met after church in May, they unanimously
voted for 'the formation of the Parish of Yarralumla' and elected their
own committee of nine, prompting Border to visit Bishop Burgmann
and discuss the options available. Their deliberations were reflected
in a letter that Border drafted on 14 July 1957: 'My dear Bishop, As
you are aware … we are of the opinion that the time is ready and
propitious [for] the creation of the Parish of Saint Luke, Yarralumla,'
one embracing 'Yarralumla (including Westlake), New Deakin and
that part of Deakin west of Melbourne Avenue and west of Empire
Circuit'. The population of the area was almost 3,000, there were
302 Anglican families in the region, 119 of them had pledged almost
£5,600 over three years and the average weekly income per family
was £123. St Paul's had not charged for stipend or parish expenses
for seven years so that there was approximately £2,000 held in trust
for a building.[21]

Moreover, the rector's 1950 application for a home for a priest
had been successful and a house was assured by September within
walking distance of the two acre site for the new 'parish buildings and
appurtenances'. The church land had an unimproved capital value of

£1,500 and £8,000 was 'sufficient for a building of a hall-cum-chapel suitable in size and dignity for the new area'. Border informed the bishop that the Parish of St Paul would provide approximately £2,500 within twelve months, comprising £750 already held in trust for Yarralumla, a grant of £500 from the parish and at least £1,300 held in a general fund set aside for the Yarralumla work.[22]

As there was no permanent place of worship, a parish could not be created but the bishop decided to separate the area from St Paul's, to name it a provisional district and to appoint a priest-in-charge. Hayden McCallum had been ordained in 1950 and appointed to the staff of St John's. He was a person 'with a rich experience of work with university students' throughout Australia and Europe.[23] In turn he had been the assistant registrar and helper to Assistant Bishop Ken Clements, a postgraduate student on a Rockfeller Scholarship in New York and was now at St John's once again.[24] The bishop believed that he should be the first rector of St Luke's. Knowing this, Border suggested that McCallum might be 'Rector of St Luke's at a stipend of £900 a year, plus £100 per year entertainment allowances and a travelling allowance of £200 per annum'.[25] The bishop agreed. As the first phase of St Luke's history came to a conclusion, McCallum moved into the house in Jervois Street, Deakin, in September 1957 and the new priest-in-charge was 'instituted into the cure of souls' on 18 October 1957, St Luke's Day.

The second stage of the parish's history, which spanned 1957 until the end of 1966 was a period of rapid growth. It saw the construction of the church, the evolution of neighbouring suburbs and the development of a worshipping community. At the first general meeting of parishioners held at the Girls' Grammar School in February 1958, it was decided to erect an L-shaped structure containing an assembly room, kitchen, toilet block, entrance hall, vestry and kindergarten room.[26] Tenders were invited in December 1958 and a loan of £9,000 at an interest rate of 5.75 per cent over nine years was secured. Construction of the steel frame and brick walls began in March 1959 and Her Excellency Lady Slim set the foundation stone on 5 April.[27] Parishioners organised working parties and collected river rocks for a stone feature wall.

Opening day on 18 October 1959 saw more than 500 people descend on Newdegate Street. Black cars conveyed the official party in style but the majority of parishioners walked across from Yarralumla or from the surrounding streets. After an opening address by the eminent theologian, Professor Norman Pittinger of New York, Bishop Burgmann dedicated the hall maintaining that 'the pioneering spirit, which laid the foundation of Australian history, was still aglow in the people' of Yarralumla and Deakin.[28] On the same day, the provisional district passed into history and the new Parish of St Luke was created, McCallum changing his title to that of rector. After serving for three years, McCallum was offered a theological scholarship to return to the United States and left in June, his place being taken by the youthful Peter Rudge, who had been ordained in 1953 and had served at Tumbarumba and Wagga Wagga for six years.

Both McCallum and Rudge realised the peculiarities of the district when in one year the parish recorded 60 baptisms (but only three marriages and three burials), a virtual children's nursery. Peter Rudge knew that social life was governed by small children and that joint functions for husbands and wives were 'almost out of the question'. Evening gatherings for women were inconvenient and meetings had to be arranged at lunchtime with youngsters in a nearby room or playing on the floor. Sunday school was an integral part of the worship. Even before the church hall had been opened in 1959, 150 children attended Sunday school, drawn from the 400 Anglican families in the area and it was necessary to hire an extra room at the school and appeal for additional teachers as numbers increased.[29] When the kindergarten section numbered 70 in March 1959, McCallum thought that the proposed new church building would be inadequate and that 'continued use of the primary school would be required for the overflow of children.'[30]

Bishop Burgmann (Reverend H McCallum to the bishop's right) on opening day, St Luke's.   © *St Luke's Archives*

Parishioners collecting rocks for the church's feature wall.
© *St Luke's Archives*

During 1959 and 1960, two Sunday schools operated, one in the Yarralumla school and the other in the church. The Yarralumla Sunday school ceased in early 1961 when the group felt isolated and not part of the 'parish family'. Consequently the 9.45am Sunday school and the 11am church service were amalgamated into a 10am service for more than 100 primary-aged children, who met together for 40 minutes and then moved into classes for girls and boys. When added to 70 to 90 kindergarten youngsters who met separately in a crowded room designed for 50, the numbers provided a challenge for the 24 teachers involved. An additional 20 young people attended the church's 'high school class' as a preparation for confirmation.[31] Rudge was tireless in his work for children and young people and even allowed basketball in the church hall.

Religious classes in schools generated a similar challenge when 345 children taxed the ability of the priests and their helpers to provide instruction at the Yarralumla school, with 'desperate' appeals for assistance being made during 1959.[32] The difficulties became more acute in 1961 as Rudge and his six assistants struggled to teach 388 lessons in fifteen classes at Telopea Park, Forrest and Yarralumla Primary Schools.[33] The effects of the postwar 'baby boom' had profound implications for the newly-formed parish, affecting both human and financial resources.

As the parish council explored the area's special (some said unique) features, they noted the rapid turnover of parishioners, the high percentage of public servants, the presence of embassies, the significant number of members of the medical profession in the district, the majority of people who worked outside the parish and the loneliness of some wives on arrival. With this information, the council sought to create an administrative structure, a pattern of worship and an outreach program designed to meet newcomers and involve them in the church. Every home was visited, new arrivals were targeted, family services were commenced, a small adult choir and a separate children's choir were created, men's teas were planned and activities for women were stressed through the Churchwomen's Union. Moreover, the bishop asked Rudge to become chaplain to the Canberra Girl's Grammar School, a weekly commitment that fortunately did not involve religious instruction classes. Both McCallum and Rudge sought to involve the community in a church that had a missionary zeal, a desire to incorporate both children and adults.[34] Fortunately the clergy had the assistance of Percy Moore, the head of the Yarralumla Nursery, who was deaconed by Bishop Burgmann and served as an honorary assistant from 1960.

After Rudge's departure, the parish experienced five hectic years during the incumbency of Canon Harold Palmer, an older priest who had been on the staff at St Saviour's Cathedral Goulburn and had served as the rector of Port Moresby, sub-Dean of Dogura Cathedral and chaplain to the Bishop of New Guinea. Whereas Rudge had conducted 156 services in 1961, Palmer recorded 275 in 1962 and 340 in 1964 and in 1965. The estimated Anglican population of the parish jumped from 2,300 to 2,800 in three years and the number of Anglican families rose from 560 to 750. The church was frequently crowded – 280 communicants were accommodated at Easter and another 346 at Christmas and the number of children attending regular services often equalled communicants. Baptismal services, numbering up to 65 annually, were conducted during the week, on Sunday afternoons and during Sunday morning services.

When Palmer spoke to the bishop in 1962, he was informed that 'the new up-and-coming district of Woden' (soon named Hughes and Curtin) would be the responsibility of St Luke's until the area 'was able to stand on its own feet'.[35] In the following two years, the priest, honorary staff and laity began visits to each new house, established regular Sunday worship in the Hughes Primary School (in February 1964), opened a Sunday school, formed a church council, conducted a canvass to attract funds and provided weekly religious instruction at the new Hughes Primary School. St Luke's parish, only five years old itself, prepared the new provisional district for the coming of its first clergyman, Steve Osborne, in February 1965. This was done without extra funds and with only the additional part-time assistance of the newly ordained Bill Ross for fourteen months as he continued his university studies at ANU.[36] With the opening of the Church of the Good Shepherd, the size of St Luke's Parish was diminished and Palmer's workload was reduced.

Meanwhile, the rector and the Sunday school teachers held a range of services at St Luke's each Sunday morning, seeking to determine the most effective way of coping with adult communicants and a Sunday school and kindergarten of up to 150 children. Palmer was encouraged to see the 'church-hall packed full' during 1963.[37] If the weather was fine, children's classes spilled outdoors and oc- cupied any space that could be found. Elizabeth Price recalled with humour in 2008 the difficulty of teaching new songs to the youngsters in the kindergarten as 'none of the teachers could sing in tune' and the young accompanist 'sort of played the piano'.[38] There was also a continuing demand for weekly instruction for 730 children at Telopea Park, Forrest and Yarralumla schools and for associated confirmation classes, and Palmer conducted Communion for 40 to 50 students at the Girls' Grammar School each week during term.[39]

Even though the number of communicants continued quite high in 1963–1964, some of the parishioners claimed that the rector's 'strong views' and rather restrained attitude 'took the joy out of youth work' and contributed to falling youth numbers. Somewhat staid in appearance and always dressed in a black suit, it was said he could offend and be abrasive at times.[40] The Sunday school numbers did fall during 1965–1966 but there were other factors involved, including the commencement of a Sunday school at Hughes nearby.

The three clergymen between 1957 and 1966 had differing ap- proaches but each had to contend with the issue of churchmanship. McCallum and Rudge were middle-of-the-road Anglicans, somewhat evangelical in style, both incorporating the community as much as possible. Harold Palmer was high church, devout and a hard worker but not perceived as being inspirational as his message was 'traditional' and without great stimulation. He contended that, while innovation was required, 'the Church is rightly conservative' and 'should preserve' much of what 'is tried and proven'.[41] The congregation included both those who appreciated Palmer's high church approach and others who were strongly evangelical and desired less ritual and greater spontane- ity. To its credit, the church was able to embrace both groups although not without some tension.

Fortunately all clergy had the unqualified support of the council, as it grappled with wider everyday matters – perennial maintenance tasks including a leaking roof, the need for additional accommodation and incessant stewardship campaigns to raise funds. The church was not affluent and it depended on the collections and pledges made by parishioners. Long-term planning was difficult because of the rapid turnover of the population. In 1961, for instance, 130 families arrived,

35 left the parish, 13 went overseas and 18 changed address, a total of 200 known changes over twelve months. It was impossible to maintain an up-to-date church roll and this hampered the distribution of weekly 'finance envelopes', the collection of pledged money and the development of accurate budgets. A canvass in 1962–63 resulted in forward pledges for £5,200 a year but the amount actually contributed in 1965 was £2,000 short. While the treasurer lamented the departure of parishioners, he commented particularly on 'the apathy' of those 'who are able to help' and 'have chosen to use the church and its equipment but not to contribute to its funds or development'. After the introduction of decimal currency, the church reserved $216 each month to repay the debt on the church building and worked on a budget of $4,000 to $5,000 each year.[42]

As 1966 came to a close, Canon Palmer announced his resignation, the deacon's position was not renewed and Percy Moore left the district. The second phase of the parish's history had come to an end. St Luke's church hall had been built and much of the debt had been repaid, the Yarralumla–Deakin area had expanded, attendances had burgeoned, a vital children's ministry had been successfully developed, a neighbouring provisional district had been launched and the church had successfully negotiated financial crises. It had been an active phase, one in which the priests and their helpers had walked or driven along new streets to meet and welcome every newcomer to the rapidly expanding district and, in retrospect, the clergy and hard-working council could take satisfaction and pride in the foundation years of the parish.[43] There were ominous signs, however, when the commencement of church services at Hughes in February 1964 effectively reduced the size of the parish and ultimately affected its financial basis.

The third phase of the church's development stretched from 1967 until 1973 (or beyond), a difficult period during which numbers fell and despondency enveloped the council. Communicants plummeted – 4,113 in 1968, 2,621 in 1971 and 2,511 in 1974 – while the Sunday school attendance of 80 in 1967 dropped to just 15 in 1974.[44] After Canon Palmer's departure in January 1967, it was seven months before the arrival of Philip Boulsover from Rockhampton and the congregation appeared to languish as they awaited a leader. The new rector, 'Father Philip', was decidedly Anglo-Catholic, a devout man who saw his ministry as sacramental and stressed the significance of liturgy to the disappointment of the evangelicals in the church. A gentle, caring and compassionate man, Boulsover arrived after the baby boom was over, when there were fewer children and when even the enrolments at the Yarralumla school were falling. With the creation of the neighbouring parish, there were questions about parish boundaries and the actual viability of the parish itself.

Financial fears also arose, although the church paid off the debt on the building with the money saved from the rector's delayed arrival.[45] The pioneering spirit of the parish waned, women took up, or returned to, work as their children grew and the enthusiasm for the church was more restricted. Fewer had time to conduct religious instruction in schools and most were uninterested. The rector decided on a mission to help revive the parish late in 1969 but the attendances were disappointingly low, some maintaining that it should have been evangelistic and based on a 'Billy Graham type approach'. When questioned about his attitude to the mission, Boulsover said he, 'did not like the methods adopted at these [evangelistic] crusades for the conversion of unbelievers' and favoured conservative Anglican practices.[46]

While there were demographic reasons for the church's decline, very few seemed to grasp the essential need for pastoral care. During the growth stage, young families had met through their children and the work of erecting and developing a new church had brought people together. The large Sunday school and baptismal services had 'allowed for a lot more to happen than did the average service'. Now there was less interaction among parishioners, fewer chances to meet beyond the Sunday service and the rector visited people less.[47] The parish council concentrated on administrative matters rather than long-term issues, the rector was concerned about the location of the altar and the effect of experimental liturgies and the church was divided over the need for an altar frontal. Finally, the 1969 Annual Meeting appointed a delegation to inform the bishop that, 'in attempting to maintain its present form of activity', the parish was 'not a viable unit'.[48]

When little change had resulted by 1972, another delegation met Bishop Cecil Warren (by now the diocesan bishop) with the same message. Some said it was the rector's form of churchmanship that hindered development while others sought a reawakening of social activities.[49] At that stage, the bishop was developing a diocesan renewal program and, accepting the challenge, he guided the church through 'a carefully worked out plan' by which it 'could strive towards renewal of the parish'. He pointed out the need for greater parish fellowship, prayer and a more zealous effort by parishioners 'to help themselves'.[50] The bishop's intervention eventually acted as a catalyst that introduced the fourth phase of the parish's development when the rector, council and congregation (goaded by Heather Clark and Elizabeth Price) gradually warmed to the need for pastoral care and cautiously introduced member support and greater congregational involvement. Small groups were encouraged in people's homes and out of these came suggestions that 'we must be concerned with people' and not with the church's liturgy only.[51]

By 1973 the wardens aimed 'to do more' to develop 'the sick and failing parish', leading Heather Clark to organise a church fete which not only raised over $1,350 but also indicated how the parish could 'work together very successfully spiritually and practically'. It was even found that 'many parishioners, not seen often at church, supported the fete'. Family services – followed by an innovatory cup of tea or coffee – brought new faces into the church and the rector commented that 'we have had some good congregations' when celebrating something special. A 5pm Communion service followed by 'tea and films' was well attended and enhanced fellowship while Ken and Margaret McKay developed fortnightly prayer and Bible study groups in private homes.[52]

After the bishop returned to the parish to outline the diocesan renewal program titled 'Impact 74', Dr Charles Price was appointed chairperson to organise the program. As part of this program, thirteen people attended a large rally in Goulburn, eighteen parishioners visited 126 families to interest them in church membership and pledging increased by 30 per cent. Meanwhile, the women conducted market mornings, art and pottery exhibitions, fetes, tapestry exhibitions and plant stalls. A branch of Anglican Women began with the help of Joan Chynoweth who resided in the assistant bishop's house next door. The number of communicants rose perceptibly from 2,638 in 1975 to 3,349 in 1978, weekly Bible studies were extended, the Churchwomen's Union arranged visits and excursions, church services were conducted at the Cotter followed by basket picnics and the church sponsored an Indo-Chinese family for six months.[53]

In a self-generating program of pastoral care and fellowship, visiting speakers were invited to the church, a men's group met every second Saturday for breakfast, prayer and inspiration, the St Luke's Day Eucharist was combined with a 'pot-luck' tea and parish dinners proved successful. The Churchwomen's Union concentrated on social and fund-raising activities; the Anglican Women looked further afield; the youth group provided activities for ten to fifteen young people of high school age; and travel talks, films and progressive dinners brought parishioners together. In the process, the number of communicants rose again to 3,456 in 1980 and there was little difficulty in introducing a modified liturgy based on *An Australian Prayer Book* and the new hymnal after 1977.[54]

The improvement was reflected in the church's financial position. In 1968 it had been reported that viability was 'brittle' as 'we just exist from month to month' but this had turned to desperation when attendances fell. By late 1971, the expenditure had exceeded income by $130 a month, the diocesan pledge had been reduced and, with inflation and increasing costs, the council believed it would be 'forced to close down our parish church about Easter 1972' unless additional funds were immediately available.[55] The church considered the possibility of developing the church site with tennis courts, a rectory, or 'a block of units for aged parishioners' (a suggestion to be repeated over some decades) but the lack of money prevented further discussion.[56]

As the church extended its programs with a greater faith in its own abilities, the treasurer reported with pleasure:

> that during 1975 we were able to cover all necessary costs, to maintain a contribution to the diocese of 10 per cent of income … and to cooperate with the diocese in building on this site a house for the Assistant Bishop and a Rectory for this parish.

The rectory cost $33,300, necessitating loans of $15,000 through the Department of the Capital Territory (a 32-year loan at a worrying interest rate of 10.25 per cent) and $14,600 through the diocese (a 15-year loan at 8.75 per cent).[57]

Under the combined scrutiny of the council members, Lieutenant-Colonel Noel Monday and his son, Ian Monday, the finances improved and by the end of 1979 the church had an annual income of $20,637, an expenditure of $18,485 and a balance of $2,152. Parishioners' pledges had risen to over $11,000 and the debt on the rectory loans had been reduced from $29,600 to $18,993. With demographic changes, the Sunday school could never return to its flourishing former condition but it continued with 20 to 30 children each week and a small youth group was maintained.[58] Prayer groups, home-based Bible studies, Cursillo, family services and special Eucharists denoted a positive spirituality among the people and the earlier displays of defeatism – so marked from 1969 to 1973 – had been checked. The parish was no longer inward-looking, concentrating on liturgical correctness with limited congregational input, but now embraced increasing fellowship, pastoral care and outreach. And so, when Philip Boulsover left in December 1981 and John Bowen was inducted the following week, there was a strong sense of optimism among the parishioners.

John Bowen, a Welshman, and his wife, Joanne, arrived in Canberra in 1973 and served at St Paul's Manuka, Binda and Tumbarumba over an eight-year period.[59] The new rector had been influenced by the charismatic movement and promoted an inclusive form of ministry that moved away from Boulsover's high churchmanship. His style readily incorporated the laity and encouraged the participation of children in an atmosphere of freedom, an approach that quickly proved popular. Most services used the modern (Second Order) Communion service, gatherings were followed by 'a cuppa and a chat', other preachers were invited to take the pulpit more often and the Sunday school numbers gradually inched up. Between 20 and 30 parishioners attended the breakfasts between the 8am and 10am services, the study groups flourished under the McKays' guidance and a Youth Fellowship group for high school students provided a meeting place for potential confirmees with 'a Christian ethos' and 'plenty of fun'.

Fellowship and spirituality were nurtured by two courses on 'Basic Christianity' organised over nine weeks for groups of twelve. Small group gatherings were promoted in the homes of parishioners, Lenten studies were organised and the 80 regular worshippers were encouraged to invite their neighbours each week. While a few left St Luke's because of the rector's approach, there was widespread support for his inclusive message and his less formal manner. Combined services were held at St Luke's with the Roman Catholic and Uniting Churches and parish camps at Burrill Pines and Caloola Farm proved popular.

The number of communicants rose from 3,757 in 1982, to 3,820 in 1983 and to 4,638 in 1984. The rector expressed satisfaction with both 'the quality and quantity' of parish life' on the 25th anniversary of the church's foundation but exhorted his friends to visit more and become more involved in healing services, Evensong and Cursillo weekends. With Bowen's emphasis on a growing church ('it was Jesus' solemn commission for us to make disciples') the Sunday school numbers rose, sometimes to 40, the four prayer groups involved 30 people on a weekly basis and it became evident that church buildings needed to be expanded to accommodate the increasing numbers.

After the completion of the rectory in 1975, the parishioners had debated whether to construct a new church or extend the existing hall, eventually opting for extensions because of the lower costs involved.

By 1983 the plans had reached the drawing board stage and the wardens were 'looking for ways' to finance the project, a goal partly achieved the following year when $18,000 was raised with promises of a further $3,000. Finally the new wing of the building was opened in 1985, providing additional meeting space and a vestry and counselling

St Luke's Deakin-Yarralumla

room for the rector. When the church was repainted by the parishioners, Bowen reminded them that the courtyard still needed to be constructed, the 'driveway put in order,' and three more projects considered – the re-roofing of the original building, the erection of aged-care units and the extension of the church itself. There was no room for complacency and funds were always a challenge.

By 1986 the church's annual income had reached over $115,000, including investments put aside for extensions, allowing the church to forward its contribution of $7,000 to the diocese and purchase a new vehicle for the rector. The loan from the diocese for the rectory had been repaid although $13,000 was still owed to the Department of Capital Territory. Of greater significance, the bank loan for the building extensions and associated costs had been repaid in full, leaving 'an effective debt to parishioners on interest-free loans' of $13,432 – a highly satisfactory result considering the total cost of extensions was $48,900.

Hence, by 1986 the parishioners of St Luke's could look back over twelve years during which they had accepted Bishop's Warren's challenge to increase their spiritual life and stewardship and 'to help themselves' with greater zeal. It had been an arduous journey as they had gradually learned the importance of fellowship and pastoral care under two devoted, compassionate clergymen and their wives, had increased their financial support of the church and had appreciated an active and satisfying involvement. And then John Bowen, who had been chaplain to the Girls' Grammar School for five years, surprised the council when he announced his resignation in September to take up the chaplaincy of St Michael's Collegiate (Girls') School in Hobart. As he left the parish, he knew that he and Philip Boulsover had reversed the fortunes of the parish but he was not aware that the fourth phase of the parish's development was likewise ending. He was to observe further developments when he returned as chaplain to Radford College in 1991.

Apart from the rectors, there were members of the laity who influenced the development of the church in profound ways. Ken McKay, a Reader at the ANU, was a biblical scholar, who led a house study and prayer group over many years and occupied almost every lay office available from councillor to lay reader. Margaret McKay was associated with the Churchwomen's Union, the Sunday school and outreach missionary programs. Charles Price was similarly involved in the council, synod, presentation board, church music, lay preaching and liturgy, not only performing his own duties but also filling in for others when the need arose. Heather Clark was chair of the council, the first woman on diocesan synod and organiser of church fetes and other fund-raising events. Others such as Betty Cromer, Eunice Burton, Joan Boulsover, Jo Bowen, Frank and Dorothy Macklin, Michael and Elizabeth Game, Ellie Devine, Noel and Ian Monday, Elizabeth Price, Molly Lesley, Alwyn Warren, Dorothy Buckmaster, Vernon and Evelyn Edge and Wendy Nielson (to name only a few) provided an important and continuing input over many years.

The fifth stage of St Luke's development commenced in 1987 and lasted until 2008, a period coinciding with another downturn in attendances, the attempts of three rectors and two bishops to revive the parish and the need to find a different solution to the parish's emerging financial woes. Moreover, churchmanship became a significant issue once again. For four decades there had been some tension within the church as it sought to accommodate the different views of parishioners, ranging from strong evangelicalism to high churchmanship. This blend of conservative Anglicanism, evangelical zeal and the input of each rector's personality and style continued to influence development. Meanwhile the economic basis of the parish became more parlous and necessitated a radical resolution.

The Reverend Dr Robert Withycombe had arrived in Canberra in 1975 as warden of St Mark's Library. With a strong academic background, he had guided the library for over a decade and had become Acting Principal of the College of Ministry until the principalship was assumed by Bishop Bruce Wilson in 1985. Withycombe's strong interest in church history, both as a lecturer and researcher, was not assuaged by his appointment to St Luke's in 1987 and, during his nine-year incumbency, he maintained close links with St Mark's and continued a number of individual research projects. As he and his wife, Susan Mary, owned a home in Hughes, they opted not to live in the rectory, which was rented out on a commercial basis, thereby assisting parish finances. 'It seemed strange' to parishioners, however, to have 'a rector living at Hughes' and, by the start of 1988, the church wardens and others were still 'adjusting' to the different circumstances.[60]

The rector, with a Moore College background and 'not averse to a degree of emotional response', was viewed as evangelical but 'not excessively so'. He soon sought to move parish life from 'Nurture and Maintenance' towards 'Evangelism and Growth'. In doing so, he had the support of the prayer and Bible study group that met twice a week (known as the McKay's 'Home Group at 41 Rawson Street'), the weekly hospital visits by Elizabeth Game and others, the play group where children socialised each Wednesday or Thursday at the church and the Sunday school that faithfully provided for 15 to 25 children. Through the leadership of Margaret McKay, contact was maintained with overseas missionaries and their work was supported in practical ways. An informal pastoral care group was formed and, with the assistance of Frances Hollinsworth, a retired social worker, provided quiet support for parishioners in need as well as for the elderly at the nearby Grange Retirement Village and Brindabella Gardens. Youth work was spasmodic owing to the lack of leadership and the attraction of larger groups at Pearce Anglican and Hughes Baptist churches but contacts with the Girls' Grammar School helped.[61]

The association between St Luke's and the Girls' Grammar School stemmed initially from the appointment of Peter Rudge as chaplain to the school in February 1962, a duty assumed by Harold Palmer until 1966. (It had earlier been performed by Ross Border.) Over the years, some of the senior girls assisted at the church, Susan Mary Withycombe taught at the school for seventeen years, chaplain Robert Willson was a regular worshipper at St Luke's and frequently helped in the conduct of services and Canon Withycombe was an elected member of the school board and conducted occasional chapel services. The association with the school was quite strong and formed part of the church's ministry.

The Churchwomen's Union continued to provide a major input into church life as it met the social and spiritual needs of its members and engaged them in constant fund-raising activities. Arranging cake stalls, luncheons, fashion parades, coffee mornings, slide evenings, jumble sales and trading tables, Eunice Burton, Dorothy Macklin, Edna Sturman and a small group of ladies organised fetes, market days, excursions and a range of informal public addresses, raising money each year for church projects and donations to mission activities. As the rector said on one occasion, any difficulties at St Luke's stemmed from the 'quantity of people, not the quality'.

Withycombe's incumbency was not without difficulties, however, and it was only a matter of time before he was faced with falling collections, pledges and investments. Church-based income declined by $7,300 in 1987. An annual attendance of 6,375 in 1986 fell to 4,002 by 1991 and then stabilised between 4,500 and 4,800. The number of communicants averaged about 2,600 in the period 1993–1995, approximately 70 a week. Moreover, the rector faced the traditional difficulties inherent at St Luke's – the number of Sunday services desired by the parishioners, the type of liturgy espoused at each, the small size of the Sunday school and the absence of vibrant youth programs. Committee systems were not always successful and, after an extensive diagnostic consultation by the Reverend Dr Brian Carter in 1992 followed by planning days in 1993–1994, renewal efforts did 'not appear' to result in 'a significant milestone of positive progress.'[62]

There was even a degree of tension between some of the older conservative members of the congregation and younger arrivals. 'The
latter wanted a future different from the practices and patterns of
the past at St Luke's which the former group struggled to preserve'.[63]
Moreover, changing demographic patterns had altered the parish. As
Charles Price pointed out in 1993, the number in the parish calling
themselves Anglican had fallen to 29.2 per cent. Whereas there had
been 65 baptisms at St Luke's in 1960, this had dropped to 19 in 1969
and had then declined further to only four in 1986. The number of
confirmations had likewise declined from 42 in 1966 to three in 1986.
Deakin's overall population had fallen from 3,510 (1966) to 2,468 in
1999 with the age group, 0–14 years, representing only 5 per cent
of the total. Hence, by 1995 there were 'growing doubts about the
long-term viability of the parish as an independent entity' and it was
decided to hold an external review on 'its future prospects'.[64]

During 1989, Withycombe who always aspired to an academic
vocation – an integral part of his life – negotiated seven months
long-service leave without parish remuneration to study and research
at Cambridge University. Susan Mary, who taught Religion and Latin
at CCEGGS, obtained leave without pay to accompany her husband
to Cambridge. In the rector's absence, Gail Tabor, a deacon, was
employed half-time and Philip Peters, an honorary priest, assumed
an increasing role in the parish together with Don Saines (who lived
in the rectory) and Robert Willson. From 1991 to 1993, funds given
by an anonymous donor allowed Withycombe to spend time at
St Mark's (teaching and researching), enabling St Luke's to employ
Pamela Phillips and later Vicky Cullen as deacons on more than a half-
time basis. When the rector travelled to London to conduct further
research for two months in December and January 1991–1992, he
house-swapped with Bill Kingston, who assisted at his own cost in
the ministry being sustained at St Luke's by Pamela Phillips, Philip
Peters and Robert Willson. Eventually, the rector resigned the parish
at the end of 1995, indicating that there is 'much I could do, but there
is much I now think others could do better'. He desired to concentrate
on his 'teaching, planning, research and writing' where he believed
he had 'been given skills and new opportunities to use them'. Philip
Peters took over as locum for five months, working virtually full-
time and declining payment, while Robert Willson provided back-up

assistance with further input from the lay readers, Charles Price and Michael Swan.[65]

When Archdeacon Allan Huggins and the bishop called meetings of parishioners to consider the parish's future, it was decided to continue as a separate entity with 'the best available rector, whether male or female and preferably one who would occupy the rectory'.[66] Facing the financial challenge of a full-time rector and the possibility of loss of rectory rental income, Charles Price led parishioners in providing a fund of $6,000 in cash donations and $16,000 in two-year interest-free loans.

Elaine Gifford had spent some years as part-time administrator at Holy Covenant Jamison and had worked closely with Jeffrey Driver as a lay reader before training at St Mark's. Ordained as a deacon in 1990, Elaine was the founding coordinator of St John's Care while acting as an honorary deacon at St John's for two years, prior to her ordination to the priesthood in 1992. After service at Batemans Bay, she was appointed to St Luke's in 1996 and arrived with husband, John, moving into the rectory later that year. She accepted the challenges involved and sought to restore a sense of stability in the parish. Over a seven-year period, physical conditions were improved as a hearing-loop was installed to assist the hard-of-hearing, the church floor was resurfaced, the courtyard area paved, church signage improved and computer facilities extended. The parish car was replaced in 2003 with earmarked funds.

These improvements were possible because the parish continued its long-term policy of setting aside reserves for maintenance, equipment and car replacement and because some of the parishioner loans were converted to gifts. The remaining loans were fully repaid after two years. Parish giving slowly increased over five years, supplemented when needed from the full-time rector reserve; income from building hire increased; and fund-raising from fetes and market mornings raised significant amounts. Parishioner confidence was further bolstered when the church became free from debt in 1998. This allowed the parish to meet its internal and diocesan commitments and to give to missions and organisations such as Anglicare and the Mogo Boomerang Ministry.[67]

The congregation of 30 to 40 responded to Elaine Gifford's broad churchmanship as she stressed dignity and order, involved the laity and reintroduced a quarterly family service. Early in 1996 *A Prayer Book for Australia* was introduced and accepted without difficulty. When the new hymn book, *Together in Song*, was released, hymns were introduced through overhead projections and people were encouraged to purchase their own hymnals. The rector quickly became involved in the healing ministry, held 'imaginative' services at Easter and Christmas, opened the rectory for various church gatherings and functions and worked with the Churchwomen's Union to provide traditional pancakes on Shrove Tuesday. A prayer chain was started, a successful weekly playgroup was recommenced and improvements were made to the outdoor play area. Moreover, as part of an outreach program, a regular fortnightly service was begun in the community hall at the Grange Retirement Village, building on the earlier efforts of Frances Hollinsworth.[68] Overall, therefore, the life of the parish was enhanced and the physical condition of the church building improved during Elaine Gifford's incumbency.

Long-term success was restricted, however, by the size of the congregation and the ageing of the population. The treasurer resigned for personal reasons in 2001 after 29 years in his position and there were increasing concerns about the solvency of the parish. Accepting that the position had improved over seven years but feeling that the input of a new rector might enhance the changes made, the rector resigned in June 2003 to take up a position as Mental Health Services Chaplain attached to St Saviour's Cathedral. Nevertheless, the constricting financial base of the parish still brought into question the future viability of the parish.[69]

Philip Peters again took over as locum and again refused remuneration for his five months of 'tireless work'. He was assisted by Robert Willson until the induction of David Clark on 29 January 2004.[70] Realising the parlous condition of the church, Bishop Browning asked Clark to try to revive the parish as it was again struggling both numerically and financially. As the rector later acknowledged, 'The parish was in serious financial trouble before I arrived ... essentially it was broke.'[71] He was able to combine two roles by leading the parish and continuing his ministry as chaplain at the Belconnen Remand Centre. David Clark – a committed Evangelical – knew that there was a devoted core of parishioners and concentrated on three aspects of the church's mission plan: gathering (worship and fellowship);

upbuilding (ministry, teaching the gifts of the Spirit); and sending (missionary support and evangelism). Seeking to strengthen faith and enable outreach, he eventually introduced the '40 Days of Purpose Campaign', an integrated program involving the individual, small groups and the congregation over seven Sundays, with an emphasis on worship, fellowship, discipleship and evangelism.

Economic difficulties were ever present, however, due to the small size of the parish. Despite the rector's best efforts, it was an impossible financial task when the church deficit for 2004 was $13,600, followed by $9,600 in 2005 and $1,500 in 2006.[72] It was only a bequest that overcame some of the problems resulting from a further deficit of $16,300 in 2007 and the wardens were forced to approach the diocese because of the parish's 'totally unsustainable financial position'.[73] Commencing 1 January 2008 the diocese contributed payment of one-day-a-week to cover the rector's ministry costs as Diocesan Chaplain at the Remand Centre. Clark reverted to a four-day week and accepted (like his predecessor) a reduced stipend. Possible solutions were canvassed in discussions with both the Girls' Grammar School and Anglicare for joint developments of the church site. It was mooted that cooperation with St Paul's or with other parishes was possible but the bishop would need to be involved. In the diocesan office, Bishop Browning contemplated the same issues and approached the new rector of St Paul's Manuka with a possible solution.

More than nine decades after the foundation of the settlement at Westridge and six decades after the foundation of the provisional district of St Luke in 1947, the parish reached a point where it was no longer viable and required diocesan intervention to survive. Archdeacon Davies had commenced services in 1949, Canon Border had assisted in the creation of the parish in 1959 and three clergymen – Hayden McCallum, Peter Rudge and Harold Palmer – had steered the young parish through its formative years. After a difficult seven-year period, the parish had been rejuvenated with the help of Bishop Warren, Philip Boulsover and John Bowen, only to be followed by further challenges during the incumbency of Robert Withycombe as demographic patterns changed. Finally, by 2008, despite the positive contributions of Elaine Gifford and David Clark, St Luke's Deakin–Yarralumla proved economically unviable as a standalone parish and needed a new direction. The scenario to unfold would witness a full circle of events as the parishes of St Paul and St Luke were recombined in a different relationship.

Notes

1. A Greig, *The Accommodation of Growth. Canberra's 'growing pains' 1945–1955. http://art.anu.edu.au/greig/selfandsociety* (1996).
2. CT, 16 February 1949.
3. CT, 17 July 1950.
4. Greg Tarrant, Personal communication, 2009.
5. CT, 17 July 1950.
6. PN, September–October 1949.
7. Greg Tarrant, Personal communication, 2009.
8. StLCC, 8 October 1957.
9. Discussion between G Tarrant and R Border as reported by Eunice Burton, Personal communication, 2009.
10. CT, 15 June 1950.
11. StPPC, 12 June 1950.
12. *The Pauline*, Christmas 1951; Lent 1952.
13. Notes supplied by Elizabeth Price, 2009; *The Pauline*, Michaelmas 1952.
14. *The Pauline*, June 1954; StPPC, 21 November 1955.
15. Elizabeth Price, Personal communication, 2009.
16. *The Pauline*, Lent 1956.
17. *The Pauline*, Trinity 1956.
18. Rector's 1956 report in *The Pauline*, February 1957.
19. StPPC, 18 February 1957.
20. StPPC, 15 April and 20 May 1957.
21. StLCC, 25 May and 14 June 1957.
22. Border to Burgmann, 2 July 1957, NLA, Burgmann Papers. MS 1998. Box 36. 'Canberra'.
23. PN, April 1950.
24. Frame, *A Church for a Nation*, p. 213; PN, July 1955; July 1956.
25. StLCC, 14 June 1957; *The Pauline*, September 1957.
26. StL, First AGM, 11 February 1958; CT, 12 February 1958; 9 February 1959.
27. StLCC, 6 January 1959; Letter from St Luke's, No. 2. September 1963; CT, 9 February 1959. A card of invitation was printed for the 'setting of the foundation stone' by the Governor-General's wife on 5 April 1959, StLCC Archives.
28. CT, 26 October 1959.
29. StLCC, 8 October 1957; 16 March 1959.

30. StLCC, 16 March 1959.
31. StL, AGM, February 1962; StL, parochial returns for 1961.
32. StLCC, 20 October 1958.
33. StL, parochial returns for 1962.
34. StL, AGMs 1958–1962; StLPC, 1959–1962.
35. StLPC, 17 September 1962.
36. StL, parochial returns, 1964; Rector's 1964 annual report; StLPC, 21 December 1964.
37. Letter from St Luke's, No. 1, August 1963.
38. Elizabeth Price, Personal communication, 2009.
39. StL parochial returns, 1964 to 1966; and Registers of Service 1963–1966.
40. This was the opinion of past parishioners in 2008 and of other clergy who knew him.
41. StLPC, 1965 rector's report,
42. StL, 1965 annual report.
43. StL, parochial returns, 1962–1966; rector's report for 1964 AGM 12 February 1966.
44. StL, parochial returns, 1968–1974.
45. StL, 1967 treasurer's report.
46. StLPC, 16 September 1968.
47. StL, Archives, paper prepared by Bob Day, 'History of the Parish', March 1986; Elizabeth Price, Personal communication, 2010.
48. StL, 1969 AGM Minutes, 16 March 1970.
49. StL, wardens' report for 1971.
50. StL, 1972 rector's report, 19 March 1973.
51. StL, 1972 Report, 19 March 1973.
52. StL, 1973 annual report.
53. StLPC, report of C Price on Impact 74; annual reports 1974–1978.
54. StL, 1980 annual report.
55. Letter to parishioners, August 1971, attached to the wardens' report for 1971.
56. StL, 1972 wardens' report, 19 March 1973.
57. StL, 1975 and 1976 treasurer's reports, 9 February 1976 and 21 February 1977.
58. StL, 1979 annual report.
59. The following section on John Bowen's incumbency is based on StL, parochial returns 1981–1986; annual reports 1981–1986; and on the recollections of parishioners in 2009–2010.
60. StL, annual reports for 1986 and 1987.
61. Robert Withycombe, Personal communication, 2009; StL, annual reports, 1987–1994.
62. StL, annual reports 1987–1995
63. Robert Withycombe, Personal communication, 2010.

64. StL, parochial returns 1965–1988; annual reports 1987–1995; *Deakin – Neighbourhood Plan, 2003*, ACT Planning and Land Authority. I am indebted to Dr SM Withycombe for helpful information.

65. Robert Withycombe, Personal communication, 2009; StL, annual reports 1998–2005.

66. StL, 1996 annual report.

67. StL, annual reports 1997–2003; Elaine Gifford, Personal communication, 2010.

68. StL, annual reports 1997–2003; Elaine Gifford, Personal communication, 2010.

69. StL, 2003 annual report.

70. StL, 2003 annual report.

71. David Clark, Personal communication, 2010.

72. StL, 2006 annual report.

73. StL, 2007 annual report.

16   Retrospective and reflection

Once again the bishop contemplated events that were to influence two adjacent parishes. With the resignation of Scott Cowdell at Manuka in June 2007, Bishop Browning met with the church's Clergy Appointments Board to discuss developments and possible replacements. At the same time, he pondered the financial difficulties of St Luke's and wondered if the two separate communities might be considered together.

Dr Brian Douglas was the chaplain at Newcastle Grammar School and a residentiary canon at Christ Church Cathedral. Following his earlier career as a deputy school principal, together with work in the Curriculum Division of the New South Wales Department of Education, he entered St John's College at Morpeth to train for the priesthood and eventually lectured at the same institution. With his qualifications, BA (Hons), BD, MTh (Hons) and PhD, and with experience in a number of parishes, he was considered to be an appropriate choice for St Paul's. While he was advised by a number of clergy that the parish was 'difficult', he accepted the challenge and arrived in the first week of 2008. Within a week the bishop raised the future of St Luke's and suggested the possibility of a 'combined district'.[1]

It was not a new suggestion. Bishop Clements had discussed the same possibility with Dr John Munro in 1969 and it resurfaced in various guises in the 1990s and during the incumbency of David Clark. When Clark moved from St Luke's at the end of April 2008 and combined the positions of warden at St David's Close, Red Hill, associate priest at St Paul's and chaplain to the Remand Centre, the way was open to formalise the new concept at the commencement of 2009. The three communities at St David's Red Hill, St Luke's Deakin and St Paul's Manuka formed the Combined Ministry District (CMD),

considered the district's mission and ministry, developed strategies
and a resource management plan and embarked on a new venture that
had 'opportunities for growth and development'. The framers of the
combined district believed that they needed 'to be creative, visionary'
and risk-takers.[2]

Another part of the jigsaw was solved
when Douglas contacted one of his colleagues
in the Newcastle diocese to raise the possibility of an appointment to St Luke's. Michael
Armstrong had a background in applied science
with particular interests in parks, recreation
and heritage and had been involved in youth
and children's work. He declined at first but
eventually accepted the challenge and was
appointed priest-in-charge in 2009.[3] As both
Douglas and Armstrong had a Newcastle dio-
cese background with its Catholic emphasis, it was expected that St
Paul's and St Luke's would reintroduce prayer book use and move towards a more advanced liturgy. Forty years after the Parish of St Luke
had been created out of a larger St Paul's parish, the two were reunited
in a combined district that afforded the possibility of expansion and
future development.

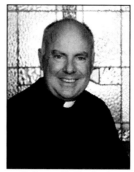

The Reverend Dr Brian Douglas
© Framing Matters, Manuka

By 2010, the parishioners at St Paul's and St Luke's could reflect
on their shared history spanning nearly a century. It was in mid-
1914 when the rector of St John's had saddled his horse, forded the
Molonglo River and ridden out to two camps to meet small groups of
workers at the Brickworks and the Powerhouse and so established two
Anglican centres on the inner south of Canberra. As the embryonic
capital had developed, Fred Ward had visited all emerging camps,
watched as they evolved into settlements and collected the workers
together for mission services in camp messes, recreation halls, old internment camp buildings and a tin shed. Other camps and settlements
grew at Molonglo, the Causeway and Westlake, three 'temporary'
centres designed to accommodate the workers involved in building
Canberra's public buildings. Anglican services at these three centres
had not lasted beyond 1949 but other settlements had developed into
suburbs where churches had been constructed and parishes eventually

created. The two most important were St Paul's Manuka and St Luke's at Deakin–Yarralumla.

There have been a number of significant dates in the history of St Paul's parish. Some remember the foundation of the original church on a vacant stretch of land opposite the Powerhouse on 1 August 1914. Closed during World War I and reopened in April 1922, the tin shed had become the centre of Anglicanism on the southside, the building eventually being extended in 1931 in the middle of an economic depression. Others recollect Sunday 11 December 1938 when Lord Gowrie set the foundation stone for the first section of a church at Manuka, while others recall the opening and dedication of the new building on 6 August 1939 just before the outbreak of hostilities in Europe. Still others think back to the creation of St Paul's parish on 26 March 1950 or the extension of the church on 18 November 1956. And more recently, some recollect the last extension in December 2001. A few kilometres away, St David's church, built and opened in 1971, formed part of the parish and catered for residents in the Red Hill area while a smaller venture at Narrabundah faltered and closed.

On the other side of Capital Hill, the Brickworks settlement – variously known as Westridge or Yarralumla – had quickly developed as a major suburb after 1947 and ten years later had been named a provisional Anglican district, carved out of the new Parish of St Paul. After a church had been constructed at Deakin and a parish created in 1959, surrounding suburbs had rapidly formed and St Luke's at Deakin–Yarralumla had become a land-locked parish that prospered until the mid-1980s but ultimately proved to be economically unviable and in need of diocesan assistance.

At the same time, two denominational schools had been created – Canberra Grammar School and Canberra Girls' Grammar School – both of which had endured two decades of financial stringency but had developed as strong institutions from the time of World War II. Anglican services had been provided at the naval base HMAS *Harman* for 25 years but had virtually ceased with the abolition of compulsory church parades. St Mark's Library had evolved and expanded to become a major national provider of vocational training and theological education. And so, of the eleven Anglican centres that had been commenced on the inner south between 1914 and 1971, only six remained in 2010 – Manuka, Red Hill, Deakin, the two denominational schools and St Mark's.

In a most significant way, the history of the Anglican Church in the inner-south of Canberra parallels the history and development of the city itself. From the time when the first workers were accommodated in tents and humpies, to the gradual development of settlements – often temporary in nature – and to the eventual emergence of permanent suburbs, the church has sought to take its message of hope to the people. Its task has not been easy and there have been times when its success has been limited but, with evident faith, the clergy and laity have provided an Anglican presence in the inner-south for almost 100 years, a testimony to faith, devotion and perseverance.

Notes

1. Brian Douglas, Personal communication, 2010.
2. 'Mission and Ministry: The Combined Ministry District of Manuka and Deakin: Three Churches, One Community', 2009.
3. Michael Douglas, Personal communication, 2010.

References

Abbreviations used

ABM	Australian Board of Missions (Anglican)
ACT	Australian Capital territory
ANU	Australian National University
AWM	Australian War Memorial
CEMS	Church of England Men's Society
CCEGGS	Canberra Church of England Girls' Grammar School
CGGS	Canberra Girls' Grammar School
CGS	Canberra Grammar School Archives
CT	*The Canberra Times*
CSU	Charles Sturt University
EFM	Education for Ministry
NAA	National Archives of Australia
NCDC	National Capital Development Commission
NGA	National Gallery of Australia
NLA	National Library of Australia
PN	*Parish Notes*, St John the Baptist Canberra
QA	*The Queanbeyan Age*
RA&P	Register of Acts & Proceedings, Diocese of Goulburn
SC	*The Southern Churchman*
StD	St David's Church, Red Hill
StJ	St John's Church, Reid
StJPC	St John's Parish Council, Reid
StL	St Luke's Church, Deakin
StLCC	St Luke's Church Council, Deakin
StLPC	St Luke's Parish Council, Deakin
StP	St Paul's Church, Manuka
StPCC	St Paul's Church Council, Manuka
StPPC	St Paul's Parish Council, Manuka
£ s d	pounds, shillings and pence (for example, five pounds, six shillings and ten pence: £5 6s 10d)

References

A. Official church records

a. Diocesan

Burgmann Papers. The *Papers of Bishop Burgmann*, Anglican Diocese of Canberra and Goulburn, NLA (Manuscripts Section), MS1998
> Boxes 24, 35, 36, 37 Letters from/to Burgmann from parishes
> Box 34 Diocesan Correspondence with Archdeacon Robertson
> Box 39 Photos

Register of Acts and Proceedings (Diocese of Goulburn) 1840–1914; 1914–1939; Index to 1914–1939

Diocesan 'Clergy and Parish Database Project' ANGHISOC75 Version 05Nov2007 (H Quinlan)

The Southern Churchman 1903–1964.

b. St John the Baptist, Canberra

Notices of Intention to apply for a Faculty / Petitions for a Faculty, St John's Archives.

Minutes of vestry meetings, 1913–1914 and minutes of parish council meetings, St John's Canberra, Vol. 1, 6 July 1914 to 31 August 1928.

Parish Clergy (and Superannuation) Cards, St John's Archives.

Parish Notes (Canberra). (Church of St John, Canberra) Vols. 1–4: September 1928 – 1962.

Register of Baptisms 1915–1941, Parish of St John the Baptist, Canberra. NLA, MS3085/54/106.

Register of Services, Parish of St John the Baptist, Canberra.
> 2 April 1899–29 October 1905.
> Vol. 1: 6 April 1919 to 26 December 1926.
> Vol. 2: 2 January 1927 to 12 September 1937.
> Vol. 3: 13 September 1937 to 15 August 1950.

St John's Archives, First Series, P14/10-P14/14 and Second Series.

c. St Paul's Manuka

Records held in NLA (Manuscripts Section)

Reference: Diocese of Canberra and Goulburn MS3085, St Paul's
Church, Manuka, Addition 28/06/1993.

Box 1:   Minute Books, Council of St Paul's, Canberra South ACT. 11
           August 1937–1962
           Pastoral Reports for St Paul's, 1937 and 1938
           Personal File of J Monro, parish council meetings 1959–1962

Box 2:   Minutes of parish council meetings 1963–1977

Box 3:   Minutes of parish council meetings 1978–1987
           Annual reports 1964, 1967, 1969–1971
           St Paul's Organs

Box 4:   Annual reports 1975–1992
           St Paul's Church Kingston
           St David's Church (4 folders) - Correspondence and Papers re
           Buildings
           St Paul's Men's Groups
           Correspondence relating to proposed new church, 1935–1939

Box 5:   Minutes of meetings of St Paul's Churchwomen's Guild and
           Union

Box 6:   Copies of *The Pauline*, 1950–1959
           Summaries of parish council minutes by subjects, 1942–1989
           Minutes of Provisional Parochial Council
           Notes from St Paul's Service Register
           'The Story of St Paul's Church' by Reverend TE Whiting

Box 7:   Special Occasions, Services and Reports
           Sunday *St John's Parish Notes* with reference to St Paul's
           Minutes of meetings of St John's parish council with reference
           to St Paul's

Service Registers, St Paul's, Canberra South
     5 January 1930 – 17 November 1933 (NLA, MS3085/13A/1)
     19 November 1933 - 31 June 1937   (NLA, MS3085/13A/2)
     1 January 1937 – 9 March 1958   (NLA, MS3085/13A/12)
     18 November 1956 – 3 June 1972   (NLA, MS3085/13A/13)
     4 June 1972 – 10 May 1978   (NLA, MS3085/13A/14)

Records held at St Paul's, Manuka (Indexed by A Ingle)

Most early records of St Paul's (Kingston) and Manuka to 1965 are to be found in the Manuscripts Section of NLA. At St Paul's, there are 28 large boxes and a filing cabinet of archived material (mainly from 1939) relating to buildings, plans, finances, outreach programs, orders of service, and registers of baptisms, marriages and burials for St Paul's, St Barnabas' and St David's. A complete index is available from the church secretary. Some of the main referenced archives are:

Annual reports 1965–2009.
Cross-Way: The paper of St Paul's Canberra, July 1967; 1971–1975.
Guild of St Martin 1970
Historic Documents 1914–1963.
Parish Council Minutes 1956 -2003.
Registers of Services, May 1978–2010.
Scripture Teaching in Schools, 1971.

d. St Luke's, Deakin

Annual general meetings, 1983- 1997.

Annual general meetings, 2004–2007.

Minutes of St Luke's Church and Parish of St. Luke's Council meetings, 1957–1960; 1960–1964; 1968–1974.

Parish Council Minutes, 1995–1997.

Parish Council Records, 1998–2004.

Photographs Collection

E Price, 'Recollections of St. Luke's in the Early Days' [Notes]. Personal communication, 2009.

e. St David's Red Hill

Cross-Way, 1977–1983.

Files in the NLA, Manuscripts Section MS3085 Box 4, titled:
St David's
St David's Correspondence and Papers re Buildings
St David's – Parish, Activities, Festivals and Publications

B.   Official Non-Church Records

Australian War Memorial
30th Battalion. *http://www.awm.gov.au/units/unit_11217.asp*
First World War Embarkation Roll, *http://www.awm.gov.au/wwi/*

embarkation/person.asp?p=932
Honours and awards (gazetted) Frederick Greenfield Ward,
http://www.awm.gov.au/honours/honours/person.asp?p=MC0391

Canberra Grammar School Archives from 1928.

Electoral Rolls for Eden Monaro, 1925 and 1928.

National Archives of Australia.
'Administration', Series A 206/1 Vol. 9.
'Brickworks', Series A414 (A414), Control # 21, Part 1.
'Canberra – Maps', Series A414 (A414), Control # 26, Attachment 1.
'Copy of address presented to Dr (sic) Canon FG Ward on his
   retirement from St. John's Anglican Church', Series A3560 (A3560),
   Control # 5560.
'Cottages for Power House Staff', Series A414 (A414/1), Control # 23.
'Ecclesiastical Building Sites', Series A414 (A414), Control # 75,
   File A3569, Vol. 74.
'Localities for Initial development'', Series A414 (A414), Control # 64.
'Public Hall Manuka Circle', Series A414 (A414), Control # 91.
'St Paul's Church Hall, Kingston', Series A659 (A659/1), Control #
   1941/1/3451.
'Workmen's Cottages Ainslie Settlement,' Series A414. Vol. 11.
National Capital Development Commission, *Sites of significance in the
ACT. 2. Inner Canberra.* National Capital Development Commission,
1988.
Yearbooks of the Commonwealth of Australia, 1901–1920; 1937,
Government Printer, Melbourne and Canberra.

Interviews, Correspondence, Notes

Acton, the Reverend Colin

Adamson, Morrie	Burton, Eunice
Armstrong, the Reverend Michael	Bruce, Joan
Arthur, Bob	Bruce, Bill
Batterham, the Reverend Ken	Bullock, Phyllis
Bertram, Canon Peter	Cameron, Trish
Blakston, Beverley	Cameron, Warrington
Body, Diana	Campbell, Robert
Boston, Joan	Campbell, Thomas
Boston, Neville	Christie, Alan
Boyd, Bob	Chynoweth, Bishop Neville
Bunyan, the Reverend John	Chynoweth, Joan
Burton, the Reverend Eric	Clark, Heather

Colman, Diana
Colwell, Frank
Cowdell, A/Prof Canon Scott
Curtis, Suzanne
Douglas, the Reverend Brian
Dowling, Gloria
Driver, Archbishop Jeffrey
Emanuel, Neale
Emerton, Val
Erskine, Chris
Farleigh, the Reverend Gerald
Foskett, Alan
Game, Elizabeth
Game, Michael
Gay, Tony
Gibson, the Ven. John
Gifford, the Reverend Elaine
Greaves, Rosemary
Gugler, Ann
Hansford, the Reverend Hartley
Hensen, the Reverend Roy
Hodge, Peter
Huff-Johnston, Bill
Huff-Johnston, Rosemary
Hyslop (nee Hardman), Janet
Ingle, Arthur
Ingle, Judy
Jackson, Gwen
Jones, the Reverend John
Kowalski, Elaine

Lehmann, Marie
McOmish, Janie
McOmish, Lachie
Moses, the Reverend John
Moyle, Audrey
Norris, Brian
Osborne, Brian
Osborne, Marcia
Peters, the Reverend Philip
Price, Charles
Price, Elizabeth
Pryce, Canon William
Raymond, Helen
Raymond, Oliver
Roberts, Margaret
Salisbury, Jean
Scott-Findlay, Eleanor
Sibly, the Reverend Geoff
Sturman, Edna
Tarrant, Greg
Tarrant, Pam
Thurlow, Bill
Thurlow, Joan
Ward, Lt.-Col. Simon (UK)
Webb, Judith
Webb, Robert
Willson, the Reverend Robert
Withycombe, Dr Susan Mary
Withycombe, Canon Robert

Published works

Books

An Australian Prayer Book, The Standing Committee of the General Synod of the Church of England in Australia, Anglican Information Office, Sydney, 1978.

G Ayre, *Visions on Rottenberry Hill,* Charles Sturt University, 2001.

B Barnes, *A Noble Experiment. A History of Holy Covenant Anglican Parish, Jamison ACT 1968–1992,* Holy Covenant Church, Cook, ACT, 1992.

J Baskin (ed.), *Wartime in Canberra – An Oral History of Canberra in the Second World War,* National Trust of Australia ACT, 2005.

A Body, *Firm Still You Stand*, St John's Parish Council, Canberra, 1986.

A Bolitho and M Hutchison (eds), *Stories of the Inner South: From a Day of Memories at Manuka Pool*, Arts Council of the ACT, 1992.

JR Border, *The Founding of the See of Goulburn*, St Mark's Library Publications, Canberra, 1956.

------ *Church and State in Australia 1788–1872. A Constitutional Study of the Church of England in Australia*, SPCK, London, 1962.

E Burgmann, *The Education of an Australian*, 1944, (Reprinted by St Mark's National Theological Centre, Canberra, 1991.)

Burrawi, The Magazine of the Canberra Church of England Girls' Grammar School, 1959–1963; 1965–1968.

Canberra Church of England Girls' Grammar School, *Reports of the Headmistress*, 1966–1974.

P Carnley, *Reflections in Glass*, Harper and Collins, Sydney, 2004.

M Clark, *History of Australia*, Melbourne University Press, 1997 reprint.

C Coulthard-Clark, *Duntroon: The Royal Military College of Australia, 1911– 1986*, Allen & Unwin, Sydney, 1986.

S Curley, *A Long Journey. Duntroon, Mugga Mugga and Three Careers*, ACT Government, 1998.

C Daley, *As I Recall. Reminiscences of Early Canberra*, Mulini Press and Canberra and District Historical Society, 1994.

V Emerton, *Past Images, Present Voices: Kingston and Thereabouts through a Box Brownie*, Canberra Stories Group, 1996.

A Fitzgerald, *Historic Canberra 1825–1945*, AGPS, Canberra, 1977.

------ (ed.), *Canberra's Engineering Heritage*, The Institution of Engineers Australia, Canberra Division, 1983.

------ *Canberra in Two Centuries. A Pictorial History*, Clareville Press and the Limestone Plains Partnership, Canberra, 1987.

L Fitzhardinge, *St John's Church and Canberra* (2nd ed.), St. John's Parish Council, Canberra, 1959.

B Fletcher, *The Place of Anglicanism in Australia. Church, Society and Nation*, Broughton Publishing, Mulgrave Vic, 2008.

A Foskett, *You May have Lived Here for a While*, The author, Canberra, 2002.

------ *The Molonglo Mystery*, The author, Canberra, 2006.

------ *More about Molonglo. The Mystery Deepens*, The author, Canberra, 2007.

A Foskett, P Johnstone and D Andrew, *On Solid Foundations. The Building and Construction of the Nation's Capital 1920 to 1950*, Canberra Tradesmen's Union Club, 2001.

T Frame, *A Church for a Nation: The History of the Anglican Diocese of Canberra and Goulburn*, Hale & Iremonger, Sydney, 2000.

------ *Anglicans in Australia*, University of New South Wales Press, 2007.

J Gibbney, *Canberra 1913–1953*, Australian Government Publishing Service, Canberra, 1988.

L Gillespie, *Canberra 1820–1913*, Australian Government Publishing Service, Canberra, 1991.

------ *Early Education and Schools in the Canberra region. A History of Early Education in the Region*, The Wizard Canberra Local History series, 1999.

A Gugler, *The Builders of Canberra 1909–1929. Part one – Temporary Camps and Settlements*, CPN Publications, Fyshwick ACT, 1994.

------ *Westlake. One of the Vanished 'Suburbs' of Canberra*. CPN Publications, Fyshwick ACT, 1997.

------ *True Tales from Canberra's Vanished Suburbs of Westlake, Westridge and Acton*, CPN Publications, Fyshwick ACT, 1999.

------ *A Story of Capital Hill*, Elect Printing, Fyshwick ACT, 2009.

P Hempenstall, *The Meddlesome Priest. A Life of Ernest Burgmann*, Allen & Unwin, Sydney, 1993.

M Hunter, *Over my Shoulder. Growing up with Canberra from the 1930s*, Canberra Stories Group, Murrumbateman NSW, 1998.

B Kaye, *A Church without Walls: Being Anglican in Australia*, Dove, Melbourne, 1995.

B Kaye (ed.), *Anglicanism in Australia. A History.* Melbourne University Press, 2002.

A Keenan (ed.), *Catching the Vision: The Foundation of the Canberra Grammar School*, Canberra Grammar School Foundation, 1997.

P Kriesler, *The Australian Economy* (3rd ed.), Allen & Unwin, Sydney, 1999.

E Lea-Scarlett, *Queanbeyan – District and People*, Queanbeyan Municipal Council, 1968.

E Lea-Scarlett and T Robinson, *First Light on the Limestone Plains – Historic Photographs of Canberra and Queanbeyan*, Canberra and District Historical Society, Hale and Iremonger, 1986.

J Lee, *Duntroon. The Royal Military College of Australia 1911–1946*, Australian War Memorial, Canberra, 1952.

G Linge, *Canberra – Site and City*, Australian National University Press, 1975.

C McGillion, *The Chosen Ones. The Politics of Salvation in the Anglican Church*, Allen & Unwin, Sydney, 2005.

P McKeown (ed.), *Deo, Ecclesiae, Patriae. Fifty Years of Canberra Grammar School*, Australian National University Press, 1979.

M McKernan, *All in! Australia during the Second World War*, Nelson, Melbourne, 1983.

J Moses (ed.), *From Oxford to the Bush. Essays on Catholic Anglicanism in Australia*, Broughton Press and SPCK, Australia, Hall ACT, 1997.

NCDC, Tech. Paper 28, *Causeway Redevelopment: A Case Study in Public Participation,* NCDC, Canberra, May 1980.

A Nelson, *History of* HMAS *Harman and its People: 1943–1993,* DC-C Publications DPUBS: 4308/93, 1993.

R Nelson, F Margan, P Breen and S Reid, *A Pictorial History of Australians at War,* Paul Hamlyn, Sydney, 1970.

F Robinson, *Canberra's First Hundred Years and After,* WC Penfold & Co, Sydney, 1927.

W Rolland, *Growing up in Canberra – Birthpangs of a Capital City,* Kangaroo Press, Sydney, 1988.

G Sorgi, A Russell and K Powell, *World Events and Australia,* Longman Cheshire, Melbourne, 1985.

E Sparke, *Canberra 1954–1980,* Australian Government Publishing Service, Canberra, 1988.

H Taylor-Rogers, *St. Paul's Parish, Canberra,* St. Paul's Parish Council, Canberra, 1992.

J Udy, *Living Stones: The Story of the Methodist Church in Canberra,* Sacha Books, Sydney, 1974.

C Warren, *A Little Foolishness. An Autobiographical History,* Church Archivist Press, Virginia, Qld, 1993.

J Waterhouse, *A Light in the Bush. The Canberra Church of England Girls' Grammar School and the Capital City of Australia, 1926–1977,* The Canberra Church of England Girls' Grammar School Old Grammarians' Association, 1978.

------ *Canberra: Early Days at the Causeway,* ACT Museums Unit, Dept of the Environment, Land and Planning, 1992.

T Whiting, *The Priest in Society,* (a family production), 1988.

M Williamson, *Malcolm Williamson: A Mischievous Muse,* Omnibus Press, London, 2007.

R Winch, *The Red Bricks of Reid. The Story of Reid Methodist Church Canberra,* Reid Uniting Church, Canberra, 1977.

B Wright, *Shepherds in New Country. Bishops in the Diocese of Canberra and Goulburn 1937–1993,* WE Wright, Moruya, NSW, 1993.

R Wyatt, *The History of the Diocese of Goulburn,* Edgar Bragg and Sons, Sydney, 1937.

Chapters in books

M Adamson, 'The Adamson family' in V Emerton, *Past Images, Present Voices. Kingston and Thereabouts through a Box Brownie,* Canberra Stories Group, 1996, pp. 1–6.

W Andrews, 'Roads and bridges', in A Fitzgerald (ed.), *Canberra's Engineering Heritage*, The Institution of Engineers Australia, Canberra Division, 1985, pp. 14–25.

B Arthur, 'The Opening of St Mark's 24 February 1957', in *St Mark's Turns 50*, St Mark's National Theological Centre, Canberra, 2007, pp. 24–30.

R Border, 'Thomas Hobbes Scott (1783–1860)', *Australian Dictionary of Biography*, Vol. 2, Melbourne University Press, 1967, pp. 431–433.

K Cable, 'Wentworth-Shields, Wentworth Francis, 1867–1944', *Australian Dictionary of Biography* Vol. 12, Melbourne University Press, 1990, pp. 443–444.

D Carment, 'Groom, Sir Littleton Ernest (1867–1936)', *Australian Dictionary of Biography*, Vol. 9, Melbourne University Press, 1983, pp. 130–133.

G Colman, 'The live firm with the live staff – JB Young's', in V Emerton, *Past Images, Present Voices*, Canberra Stories Group, 1996, pp. 51–57.

S Cowdell, 'On Loving the Church', in T Frame and G Treloar (eds), *Agendas for Australian Anglicanism*, ATF Press, Adelaide, 2006, pp. 249–270.

P Curthoys, 'State-support for churches 1836–1860', in B Kaye (ed.), *Anglicanism in Australia. A History*, Melbourne University Press, 2002, pp. 31–51.

C Daley, 'The growth of a city', in H White (ed.), *Canberra. A Nation's Capital*, Angus & Robertson, Sydney, 1954, pp. 33–65.

B Dickey, 'Secular advance and diocesan response 1861–1900', in B Kaye (ed.), *Anglicanism in Australia. A History*, Melbourne University Press, 2002, pp. 52–75.

L Fitzhardinge, 'In search of a capital city', in H White (ed.), *Canberra. A Nation's Capital*, Angus & Robertson, Sydney, 1954, pp. 1–13.

------ 'Old Canberra and district', in H White (ed.), *Canberra. A Nation's Capital*, Angus & Robertson, Sydney, 1954, pp. 14–32.

B Fletcher, 'Anglicanism and the shaping of Australian society', in B Kaye (ed.), *Anglicanism in Australia. A History*, Melbourne University Press, 2002, pp. 293–315.

------ 'The Anglican ascendancy' in B Kaye (ed.), *Anglicanism in Australia. A History*, Melbourne University Press, 2002, pp. 7–30.

T Frame, 'Recapturing the vision splendid: The 1933 Anglican inter-diocesan Oxford movement centenary celebrations held in Wagga Wagga', in J Moses (ed.), *From Oxford to the Bush. Essays on Catholic Anglicanism in Australia*, Broughton Press and SPCK, Australia, Hall ACT, 1997, pp. 146–171.

------ 'Local differences, social and national identity 1930–1966', in B Kaye (ed.), *Anglicanism in Australia. A History*, Melbourne University Press, 2002, pp. 100–123.

R Frappell, 'Imperial fervour and Anglican loyalty 1901–1929', in B Kaye (ed.), *Anglicanism in Australia. A History*, Melbourne University Press, 2002, pp. 78–99.

D Garnsey, 'Struggle and development, 1948 to 1958', in P McKeown (ed.), *Deo, Ecclesiae, Patriae. Fifty Years of Canberra Grammar School*, Australian National University Press, 1979, pp. 104–134.

H Jones, 'Electricity', in W Andrews (ed.), *Canberra's Engineering Heritage* (2nd ed.), The Institution of Engineers, Australia, Canberra Division, 1990, pp. 127–140.

P Hempenstall, 'Burgmann, Earnest Henry (1885–1967)', *Australian Dictionary of Biography*, Vol. 13, Melbourne University Press, 1993, pp. 300–301.

D Hilliard, 'Pluralism and new alignments in society and church 1967 to the present', in B Kaye (ed.), *Anglicanism in Australia. A History*, Melbourne University Press, 2002, pp. 124–148.

M and M O'Brien, 'At the cutting edge', in *Settlers Stories [1913–1975] – Why they Came and Stayed in Canberra*. Canberra Stories Group, 2000, pp. 46–47.

B Porter, 'A backward glance', in P McKeown (ed.), in *Deo, Ecclesiae, Patriae. Fifty Years of Canberra Grammar School*, Australian National University Press, 1979, pp. 1–17.

J Pulford, 'Deo, Ecclesiae, Patriae', in P McKeown (ed.) *Deo, Ecclesiae, Patriae. Fifty Years of Canberra Grammar School*, Australian National University Press, 1979, pp. 18–48.

L Radford, 'The Oxford Movement. I. Its antecedents', in J Moses (ed.), *From Oxford to the Bush. Essays on Catholic Anglicanism in Australia*, Broughton Press and SPCK, Hall, ACT, 1997, pp. 4–7.

G Shaw, 'Australia's Anglicanism: A via media?' in J Moses (ed.), *From Oxford to the Bush. Essays on Catholic Anglicanism in Australia*, Broughton Press and SPCK, Australia, Hall ACT, 1997, pp. 257–262.

W Shellshear, 'Railways', in A Fitzgerald (ed.), *Canberra's Engineering Heritage*, The Institution of Engineers, Australia, Canberra Division, 1983, pp. 47–71.

M Steven, 'Campbell, Robert (1769–1846)', *Australian Dictionary of Biography*, Vol. 1, Melbourne University Press, 1966, pp. 202–206.

J Vockler and B Thorn, 'Barlow, Christopher George, 1858–1915', *Australian Dictionary of Biography*, Vol. 7, Melbourne University Press, 1979, pp. 176–177.

R Withycombe, 'St. Mark's at fifty: A brief history', in *St Mark's turns 50*, St Mark's National Theological Centre, Canberra, 2007, pp. 31–44.

D Youngman, 'Organs and organists', in H Taylor-Rogers, *St Paul's Parish, Canberra*, St Paul's Parish Council, 1992, pp. 81–85.

Articles and pamphlets

'1307.8 – Australian capital Territory in Focus' 2007, *Australian Bureau of Statistics*, http://www.abs.gov.au

Australian Imperial Force – Nominal Roll. 8th Infantry, 30th Battalion', AWM, http://www.awm.gov.au/units/unit_11217.asp

'Anglo-Catholic', http://www.answers.com/topic/anglo-catholicism

'A recollection of Bishop D Garnsey', *Anglican Historical Society Journal*, October 1994, p. 35.

'Bishop Kenneth John Clements', *Anglican Historical Society Journal (Diocese of Canberra and Goulburn)*, No. 13, April 1992, pp. 1–2.

A Body, 'The cross beside the lake – some background notes', *Diocesan Historical Society Journal*, April 1986, No. 1, pp. 3–8.

T Campbell, 'Canberra's national 'cathedrals': Whatever happened to them?' *Canberra Historical Journal*, New Series No. 53, March, 2004, pp. 28–42.

N Chynoweth, 'Church history: A bicentennial reflection', *Anglican Historical Society Journal (Diocese of Canberra and Goulburn)*, No. 6, Oct. 1988, pp. 24–27.

------ 'Lawrence Maxwell Murchison, Priest 15.1.1919–19.11.93', *Anglican Historical Society Journal (Diocese of Canberra and Goulburn)*. No. 17, Apr. 1994, pp. 1–3. [Eulogy delivered for the Reverend Canon LM Murchison, 22 November, 1993.]

------ 'Neville Chynoweth', Interview tape, NLA, Oral History Section, 1995.

Civilians employed at the Royal Military College of Australia, Duntroon, from 1911 to 1931, Mimeo, R Howarth, Archivist, (November 2000), (ACT Heritage Library).

V Emerton, 'St Paul's in the tin shed', *Newsletter of the Canberra and District Historical Society*, Newsletter 389, October/November, 2003, pp. 5–8.

J Fergus, '*Canberra in the depression – A policy of neglect*,' History assignment, 1981, Canberra and District Historical Society, File: 'Depression'.

D Garnsey, 'The diocese between 1938 and 1958 – Reminiscences', *Anglican Historical Society Journal (Diocese of Canberra and Goulburn)*, No. 11, April 1991, pp. 1–8.

------ 'Laurie Murchison', *Anglican Historical Society Journal (Diocese of Canberra and Goulburn)*, No. 18, Oct. 1994, pp. 35–36.

A Greig, 'The accommodation of growth: Canberra's *growing pains* 1945– 1955', *Canberra Historical Journal*, New Series, No. 57, 2006, pp. 13–34.

F Hawkins, 'St David's Red Hill – The planning decade, 1962–1972', *Anglican Historical Society Journal (Diocese of Canberra and Goulburn)*, 5, April 1988, pp. 13–19.

F Hawkins and B Thorn, 'St David's Red Hill, Canberra: Part 2 – The seventies', *Anglican Historical Society Journal (Diocese of Canberra and Goulburn)*, 8, October 1989, pp. 26–35.

'History of the US Embassy', *http://canberra.usembassy.gov/history.html*

'HMAS *Harman*', *http://www.navy.gov.au/*HMASHarman

B Holt, 'Canberra during World War II', *Canberra and District Historical Society Newsletter*, May 1983, pp. 11–13.

'Mission and Ministry: The Combined Ministry District of Manuka and Deakin: Three Churches, One Community', 2009. StP Archives.

'*Our parish and our church: St Paul's Canberra*' (1960), St Paul's Publication, (NLA, Np 283.9471 CAN.)

R Pierard, 'Evangelicalism', *http://www.mb-soft.com/believe/text/evangeli.htm*

J Pulford, 'William John Edwards 1891–1967. Canon of St. Saviour's Cathedral', *Anglican Historical Society Journal*, April 1995, No. 19, pp, 16–21.

Recommended for Mention, 8th Infantry Brigade, 5th Australian Division, 9 March 1917, AWM, *http://www.awm.gov.au/cmsimages/awm.pdf*

'Robert Garran', *http://en.wikipedia.org/wiki/Robert_Garran*

M Robertson, 'The Ven. Charles Shearer Robertson: Some memories', *Anglican Historical Society Journal (Diocese of Canberra and Goulburn)*, No. 19, 1995, pp. 2–15.

W Stegemann, 'For better, for worse – The Monaro Grammar School, 1908–1928', *Anglican Historical Society Journal (Diocese of Canberra and Goulburn)*, No. 2, Oct. 1986, pp. 19–24.

------ 'The Community of the Ascension', *Anglican Historical Society Journal (Diocese of Canberra and Goulburn)*, No. 4, Oct. 1987, pp. 1–10.

'The southern visitations of Bishop Broughton 1837–1852', Goulburn Diocesan Church House, 1936.

R Wench, 'The cathedrals that didn't happen and the early urban churches of Canberra', *Canberra Historical Journal*, March 1977, pp. 15–21.

'The Church Act, 1836', *http://www.sl.nsw.gov.au/discover_collections/history_nation/religion/places/act.html*

'The Oxford Movement', *The Columbia* Encyclopedia (6th ed.), 2008, *http://www.encyclopedia.com/doc/1E1-Oxfordmo.html*

T Whiting, 'The Story of St Paul's *Church*, 'Canberra South from the Day of its Inauguration, 4th August 1914 to the Establishment of the Church at Manuka between the Years 1937–1944', NLA, MS3085, Box 1.

R Willson, 'Jane Barker's Letters from Canberra', *MARGIN: Life & Letters in Early Australia,* April 2008, *http://findarticles.com*

J Woolven, *A Stitch in Time. Charles Shearer Robertson – Recollections and Reminiscences of some who knew him.* Mimeo, 1992, pp. 22 ff.

Newspapers / Newsletters

ABM Review (Australian Board of Missions), 1956.

The Canberra Times 1926–2010

Community News, The [Canberra] 1925–1927

Federal Capital Pioneer December 1924-August 1926

Federal Capital Pioneer Magazine October 1926-August 1927

Newsletter: St Mark's Institute of Theology, 1962–1971 (NLA, Nq 026.283 SAI).

The Queanbeyan Age 1912–1926

The Queanbeyan-Canberra Advocate 1925

Index